THE THIN RED LINE

THE THIN RED LINE

An Eyewitness History of the Crimean War

JULIAN SPILSBURY

Weidenfeld & Nicolson
LONDON

ISBN-10: 0 297 84625 6
ISBN-13: 978 0 297 84625 3

Weidenfeld & Nicolson
The Orion Publishing Group Ltd
Orion House
5 Upper Saint Martin's Lane
London, WC2H 9EA

Printed in the United States of America

To my mother

ACKNOWLEDGEMENTS

Among the many people who have helped me research and write this book I owe particular thanks to the staffs of the London Library, the British Library and the National Army Museum; to the staff of PSW, Alcester, Warwickshire; to Mr James Falkner; to Major Roger Chapman of The Green Howards for permission to quote from his *Echoes from the Crimea* and for his generous assistance with source material; to Major David Harrap, and Mr Scott Flaving of The Duke of Wellington's Regiment for the use of extracts from the Diary of Major Mundy; to Lieutenant-Colonel Peter Crocker of The Royal Welch Fusiliers for the diaries of Boscawen Trevor Griffith; and to Michael Leventhal of Greenhill books for permission to quote from the letters of Colonel George Dallas. Extracts from the letters of Henry Clifford appear with the kind permission of Penguin books. Acknowledgement is due to the *Illustrated London News* and the National Army Museum for permission to reproduce the colour plates. I am also indebted to Ian Fletcher of Ian Fletcher Battlefield Tours for getting me to, from, and around Sebastopol and to Patrick Mercer MP for his unfailing help and encouragement, and for repeatedly pointing me in the right direction – metaphorically in England, literally in the Crimea.

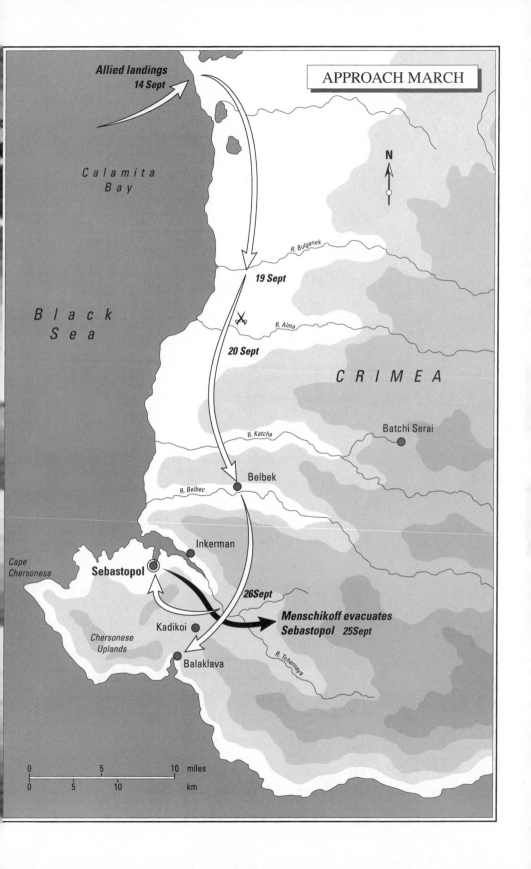

APPROACH MARCH

Allied landings
14 Sept

Calamita
Bay

N

R. Bulganek

19 Sept

R. Alma

20 Sept

Black
Sea

CRIMEA

R. Katcha

Batchi Serai

R. Belbec

Belbek

Inkerman

Cape
Chersonese

Sebastopol

26 Sept

Menschikoff evacuates
Sebastopol 25 Sept

Kadikoi

Chersonese
Uplands

R. Tchernaya

Balaklava

0   5   10 miles
0   5   10   km

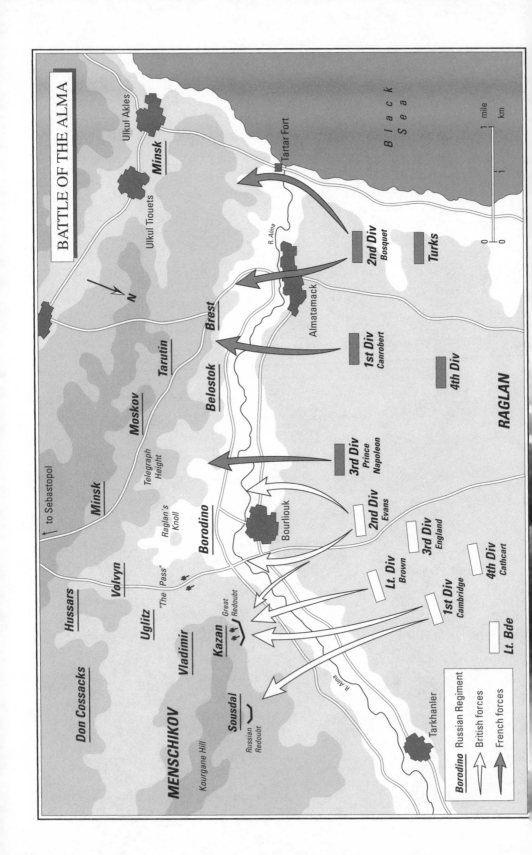

BATTLE OF THE ALMA

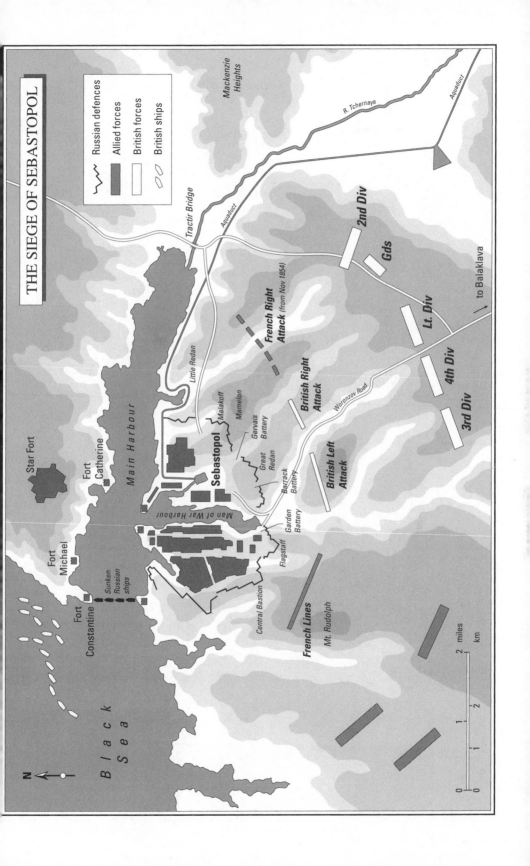

THE SIEGE OF SEBASTOPOL

Russian defences
Allied forces
British forces
British ships

Mackenzie Heights

R. Tchernaya

Aquaduct

Tractir Bridge

Aquaduct

2nd Div

Gds

Lt. Div

4th Div

3rd Div

to Balaklava

French Right Attack (from Nov 1854)

British Right Attack

Woronzov Road

British Left Attack

Little Redan

Malakoff

Mamelon

Gervais Battery

Great Redan

Sebastopol

Barrack Battery

Main Harbour

Garden Battery

Man of War Harbour

Star Fort

Fort Catherine

Flagstaff

Central Bastion

French Lines

Mt. Rudolph

Fort Michael

Sunken Russian ships

Fort Constantine

Black Sea

N

2 miles

2 km

0   1   2
0   1   2

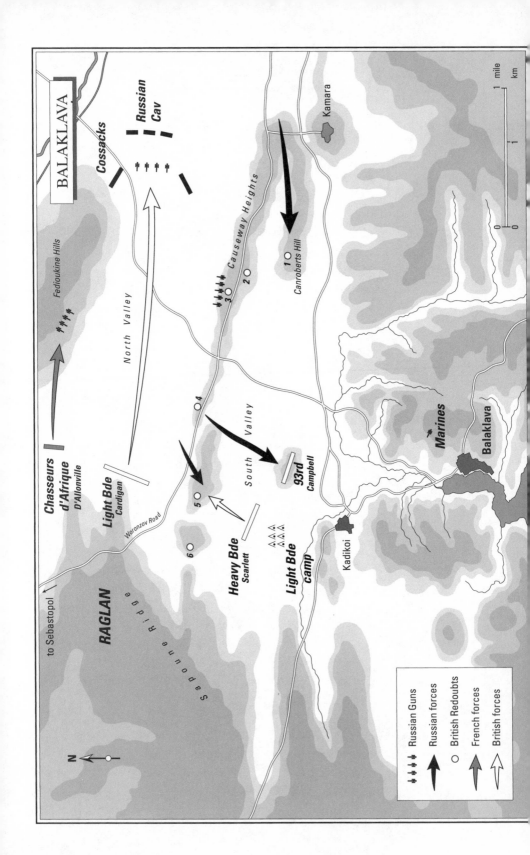

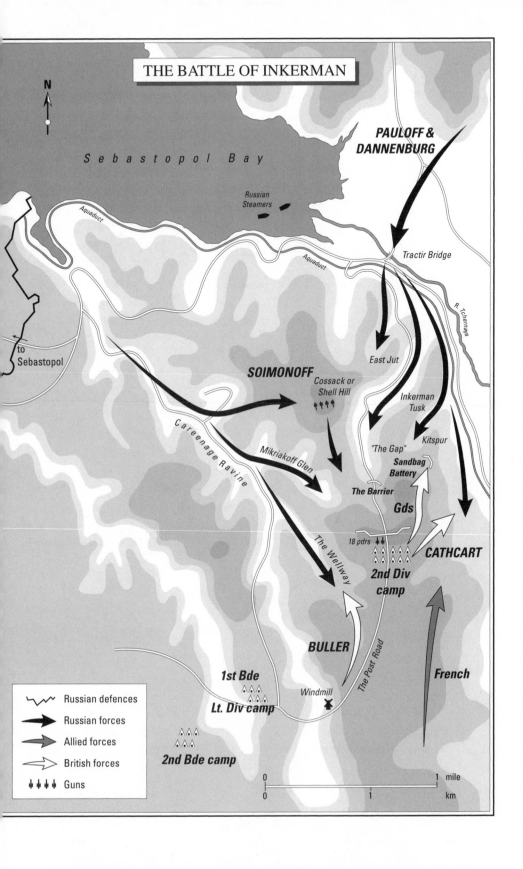

THE BATTLE OF INKERMAN

N

PAULOFF &
DANNENBURG

Sebastopol Bay

Russian
Steamers

Aquaduct

Aquaduct

Tractir Bridge

R. Tchernaya

to
Sebastopol

SOIMONOFF

East Jut

Cossack or
Shell Hill

Inkerman
Tusk

Careenage Ravine

Mikriakoff Glen

"The Gap"

Kitspur

Sandbag
Battery

The Barrier

Gds

The Wellway

18 pdrs

CATHCART

2nd Div
camp

BULLER

The Post Road

French

1st Bde

Windmill

Lt. Div camp

2nd Bde camp

Russian defences

Russian forces

Allied forces

British forces

Guns

0   1 mile

0   1 km

CHAPTER ONE

'We have on our hands a sick man – a very sick man; it will be a great misfortune if one of these days he should slip away from us, especially before all necessary arrangements are made.'

These words – spoken by Tsar Nicholas I to the British Ambassador at a reception in St Petersburg in 1853 – set the scene for the Crimean War. The 'sick man' was Turkey, which had, over the previous two hundred years, declined from superpower status, losing, in the 1820s, Egypt, Syria, Greece, Moldavia and Wallachia (modern Romania) and keeping only a shaky grasp on what remained. The watchers at the sick man's bedside were Austria, Britain, France and Nicholas's Russia. If Turkey's European dominions – comprising the Balkan states, much of modern Bulgaria and its own capital, Constantinople (modern Istanbul) – were up for grabs, these would be foremost among the grabbers. To the Tsar, they represented that recurring dream of Russian statesmen: a warm-water port – and one with free access to the Eastern Mediterranean.

Russia's dream of being a Mediterranean power was a nightmare for France and Great Britain. For France – already a Mediterranean power, and wanting no rivals – there was the fear of Russian interference with her North African Empire and, worse, the prospect of a Russian fleet off Toulon. For the British, already – in India – casting anxious eyes over the Himalayas at Russian expansion into Central Asia, there was the prospect of a Russian threat to communications with India, via Egypt and the Red Sea.

If the cause of the war was simple enough, the pretext was more complicated. As spiritual heir – in his own eyes at least – to the Byzantine Emperors of Constantinople, the Tsar saw himself as Protector of the Orthodox subjects of Sultan Abd-ul-Mejid's empire. In this the Tsar may have been sincere, but in practical terms he was claiming a 'right of intervention' on behalf of one third of the Sultan's subjects. A riot in Bethlehem brought things to a head. Access to the holy places in Palestine, especially the Church of the Nativity and the Church of the Holy Sepulchre, had been a bone of contention between Latin and Orthodox monks for centuries. Now the Latin Church attempted to assert old rights, backed by a new champion.

Napoleon III, who had become President of France in 1848 and proclaimed himself Emperor in 1852, maintained his rule over a fractious population by constantly producing rabbits out of a hat. This was his latest: Napoleon re-invented himself once more, this time as spiritual heir to the Crusader kings and protector of Latin Christianity, which no doubt played well with the Church in France. The placing, by Latin monks, of a silver star adorned with the arms of France over the Sacred Manger, and their seizure of the keys to the church, caused a riot, in which some Orthodox monks were killed. The Russians were quick to blame the Turkish police for complicity in these murders, and demanded the restitution of its rights to the Orthodox Church.

A rebellion in Montenegro further complicated matters. Austria – a regional power with her own interests in the Balkans – demanded the withdrawal of Turkish forces which, under Omar Pasha, were acting against the rebels. Enter Prince Menschikoff, a man we shall see much more of. Brilliant, witty, sarcastic, and no friend to the Turks – he had been castrated by a Turkish cannon ball in a previous war – he was the Tsar's Ambassador in Constantinople, and as such he backed the Austrian demand, adding that a refusal to withdraw Omar Pasha's forces would be treated as a declaration of war. To the Turks this was unacceptable – as it was meant to be. When the Sultan, assured of British and French support by the presence of both their fleets at the Dardanelles, refused, Russian forces crossed the river Pruth and entered Moldavia.

Even at this stage it was hoped that Austria – who, after Turkey, had most at stake in the region – might yet bring her influence to bear against the Russians. Emperor Franz-Josef, however, grateful for Russian help against his own people in 1848, held back, and the Russians' southward advance continued. The Turkish position in Europe was defended by two east-west barriers: the Danube, which formed its northern border, and the Balkan mountains, which split what is now Bulgaria into a northern and a southern half. It was towards the Turkish defences along the Danube that the Russian advance was directed; once across this and through the Balkan passes, they could be in Constantinople within weeks. Despite recent reforms – and the presence of foreign instructors, many of them English – little was expected of the Turkish army.

On 5 October 1853, with the Russian army now lining the north bank of the Danube, the Sultan declared war on Russia. At first the Russians, attacking on a wide front, suffered a number of reverses, most notably at Oltenitza on 4 November, but then, on 30 November, a Turkish naval squadron under Osman Pasha was utterly destroyed by ships of the Russian Black Sea fleet at Sinope. The French and British press denounced Sinope as a massacre – and one which was all the worse for occurring practically under the noses of their own fleets. By April, public opinion in both countries was clamouring for action. France declared war on 26 March, Britain the following day.

It was decided that the Army of the East should be based around five infantry divisions – the Light Division, the 1st, 2nd, 3rd and 4th Divisions. Each division was subdivided into two brigades, each of three battalions. Each battalion was between 750 and 800 men strong, giving each division six battalions, and an approximate strength of 4,800 men. In addition there was to be a cavalry division, divided into two brigades, the Heavy Brigade and the Light Brigade, each of which consisted of five regiments and had a total 'sabre strength', of 1,000 men. Including the artillery – a total of 60 guns and crews, a siege train and engineers – the total force comprised, officially, 26,095 men.

How ready was Britain to deploy and maintain a force of this size? Writing four years after the war, Lieutenant-Colonel Adye, Royal Artillery, who had served in the Crimea, estimated that to maintain an army of roughly 20,000 men on active service required:

20,000 men in the field.
A further 20,000 trained men as a 1st Reserve.
A further 20,000 men under training as a 2nd Reserve.
General Staff, Medical Staff and Commissariat Staff – consisting of carefully selected officers educated and accustomed to their duties.

Transport for the conveyance of food, reserve ammunition, camp equipment, medical stores, engineer stores, a pontoon train, and siege train.

Adye concluded: 'One may almost put the pen through every other item except the first. When the 20,000 men had left England, the country was almost drained of its soldiers; of reserves, consequently, there were next to none.'

Regiments destined for the East were brought up to strength by accepting drafts of volunteers from other regiments. Garrisons throughout Britain and the Mediterranean were denuded. The 95th (Derbyshire) Regiment preparing, at Weedon, to embark on its first ever campaign received volunteers from the 6th, 36th, 48th and 82nd Regiments. When the 55th (Westmoreland) Regiment was ordered out from Gibraltar they received 150 volunteers from the 92nd Highlanders; another 100 joined the 30th. Captain John Hume of the 55th – whom we shall see more of during the campaign – was highly impressed with the quality of the men his regiment received; he wrote, 'They did splendid service during the war.' He added: 'It was a cruel thing, almost to destroy a fine Scotch Regiment with such a historical record as the 92nd had, and it was a long time before it recovered from the loss of so many good men.'

The administration of the army was a tangle of prerogatives and responsibilities: the Commander-in-Chief commanded all troops in Britain, but not those overseas; the Master-General of the Ordnance was responsible for the Royal Artillery and Royal Engineers; the Medical Department was a law unto itself, and – most ominously of all – the Commissariat was a branch of the Treasury. In most respects this was the same army that had fought in the Peninsula under Wellington: apart from a few tinkerings by Prince Albert, even its uniforms were virtually unchanged. Most of its commanders had learned their trade under the Iron Duke, who had died only two years earlier, and whose iron hand had generally applied the handbrake when any project of reform was proposed. Nor were its formations – brigades and divisions – tactical units in any meaningful sense. Large-scale manoeuvres were very rarely practised, were entered into reluctantly by many regimental commanders, and were generally shambolic. This was not so much an army as, in Prince Albert's words, 'a mere aggregate of regiments'.

Worst of all, this 'army' lacked the one thing the Peninsula army did have: a baggage train. Wellington's wagon train, painstakingly built up over years of campaigning in Spain, had been disbanded in 1814 as a unnecessary expense. In future, it was decided, wagons and carts, and the horses, mules or oxen to pull them, would be provided by local purchase in the theatre of war. What had proved difficult in Spain forty years earlier was to prove more so in Bulgaria in the months to come, and well-nigh impossible in the Crimea. The result was, as Adye put it, 'As to transport, or any means of moving the impediments, provisions, or ammunition, nothing of the kind existed! The army, such as it was, was perfectly immovable.'

It wasn't all bad news, however. It was an all-volunteer army, the only one in Europe. Its regiments had a fighting tradition second to none, and high morale. If the commanders were mostly old men, they had at least seen a good deal of active service and, at regimental level, the army was officered by men drawn from the upper-middle classes and gentry who generally were devoted to their men, and took their profession seriously.

The other ranks were tough, hardy men drawn from the fields and factories. A high proportion of the men, whatever their regiment's supposed county affiliation, were Irish. At this time – after the Famine but before large-scale emigration to America – the army offered an escape from poverty for many Irishmen, both Catholic and Protestant. They were often men of high calibre, denied opportunities elsewhere, and they were to prove their worth time and again. Often outcasts, and despised by civilians – at least in peacetime – the soldiers were patriotic and fiercely loyal to their regiments, and the bond between officers and men was a strong one.

So the raw material was good, and, with the natural ebullience of early Victorian England, it was generally agreed that given a fair crack at the enemy, 'Bill, Pat and Sandy' (the English and Welsh, Irish and Scots soldier) would give a good account of themselves. This, the first major war of Queen Victoria's reign, and the first against a European power since Waterloo, was popular with the public. The cause was just: war fever gripped the land. Henry Russell's popular hit 'Cheer, Boys, Cheer!' – a song about emigration – was rapidly becoming the 'Tipperary' of this war.

5

Cheer, Boys, cheer,
For country Mother country,
Cheer, Boys, cheer
For a willing strong right hand,
Cheer, Boys, cheer,
There's hope for honest labour,
Cheer, Boys, cheer
For a new and happy land.

It was played in music halls, bawled out in grog shops, belted out by regimental bands as they marched to railways stations across the kingdom. The 1st Royal Fusiliers, commanded by Lieutenant-Colonel Lacy Yea, left supposedly progressive, pacifist Manchester for embarkation at Southampton amidst cheering crowds. Watching them was newly enlisted Private Timothy Gowing, son of a Baptist minister from Halesworth in Suffolk. Gowing, a strapping six-footer – he had once laid out two footpads who attacked him as he drove his father's livestock to Norwich market – was not going with them; he would join them when his training was completed. Even so, he shared in the pride of the moment, writing, 'In marching out of the barracks at Manchester to the railway station, one could have walked over the heads of the people, who were wrought up to such a pitch of excitement as almost amounted to madness.

'Our inspiring band in front struck up "The British Grenadiers", "The Girl I left Behind Me", "We Are Going Far Away". Fathers shook hands with their sons and bade them farewell, while mothers embraced them; and then the band struck up "Cheer, Boys, Cheer!" which seemed to have a thrilling effect upon the multitude and to give fresh animation to the men. The expressions from the vast crowd, as our men marched along, were:

' "Pur them, Bill!"
' "Remember Old England depends upon you."
' "Give them plenty of cold steel, and then pur them!"
' "Keep your pecker up, old boy – never say die!"
' "Leave your mark upon them if you get a chance!"

'At last the noble old corps reached the railway station, and then there were deafening shouts. Some cried, "We'll meet again, and give you a warm reception when you come back." Then after one hearty "God bless you" from a vast multitude, away they went behind the iron horse.'

In public houses and gin shops departing soldiers were lionised. Private Albert Mitchell of the 13th Light Dragoons – soon to form part of the Light Brigade – was billeted with a comrade at an inn in Portchester, near Portsmouth, where the landlord and his daughter gave them the run of the house: 'I believe they both thought, that as we were going to fight the Russians, that we should never return to Old England again, and that no matter what they did for us, they could not do too much. Many times we spoke of their kindness to us when we were far away.'

When he and his comrade, William Nicholson, received orders to march next morning to the dockyard to embark: 'Soon after a party of the Hampshire Yeomanry pulled up at our inn for refreshment. They were going to Fareham for drill. On seeing me and my comrade they all dismounted, placed their horses in the yard and entered the house with us. They were very kind to us, and I am sure had we been drinking men, we might have drank to our heart's content. After having taken a glass or two of beer with them, they were very anxious for us to give them a lesson at the sword exercise. We did so, and very creditably they got through it. They then mounted and started for Fareham and on their return in the evening brought several of their comrades with them; and by that time we had our horses done up for the night and packed our valises for the morning, for we were to march at 6 a.m.

'In a short time several of our men from other billets dropped in, so, altogether, we had a large party, and very comfortable we were, singing and drinking until near daylight.

'At last we broke up. The Yeomanry started, and our comrades from other billets rolled home, and me and Nicholson turned in for a couple of hours. Little did I think when I jumped out of bed at 4 a.m. that it was the last time I should see a bed for two years and nearly a month. But so it was; and I have no doubt it was the last for ever for some of our party – for many of them were left behind poor fellows.'

Command of the army was given to the Master-General of the Ordnance, Lord Raglan. The eleventh son of the Duke of Beaufort, and then Lord Fitzroy Somerset, he had served the Duke of Wellington as Military Secretary from 1810 onwards and had lost his right arm at the Duke's side at Waterloo. He married the Duke's niece and continued as his secretary throughout his years as

Commander-in-Chief. Denied that post on the Duke's death – it went to Lord Hardinge – he had instead been made Master-General of the Ordnance, and created the first Lord Raglan. Hard-working, dedicated to the army, possessed of a cool courage, courteous, and modest to the point of self-effacement, Raglan is almost the archetypal perfect English gentleman. The only problem was that he had never commanded troops in the field in any significant numbers.

The army's initial deployment was to Gallipoli, a small town on the Dardanelles which few Englishmen had heard of, but where the grandsons of this army would fight against the offspring of Turks they were now going out to assist. Sir George Brown, another Peninsular veteran, now designated Commander of the Light Division, was to command there a force of 18,000 British troops. Some 20,000 French were also to assemble there. Sailing from Marseilles and Toulon rather than Southampton, Portsmouth, Plymouth and Liverpool – and not waiting in Malta for hostilities to begin, as the British had done – they arrived first and bagged the best of the available accommodation and food. This was a pattern that would repeat itself, and cause friction between the Allies. By the end of May other units had gone on to Scutari, across the Bosphorus from Constantinople, and by June, with the situation in Bulgaria becoming critical, it was agreed that the Allied armies should concentrate at Varna in Bulgaria.

After their bloody nose on the Danube, the Russians had regrouped and concentrated an army of 50,000 men, under General Paskevitch, against Silistria. This Danube fortress – which the Russians had taken before, in 1829 – was held by 12,000 Turks. Its capture this time would enable the Russians to cut off any Turkish forces in the Dobrudja region, and give Paskevitch a bridgehead for operations southwards against the Balkans. Varna, on the coast, offered the Russians a way round the Balkans, should they choose not to risk storming the Balkan passes. The Allied armies would plug this gap in the Turkish defences until they were up to strength and acclimatised, at which point they would move north to assist the Turks. The best Omar Pasha, the Turkish commander in Bulgaria, could hope was that Silistria could hold out until then.

The voyage out to the East was a pleasant Mediterranean cruise for some, a nightmare for others. It was particularly hard for the horses. Trooper Albert Mitchell's regiment, the 13th Light Dragoons, were on *Culloden*, an East India merchantman. He wrote, 'The hold ... was fitted up as a stable, each horse being provided with a separate stall. They were placed with their heels towards the ship's side, and heads towards each other, with a passage between them, so we were able to walk down between them. There were strong mangers fixed beneath their heads, to which they were fastened by double halters, so that once they were fastened there was no chance of lying down when they were on board ...

'I think there is no time that will prove whether a dragoon is a good horse-master so well as the time they are on board ship. They require much attention, the motion of the vessel being altogether a new thing to them, many soon begin to show signs of sickness unless they are well attended. Some men would spend all their time coaxing their horse to eat, bathing the face and nostrils with vinegar and water or salt water. We were employed several hours each day removing the dung &c., from the stalls, and hoisting it on deck in large baskets to be thrown overboard.'

His training now completed, Timothy Gowing was sailing to Varna to rejoin the 7th Fusiliers. He too had an unpleasant voyage: 'It is not very comfortable on a troopship, shut up with scarcely standing room, constantly being pitched and tossed about, especially if you should happen to lose your balance and come down "soft upon the hard" with your face in contact with some of the blocks, and have a lot of sailors grinning at you – for they do not seem to have any pity for a poor fellow staggering about like a drunken man.'

It was different for Captain John Hume, sailing from Gibraltar with his regiment, the 55th Foot, who remembered: 'As soon as we got our sea-legs the voyage was very enjoyable. The band under Senor de la Vega, our excellent bandmaster, played every evening weather permitting, when some danced, others read or played games and some slept. A few Minié rifles has been served out to the regiment for instruction in the use of the new weapon, and practise went on whenever the sea was smooth enough for the men to stand steady.'

This new weapon, the Minié rifle, named after the French colonel who had designed it, was replacing the smooth-bore 1842 percussion musket. By the time the army actually engaged the Russians, every division except the 4th had been issued with it. Fired, like its predecessor, by means of a percussion cap, which was fitted over a hollow nipple and ignited the powder in the barrel, its rifling made it slightly harder to load, but gave it greatly increased power and accuracy. Firing a conical bullet rather than a ball, it was reliably accurate at over three hundred yards, which was more than three times the range of the smooth-bore muskets issued to the Russians. Marksmen could bring a man down at seven hundred yards. In previous wars, infantry had fought shoulder to shoulder, and light infantry had fought in loose, open formations. Issuing rifles to every soldier made every man a potential light infantryman. This was a lesson that the British were to learn over the next few months. To the troops being issued with these new weapons *en route*, the Minié must have looked like just another new firearm; few officers or men realised yet that they were holding in their hands a potential battle-winner.

We join the British army at Varna. Here, on the coast of Bulgaria, Lord Raglan – having come out by way of Paris and Constantinople – established his headquarters in a small house at the back of the town. A general's headquarters staff was known in the nineteenth century as his family; in Lord Raglan's case this was almost literally true. Four of his ADCs were his nephews, including Lieutenant Somerset Calthorpe, who on 24 June, recorded his first impressions of the town: 'The town itself is like all the rest of the Turkish towns, with its ill-paved streets and tumbledown houses, and, as usual, smells of every sort of abomination. It is swarming with troops, English, French and Turkish. One great drawback to the town is the want of water, and what little there is is very indifferent . . . There is a great deal of drunkenness here.'

Around Varna were four of the five divisions. The 1st Division – consisting of a Brigade of Guards and a Highland Brigade – and the 2nd Division were encamped nearby. The Light Division was thirteen miles way at Aladyn. Two more infantry divisions, the 3rd and 4th, were yet to join the army. The Cavalry Division, consisting of the Light and Heavy Brigades, was twenty miles away at Devna.

There were also 20,000 French troops in the vicinity. If the alliance at the higher levels was an uneasy one – Lord Raglan was apt, in forgetful moments, to refer to the enemy as 'the French' – at the lower levels, the relationship was extremely cordial. 'The French and ourselves got on capitally,' said Timothy Gowing, 'particularly the Zouaves, whom we found a very jolly set, though they afterwards proved themselves a troublesome lot to the enemy.'

These Zouaves – originally North African troops from the Kabyle tribe of Zouava – were by now all-French units, but maintained the oriental uniform of baggy red trousers, blue tunics and kepis. They struck up an instant affinity with the Highlanders – Britain's own exotic shock troops – as Captain Wilson of the Coldstream Guards observed: 'Of all our intimacies, the most remarkable was the love at first sight which glowed in the bosoms of *Zou-Zou* and the High-landman. Charmed, most like, by one another's singular and attractive costume, honouring one another's glorious antecedents, these *corps d'élite* became inseparable.'

Marshal St Arnaud, the French Commander-in-Chief, was cheered extravagantly whenever he appeared among British troops, an attention he both enjoyed and courted. In this he differed greatly from Lord Raglan, who followed his revered old Chief in all things. He shared the Duke of Wellington's view that the troops had no business cheering their officers – it came close to an expression of opinion. Hating all forms of ostentation, the soldiers' enthusiasm pained him and he tried to do his rounds of the camps with as little show as possible. This would lead, in due course, to the unfair accusations that he was uncaring, remote and unwilling to show himself among them.

Every regiment in the army had brought a certain number of women: soldiers' wives who acted as laundresses, seamstresses and, on occasion, as unpaid medical orderlies. The traditional allotment of six wives per hundred men had been reduced to four at Lord Raglan's insistence. Ladies were another matter entirely: they were actively discouraged – not that all officers' ladies let that stop them. Among these latter was Frances Isabella Duberly, known as Fanny, wife of Henry Duberly, Paymaster of the 8th Hussars. From the moment the 8th, part of the Light Brigade, received their marching orders for the east, she determined to accompany her husband, and did so despite Lord Raglan's misgivings and Cavalry Division Commander Lord Lucan's outright hostility. Blonde, attractive, witty and twenty-four, she made herself popular with officers everywhere, and, despite her portrayal in film and some fiction, there is no hint that she was ever anything other than a faithful, loving wife to her *Dear Henry.* Any disapproval she incurred was because she was a woman poking her nose into things best left to men.

Fanny and her husband arrived at Varna with the 8th Hussars on 8 June. She wrote in her journal: 'The landing-place gave me a better idea of "war-time" than any description could do. It was shadowing to twilight. The quay was crowded with Turks, Greeks, infantry, artillery and Hussars; piles of cannon balls and shells all around us; rattle of arms everywhere; horses kicking, screaming, plunging; and "Bob", whom I was to ride, was almost unmanageable from excitement and flies. At length, horses were accoutred, and men mounted, and, nearly in the dark, we commenced our march, Henry and I leading.'

With only 12,000 Allied troops around Varna there was little Raglan or St Arnaud could do to aid the Turks until the armies were up to strength. Camp life settled into a routine which soon grew tedious. With the Coldstream Guards, in the 1st Division, was Captain Townshend Wilson. His description of camp life at Aladyn gives a good picture of life throughout the army in those early summer months: 'Our day may be divided into three portions: the first being devoted to drill and exhaustion; the second, to torpor and tobacco; the third – and most agreeable, to foraging and feeding.'

The hours between 7.30 and 10 a.m. were the hottest of the day, a new experience for regiments fresh from England or Ireland: 'Unfortunately these considerations were, in some quarters deemed unimportant; a little heat, more or less, being pooh-poohed by certain inexperienced *mounted* officers; consequently, the men on foot suffered greatly. It was a sorry sight to see tall fellows fainting on parade like schoolgirls.'

After breakfast, during the hottest part of the day, the regiments would: 'lapse into a state of semi-coma; would for the most part, compose itself to the enjoyment of a *siesta* in tents as hot as ovens; the thin canvas of course offering but feeble resistance to the blaze overhead. Take a stroll through the camp and you will find the majority ... overcome with heat and idleness, stretched flat or snoring on the ground; while a small scattered minority of livelier temperaments regale themselves with some greasy jewel of a French novel, or, more precious acquisition, a newspaper.'

Officers and men made efforts to improve their situation: 'In order to increase our confined domestic accommodation, we set about building arbours; and so expeditiously did the work proceed, that, in a few days, officers and soldiers had constructed a number of cool retreats, in which they afterwards fed, smoked and slumbered, during the mid-day heats.'

At about three as the day cooled officers and men would disperse in search of food to augment their rations: '. . . cabbages and chickens, eggs and sucking pigs . . . Towards six – the dinner hour in most companies – the foragers begin to drop in, some pretty heavily laden with good things, others with haversacs altogether empty. As one man will live, where another starves so would Ensign Jones pick up "grub" where Lieutenant Robinson saw naught but dust and ashes.'

Officers in particular became careless of their dress – sporting civilian shooting jackets and the low-crowned, wide-brimmed 'wide-awake' hats popular with artists and Bohemians. Having suppressed, at least temporarily, the British officers' traditional reluctance to dress alike, Lord Raglan addressed himself to the question of the uniforms themselves: 'The sword may be worn,' he complained in an order, 'the jacket may be the regimental jacket, and the cap may be the uniform forage cap; but such want of care is shown in wearing the uniform in a becoming manner, that it is difficult to recognise the officers in some cases as officers at all. The shell-jacket is allowed to fly open, shewing underneath a red-flannel shirt, with nothing round the neck, not even a white shirt-collar. Often a turban is worn over the forage cap; the chin unshaven; and there is an absence of what is befitting the appearance of an officer in the whole person.'

In the conditions in the camps, shaving became increasingly difficult – with the inadequate supply of hot water, and blunt razors, facial abrasions became a medical problem. Subalterns, as subalterns will, began to grow regrettable moustaches, whiskers sprouted on field-officers, and the men shaved less and less regularly. When senior officers, most notably Sir George Brown, the Light Division commander, tried to clamp down – the medical officers protested. The argument raged on, was taken up by *The Times* newspaper and was eventually referred to the War Minister, the Duke of Newcastle. He, said Captain Wilson: 'like a sensible man – broke up the agitation by issuing an order to the effect, that officers and soldiers might henceforth consult their own tastes with regard to the preservation or extirpation of whiskers and moustachios. Thus did the beard triumph! thus it was that the army, from being a band of shavelings, gradually assumed the grisly presence of a host of Esaus.'

The arrival of new units was always a welcome diversion from camp routine, and a boost to morale. Fanny Duberly saw the Lights arriving at Devna: 'Part of the Light Division marched up this morning, and encamped on the opposite side of the valley. The Rifles marched in first; next followed the 33rd, playing "Cheer, boys cheer" and cheerily enough the music sounded across our silent valley, helping many a "willing strong right hand" ready to faint with heat and fatigue. The 88th Connaught Rangers gave a wild Irish screech (I know no better word) as they saw their fellow countrymen, the 8th Royal Irish Hussars, and they played "Garry Owen" with all their might; while the 77th followed with "British Grenadier."'

Great efforts were made to keep the men occupied. John Hume of the 55th, in the 2nd Division recalled: 'Everything was done by the officers to amuse the men: sports, cricket, and racing were continually going on; early parades for drill, practising entrenching, making gabions and fascines, and learning to use the new rifle kept everyone well employed.'

The cavalry, too, were kept busy. Trooper Mitchell of the 13th Light Dragoons, a regiment of the Light Brigade, wrote: 'We had plenty of drill here, generally early in the morning. Lord Cardigan seemed determined that it should not be for want of practice if we were not perfect. One of his favourite manoeuvres was to advance a squadron to the front, and at a given signal for every man to disperse and go where they pleased. He would then order the "Rally" to be sounded to see how quick we could get into our places again. This with skirmishing drill, charging in line and by squadrons, outpost drill etc was principally our work while here.'

Inevitably, boredom and frustration took their toll. With cheap Turkish liquor plentiful, discipline had to be rigidly enforced. Trooper Albert Mitchell witnessed the punishment of a trooper of the Light Brigade who had struck a sergeant.

'The prisoner was ordered to strip all except the overalls and boots. He was then strapped to the cart wheel by the wrists and ankles, his body slightly leaning towards the wheels. A couple of farriers were already stripped for the work. They were each to give him twenty-five lashes. This was the first time it had fallen to my lot to see a fellow soldier flogged. I wish it had been the last. The doctor stood by ready to stay the proceedings if he considered the man was unable to bear the punishment. The regimental sergeant-major gave the word, one, and down came the lash on the man's bare back. After a few lashes, which always fell in the same place, in an oblique direction, from the right shoulder to the left side of the back, we soon saw the flesh change colour.

'At this sight four young men in the ranks of the brigade fainted, and were carried to the rear. Still the work went on as though nothing had occurred, until he had received the first twenty-five lashes. It now became the turn of the other farrier to give the next instalment of lashes, and, as he happened to be left-handed, it caused the man double punishment, as instead of being flogged on the same part as before (and which had become callous and benumbed), he was now flogged so that the lashes fell from the left shoulder to the right side of the back, thus inflicting a large wound or raw place on the back in the shape of an X. After he had received the full complement, a cloak was thrown over him, and he was marched back to the hospital tent, where his back was dressed, and in a few days he was out and at his duty.'

Mitchell noted with approval that, among the French, defaulters were put to useful but onerous work – digging latrines and graves, gathering firewood and fetching water – which would otherwise have to be done by good men.

Elsewhere, British forces had already been engaged. In April a British squadron had bombarded the Black Sea port of Odessa, devastating the town's military installations. Five British ships had been damaged; the steamer *Tiger* had run aground and her crew had been taken prisoner. The *Tiger*'s commander, Captain Giffard, was severely wounded; his wife was allowed to join him in captivity. When he died, the wife of General Osten-Sacken, Odessa's Governor, cut off a lock of his hair and sent it to his mother.

As the weeks progressed with no sign of action, rumours – known as *shaves* – abounded. Fanny Duberly recorded in her journal: 'Friday, 16th [June] – A report was rife in camp that 57,000 Austrians were marching to our assistance against the Russians; also that the whole force, English and French, will be under immediate marching orders for Silistria, as 90,000 Russians are investing the town.'

By the following day she added: 'They inform us today that the Austrian force is 300,000, and it is uncertain upon which side they will fight.'

In the Guards' camp, in the most fashionable of the arbours – the 'Guards Club' established by Colonel Cadogan of the Grenadiers – Captain Wilson heard various schemes confidently predicted: 'In a fortnight at furthest, an appalling chastisement would overtake the Tsar ... the destruction of Anapa ... a second attack upon Odessa, in which attack the land forces were cast for great parts ... the crumpling up of Muscovy, that must surely follow an advance upon Moscow.'

It was generally assumed, however, that the Army of the East, assisted by the French, would soon be called upon to fight in Bulgaria. Any day now Silistria would fall and the Russians would push on south with, first, Adrianople, and then Constantinople as their goals. Then all that would stand between Prince Gortchakoff's army and the Turkish capital itself would be the British and French armies.

In the camp of the Light Division, with the 2nd Battalion the Rifle Brigade, was Henry Clifford. Clifford, third son of Lord Clifford of Chudleigh, was an untypical army officer: not only was he a Roman Catholic in a predominantly Protestant officer corps – Catholics had only been allowed into the army as officers since 1829 – but he had been educated at the University of Fribourg, spoke fluent French and had travelled widely on the Continent. He was a man of artistic tastes and sensibilities.

Clifford had been an officer since 1842, and had recently seen active service in South Africa, in the Kaffir Wars. With him on campaign was Jacob, his African servant. Chafing at the army's inaction like everyone else, Clifford wrote home: 'It is very hard to get any correct information in Camp ... yesterday Omar Pasha sent word from Schumla that Silistria could not hold out more than five days longer if we do not go to help him. I believe we shall start the moment it is practicable ... The Russians are strongly encamped, and seem to say "Here we are, all ready for you to come and see what we are made of." Silistria must be taken and every day we expect to hear the bad news.'

*

The news, when it came six days later, was surprising. Wilson and his guardsmen heard it from their divisional commander: 'On Sunday June 25th, immediately after divine service, the Duke of Cambridge informed the first division, how a *Tatar* (courier) had just communicated to Lord Raglan the wonderful tidings, that the Russians ... had, on a sudden, raised the siege, and recrossed the Danube. Paskevitch, it turned out, apprehensive of the proximity of the allies (he knew not their immobility), had strained every nerve in a final furious burst upon the *tabias* (outworks) defending the town. That burst was beaten back with terrific carnage: wherefore the old Muscovite Marshal decamped.'

Among the British, the defence of Silistria was ascribed to the presence of two or three British officers, acting as military advisors, and the Russian evacuation to the threat posed by the Allied armies at Varna. In reality, it was due more to the arrival of 50,000 Austrian troops on the borders of Moldavia and Wallachia, and Austria's demand, backed by the Prussians, that Russia withdraw. Had Austria acted earlier, the entire war might have been avoided.

On hearing the news, Lord Raglan immediately sent orders for Lord Cardigan, commanding the Light Brigade, to take three squadrons and make a reconnaissance of the Dobrudja to ascertain beyond a doubt that the Russians had retreated from Bulgaria.

James Brudenell, 7th Earl of Cardigan, was – and still is – a controversial figure. Notorious for his affairs and duels, he seemed to many of the general public, the Press and the army, to exemplify all that was worst about the purchase system. A childhood riding injury left him prone to mood swings and violent rages, and he had an ability to divide a command that was almost a gift. At the age of thirty-five he bought himself the Colonelcy of the 15th Hussars, but was later dismissed from command for spying on his officers.

However, as one of the country's wealthiest peers, he enjoyed Royal favour and was soon back in command, this time of the 11th Light Dragoons (soon to be Hussars). Here he went on as before – creating cliques, showing partiality for the wealthy and well-connected and contempt for older, poorer officers, and reserving an especial venom for any who had served in India. One of his few redeeming features – apart from courage – was an instinctive and genuine sympathy with women, and it was this that had brought him into conflict with his superior, Lord Lucan, the commander of the Cavalry Division. Lucan, in many ways a similar character to Cardigan, was his brother-in-law and, according to Cardigan, had treated his sister abominably. The fact that the two men – who had almost come to pistols over the matter – were now barely on speaking terms, did not augur well.

Lucan was regarded as a harsh disciplinarian but an experienced officer – he had served on the Russian General Woronzov's staff in a previous war against the Turks – but many had their doubts about Cardigan's competence . . . and this was the man who was now to be the eyes and ears of the Army of the East.

Fanny Duberly at the Light Brigade camp recorded: 'Was awoke at four o'clock from a profound sleep, by the words, "A general order for the regiment to be prepared as soon as possible to march thirty miles." All the camp was alive. No tents were to be struck but everyone was to move. We could make nothing of the order, until we heard that the Russians had abandoned the siege of Silistria, and had crossed the Danube. We still dressed in hot haste, wondering at the order, when an aide-de-camp came up to say that only a squadron of the 8th and a squadron of the 13th were to go; and that they were to march towards Silistria to make a reconnaissance of the Russian army.

'The order to "bridle and saddle" was given, and all was ready for a start, when a counter order arrived – "The squadrons are to wait until three days' provisions are cooked", so that of the whole regiment roused at four, two troops went away at half-past ten. If it takes six hours and a half to get two squadrons under weigh, how long will it take to move the whole British force?'

The start of this – the infamous Sore-Back Reconnaissance – was a portent of what was to follow. The force marched for seventeen days, heavily laden with much unnecessary lumber, at a scorching pace set by Lord Cardigan himself. Marching from dawn to dusk in blistering heat, lying out under the open sky at night, resulted in a steady deterioration in both men and horses. On 11 July Fanny Duberly saw the force return: 'The reconnaissance, under Lord Cardigan, came in this morning at eight, having marched all night. They have been to Rassova, seen the Russian force, lived for five days on water and salt pork; have shot five horses, which dropped from exhaustion on the road, brought back an araba full of disabled men, and seventy-five horses, which will be, as Mr Grey says, unfit for work for many months, and some of them will never work again. I was out riding in the evening when the stragglers came in; and a piteous sight it was – men on foot, driving and goading on their wretched horses, three or four which could hardly stir. There seems to have been much unnecessary suffering, a cruel parade of death, more pain inflicted than good derived.'

Those who had doubted Cardigan's competence now seemed vindicated. Captain Wilson of the Guards noted: 'Not the least curious part of the story is a statement that the Turkish lancers, who also accompanied the Earl, suffered no losses whatever. How are these things to be explained? Are we to ascribe our calamity, for calamity it assuredly was, to the avoirdupois weight of the light dragoon; or the campaigning inexperience of the commander? To a little of both perhaps.'

At whatever expense, Cardigan's Sore-Back Reconnaissance had established that the Russians had cleared out of Bulgaria lock, stock and barrel. Cheering as the news was to most of Europe, who had followed the siege anxiously, among the Allied High Command rapture was modified – the Turks had shot their fox. Raglan's instructions from the Government had made it explicit that his primary purpose was the defence of Constantinople, but that if that threat was removed, it was essential that a blow be struck at the southern extremities of the Russian Empire. No blow could be more effective than the taking of Sebastopol.

Sebastopol, at the southern tip of the Crimea, was described by some at the time as the Liverpool of Southern Russia, although it could more accurately have been matched with Portsmouth. The Black Sea fleet which had massacred the Turks at Sinope was based there. If Russia as a Mediterranean power was unacceptable, Russia as a Black Sea power was scarcely less so. Even if the Russians were to evacuate Moldavia and Wallachia completely, and withdraw all forces beyond the River Pruth – which they did by 2 August – Russia retained the ability to launch a new offensive the moment the British and French departed, as long as the Black Sea fleet was in being. Without that protection on its seaward flank, any Russian offensive through Bulgaria was impracticable. The naval base at Sebastopol, its forts and arsenal, were a dagger pointed at Constantinople. The idea of an attack on it had been discussed in political and military circles as early as December 1853. The Duke of Newcastle, Secretary of State for War and the Colonies, summed up the British official position in a letter: 'Unless we destroy Russia's Black Sea fleet I do not see my way to a safe and honest peace.'

This view was ratified on the afternoon of 28 June at a Cabinet meeting – at which most of the members dozed off – in a hot, stuffy room in Richmond, where the Cabinet had gone to escape the cholera that was abroad in London. By 16 July, Newcastle's letter, written the next day, reached Raglan at Varna. In it he urged the reduction of Sebastopol and the taking or destruction of the fleet there: 'The confidence with which Her Majesty placed under your command the gallant army now in Turkey is unabated, and, if upon mature reflection, you should consider that the united strength of the two armies is insufficient for this undertaking, you are not to be precluded from the exercise of the discretion originally vested in you, though Her Majesty's Government will learn with regret that an attack from which such important consequences are anticipated must be any longer delayed.'

'Nothing but insuperable impediments' the letter continued, should stay Raglan's hand. A similar letter from the French Emperor, long an advocate of an attack on Sebastopol, had been sent to Marshal St Arnaud.

Raglan had reservations. The year was already far advanced and the prospect of the army sitting before Sebastopol through a terrible Crimean winter was an alarming one. He had no idea of the strength or dispositions of Russian forces in the Crimea. Co-operation with his French and Turkish allies had already proved problematic. He had insufficient land and sea transport, insufficient troops, insufficient reserves and no plan.

Raglan and his second-in-command, Sir George Brown, were wont to ask themselves, in difficult situations, what their mentor, the Duke of Wellington, would have done. The answer must have been clear: he would have declared that the impediments *were* insuperable and vetoed the scheme.

There were, however, political considerations. Newcastle's point about the impossibility of a lasting peace without the destruction of the Black Sea fleet and its base was a valid one. As *The Times* wrote on 24 July: 'The broad policy of the war consists in striking at the very heart of the Russian power in the East, and that heart is at Sebastopol.'

Above all there was public opinion. This was a just war, and a popular one. The fact that its immediate cause – the occupation of the Danubian provinces and the threat to Constantinople – had vanished, was immaterial. The British and French armies had departed for war with great fanfare. French troops had paraded before the Emperor on the Champ de Mars; Queen Victoria had waved the Guards off from the balcony of Buckingham Palace. Were these magnificent troops now to come slinking home without having fired a shot because the despised Turks had seen the enemy off without their help? Then there was the Tsar, tyrant ruler of a slave nation. The Queen spoke for the nation when she wrote of the causes of the war: 'It is the selfishness, and ambition, and want of honesty of one man and his servants which has done it.'

With all his reservations, on 18 July Raglan began planning for a descent on the Crimea. Replying to Raglan's letter announcing the decision, the Duke of Newcastle wrote: 'I cannot help seeing through the calm and noble tone of your announcement of the decision to attack Sebastopol that it has been taken in order to meet the views and desires of the Government, and not in entire accordance with your opinions.'

Raglan was not the only one with reservations. Five days later, Henry Clifford wrote home: 'Everyone is convinced of one thing and that is, that if an attack is made upon Sebastopol, with the best possible management and under the most favourable circumstances the loss of life will be very great on our side. The least sanguine look upon the plan as that of a madman and the taking of the place as impossible.'

By now, though, most of the army had other worries. That same day Fanny Duberly wrote in her journal: 'The cholera is come among us! It is not in *our* camp, but it is in that of the Light Division, and sixteen men have died of it this day in the Rifles.'

Throughout that summer the disease had been prevalent throughout southern Europe. In July it caught up with the armies in Bulgaria. At first sight Varna had appeared a healthy location; in fact its contaminated water-supply – a problem exacerbated by the presence of some 60,000 extra humans – made it a perfect breeding ground for the *Vibrio cholerae* bacteria. Cholera was nothing new –

it killed more British soldiers in the nineteenth century than bullet, bayonet and shot combined.

Cholera had killed many thousands in Britain in 1848, and was abroad now in London where, in the Middlesex Hospital, a well-bred lady with the outlandish name of Florence was already – to the horror of her well-bred family – tending to the sick prostitutes of Soho. The sickness began with severe vomiting and diarrhoea, then progressed to violent cramps in the stomach, legs and feet, sometimes so severe that victims screamed out in pain, or even shot themselves. The end was almost inevitable: coma and death.

The only solution was to move, and they did. The Light Division went to Monastir, from where Henry Clifford wrote home: 'We have been obliged to change our Camp, and fly from an enemy who is perhaps more dangerous than the Russians to us. I mentioned in a few lines I wrote from Devna the other day, I think the 23rd or 24th instant, that *Cholera* had broken out in camp and that we had lost some men. On the night of the 25th at 9 o'clock the cases became more frequent, and before 8 in the morning we had lost 19 men. The medical men advised a move of Camp, and said the men considered themselves doomed if they remained at Devna.'

Complaining of the monotony of camp life Clifford added: 'The Cholera was some excitement, but that is over.'

It was far from over. In July, 600 army men died in a fortnight. Colonel Sanders of the 19th, another Light Division regiment, wrote in his journal: 'Cholera increasing and men dying very fast. Every case taken in at Varna hospital has gone to the grave. Fifteen dead these last two nights.'

Private Howells, of the same regiment, recalled: 'It was a dreadful time, stray men were suddenly seized in the grip of cholera and died in great suffering in the course of two or three hours. Few who were seized escaped – they died before my eyes – and there was no one, neither a doctor nor anyone else able to lend them a helping hand. There was no such luxury as a coffin to be had, men were buried in their grey blankets.'

The regiment moved camp with rest of the division, and Margaret Kirwin, a soldier's wife, wrote: 'No sooner had we gone than the Turks opened up the graves and took the blankets from around the dead men. We were then ordered to bury them without any covering, except the branches and brambles that we picked up.'

With severe attacks of the disease, death occurred within hours of the first onset. Mrs Kirwin remembered one pitiful case following the regiment's move to Monastir: 'There was one sergeant in particular of the 19th, Murphy was his name and he had come in from a long day's march protecting the Colours. Mrs Murphy, his wife, a nice respectable woman, came to me for the loan of a frying-pan and before she had the beef-steak fried, her poor husband was dead.'

By early August Henry Clifford had repented of his earlier optimism, writing to his brother: 'The Cholera came at a time when we were all low spirited and disgusted with the tiresome life we are leading and it has had a very great effect on the spirits of both Officers and men. We have been more fortunate than the French who have lost very great numbers, but with us it has been as I say, very sad times, funerals, day after day, not a day without one since it broke out ... Fine young men in perfect health are taken with it and die in four or five hours. I grieve very much for a young Officer of the 77th who came out here with a Draft from England. He came up here on the Tuesday, was taken ill on the Wednesday morning and buried that evening.'

Nor were the Fleet immune – HMS *Britannia*, the flagship, lost 139 out of a crew of 985. Aboard HMS *Queen* was Midshipman Evelyn Wood, a nephew of the Captain. Wood thought the navy was better equipped to deal with sickness: 'One great advantage of the Naval Service lies in the fact that a crew virtually goes on active service each time a ship leaves harbour. Nevertheless, although we were amply supplied with every requisite, our casualties were greater, because the men were concentrated in one place. The French flagship lost 140, of whom 40 died the first night; our flagship lost about one tenth of the ship's company; and none escaped except H.M. ships *London* and *Queen*.

'The screams of a sufferer when seized with cramp often brought on other seizures, and the scenes on a middle or lower deck were trying even to strong nerves. We went to sea to try and shake off the disease. A few days later, so many men were enfeebled by intestinal complaints, that some of the ships, carrying crews of 700 to 1,000 men, had not sufficient Effectives to work the sails; and when the Admiral wanted his boat, officers had to prepare it. I was sent aboard the flagship with a party to furl sails, and while the epidemic lasted we went at sunrise and sunset daily, to bury her dead.'

By the first week of August eight per cent of the British army were suffering from the disease. The 8th Hussars had a quarter of their men in hospital, and the Light Brigade were borrowing buglers to blow the Last Post over the graves of their dead. In the Heavy Brigade the 5th Dragoon Guards lost 34 men and 3 officers, the 4th Dragoon Guards 23 men. In the 5th Dragoon Guards, the severity of the sickness occasioned an almost unheard-of occurrence, as Sergeant Major Henry Franks described: 'We had a Turkish waggon or "Arabi", drawn by two large oxen, or a sort of buffalo, and a native or Bulgarian driver. This conveyance was used chiefly in bringing the rations or forage for the use of the Troops. It was also used by the officers' servants for the foraging of the officers' chargers, and was in and out of the camp several times in a day, so it was not thought unusual when the waggon was seen to leave the camp, with its driver, and accompanied by James Gamble (the Colonel's servant). It was remarked that there seemed a large quantity of grass in the waggon when it was taken out of the camp, but no further notice was taken of it at the time ...

'At length night came, and then it was found out that Colonel le Marchant was gone. He had deserted his regiment in a mean and cowardly manner. Gamble, the servant, returned two days afterwards with the waggon and oxen, and he produced a pass signed by the Colonel, giving him leave of absence for five days. Gamble stated that he had covered the Colonel up in the waggon with grass, and had accompanied him to Varna, about forty miles distant from our camp. They had travelled all night, and when at Varna the Colonel had gone aboard one of the ships in the Bay, but he did not know the name of the ship. This was the last time we ever saw Colonel le Marchant, nor did we ever hear anything more of him.

'It is not often that we hear of a Colonel of a Regiment deserting, and of course it was a surprise to many people who had no knowledge of the man; but he was an exception to all the Colonels I ever saw – he never seemed to take the slightest interest in the Corps from the day he joined us at Ballincollig. I don't think he ever once visited the Hospital Tents, which were crowded with sick men, and they got it into their heads that he didn't care whether they lived or died.'

With men dying or sick, there were fewer to attend to the horses, which were themselves suffering: from heat by day and cold dews by night, from lack of forage, and equine diseases. Commenting on the state of the 5th Dragoon Guards, Captain Wilson of the Coldstream noted: 'The 5th Dragoon Guards, which on landing in the East, were deemed the flower of the Heavy Brigade – so stalwart the men, so full of bone and breeding the horses – had greatly suffered. The senior officers were sick, the best non-commissioned officers were dead, the horses were perishing wholesale ... thus, a few weeks of the deceitful Bulgarian glades had disorganised a most distinguished corps more effectually than months of ordinary fighting probably would have done – pestilence hits harder than big guns.'

Worst hit among the infantry were the Light and 1st Divisions. The Guards were moved from Aladyn to escape the foul air from the marshes, which some medical opinion blamed for the disease, but Wilson reported: 'Barely had the tent-pegs got hold of the new ground, before a soldier of the Scots Fusilier Guards was writhing in his last agony; then a woman was cramp-wracked; now a pause, and men try to believe that the pestilence has passed by, that the demon has gorged himself with enough of victims. Alas! he is not satiated, but he gathers up his strength for a terrible raid among the guardsmen. By Monday, 7th of August, the scourge had reached the intensity of bitterness. The hospital marquees having been crowded long since, every morning, noon and night, saw us providing fresh accommodation for the dying, by pitching bell-tents near the surgeons' quarter. In each of these canvass ovens lay, huddled together, fifteen patients. Hence, in each tent, every stage of the epidemic was personated; the strong man wrung with the first spasms; the doomed wretch cold, pulseless, livid, with myriads of flies swarming in and out of his open mouth, and clustering upon his fixed eye-balls; the blue swollen corpse just rid of unspeakable torment. Was there a soldier of the division that gazed unappalled on those immedicable heaps of tortured humanity – the quick gasping and screaming beside the stark dead?'

Within divisions some regiments suffered less than others. Captain John Hume of the 55th (Westmoreland) Regiment had his own theory as to why. In his Division, the 2nd: 'The 95th suffered severely, losing many men ... The 30th and 55th, although they were camped close to the 95th, lost only a few men in Bulgaria from cholera – a proof, I think, that those regiments were acclimatised by being so long stationed at Gibraltar. The 95th . . . came straight from England. The 41st, 47th and 49th – Mediterranean regiments – lost very few men.'

That cholera was due to bad sanitation water was not discovered until 1883. A London doctor, John Snow, had already discovered that boiling drinking water could prevent cholera but his findings went largely unrecognised. Instead the disease was put down variously to miasma from the swamps and lakes around Varna, lack of acclimatisation, or the soldiers' prodigious consumption of fruit. Cholera belts were issued, which proved entirely useless. Those who did not die were left debilitated and demoralised.

It was not only in Bulgaria that British soldiers were dying of cholera. The 97th Regiment were at Piraeus, Athens harbour, along with 4,000 French troops, to encourage King Otho of the Greeks to stay neutral. Among them was Captain Hedley Vicars, who wrote to a family friend on 19 July: 'We are now in quarantine, as the cholera has broken out amongst the French. They have lost two officers and one hundred men. We have not lost a man; but it is a solemn time, and loudly calls upon each of us, "Prepare to meet thy God." '

It is generally assumed that the officer corps of the Victorian army was found from the aristocracy. Certainly the lisping cavalry plunger and the drawling dandy of the Guards could be found in the camps at Varna and later in the Crimea, where both would show their quality. The bulk of the Queen's officers, however, were drawn from the gentry; they were often younger sons, or sons of younger branches of landed families. Connected to land but not drawing an income from it, dependent on whatever interest their families or friends could muster, such men were generally serious-minded and dedicated to their regiments, their profession and their men. Hedley Vicars, the son of a Captain of Engineers, was one such man. He had been commissioned into the 97th in 1843 and served with them in the West Indies and Canada. Here, under the influence of Dr Twining, the garrison chaplain of Halifax, Nova Scotia, Vicars had become *serious* – he had been *saved*. He abandoned the reckless, spendthrift life he had formerly embraced, became a Sunday school teacher, visited the sick, read scriptures and prayed with the men of his company. One should not underestimate the potency of religion at this time, and its effect on men who had been recruited from society's outcasts. Before his regiment sailed from England, it was reported of Vicars that: 'Since Mr Vicars became so good, he has steadied about four hundred men in the regiment.'

They needed steadying now. Within a week of his previous letter, twenty-seven men of the 97th had died of cholera. Vicars wrote to his family: 'Do you remember poor young Reynolds, the soldier whom you noticed particularly when you gave the hymn books to the men at Kensington Barracks, and those kind words of parting counsel which they have never forgotten? I buried him and another comrade last night. I had intended speaking a few words to my men over the open graves of their dead messmates; but it was as much as I could do to get through the service; and as soon as I began to speak to them afterwards I could not for the life of me help crying like a child. The men cried and sobbed around me. It was of no use to try to go on, so I ordered them to "fall in", and we went mournfully back to the barracks.'

Vicars was constantly visiting the sick – he gave a graphic account of the agonies of one of his men: 'Poor fellow, he suffered most dreadfully; it was quite painful to stand by his bedside. I remained with him for nearly an hour, and spoke to him from time to time of Jesus Christ. But whenever the cramps came on, his screams quite drowned my voice. On leaving, I shook hands with him (his were black and cold) and told him to "behold the Lamb of God which taketh away the sins of the world", to look on Jesus, whose blood cleanseth from all sin. When I mentioned the name of Jesus he gave me such a wonderful look, full of peace and resignation. In less than four hours afterwards his soul had fled.'

For many of the enlisted men, without homes or families, their officers were the only people who had ever taken an interest in them. In some regiments it was even the custom for officers to give each of their men an individually chosen present at Christmas. This produced a strong bond between officers and men, and occasioned many instances of soldiers risking their lives to save their officers. On 23 August, by which time the 97th had lost 118 men to cholera, Vicars was visiting the hospital four or five times a day: 'I went especially to see Egan, an old soldier, who had been seventeen years in my Company. Poor fellow! he was so grateful; he said, when I wished him good-bye for the last time, "God bless *you*, Sir; and may the blessings of an old man rest upon your head, for coming to see and talk with an old comrade, when stretched out like this. Yes, Sir, and you have the love and blessing of every man in the regiment." I just tell you what he said, because it will give you pleasure. I feel myself that I have not done a quarter of what I ought to have done.'

By late August the cholera at Piraeus was past its worst. It was the same with the army in Bulgaria, but by then the damage was done. The French had suffered more than the British, and the Turks had suffered worst of all. By September 1854, seven thousand Allied soldiers had died and a further fifteen thousand were in hospital without a shot, so far, having been fired in anger.

Shots had been fired elsewhere in the world. An Anglo-French fleet commanded jointly by Sir Charles Napier and the French Vice-Admiral Deschenes had been operating in the Baltic since the spring. Having failed to entice the King of Sweden into the war, the fleet had reconnoitred Kronštadt and Šveaborg, decided against attacking either, and captured Bomarsund, on the Åland islands, instead. A small British squadron had blockaded Russia's White Sea ports and, in the Pacific, an attack on Petropavlovsk was beaten off with heavy casualties.

At Varna, by the end of August preparations for an expedition to the Crimea were under way. Transports were assembled at Varna and Balchik, boats were lashed together in pairs and provided with platforms for the transport of guns and horses; temporary wharves and landing stages were constructed for the loading of ships. The final lot of reinforcements for the initial landings were brought up to Varna. Among the last of these units to arrive was the 4th Light Dragoons, commanded by Lord George Paget. George Augustus Frederick Paget was the sixth son of the Marquis of Anglesey, who – as Lord Uxbridge – had commanded Wellington's cavalry at Waterloo. Anglesey's laconic remark to Wellington as a cannon-ball took off his leg – 'By God, Sir, I've lost my leg' – had elicited the brisk Wellingtonian response, 'By God, Sir, so you have.'

To many of the army's commanders, Paget was the son of an old and valued friend. A thoughtful soldier – he had already proposed a scheme for the establishment of an army reserve – Lord George had been about to resign his commission, following his marriage to his cousin Agnes, at the outbreak of war.

Almost immediately on arrival at Varna, Lord George paid a courtesy call on an old friend of his father's: 'My first visit, of course after attending to the details of disembarkation, was to Lord Raglan, who soon sent for me into his bedroom, where he transacted his business. He looked well, though rather pale and worn. He was much interested as to the details of my father's last illness and death, which had occurred since his departure from England, and his expressions moved me much.

'What a strange combination of circumstances that I, a mere subaltern, should have detailed to him, on the first day of my arrival at what may almost be termed the seat of war, the last moments of an old comrade in the Peninsula and Waterloo.'

Paget dined with Lord Raglan the following evening, and noted: 'They were in good spirits about the expedition, but with our present state of sickness, consider it a very grave undertaking, especially with our ill-developed commissariat, which, however, is believed to be better than the French.'

Time would tell. As to the state of the troops, Paget could see for himself. As new arrivals, Paget's regiment had been spared the ravages of cholera, but in his journal he noted the weakened state of many of the infantry marching down for embarkation: 'A party of the 1st Division just marched by our camp, many quite faint. Our fellows turned out, and carried their arms and knapsacks for them to the destination close by.'

The general reaction to the embarkation orders was one of relief. Trooper Albert Mitchell was on hand when Lord Cardigan received the news: 'We were in lines grooming our horses, Lord Cardigan came round. He was conversing with our colonel close by where I was at work, when suddenly his lordship exclaimed: "Hullo! a cocked hat, by Jove!" and looking up at the same time I saw a staff officer cantering across the plain towards the camp from the direction of Varna. He soon espied his lordship, and riding up to him, gave him a dispatch. It was at once opened, and as soon as it was read, Lord Cardigan turned to the colonel, saying: "Hurrah Doherty, we are for the Crimea! We march to-morrow morning for Varna for immediate embarkation." The news soon flew through the camp. Trumpeters were sounding "Orders", orderly sergeants were running with order books to take orders, and everyone was in the highest spirits, for we had been at this place long enough.'

Mitchell spoke for the whole army: their 'New and Happy Land' was a plague spot: 'Better to be shot in the Crimea than die of cholera here,' said one Guards officer. For all his doubts about the coming expedition, Henry Clifford wrote to his brother: 'All are very anxious to go, and there are but few in Camp who would not prefer certain death to the life they spend in camp here.'

Preparations for the invasion were hampered by a major fire in Varna on the night of 10 August. At 10 p.m. Lord George Paget noted in his journal: 'A fire is raging in the town, and spreading rapidly. The commissariat stores are evidently on fire, which will baffle all previous arrangements, and we shall no doubt starve in the meantime. The Greeks no doubt at the bottom of it; all it is believed in the pay of Russia.'

The following day he added: 'Five Greeks were caught setting fire to buildings by the French, who immediately bayoneted them. They do things better than we do in this way.'

According to Somerset Calthorpe: 'Our commissariat sustained a considerable loss in the fire; Mr Filder, the Commissary-General, says to the amount of 20,000*l*. It chiefly consists in rations of biscuits, of which 450,000 have been destroyed; also a large quantity of regimental uniforms.'

Despite this setback, embarkation began on 24 August, with infantry being ferried to the ships on the boats of the fleet; cavalry, artillery horses, wagons and guns crossing on improvised rafts. The French, short of troopships, decided to cram their 30,000 soldiers on their men-of-war; the Turks did the same with their 6,000 men. As a result only the Royal Navy – who would not hear of such a thing – were in any condition to engage the Black Sea fleet, should they choose to attack this armada at sea. The loading of the British army into 29 steamers and 56 sailing ships was carried out in a matter of days, but it was not without its complications. Captain Wilson, with the Guards, encountered one of them: 'What was to become of the women? ... some commanding officers, supposing (as they had reason to do) that it was intended to dispatch the entire bevy to Scutari, where they could be housed and fed, out of harm's way, had prevented wives accompanying their husbands on board ship. This naturally incensed the ladies – "they'd have their rights!

no *giniral* or *cornel* either should humbug *them*! A pretty thing, indeed, to be after parting a man and wife, as if they was work'us folks!" so they resorted to those powerful female weapons – tears and scolding; the air was rent, and the ears of the kind adjutant-general split with a shrill bewailing! the result may be anticipated: we were one morning rather surprised than delighted to perceive the approach of boat-loads of the excommunicated "misseses".'

Soldiers wives were one thing, officers' ladies quite another. Fanny Duberly, determined to accompany her husband to the Crimea, had enlisted Lord Cardigan, always a soft touch where ladies were concerned: 'Lord Cardigan, immediately on my arriving at Varna, went to head-quarters to ask Lord Raglan's permission for me to accompany the troops to the Crimea. Lord Cardigan was at the trouble of bringing me Lord Raglan's answer himself. It was a decided negative. "But" added Lord Cardigan (touched perhaps by my sudden burst of tears, for I was so worn and weak!), "should you think proper to disregard the prohibition, I will not offer any opposition to your doing so." '

Accordingly, when her husband's regiment boarded the *Himalaya*, Fanny disguised herself and went down to the shore: 'Lord Lucan, who was there, scanned every woman, to find traces of a lady; but he searched in vain, and I, choking with laughter, hurried past his horse into the boat. Here the crew received me very hospitably, gave me some water, and a compliment on the clearness of my cheeks, which "did not look as though I had done much hard work in the sun", and finally put me safely on board the *Himalaya*, where I was immediately handed down to my cabin.'

By 6 September both fleets had assembled in Balchik Bay, the general rendezvous, fifteen miles north of Varna. The following morning the ships got underway: the merchant steamers wheeled around, attached tow-ropes to the huge East Indiamen and then, with the British in five great columns – each carrying a division – the combined armada set off for the coast of the Crimea. Sea air, ship's rations and the prospect of action at last had a restorative effect on the men. The Coldstream Guards even received a reinforcement, as Captain Wilson recorded: 'We had not been at sea twelve hours, before one of the women, whose coming on board had been alluded to already, presented the good sergeant, her husband, with a pledge of mutual endearment, in the thumping shape of a rosy daughter. Some sentimental individuals suggested that the infant should be baptised "Euxina", in compliment to the great water on whose boisterous bosom she had entered this wicked world; but no romantic reasoning could persuade the parents to adopt so pagan a name. "Thank you, gentlemen, but we've settled on Charlotte Elizabeth, as being more Christian-like," was the pious reply of the worthy but unimaginative papa.'

Cholera, however, was still claiming victims – Wilson's regiment lost nine men to it two days later. On board the *Himalaya* Fanny Duberly wrote in her journal: 'Since I have been here death has been amongst us. Poor Captain Longmore, who on Friday helped me up the ship's side, was dead on Sunday morning – "Stretched no longer on the rack of this rough world." Death with such inexorable gripe appears in his most appalling shape. He was seized but on Friday with diarrhoea, which turned to cholera on Saturday, and on Sunday the body was left in its silent and solemn desolation. During his death struggle the party dined in the saloon, separated from the ghastly wrangle only by a screen. With few exceptions, the dinner was a silent one; but presently the champagne corks flew, and – but I grow sick, I cannot draw so vivid a picture of life and death. God save my dear husband and me from dying in the midst of the din of life!'

The diners' attitude might appear callous, but the Victorians lived with death. Letters from England were as likely as letters from the Crimea to contain news of sudden bereavement. Only a few weeks earlier Henry Duberly had received news from home of his stepsister's death, followed a few days later by the death of a close relative's baby.

On 8 September, with the Allies' fleet now strung out across the Black Sea, Lord Raglan in the steamer *Caradoc* caught up with the *Ville de France* and the French commander, Marshal St Arnaud. St Arnaud, a veteran of French campaigns in Algeria, was too ill to leave his ship (he had stomach cancer), and Raglan could not, with one arm, board the French vessel, so the discussion was carried out via intermediaries. St Arnaud finally agreed to abide by Raglan's choice of landing site. On 10 September the *Caradoc*, with a group of British and French officers aboard – including St Arnaud's second-in-command, General Canrobert – set off to reconnoitre the Crimean coast and the port of Sebastopol. Somerset Calthorpe was among them: 'Soon after four a.m. steam was up and we started for Sebastopol, going thirteen knots. At a quarter to five a.m. we first caught sight of the town, or rather the fortifications, which looked like a small white spot on the horizon: it was not yet day and we were five miles off; twenty minutes later we were within two miles and a half; and, as day broke, the town with its beautiful harbour appeared before us, each moment getting more distinct, and every house and window lighting up with the morning sun. It reminded one of a scene at a diorama, as it got clearer and clearer . . .

'We remained for upwards of half an hour gazing at the scene before us, with an interest deeply excited by the thought that there lay the prize for which we were going to fight, the great object of the ensuing campaign. The fortifications looked of immense strength, and appeared to bristle with guns. Our being there did not apparently cause any commotion, although probably the early hour prevented people being about in any numbers. We counted twelve large ships of war in the great harbour, but we could distinctly see the masts of many more in the inner harbour and Dockyard Creek.'

Later that day they steamed north up the Crimean coast looking for a suitable landing site. Flying a Russian flag, so as not to arouse suspicion, they examined and rejected in turn the mouths of the Belbec, Katcha, Alma and Bulganak Rivers before halting at a wide sandy beach, about 35 miles north of Sebastopol, and just south of the small port of Eupatoria – where a jolly party of Russian civilians were bathing.

Meanwhile, back at the fleet, preparations were in hand for the forthcoming landing, wherever it would be. On board the *Timandra* was Captain John Hume's 55th Regiment. Earlier in the day he and his brother, also a Lieutenant in the 55th, had gone skylarking, borrowing the ship's lifeboat to visit the frigate *Highflyer*, where their brother, Gustavus, was with the 38th. Now back on *Timandra*: 'Officers were to be seen pacing up and down, marching up and down the decks with the kits they were to land with strapped on in various ways. As there was no transport, officers and men had to depend on what they carried themselves when they landed. This included three days' rations of salt pork, biscuit, and rum. I am afraid that some of the junior officers were much amused at seeing the old officers practising for the coming marches.'

On board the *Megara*, Henry Clifford was not laughing. He was recovering from a severe bout of sickness, and he was filled with foreboding about the state of the army. A few days earlier he had written to his brother: 'It is a thousand pities our army did not go at Sebastopol on first leaving England when in rude health and full of spirits and enthusiasm. All these have vanished. The papers may tell you what they like but our army is not what it was on leaving England. We have been kept in idleness with hundreds falling around us by cholera and fever and everyone feels the greatest debility and repugnance to active exertion of any kind. I hope I may be able to write in a few days and tell you Sebastopol is taken, but I doubt it.'

At 7 a.m. on 11 September the *Caradoc* rejoined the Allied fleet, now assembled at Cape Tarkan. To Somerset Calthorpe it was an inspiring sight: 'The whole of the immense flotilla was at anchor in 22 fathoms water, and wonderful it was; such a forest of masts, yet quite out of sight of land: it was very calm, hundreds of boats were going about; you fancied that you were inside some great port, and wondered where the land could be.'

Soon boats more were moving about that great port bearing news of Lord Raglan's decision. Within the next few days the Allied armies would land on that wide sandy beach, in the ominously named Calamita Bay.

CHAPTER TWO

On 14 September 1854 the Allied armies invaded the Crimea. The French were the first ashore, at 7 o'clock, running up a Tricolore on their half of the beach, which seemed to the British to have grown overnight. The suspicion that they had moved the marker buoy that separated the two fleets, giving themselves the whole of the intended landing zone, did little to improve co-operation between the two armies. It was not until 9 o'clock that the British, having shifted to another beach slightly further south, were able to bring the first landing craft alongside their ships. According to Somerset Calthorpe: 'Sir G. Brown and General Airey and their staffs were the first English ashore; half a minute afterwards a boatload of the 7th Fusileers landed. It was then 20 minutes to 10 a.m. By 10 o'clock the French had 6,000 men ashore and we about 70.'

Timothy Gowing was one of them; he wrote: 'It was a toss-up between us and a boat-load of the 2nd Battalion Rifle Brigade as to who should have the honour of landing first on the enemy's shore; but with all due respect, I say the Fusiliers had it, though there was not much to boast of, as it was afterwards said the Rifles were a very good second.

'We were not opposed in landing; a few Cossacks were looking on at a respectful distance but made no attempt to molest us. It would have been madness on their part to have done so, considering the enormous force we could have brought to bear on them.'

From the deck of their troopship Captain Wilson and his Coldstream Guardsmen watched the Cossacks, 'scurvy-looking knaves in grey watch-coats, mounted on active, shaggy ponies, and armed with long, unpleasant-looking flag-less spears are watching our proceedings; anon, a more important actor treads the stage; an officer in green uniform, who, after coolly examining us through a portentous spy-glass, scribbles the result of his researches in a

35

note-book. As he writes, we observe some of the dingy cavaliers, above mentioned, clustering round him; to receive orders probably, for, in a few minutes, both officer and troops are spurring hard in all directions.'

It had been decided that the troops were too weak to carry their knapsacks; officers and men should wrap carry their kit wrapped in blanket and greatcoat and slung over their shoulders. According to Wilson, even the Guards, waiting on deck for their landing craft, looked a ragged crew. He recorded the proceedings: 'It would be difficult to imagine more hideous figures than most of us cut, when girded for work; officers of small stature, in particular, looking like animated lumps of undigested packages, all cloak, bundle, and hairy cap. The rank and file too, by no means, presented a comfortable appearance. Riding on their backs, in every conceivable and inconceivable trim, were those preposterous conformations of watch-coat, blanket, and "sundries", garnished with cooking utensils of various sorts. Greasy haversacs (severally pregnant 4lbs. of pork, three days' biscuit, and a ration of rum) together with the wooden water kegs, had resting places on the left hips. Sixty rounds of ammunition reposed on each man's loins. The Minié rifle was the object of every right hand's solicitude, and all perspiring heads were imbedded in towering shakoes of bearskin. It's our turn at last: a huge flat, towed by a man-o'-war's boat, pulls alongside, and one by one we tumble out of the dear old ship, amidst valedictory hurrahs from her tars; screams of "Keep yer 'pecker' up chaps" from the more strong-minded of the deserted females; and an hysteric flourishing of damp handkerchiefs by the younger matrons.'

By 3 p.m. most of the 1st and 2nd Divisions – roughly 14,000 men and 12 guns – had landed. Morale was high. 'Lord Raglan rode round the whole of the outposts . . .' wrote Calthorpe, '. . . Wherever he went today the troops cheered him, and indeed all seemed animated with the most enthusiastic spirits.'

It didn't last. During the afternoon the initially fine weather turned to intermittent rain. By the evening the rain was coming down in torrents and a hurricane was blowing. It was a portent of things to come. 'There was not a single tent for the English army,' wrote Timothy Gowing, 'so much for management! Thousands of Britain's sons who had come to fight for Queen and Country were thrown ashore, as it were, without shelter of any kind . . . Even as bad off as we were, our position was to be envied, for, although we were drenched to the skin, we were on terra firma; the poor marines and sailors in the men-of-war boats were towing large rafts, with horses, guns and detachments of artillerymen, amid a heavy swell from the sea, that was now running high – it was as dark as pitch, the horses almost mad with excitement, kicking and plunging. A number of poor fellows found a watery grave, rafts being upset in the heavy surf while attempting to land, the sea dashing with all its majestic force upon the sandy beach, although we could not see it. We made fires as best we could, with broken boats and rafts.

'The first night in the Crimea was a night long remembered by those who were there. It came on to rain in torrents, while the wind blew a perfect hurricane, and all, from the commanders down to the drummer boys, had to stand and take it as it came. And the rain did fall, only as it does in the tropics.'

With the 55th, John Hume and his men marched inland about four miles: 'It was quite dark when we halted; rain came down in torrents. We were told to make ourselves comfortable for the night! What a night that was! I have spent many uncomfortable nights, but that beat all for utter misery. Sleep was quite out of the question. Any one lying down got drenched. The only thing was to walk up and down watching the attempts of the men to light fires from weeds they collected off the bivouac ground ...

'Our first night in the Crimea decided the fate of many poor fellows who otherwise might have lived to meet the Russians. Cholera stuck to the army, and the night of 14th of September helped to spread the terrible disease.'

Those on board ship did not fare much better. Below decks on the *Jason* was Trooper Mitchell, who described the scene. 'The rain poured down the hatchways with such force that it soon flooded the floor on which we lay. When we arose in the morning we found our blankets were soaked in wet. The men who had landed were obliged to hold their horses all night, they could not lay down for a short time; had they done so, the sand being soft, their bodies would soon form a hollow which would soon fill up with water.'

When his turn came to go ashore Mitchell was nearly prevented: 'I was already dressed and accoutred on deck, and happening to pass by where the colonel was sitting. He asked me if I had lately come out of hospital? I answered, "No Sir." The doctor was standing near, and the colonel asked him if I had? He replied, "No, not since we had left England." They both said I looked badly, but I told them I felt quite well. They then told me if I did not feel equal to starting on the campaign now was my time to speak. I again assured them I had not fear, but that I would be able to get alone as well as the rest. Where the regiment went, there I wished to go, and should be very sorry to be left behind. They said no more, so I took it for granted I should land.'

Mitchell just had time to visit the sick bay, to see his comrade, Nicholson, who had been with him at the inn in Portchester, and who was now recovering from fever.

The trooper wrote, 'He was to remain on board with many others to be sent down to Scutari. I am sure when I shook hands with him, I had but poor hopes of seeing him again, for he was in a very low state. He was a young married man, and he gave me his wife's address so that I might write in case anything should befall him. I gave him my mother's address in case he should survive me. Those were moments which would touch the heart, be it ever so callous. Soon I heard my name called, saying, "Your horse is in the boat," so after another shake of the hand, and "Good-bye, God bless you, old fellow," I hurried off, down the companion ladder, and was soon on board the horse boat by my horse's head. Poor fellow, he knew me, and began smelling at my haversack for biscuit. I gave him a piece or two, but could not spare more, as I could not tell when I might get more.'

The day was dry but high winds hampered the landings. It was not until the afternoon of the following day that the disembarkation of the cavalry was complete. Officers were restricted to one horse each, and Fanny Duberly was without her beloved pony, 'Bob', and so had to say goodbye to Henry when the 8th Hussars landed. She described the separation: 'At ten o'clock today, with a failing heart, I parted from my dear husband, and watched him go ashore; whilst I, alas! having no horse, cannot follow him, but must go on board the *Shooting Star*, and get round by sea. How I hate it! How much rather I would endure any hardship than be separated from him at this time! But my reason and strength both tell me it's impracticable, and so I must make up my mind to it.'

Lord George Paget's regiment, the 4th Light Dragons, were the last to land. For the time being they were detached from the Cavalry

Division and told to bring up the rear with General Cathcart's 4th Division, the last of the infantry to land. For this, Paget commented in his journal, he was truly thankful, adding later: 'In saying this, I meant nothing as regards Lord Lucan. I always received every consideration from him, and there was no one under whom I would rather serve; but I certainly had misgivings as to my position relatively to him and Lord Cardigan combined.'

The two earls had been bickering ever since Cardigan had arrived at Varna, Lucan, supposedly in command of all the cavalry, had been left behind at Scutari with the Heavy Brigade and, after they had gone on, alone. In his absence Cardigan had assumed, and been allowed, the role of cavalry commander – and found it hard, once Lucan caught up with his command, to revert to being a subordinate. Lord Raglan, himself impeccably mannered and hating anything resembling a scene, had simply resolved to keep the noble brothers-in-law apart as much as possible.

For the forthcoming advance Paget noted: 'The French have secured for themselves the right flank, that protected by the ships and nearest the provisions, which gives the English the post of honour and hard work.'

In fact, it made sense that the British – as the two armies marched with the sea on their right – should take the landward side. Theirs was the only army that had any cavalry to scout ahead and defend the flank of both armies from an attack from the Crimean interior. As for provisions, the French had yet again proved themselves the better foragers. Part of the problem was that Lord Raglan, as usual following Wellingtonian precedent, had insisted that everything locally procured should be paid for – a process both time-consuming and expensive. The French, following *their* Napoleonic tradition, simply helped themselves. They had made good use of their two hours' start on 14 September and had helped themselves to most of the *arabas* – native carts – in the area.

The British had brought no wagons with them – even the ambulance wagons, painstakingly collected in Bulgaria, had been left behind after being judged too frail for the rough terrain of the Crimea. One British Quartermaster-General, Lord Ros, had already buckled under the task of procuring food, fodder and transport for the army. The best efforts of his successor, General Airey, had so far produced only 350 wagons, 67 camels and 253 horses, 45 cartloads of poultry, corn and flour and 1,000 head of livestock. Inadequate supply and lack of transport were to dog this army to the end of the campaign.

In the days that followed the landing St Arnaud, the French commander, made little secret of his frustration at the delays of the British. His army was ready, he repeatedly told Lord Raglan, so were the Turks – how much longer would the British be? The contrast between the styles of the two commanders struck Lord George Paget forcefully: 'I was riding today with the Duke of Cambridge (Commander of the 1st Division) about the French camp, when we fell in with St Arnaud, and the contrast between him and Lord Raglan, whom we had just left, was very typical of the two nations. He had a staff of about twenty; two Chasseurs d'Afrique as advanced guard, and a sort of body-guard besides, with an orderly close to him, carrying a beautiful silk tricolour standard. We rode with him to Lord Raglan, who came out in a mufti coat to meet him, and looked *less* like a commander-in-chief and *more* like a gentleman.'

If he was rattled by St Arnaud's urgings, Raglan did not show it; nevertheless on 18 September, concluding that the transport situation was unlikely to improve, Raglan agreed that both armies should commence the march on Sebastopol the next day. The tents that had been landed to give the men a few nights' shelter would have to be sent back to the ships – the reserve ammunition would have to be given priority on what few wagons there were. Apart from that, the army would survive on what each man could carry.

On the morning of 19 September the Allies began their march. Their objective, Sebastopol, lay thirty-five miles away, at the southern tip of the Crimea; the armies would march southwards down the coast with the sea on their right. At right angles to the Allies' route ran four rivers*, at any one of which the Russians might be expected to make a stand. The British would take the left, landward, side of the advance; the French, followed by the Turks, would take the right, marching under the protection of the combined fleets.

It is difficult to exaggerate the importance of Allied sea-power in this campaign. It was the Allies' control of the Black Sea which had

* See Map 1.

allowed the armies their untroubled passage to the Crimea – the Russian Black Sea fleet being in no position to mount a challenge at sea – and had underwritten their unopposed landings. From a soldier's point of view the British and French men-of-war represented vast floating batteries of heavy artillery whose combined firepower could destroy an army. It was these fleets which currently constituted the Allied armies' supply base and hospital, and guaranteed its communications. In the event of a reverse on land they offered a powerful fire-base under whose guns the Allies could rally. In the last resort, they were an escape route.

There was the usual delay while the French – who had been ready since 6 a.m. – fumed and the British packed up what couldn't be carried and hauled it down to the beach.

'This took a long time,' wrote Calthorpe, 'and occasioned the troops employed much labour and fatigue. Part of the 4th Division, under General Torrens, and the 4th Light Dragoons being left to see the beach cleared of all the stores, &c and also the sick embarked, of which I am sorry to say there were no inconsiderable number. All this delayed the movement of the troops, and they actually did not march till near 9 o'clock.'

When they did, the army set off in five great divisional columns, protected on front and flanks by riflemen and cavalry, with two divisions leading. On the left was the Light Division, commanded by Sir George Brown – Peninsular veteran, martinet, advocate of 'pipe-claying, close-shaving and tight-stocking'. Brown's Division contained some the army's finest regiments, the 77th East Middlesex, the 88th Connaught Rangers, the 19th Green Howards, the 23rd Royal Welch Fusiliers, the 33rd Duke of Wellington's, and Timothy Gowing's 7th Royal Fusiliers. To their right marched the 2nd Division, commanded by Sir de Lacy Evans. Evans had served in the Peninsula and America, had been present at the burning of the White House in 1814, and had commanded a force of 10,000 British volunteers in the Carlist Wars in Spain in 1835. In his division were the 95th Derbyshire (not to be confused with the 95th of the Napoleonic Wars, who were now re-designated The Rifle Brigade), John Hume's 55th Westmoreland, the 30th Cambridge, and the three regiments collectively known as the 'Forties': the 41st, 47th, and 49th, the Welch, Lancashire and Hertfordshire Regiments respectively. Much has been made of the age of these two commanders, but de Lacy Evans was one of the army's most respected officers, and both men knew how to put themselves at the head of a division and go straight at the enemy.

Behind the Light Division was the 1st Division, commanded by HRH the Duke of Cambridge, the Queen's cousin, and – so far – untried in battle. His division contained a Guards Brigade – the 3rd Battalion Grenadier Guards, 1st Battalion Coldstream Guards and 1st Battalion Scots Fusilier Guards (as the Scots Guards were then known), and a Highland Brigade, the 42nd, Black Watch, and the 79th Cameron and 93rd Sutherland Highlanders. To their right marched the 3rd Division under Sir Richard England. Bringing up the rear and guarding the baggage was that remnant of Sir George Cathcart's 4th Division that had not been left to clear the beaches.

As Cathcart's division was the last to land, it was natural that it should form the rearguard – and given the army's dire transport situation, guarding the baggage from marauding Cossacks was a vital task – but it may not have suited General Cathcart. Sir George Cathcart was one of the army's rising stars; as a young man he had been an ADC to the Duke of Wellington at Waterloo. More recently he had successfully commanded the army in the same Kaffir War in which Henry Clifford had served. Travelling out with him, Surgeon Munro of the 93rd thought: 'Sir George Cathcart was very courteous to us all, but there was a condescension and dignity in his manner that reminded one of the "Grand Seigneur".'

Cathcart had good reason – before he left for the East he had been given, by the Duke of Newcastle, the War Secretary, a dormant commission, by which he would succeed as Commander-in-Chief should anything happen to Lord Raglan. Already Cathcart was feeling left out of things, and his frustration was to grow in the weeks to come.

The march began in bright sunshine. With Colours flying and bands playing it was a stirring sight. Wilson thought: 'The advance of those superb battalions of ours was an august, a moving spectacle. It was a sight that made every man-at-arms thank God he had been born an Englishman.'

Soon, however, the heat began to take its toll. Calthorpe recalled: 'The day was excessively hot, and many men fell out from exhaustion. There were frequent halts during the march to allow stragglers to join their regiments again. No ground could be found better adapted for the movement of troops than that we marched over; the only want was water and this was what made the troops suffer so much.'

Lack of drinking water had been a problem from the beginning, and contributed to the worsening condition of men and horses. General Airey had only managed to find one drinkable spring near the landing beaches; the few others were brackish, and so many men had not been able to fill their canteens. The salt pork that was the soldiers' main ration added to their sufferings. Men already weakened were prey to renewed bouts of sickness.

'For the first two hours,' says Wilson, 'we bore the fatigue and the almost vertical glare tolerably well; but afterwards men began to "fall out" and cases of wretches rolling over and over again on the ground, biting the dust, and screeching in the red-hot pincer-like grip of cholera became more frequent.

'And now an astonishing fact became patent to all – we had no ambulance! We had invaded an enemy's country without means of transporting the sick and wounded beyond a few "stretchers" in the hands of bandsmen and drum-boys. The sick and wounded of 27,000 British soldiers were to be carried bodily over burning steppes where water was not, by drummers and fifers!'

As well as stragglers, the army's route was littered with items of equipment abandoned by the exhausted men. Bringing up the rear on this fourteen-mile march was Lord George Paget's regiment: 'I never saw such a scene as the last five miles of it,' wrote Paget. 'An occasional shako and mess-tin lying on the ground first bore evidence that the troops in our front had begun to get fatigued and to flag. In the innocence of our hearts we began by picking these up. A little further a man, and anon another, were found lying down, knocked up; we used our persuasive powers to make these move on, sometimes with success. This went on gradually increasing, till ere a mile or two was passed the stragglers were lying thick on the ground, and it is no exaggeration to say that the last two miles resembled a battlefield! Men and accoutrements of all sorts lying in such numbers, that it was difficult for the regiments to thread their way through them.'

When the army reached the first of the rivers, the Bulganak, discipline almost broke down. John Hume's 55th were among the first to reach the water.

'It was quite impossible to keep the men in the ranks when we got near water, and the stream was soon thick with mud ... While we halted the artillery and cavalry were ordered to the front, as a Russian force of about 8,000 men was drawn up on some heights not very far off, and the first brush with the enemy took place.'

It was Cardigan who went forward for this, the first clash between British and Russian forces in the Crimea. As the infantry were drinking greedily from the muddy stream of the Bulganak, a line of Cossack skirmishers was seen beyond the river. Lord Raglan ordered Cardigan forward with the advance guard. To drive off the Cossacks, Cardigan sent out skirmishers from the 13th Light Dragoons to engage them with carbines. One of them was Albert Mitchell. He wrote, 'Their skirmishers were more numerous than ours, and they soon opened fire, which we promptly returned. They were better situated than we were on top of the hill, they could easily rein back out of our sight and then come forward and fire, and then back again. We being only halfway up the hill had no cover. I was the third file from the right of the line, and opposite to me I saw a man, who I supposed was an officer or non-commissioned officer. He appeared to be directing the left of their skirmishers, as he was continually shouting words of command. I fired several shots at him, and believe he was hit by the last shot, for he reined back out of sight, and the next moment a riderless horse was galloping along the crest of the hill. At any rate, he did not show himself any more. I expect we had been nearly half an hour skirmishing. They hit none of us, a few of theirs got hit, which proved that bad as our carbines were, theirs were worse.'

While this had been going on Lord Lucan had joined Cardigan. The two men were arguing. Cardigan was urging a charge; Lucan, quite rightly, refused to let him. What neither man could see from their position was that beyond the line of Cossacks was a mass of Russian infantry – men of the 17th Division, and guns. Lord Raglan could see this, and – reluctant, because of the present state of the army, to bring on a general engagement – sent General Airey to insist that the cavalry withdraw. By now the Russians had brought up a battery of guns and the Royal Horse Artillery were replying.

Presently the British cavalry withdrew in perfect order, as if at a field day on Hounslow Heath, while the horse gunners, together with a battery from the Light Division, traded shots with the Russian guns.

Standing beside his uncle, Lord Raglan, Somerset Calthorpe watched the engagement. 'The whole affair was the prettiest thing I ever saw, so exactly as one had seen it done dozens of times at Chobham and elsewhere. If one had not seen the cannon-balls coming along at the rate of a thousand miles an hour, and bounding like cricket balls, one would really have thought it only a little cavalry review,' he wrote.

It was less pretty on the receiving end. Albert Mitchell saw: 'Several shells burst close to us, and some fell in the ranks; one struck a troop horse a few files on my left. It struck him in the side, and bursting inside the horse, cleaned him out as though a butcher had done it. His rider and the next man were both wounded and taken to the rear, and afterwards sent to England.

'We claim to have the first casualty in the war. Sergeant Priestley, of ours, was allowed to be the first British soldier wounded in the Crimea. He lost a leg. It was said afterwards that Her Majesty the Queen presented him with a cork leg, also that he obtained an extra grant of pension on that account.'

If the Light Brigade had given and taken first blood, it was little consolation to Lord Cardigan. Lord Lucan had rubbed him up the wrong way once more, denying him his charge, and the jeers of the Cossacks as his command had withdrawn were nothing to the jeers of the infantry as they arrived back in the British lines. To foot-sore infantrymen it must have seemed that the cavalry had an easy time of it, and their supposed humiliation was by no means unwelcome. A soldier of the 41st summed up his comrades' feelings when he wrote, 'Serves them bloody right. Silly peacock bastards!'

Although Lord Lucan had behaved quite correctly, the blame for the Bulganak affair attached itself to him. It was here that he acquired the nickname 'Lord Look-on', which was to dog him – and the cavalry as a whole – in the weeks to come.

As the British declined to be drawn into action, the Russians, in accordance with their instructions, withdrew. Their commander, Prince Menschikoff, had selected a position a few miles further south, where he was confident he could delay the Allies for at least three weeks, if not defeat them entirely. As evening drew on, the

Allies advanced once more, onto the high ground south of the Bulganak. Across the plain to the south ran the next river line, that of the Alma. On the heights beyond they could see, in the twilight, the camp fires of the Russian army, barring the road to Sebastopol.

The army settled down to pass another night in the open. Pickets were thrown out, men gathered what they could to make bivouac fires and huddled round them, wrapped in blankets and cloaks. Every man knew that on the morrow they would be taking part in the British army's first major battle since Waterloo. For most of the men it would also be their first battle. For the officers of the 95th Derbyshire – in Evans' 2nd Division – it was to be their regiment's baptism of fire. Inevitably the hushed conversation among the officers turned to the prospect of being wounded. Captain Heyland was of the opinion that if he must undergo an amputation, he would rather lose an arm, while Ensign Boothby declared he would rather lose a leg. Both men would have cause to remember this conversation before another sun had set.

Albert Mitchell and his fellow troopers had already had their baptism of fire. Now they lay down, 'each man behind his horse and soon asleep. I had slept about a couple of hours when I was awakened by some one shaking me and saying, "Wake up you fool." I must have required a good deal of waking for he had to repeat his polite request several times. On looking about me, I saw a man of my own troop with two camp kettles and a pannikin in his hand. He filled the pannikin from one of the kettles and gave me a drink. I did not require twice asking, for I smelt it was rum. He then filled my water barrel, and went to several others and served them the same as he had done me. I asked no questions, but turned down again and was asleep in two minutes.'

With the 7th Royal Fusiliers, Timothy Gowing said he and his comrades, 'sat talking for some little time of our homes and friends far away. My comrade had just had about an hour's sleep when, on waking, he told me he had a presentiment that he should fall in the first action. I tried to cheer him up and drive such nonsense out of his head. I thought he was not well, and he replied that he was very ill, but should be out of all pain before tomorrow's sunset. However, he was determined to do his duty, let the consequence be what it might.

'"Come," he continued, "let's walk about a little. I am getting cold." Afterwards, getting hold of my arm, he stopped, looked me full in the face, and twice repeated the solemn words: "Eternity, Eternity, know and seek the Lord while He may be found. Call upon Him while He is near, for you cannot tell what tomorrow will bring forth, and it may be too late then."

'Then he repeated parts of hymns which I had often heard sung when a boy; we pledged that we would do all that we could for each other, in life or death.'

The influence of religion on men at this time – even men drawn from the lowest reaches of society – was enormous. Gathering more sticks for his fire, Captain Wilson heard a Coldstream Guardsman who had gone aside to pray. His was only one of the many thousands of prayers addressed to God, or Allah, that night by the men of the four armies mustered by the Alma, but it may speak, with suitable amendments, for all of them.

Wilson recorded, 'I heard a voice speaking in terms of extraordinary earnestness. I looked and listened, and there, within twenty paces, but far too absorbed to heed my approach, his clasped hands stretched towards heaven, intense emotion ennobling his hard sun-burnt features, knelt a private soldier pouring forth prayer. He asked forgiveness for his sins, through the atonement of the Redeemer; he implored the Almighty protection in the impending strife, for the sake of his wife and children left in England; he entreated the Divine blessing on every officer, non-commissioned officer and private of his battalion – on every living soul in the Allied host.'

CHAPTER THREE

It was what the French called *un position magnifique*. From the southern bank of the Alma river the ground rises in smooth grassy slopes to a line of downland between three hundred and five hundred feet above sea level. An army occupying these heights of Alma could dominate the river and the approaches to it, including the main road to Sebastopol. At the western end of these heights, where the slopes are so steep as to be almost inaccessible, three hundred and fifty-foot cliffs plunge into the Black Sea, where an old Tartar fort guards the mouth of the river. The heights continue for about two miles along the south bank, then curl away to the south before returning to the river in a series of gentler slopes. There were, at the time, two river crossings; at Almatamack, a mile inland, there was a ford; and at Bourliouk, three miles inland, the main road crossed the river over a wooden bridge, then climbed the heights via a gorge flanked by Kourgane Hill to the east and Telegraph Height to the west.*

Here Prince Menschikoff had disposed his army, some 35,000 men: 42 infantry battalions, 16 cavalry squadrons, 11 squadrons of Cossacks and 84 guns – a mixture of field guns and heavier guns, 'guns of position'. The Russian artillery were regarded as an élite corps. The Russians set great store by their guns which, by comparison with musket or rifle fire, or cold steel, were by far the biggest killers on the battlefield. Artillery ammunition at this time consisted of roundshot, shell and grape. Roundshot – cannonballs – used at longer ranges could kill whole files of men at a time, and then bounce on to kill more further on. Shell was a hollow ball packed with explosives which, fitted with a time fuse, would explode among the enemy, the fragments causing casualties. A more

* See Map 2.

lethal type contained musket balls which – the shell being timed to explode fifteen feet above the enemy's head – would shower bullets down on him. This was also known as Shrapnel after its inventor. The fuses in these shells were surprisingly accurate and good gunners could direct their fire with lethal effect. At closer ranges gunners used various grades of grapeshot, or canister. This consisted of clusters of muskets balls of varying sizes – grape being the largest – and the effect was similar to a burst from a machine-gun. The Russian defence plan was largely based on the devastating effect of these kinds of munitions from massed guns over ground devoid of cover.

Considering his left practically immune to direct assault because of the nature of the ground, Menschikoff posted the bulk of his cavalry on his right. Here the ground was better for them, they could protect his own landward flank, and fall on the Allies' left if (or more likely, when) they attempted an assault across the river. In the centre he correctly identified the Kourgane as the key to the position, and here he placed his headquarters. To protect it he had constructed two earthworks – redoubts – on the forward slopes: the Great Redoubt and the Lesser Redoubt. These redoubts were earthworks three to four feet high; the Great Redoubt contained twelve heavy guns, 24- and 32-pounders which were chiefly designed to fire down onto the river and on any troops approaching it, but could also fire onto the bridge at Bourliouk and beyond. The Lesser Redoubt – slightly higher up the hill, and containing nine guns – was intended to protect the flank of the Great Redoubt, but could also fire on frontal attackers. The ground in front of these batteries – on both sides of the river – had been swept clear of cover and the ranges had been marked out with painted stakes. Both of these batteries were flanked and backed up by dense columns of infantry, with still more in reserve above. The post road itself, which ran to the right of the Kourgane (looking southwards from the Allied position) through what was known as the Pass – was protected by two artillery batteries – sixteen guns in all – known the Causeway Batteries. These batteries were supported by a total of 11 battalions of infantry.

These two positions, the Great Redoubt and the Pass,* were to be

* See Map 2.

the objectives of the British – the Light Division and 2nd Divisions respectively – in the battle to come. Facing the French on Telegraph Hill and the heights to the west was the left wing of the Russian army, consisting of 13 battalions of infantry and twenty field guns – a total of 10,000 men.

Somerset Calthorpe, riding with Lord Raglan's staff, wrote on his first sight of the enemy massed on the heights of Alma, 'About 11 a.m. we came in sight of the heights of the Alma. The Army was then halted, and the allied Generals advanced to the front of our skirmishers, and reconnoitred the enemy's position. Even at this distance we could see that it was a position of immense strength; and what appeared at first sight as dark patches of underwood on the side of the hills, proved to be masses of infantry when examined with a telescope.'

The Allied staffs – St Arnaud, desperately ill and kept in the saddle only by will-power and excitement at the prospect of action, and Lord Raglan, his usual imperturbable, amiable self – rode forward to finalise the Allied plan of attack. In a letter home, Calthorpe summed it up: 'The Division of General Bosquet, supported by the division of Turks, were to endeavour to cross the river Alma at its mouth, and under the protection of the guns from our ships of war, to gain the heights, and in that manner turn the Russian left. This done, the two other divisions of the French army were to ford the river, and the English the same; but it was clearly understood that the English were not to advance to the attack until the French had gained the heights nearest the sea, and turned the Russian left.'

The task ahead for the British army – once the French had ascended the heights and were rolling up the Russian left – was no easy one. First, they would have to face an advance under artillery fire over open ground, then a battle through broken ground, enclosures and vineyards down to the river, then a river crossing, then an assault uphill against entrenched batteries supported by massed infantry. All of this would have to be done under a constant fire from massed heavy artillery.

The Russian infantry were deployed, and would fight, in the massed columns of attack that had served them so well in the wars against Napoleon, and which the French themselves were still employing. These battalion columns – rectangles of about 800 men, usually thirty-two paces across and twenty-five deep – were easy to manoeuvre, had an intimidating effect on the enemy, and prevented individuals breaking off and running away. If its massed ranks were highly vulnerable to artillery and its narrow frontage meant that only the first two or three ranks could fire, this was of secondary importance to the Russians, whose smooth-bore muskets were only accurate up to about one hundred and fifty yards. The beauty of the column from the Russian point of view was that it delivered men onto the objective *en masse*, ready to employ their favoured weapon: the bayonet.

'Thrust the bayonet with force,' wrote Alexander Suvarov, the Russian army's eighteenth-century hero. 'The bullet misses, the bayonet doesn't. The bullet's an idiot, the bayonet's a fine chap. Stab once and throw the Turk off the bayonet. Bayonet another, bayonet a third; a real warrior will bayonet half a dozen and more. Keep a bullet in the barrel. If three should run at you, bayonet the first, shoot the second and lay out the third with your bayonet. This isn't common but you haven't time to reload . . .'

These very words were drummed into the Russian peasant soldier, and remained an essential part of their military doctrine well into the twentieth century. The British would face these tactics in the thin, two-deep line that had served them well under their nineteenth-century hero, Wellington. Designed to maximise firepower, the line deployed the fire of every man onto the advancing enemy columns and, if all went according to plan, would stop them in their tracks. First the column would halt, then waver, men would start melting away – usually from the rear – and then the whole column would turn tail. At this point the officers of the line would order a bayonet charge, which would sweep the enemy from the field. British lines had beaten French columns from Vimeiro to Waterloo, but they required good command and control from officers and NCOs and great steadiness from the men. The coming infantry clash would be a classic one of line against column. So far, so Napoleonic, but this time there was a new factor of which one side knew little, and the other side had barely understood: the deadly power of the Minié rifle.

While the generals had conferred on a knoll well forward, the British had waited in their two great lines, the Light and 2nd Divisions forward, the 1st and 3rd Divisions in support. To Albert Mitchell, with the 13th Light Dragoons: 'It was a grand sight indeed.

There were the Guards and Highlanders in all their glory, their accoutrements glittering in the sunshine; the bearskins of the Guardsmen, and the bonnets of the Highlanders causing them to appear at a distance almost as large as a body of cavalry. The Riflemen were in front of the whole laying down in skirmishing order, ready to spring up at a moment's notice.'

Among the Highlanders, Surgeon George Munro took the opportunity to look at the faces of the men around him. 'During this halt there was opportunity to observe how the prospect of battle affected different individuals. There was general expression of satisfaction that at last, after long months of weary waiting, the anxiously looked-for day was at hand on which we were to meet and measure our strength with the enemy. Even those who were ill and dispirited (and there were many such who had contracted disease in Bulgaria) brightened up apparently to health and strength for the occasion. On every face there was visible an anxious look, betokening the consciousness that some event of great moment was impending, to meet which and attain success would test the strength and require the courage of every man. Those who had seen war before, and they were very few, were perfectly calm, and made their preparations in a quiet methodical manner; of those who had no previous knowledge or experience of war, and they were the great majority of the army, some were restless and hurried in their words and movements, others silent, or calm in speech and manner. Some lay on the ground examining the distant Russian position through their field-glasses; others stood in little groups, conversing in low voices, about the expected battle, and how it would be fought.'

Presently, Sir Colin Campbell, commander of the Highlanders, gave the order for the men to get loose half of their cartridges, and the noise and clinking of equipment seemed curiously loud. Shortly afterwards, right across the army, officers could be heard giving the order: 'With Ball cartridge, load!' Many that were there remembered the effect those words produced. Here was the moment that every soldier had both dreamt of and dreaded: the moment of live ammunition. Captain John Hume had drawn comfort earlier in the day during the advance when, as he recorded, 'During one of the halts Major Rose said to my brother and me, "Boys, have you got your prayer books? Let us read the 91st Psalm together." We read that beautiful and most appropriate Psalm for those about to be engaged in battle, and we resumed our march feeling that nothing could harm us unless it was God's will.'

How many more men, about to advance into a murderous hail of roundshot, grape and canister, now muttered the words of that Psalm, heard at countless church parades in England or Ireland, Malta and Gibraltar, the Cape or India?

> Thou shalt not be afraid for the terror by night; nor for the arrow
>   that flieth by day;
> Nor for the pestilence that walketh in darkness; nor for the
>   destruction that wasteth at noonday.
> A thousand shall fall at thy side, and ten thousand at thy right
>   hand; but it shall not come nigh thee.

The French advance began at one o'clock. General Bosquet's Division, laid down their knapsacks and, followed by the Turkish contingent, ascended the heights, one brigade at the river's mouth, the other by the steep track that led up from Almatamack. The powerful and accurate fire from the Allied fleets rendered the heights closest the sea untenable to the Russians, and Bosquet's right-hand brigade quickly gained a lodgement there. Bringing up his artillery Bosquet was soon firing into the Russian left flank and, although outnumbered, was making an impression on the Russian guns deployed against him. Instead of applying further pressure with his infantry, however, Bosquet now waited for reinforcements. The next division inland from Bosquet was Canrobert's, then that of Prince Napoleon, the Emperor's cousin.*

St Arnaud's orders to these two were simplicity itself – 'With such men as you I have no orders to give. I have just to point at the enemy' – which left him in the clear if things went wrong. Canrobert's Zouaves pushed up the heights in fine style, driving the Russian skirmishers before them, but the tracks leading up to the plateau here were inaccessible to the artillery, which had to be sent round to the right, to try to ascend by the track used by Bosquet's left brigade. It was a fast tenet of French military doctrine that infantry must never advance without artillery support, so Canrobert's drive ground to a halt. Next to him, Prince Napoleon's division had made even less progress, held up by vineyards, the

---

* See Map 2.

river and strong opposition from Russian troops on Telegraph Hill. All of this had taken place to the right of the Sebastopol road. To the left, the British stood and waited.

Meanwhile Lord Raglan and his staff were waiting to hear from the French. Where they were standing, on the Sebastopol Road, they were within range of the Russian guns. Two horses were killed, the shot that killed the second almost touching Lord Raglan's back. Calthorpe noted his uncle's coolness under fire: 'He took no more notice of the firing than if he had been at a review. All his thoughts were turned to the French, for he had expected before this to have heard from Marshal St Arnaud, that he had successfully turned the Russian left. He accordingly despatched Commandant Vico to see how they were going on. Vico had not been gone a moment when a French staff-officer came galloping up (I think from Prince Napoleon), begging Lord Raglan to advance, and adding, "*Nous sommes massacrés!*" Lord Raglan thought it no use remaining any longer, although he had heard nothing from the Marshal . . .

'He consequently ordered the whole line to advance.'

From out of Raglan's Headquarters group, ADCs rode to take the orders to the leading divisions. The order to de Lacy Evans' 2nd Division was carried by an excitable young cavalry officer, of Irish extraction and Continental upbringing, by the name of Louis Nolan. It was not the last attack order Captain Nolan would carry in this campaign.

As the French had begun their advance, the British army had moved forward in column. Almost at once the Russian guns had opened up with roundshot. In response the British deployed into line. The two-deep line made a much less satisfactory target for artillery than close-packed columns. For the coming attack on the heights of Alma the British deployed into two such lines which – although not the terms used at the time – will be referred to as the Assault Line and the Support Line. The Assault Line comprised the Light Division on the left and the 2nd Division on the right; the Support Line, of the Guards and Highlanders on the left and the 3rd Division on the right. Private Bloomfield was with the Light Company of the 95th Foot (The Derbyshire Regiment) in the Assault line. Each battalion had two élite flank companies. The Light Company – generally called the Light Bobs – consisted of especially agile men who were crack shots. They usually spread out in skirmish order in front of the battalion. The other flank company was the Grenadier company – nick-named the Hulks or Crushers – composed of the biggest, most powerful men in the regiment. Every battalion had a Grenadier company – not to be confused with the Grenadier Guards who, naturally, considered themselves élite *battalions*. The 95th were a new regiment, and Private Bloomfield – a Light Bob – remembered that: 'Every man seemed in high spirits, this being the Regiment's maiden Battle. After we had fallen in and got steady, I cast my eye along the line and wondered how many of these brave men were never to see the sun rise again ... Our Light Company Officer drew his sword, stepped to the front and called out in a light clear voice. Light Company – Advance.'

All across the Assault Line that order was repeated and men clambered to their feet and shook out into formation. Then, preceded by a thin line of skirmishers, the Assault Line – with a frontage of two miles and a depth of two men – advanced across the open ground towards the river. The Support Line – the Guards, the Highlanders and the 3rd Division – halted and stood at ease at the extreme range of the enemy guns. Wilson, with the Coldstream Guards, wrote: 'For a time, we had nothing to do but to strain anxious eyes on our advancing comrades ... Sad to relate, the first overt act of Brown's "lambs" was in defiance of "regulation"; no sooner were they in good earnest on the road to death or glory, than, with one accord, plucking their forage caps out of the haversacks, they chucked away their detested shakoes; most of the camp-kettles, too, shared a like fate, so that, in one particular spot, the ground was absolutely strewed with abandoned articles of infantry equipment.'

It wasn't just the shakoes – the full-dress headgear – that went. Sir George Brown, the division's commander, was a devotee of the stock, the tight black leather collar designed to keep the soldier's head up. Private Howells of the 19th saw: 'men in the ranks instinctively pulling off their stocks and fixing them under their left shoulder straps. Many threw them away altogether. Every man was determined to do his best – and he did it well. It was contagious, the throwing off of these stocks that day. There was no order for it and I certainly heard no order against it. The men knew that their stocks were an obstruction and they threw them away. That was the beginning of the end of the stocks.'

Lighter, and doubtless more comfortable, the Lights pressed on, flanked by de Lacy Evans' 2nd Division. The Russian fire intensified. Wilson continued: 'A tremendous cannonade was pouring on the advancing troops; hence red dots began to speckle the plain, and sometimes a great gap was, on a sudden, cut in the unshaken line. And now, the round-shot, its duty done in front, or else having missed aim altogether, came sneaking towards the supporting divisions with such a gentle glide, that the men could hardly be persuaded to lift a leg, to allow the dying missile to pass unobstructed through their ranks. "Why, Lord love you, sir, it's no more hurtful nor a spent cricket ball," they said; however after a poor fellow had lost a foot in an attempt to arrest one of these perfidious sliders, the soldiers grew wary.

'Notwithstanding the awe of the occasion, the antics of a pretty little Maltese terrier, belonging to the jolly drummers of the Coldstreams, drew loud laughs from the light-hearted soldiery. Whenever a ball hopped along the ground with more liveliness than usual, little "Toby", darting from his bed among the drums and fifes, would give tongue in chase as friskily as though he hunted a mouse.'

With the Grenadier Guards, Captain and Adjutant George Higginson took the time, as Surgeon Munro had done with the Highlanders, to examine the faces of the men around him. 'Even in our new position some half-spent round shot now and then found a victim, and I looked with considerable interest at the countenances of our men as a gunner belonging to a battery formed up on our right flank, struck full on the head by an eighteen-pounder shot, fell lifeless from the limber. I could trace in their expressions at first astonishment, followed by one of sternest resolution.'

As the Assault Divisions marched down towards the river, the right-hand division, the 2nd, found themselves crowded from their right by the French – themselves crammed in between the British army and the sea. The regiments of the 2nd Division began to edge to their left. Lieutenant Carmichael of the 95th Foot recalled: 'We were ordered to take ground to our left two or three times, reforming line after each movement. We were under fire of round shot at the time, and several men were knocked out of the ranks, one man being Captain Eddington's servant, Thos. Avery, who was in the centre of the rear rank, where he was placed, as he was not a Grenadier, but only attached to the Company, to be with his master.'

This constant edging to the left led to the 95th Regiment losing touch with its own division and becoming entangled with the Light Division. Lieutenant Carmichael continued: 'Whilst we were being halted and moved more and more to the left, the 30th and 55th were progressing ... the 7th Fusiliers, the right Regiment of the ... Light Division came up in line behind us – they were halted, and then were ordered to pass through our line – this they did, and we then we were ordered to pass through them.'

Observing this confusion from the Support Line, Sir Colin Campbell, at the head of his Highland Brigade, observed to his ADC: 'By God, those Regiments are not advancing like English soldiers.'

If the thin British line maximised firepower and presented the enemy's guns with a more difficult target, it had one great disadvantage over the column: it was hard to maintain. What is difficult enough over a level parade ground becomes well-nigh impossible over rough ground, through vineyards and walled enclosures, and under fire. This crowding was to have its effect on the unfolding battle – but meanwhile, confused or not, the advance continued. Major Norcott was second-in-command of the 2nd Battalion, the Rifle Brigade. These were the old green-jacketed skirmishers from Wellington's day, and, as usual, were out in front.

Norcott described the scene: 'Our skirmishers might have been 300 yards in front. I rode with them. As we descended the downs, we suddenly saw smoke and flame burst out from what turned out to be a sunken road, but from which having a fall of some 6 or 7 feet into it, had been hidden from our view, and so hindered us from seeing the cause of this fire and smoke ... All became clear in a minute. Simultaneous with the outburst of smoke and flame, there came such a singing, such a continuous stream of balls, as to make one's horse quite uneasy and the men astonished. There came a volume of white wool from a distant hill, then another, then six, seven, eight, then fifty. Eventually a hundred guns belched forth their iron load and the earth was torn and rent with their violence.'

As he and his comrades advanced, Private Bloomfield of the 95th noticed that the enemy had marked out the ranges for their guns. 'We advanced on to some white posts about 500 yards away. As soon as we got in line with these posts, Wiz— Wiz— came the shots from the guns of the enemy; we lay down immediately. While we lay here most of the shots were dropping about 10 yards in front of us and flying over our heads. Little did we think at the time those shots were flying over our heads, that they were catching the third line. There were very few of my company hit at this spot.'

With the 55th to Bloomfield's right, Captain John Hume described his first time under fire: 'Most of us for the first time found ourselves under a hot fire of round shot and shell – a curious and by no means pleasant experience. There was an involuntary movement amongst the men to cower and crowd together when the first few round shot passed over us, and there were few who did not duck their heads. All, however, soon got accustomed to the sound and saw that there was much more danger in crowding together than in opening out.'

Advancing with the main body of the Assault Line three hundred yards behind was Corporal Timothy Gowing of the 7th Foot, The Royal Fusiliers, who attempted to explain: 'To describe my feelings in going into action, I could not. As soon as the enemy's round shot came hopping along, we simply did the polite – opened out and allowed them to pass on; there is nothing lost by politeness, even on the battlefield. As we kept advancing, we had to move our pins to get out of their way. Presently they began to pitch their shot and shell right amongst us, and our men began to fall. I know that I felt horribly sick – a cold shivering running through my veins – and I must acknowledge that I felt very uncomfortable; but I am happy to say that feeling soon passed off as soon as I began to get warm to it. It was very exciting work, and the sights were sickening.'

As well as the guns on the far side of the river, the Assault Line now came under fire from Russian skirmishers posted in the vineyards, gardens and orchards on the near bank, as well as in the village of Bourliouk, which, to add to the confusion, the Russians now set on fire. Norcott and his Riflemen: 'neared the road, not firing a shot. How could we? We saw nobody! The village now showed through the smoke and flame. We neared it and the walls with the vineyards. The men more than once asked me should they push on to the wall, and at a sham fight, I should have done so long before. I feared, however, any undue idea of danger, and saying, "All right, all right; let us be cool; a few yards more," walked on till within 40 yards of the wall which we then gained by a rush, lying under and looking over it, endeavouring through the thick smoke, to catch sight of the hornets that filled the air with rifle balls.'

To Norcott's right, with the 95th, Private Bloomfield heard: 'The Advance at the double sounded. We sprang to our feet and doubled about 50 yards, here we were met with a shower of lead from the enemy's skirmishers, we lay down, fired, then advanced and so on until we came within 40 yards of a village. All in a moment the village was in flames, the smoke from it almost suffocated us. Our Captain then shouted out, "Follow them up my lads," and we did through fire and smoke.'

The Assault Line's skirmishers were now embroiled in a full-scale fire-fight in the village and the vineyards. Captain Morgan, advancing with the main body of the 95th, saw: 'Now commenced a spattering fire between the skirmishers on both sides. It lasted about twenty minutes, when a dense smoke obscured everything. The enemy had fired the village in a hundred places at the same time ... we got the order to lie down, also the Brigades behind us the same. When in this position a good many shots fell in our ranks. One fell about two yards from me ... A few seconds after, a shell burst on the right of the Grenadier Company. I thought at the time it carried away the entire section but not one was touched. A shell fell into No 1 Company carrying great destruction with it; fragments of shakoes, blankets, clothes and human flesh were carried up in the air. It was a horrid sight but many similar were occurring every minute. We lay there being pounded for a considerable time.'

Again dogs provided light relief. Sitting his horse among de Lacy Evan's staff, Colonel Lysons saw: 'the men ... much amused and excited by the coursing of a beautiful greyhound, which kept chasing hares about the plain in front of them. A little dog belonging to Captain Foreman, Rifle Brigade, created much amusement by the angry way in which he chased and barked at the round shot as they bowled past him along the turf. Later, when the troops began to move, the hares became bewildered, and many of them ran into the ranks and were captured and carried away, some by poor fellows who never lived to enjoy their supper.'

While the main body endured this pounding, deployed in lines that would not have been out of place at Waterloo, the British skirmishers were engaged in a kind of fighting more familiar to a modern soldier. Working forward in small groups, making use of what cover there was, they fought to clear the village and the enclosures of Russian riflemen. Private Bloomfield, with the 95th's skirmishers recalled: 'As soon as we got through this burning village, we met the enemy's skirmishers full in the face, and at it we went, and no mistake, we had a proper pitched battle ... We rushed on driving the enemy's skirmishers before us. Some of these skirmishers even got up trees, so they could get a good shot at us, but we saw them and brought them off their perch. Some of these when falling from the tops of the trees – after being shot – would catch either their feet or clothes in some parts of the tree and hang there for hours.'

Over to the left, Norcott's Green Jackets, specially trained for this kind of fighting, cleared the vineyards to their front and pushed on towards the river. Norcott was lucky: 'Not a man of mine had been hit. How I escaped this road, shot and grape tearing up the earth within 6 feet of my horse's feet I know not. I got my supports well jammed up, but many were the hairbreadth escapes.'

As the skirmishers pushed on through, the main line was ordered up behind them. As they came on, Norcott took his men on down to the river. 'At length the line came up and, without a moment's pause, I threw Fyers' and Erroll's Companies over the walls and into the vineyards. Pushed my supports ... down by a road that led through these to a farmhouse, and, pressing on under a murderous fire from rifles whose whereabouts it was impossible to conjecture, we crossed the river.'

Meanwhile, the main body of the Assault Line was following up behind, working its way through the tangle of walls and enclosures and the burning village of Bourliouk. To the skirmishers, used to working in loose formations, this had posed no problem, but for the battalion and Grenadier companies – trained to advance and fight shoulder-to-shoulder – it was a different story. Already entangled during the initial advance, the 7th and the 95th became even more so as they entered the burning village.

'Both regiments were then close to the walled vineyard on the left of the road, and a post house building on the right,' wrote Lieutenant Carmichael. 'Both corps then took shelter under these protections, as the Russian fire on the road, and generally was very heavy – I being on the right was behind the post house and officers and men of the 7th were also there – after a short time, the order was given to advance, but as you may imagine the line formation was lost.'

As Captain Morgan of the same regiment approached the village, 'the Enemy changed their round shot for grape and canistre; now the work of death began in earnest. We again got the order to lie down, and the 7th Fusiliers passed over us. Again we advanced. We were nearing the river where the Grenadier Company were in front of a farmyard.

'General Pennyfather ordered us to get close under it and we found the greater portion of the Light Company there. A great portion of the Regt in a few minutes were collected there; at the time grape and canistre were falling like rain. A company of the 7th Fusiliers now came up to avail themselves of the cover.

'Great confusion appeared to reign. Generals and Aide de Camps rode about not knowing exactly what was to be done – at least so it appeared to me,'

Over to the right, the 55th had cleared the village in good order, avoiding entanglement with the other regiments. Now they were ordered to lie down once more, Captain John Hume remembered, 'under the fire of some of the enemy's heaviest batteries, which were throwing shot and shell very thickly. As we were lying down most of the shot passed over us; a few fell into our ranks; a round shot passed through a man who was lying in front of me and close to my brother. One of the guns in the large Russian battery was pointed exactly in my direction. Whenever I saw that gun fired I looked out a bit. I begged Major Whimper to get off his horse, but he would not. A round shot, spent, rolled to his horse's feet.'

In all regiments senior officers had to remain mounted – in the noise, smoke and confusion of battle the only sure way to exercise command was to gallop up and down the line and deliver orders personally. So, as the junior officers, NCOs and men hugged the ground, the commanders sat their horses – conspicuous targets, as the high casualty rate among them testifies. Hume commented: 'None of our field officers dismounted. Colonel Warren sat like a statue behind the centre of the line, with a single glass to his eye; he never moved when the shot and shell passed close to him. Lieutenant-Colonel Daubeney on the right of the line was equally cool and collected . . . We could see the round shot, after they passed us, ricocheting over the plain looking like cricket balls.'

Also sitting his horse under fire, though not for the first time, was the 2nd Division's commander, Sir de Lacy Evans. Knowing the importance of keeping up the momentum of the attack, he made the decision to split his division and pass the blazing village on either side. Two regiments passed round it to the right while the remainder crowded through the centre and left. To their left, the Light Division – under Sir George Brown – had the easier ground, but even so, as the regiments approached the river, order suffered.

The depth of the river varied along its winding course to the sea. Some men waded across easily, some swam, some sank, some drowned – and all the time the Russian guns raked them with grapeshot and shell. Near the bridge, where Private Bloomfield was wading across with the Light Company of the 95th: 'Showers of lead came over, thinning our ranks fast. We dashed into the river, but before we got across, the river was red with blood. The river was full of bodies. Some parts of this river were very deep and some parts shallow. I happened to be one of the lucky ones, I got over where it was rather shallow.'

The Light Division had entered the river too. Corporal Timothy Gowing wrote: 'Up to the river we rushed and got ready for a swim, pulling off knapsacks and camp kettles. A number of our poor fellows were drowned, or shot down with grape and canister – which came among us like hail – while attempting to cross. Our men were falling now very fast. Into the river we dashed, nearly up to our arm-pits, with our ammunition and rifles on the top of our heads to keep them dry.'

To Gowing's left, Major Mundy, commanding the left wing of the 33rd, described how 'The men fell about me like leaves and my charger would not move (without being shoved on behind) to cross the river, with balls splashing all about.'

Unsure of the river's depth, some men paused at the water's edge. Private Kirwin of the 19th was close behind his officer. 'Lieutenant Barret raised his sword and said, "Men, now follow me." I stopped to pause, and said to myself, "I cannot swim." I followed the officer two steps in rear, so that if the officer went under, I would go back. No one knew the depth of the river. Every soldier had to put his pouch under his arm to save his ammunition, and his firelock on top of his head.'

Nearby Lieutenant Lidwill, also of the 19th, reached the river's edge to find: 'We were treated to a hot recognition by a discharge of shot and shell, which was the liveliest cross-fire we had yet experienced. The water, dirty and discoloured from the passage and re-passage of the enemy, was of uncertain depth. On my right and left were a number of our men huddled together, peering into the stream under our feet, and so heavy were they that the bank gave way and we all, with a shout, fell into the water. Everyone catching hold of his neighbour. We were immediately waist-deep in the clay and water and crossed to the south side.'

Their commander, Major Unett, although on horseback, had a more difficult crossing: 'My mare got into a hole in the water and was all under for some time, except her head and neck. I dismounted and got her to the side and attempted the high bank, which was nearly perpendicular and very slippery. I struggled to get up sticking my fingers into the grass and she, by desperate struggles, came up by my side as I had hold of the bridle. Shot falling all this time very thick I mounted and pushed on. We got into something like a line under the crest of the hill.'

The hill Unett refers to was in fact a ten-foot-high earth bank on the far side of the river, which offered a brief respite from the murderous Russian fire for the men of both assaulting divisions. On the narrow strip of land between this bank and the water, all along the front of both divisions, officers and men now tried to marshal the troops into some kind of order.

Once across the river, the British advance split into two: on the right, the attack on the Pass, and on the left, the attack on the Great Redoubt. On the right, de Lacy Evans' 2nd Division – split by the burning village – had effectively lost the 95th Foot and most of the 55th to its neighbouring division. Brigadier Adams had crossed to the right of the village with two battalions, and with the remaining three Evans himself attempted to advance on the Pass through which ran the road to Sebastopol.

It was a hopeless task. Deploying as best they could on ground bare of cover, Evans and his men faced 16 guns supported by 6 battalions of infantry, as well as a flanking fire from the Great Redoubt. Already reduced by casualties – the 2nd Brigade alone had lost a quarter of its men before crossing the river – the best they could do was hold their ground and 'make a front' to the enemy, inching forward when the chance arose.

To their left the Light Division was, if anything, in greater disorder. Confined on its little shelf of land between the river and the earth bank the whole division was little more than a crowd. The ordered line in which they had advanced to the Alma was now twisted into a succession of 'S' bends by the river's course – instead of two-deep, they were twenty-deep in places. All order was lost, with companies, even regiments, jumbled together. In places Russian skirmishers ran to the bank and fired down onto their heads; from a position lower down the river another group set up flanking fire.

Major Norcott, who had already climbed the bank with his Green Jackets, now saw the Russian columns on either side of the Great Redoubt starting to advance down the hill. Galloping down to the river he: 'begged all hands for Heaven's sake, to get into two deep. One is bold in action and says what one thinks. To General Codrington, to Colonel Blake, to Chester, Saunders, it was all the same thing: "By Heavens, they are only 150 yards from you. You will annihilate them. Only get into two deep."

'It was impossible. The men, dead beat, sat down. Some to drink water, others literally pulling out bread and meat and beginning to eat!'

Apart from Norcott, few of the divisions, officers or men, had ascended to the open ground above. The Divisional Commander, Sir George Brown, was one who had – he now sat his horse alone in the open, blinking myopically at a bemused group of Russian skirmishers. Below him on the bank, Sir William Codrington was acutely aware of the danger of the situation. Seeing the condition of his brigade and sensing that their precipitate advance across the river could turn into an equally precipitate retreat at any minute, he spurred his grey Arab up the bank, bellowing, 'Fix bayonets. Get up the bank and advance to the attack!'

Within seconds the whole of Codrington's Brigade – the 7th, 23rd and 33rd all jumbled together, as well as the 19th on their left and most of the 95th on their right – were scrambling up the earth bank and out onto the grassy slope that led up to the Great Redoubt five hundred yards away. The guns in the redoubt were silent for a moment, unable to fire while their own skirmishers withdrew. Even so, there was no time to form, no time for parade-ground order in the cannon's mouth.

As junior commanders tried to shake their men out into some sort of line, and knots of men – sometimes of different regiments – fell in under the nearest officer or NCO, Timothy Gowing's commanding officer, Colonel Lacy Yea of the 7th, could be heard urging his men:

'Never mind forming, for God's sake! Come on! Come on, men! come on anyhow!'

Lacy Yea was a strict disciplinarian, heartily disliked by his men on Home Service. Before the battle he had written to his sister, 'The Russians are before me and my own men are behind me, so I don't think you will ever see me again.'

That such a man, such a stickler for drill and dressing, should shout such an order – 'Come on anyhow!' – showed the urgency of the situation. Nor did his men hesitate: they came on anyhow. Now the Russian gunners and the advancing Russian infantry saw something amazing. Mixed up as they were, the men of the Light Division – the bottle-green Rifles, the 19th Green Howards, the 23rd Royal Welch Fusiliers, the 33rd the Duke of Wellington's, the 7th Royal Fusiliers, and the 95th Derbies – in a hastily formed, ragged line, began moving up over the open ground towards them. This force, already cruelly punished by the Russian guns and disordered by the ground they'd had to cross – this rabble which the advancing Russian infantry thought they were about to sweep back into the river – was actually about to attack *them*. It seemed incredible to the watchers on the heights that any infantry could dream of attacking in such a formation. The first thought of many as the Lights emerged from the smoke in the river valley was that this was the head of a gigantic column. Surely, this loose swarm was a line of skirmishers – the main assault force must be close behind – but as they hastily deployed, almost in the faces of the Russian guns, it became clear that this was all there was. If the division was deployed too deep, and too bunched for the liking of its own officers – still shouting their mantra, 'Two-deep, two-deep!' – to the Russians it seemed hopelessly fragile and pitifully understrength. Yet still they came on.

As they did so they were met by a storm of roundshot, grape and musketry. Corporal Timothy Gowing of the 7th recalled: 'From east to west the enemy's batteries were served with great rapidity, hence we were enveloped in smoke on what may be called the *glacis* and could not see much. We were only about 600 yards from the mouths of the guns; the thunderbolts of war were, therefore, not far apart – and death loves a crowd. The havoc among the Fusiliers, both 7th and 23rd, was awful.'

Major Unett of the 19th described the scene. 'The firing now was awful and many were hit. Our line was not well formed under such a plunging fire; it was impossible to form line. Sir George Brown came and said to Colonel Sanders, "Go at them!" He rode in front of the line and waved his sword. The line got more confused. I was on the right of the line, to which they seemed to crowd, and instead of being two deep we had become fourteen or fifteen deep.'

From the left of the British line, Major Norcott watched the division advance. 'On . . . they went, mobbed as they were, gallantly and desperately, but halting and firing all the time. The enemy's columns retired before their onward move. I, in the meantime, who had offered General Codrington to take them into action, brought up the left of my whole line of skirmishers, throwing in a flanking fire and advancing at the same time rapidly.'

The 7th Fusiliers, on the right of the line, now began a fire-fight with a column of the Kazan Regiment, which was to last for most of the battle.

'Up the hill we went' wrote Timothy Gowing of the 7th,' step by step, but with a fearful carnage. The fighting now became very exciting, our artillery playing over our heads, and we firing and advancing all the time. The smoke was now so great that we could hardly see what we were doing, and our fellows were falling all around; it was a dirty rugged hill.'

Within minutes the 7th had lost 12 of their officers and nearly a quarter of their men. One of their Colours disappeared, clutched by a dead ensign buried under dead Fusiliers. Their line wavered, fell back, then advanced again. Gowing continued: 'When one gets in such a hot corner as this was, one has not much time to mind his neighbours. I could see that we were leading; the French were on our right and the 23rd Fusiliers on our left. We got mixed up with the 95th. Someone called out, "Come on, young 95th – the old 7th are in front!"

'The fighting was now of a desperate kind. My comrade said to me, "We shall have to shift those fellows with the bayonet, old boy" – pointing to the Russians.'

Seconds later his comrade fell, shot through the mouth.

The men of the 95th Gowing could see were from the Light Company. The 95th had become detached from their own division, the 2nd, and once across the river simply headed for the nearest fight. Lieutenant Macdonald, of the 95th's Light Company, had crossed the river and then 'tried to find my own Regiment but not succeeding I found my own men and stragglers and marched up to the 55th who were peppering away . . . and preparing to charge and joined them having got leave from their Colonel to take the right. Here we advanced up the hill and here I thought my end had come for I received a ball in my breast which would have knocked me down but for the man behind who however was knocked down. I thought I was killed and tore away my belt and to my great thankfullness discovered that the ball had been stopped by a small ornament on my belt.'

Among Macdonald's men was Private Bloomfield. To his left, he saw the 2nd Division's other stray regiment, the 55th: 'The 55th Regiment came up, in line, my company formed up on their right. They (55th) then commenced firing. The Colonel of the 55th Regiment ordered his men to cease firing and prepare to charge, as the enemy was making a desperate stand. The men would not obey the order, but kept firing at the enemy. At last he rode to the front of his Regiment with the colours in his hand, he held them up in front of his Regiment . . .

'He then again ordered his regiment to get ready to charge, but the men still kept up a steady fire and would not obey their Colonel.'

The men were probably right. The Minié rifle was a new weapon; most regiments had been issued with it only en route to the Crimea. Few in the infantry at this stage fully realised its tactical significance, as Major Hume of the 55th later admitted: 'There had been so little time since the Minié rifles were issued to train men to the use of them. Had they known more of the powers of the rifle the losses inflicted would have been much greater.'

Yet if some officers, wedded to the 'cold-steel' school of tactics, wanted to close with the enemy and give the Russians the kind of fight they were hoping for, the men actually using the new rifle were already seeing its effect. For the fact was that the Minié fire was ripping through the Russian columns, killing one, two, sometimes three, men per round.

Before the Colonel could get his bayonet charge, Private Bloomfield saw: 'The enemy . . . began to retire, they covered their retreat by a long line of skirmishers. My company then got the order to advance, and as we advanced their skirmishers stood their ground, until we got within point-blank range of them; still we advanced steadily on, our men falling fast (shot).

'As we advanced, one of the Russian Imperial Guards (a man about 7 feet in height) stood his ground. He kept loading and firing as cool as if on parade, and every time he fired a man of ours fell. A Staff Officer who had been watching this Russian, came up and said "Isn't there a man here that can knock that chap over?" He had hardly got the words out of his mouth when the Russian fell (shot). The Staff Officer then remarked, "What a pity a man like him should be shot. He's as brave a man as ever I saw."

'We marched past this brave Russian, he was almost dead, I couldn't help but pity the poor fellow, as he lay there in his blood. He looked a stern and determined Soldier.

'As we advanced we were constantly stepping over the dead and wounded of the enemy. Most of the wounded were crying out for water. A man of my Company gave a wounded Russian a drink of water, and as he left him, the Russian rose on his elbow, took his musket in his hand, and fired at the man that gave him the water. The bullet passed close by the man's head. The man turned round immediately and ran his bayonet through the body of the Russian.

'At this moment General Pennefather was passing by, and saw what the English Soldier had done, but didn't happen to see what the Russian Soldier had done. He at once ordered a man of the Regiment to shoot (on the spot) the man that had stabbed the Russian. It happened that some one explained the whole affair to the General, so he let the man off, but told him that he had a good mind to bring him to a Court-Martial.'

There were to be many more stories like this before the day was over. For the Russians – schooled in war against the Turks and now fighting to defend the soil of Holy Russia – this was war to the knife.

Over on the left of the British line the 19th were also up against a Russian column. As they closed to within a hundred yards, Lieutenant Lidwill of that regiment noticed, 'The effect of our fire was very noticeable. I saw the men in the great column, both in front and flank, wasting away ... The strength of the enemy seemed enormous and, having advanced closer, looked like the dense crowd as you see it at Epsom on the Derby Day.'

This was a very different crowd, though. 'Their strange drab coats and ugly heavy-looking helmets looked anything but sightly, though, perhaps, martial. Between these columns and the earthwork were skirmishers kneeling and one very big man used to come out of the battery, kneel and fire, as I thought, at myself. So I shouted for Sergeant Owen, who was a splendid shot, and I pointed out to him what I wanted. Owen straightway fired and this troublesome fellow fell forward.'

As the regiments on the right and left of the Light Division battled it out with the Russian infantry columns, those in the centre, the 23rd and 33rd, most of the 95th including the Colour Party, plus elements of both the 7th and 19th had, from the moment they had emerged from the river, been advancing head-on at the Great Redoubt. The brief respite they had enjoyed while the Russian skirmishers withdrew was followed by a storm of roundshot, grape and canister. A frontal assault on a 12-gun battery uphill over three hundred yards of open ground was a thing near-impossible. Yet in clumps, in ragged lines, in mixed groups of companies and regiments, often under officers and NCOs they'd never seen before, too breathless to shout, too eager to stop and fire, the men of the Light Division surged up the slope into the teeth of the guns. The two-deep line they had been trained in was all-but abandoned now as the men of five regiments closed in on the one obvious objective: ahead and above them, the earthwork. It was blanketed now in smoke. Behind that smoke were the guns and the gunners who had inflicted such punishment, that had slaughtered so many of their comrades and were still ploughing bloody furrows through their ranks.

Captain Morgan of the 95th had lost touch with most of his unit in the burning village. Crossing the river he had run up and joined a large body of men he saw battling it out with a Russian column.

'When I came up I found them to be made up of parts of different Regiments; all order was lost and the enemy's fire was cutting them up frightfully,' he wrote. 'I saw the Colours of the Regiment; Davies was carrying one and I think a sergeant the other. Hume was with them. There was only about ten men. Hume called me and gave me the Regimental Colour. We fell in with the few men we had and showed them the best front we could keeping up a fire. Our position was not at all a pleasant one, but a few more men joined us.'

Colour Parties – the regiments' rallying-point – were obvious targets for sharpshooters. Morgan soon found himself with a problem similar to Lieutenant Lidwill's – being singled out by an enemy marksman. The Colour carried by Morgan was struck twice, and another bullet tore through the shoulder of his tunic, striking Private Keenan in the throat. Seeing that the Russian who had fired the shot was reloading, Morgan – an excellent shot himself – called for a rifle and brought the man down.

The casualties in the centre regiments were horrific. Command and control were well-nigh impossible in the smoke and confusion, the roar of the enemy's guns and muskets and that flat crack of the Minié. Yet, almost by instinct, the men of the three centre regiments, and those on the flanks not engaged with the Russian columns, closed into the centre, filling up the lanes in their ranks raked by the enemy artillery – and as they closed in, they rushed on.

The Russian musketry was ineffective compared to Minié fire – to which the number of spent bullets and rounds lodged in equipment would testify – but their gunners, firing canister now as well as shell, took a fearful toll. Private John Kirwin of the 19th saw: 'shot from the twelve-gun battery that cut the bowels out of four men. There was a young man who came out in the last draft from Varna: when he saw the four men shot dead, he let out a shout, and was for running away when Lieutenant Clay of the Light Company upraised his sword over his head and said he would cut the head from off his body if he attempted to run away. His words drew my attention – I laid my hand on the young man's shoulder and told the officer that he was a bit frightened and told him he would make a good soldier yet.'

Sergeant Usherwood, also of the 19th, was facing the main battery when a shell landed between him and his friend. 'No sooner than it fell it exploded with a most dazzling light covering myself with earth and inflicting on my companion a most severe wound on the right side of his head. After collecting together my scattered thoughts, I found him lying upon his face in a pool of blood only about seven yards distance from me. Lifting him up he appeared at first like one who had truly just departed this life. Then quickly afterwards he came to in all the vigour of manhood minus that strength of nerve and spirit as wont to be within himself. Handing to him a handkerchief which, I had in my haversack I said, "You had better go down to the river's bank out of the way and, if possible, see the doctor." I then hurried on into the fight going on to the battery opposite us.'

Ensign Cardew was hit in the leg. 'I felt as if a hot iron had been run through my leg just at the bottom of the calf of my leg. It dropped me for a second. I felt and saw a hole on either side of my trousers; so concluded justly that the ball had passed through. I got up again and limped along leaning on the arm of one of our sergeants. Then, by jove, I felt a tremendous lump on my cheek and fell to the ground, stunned. At the same time the sergeant I was with fell shot through the thigh. I was then carried a few yards to the rear and placed on some hay, where I lay in great pain for about three hours.'

Yet still the Light Division, 2,000 strong and falling – men who had never been under fire before in their lives – scrambled on up the slope. The Russian artillery were in a dilemma. Despite their fire, despite all their sponging, loading and firing – over open sights over specially prepared ground – the enemy's ragged line seemed unbreakable, and it was getting uncomfortably close. The columns of the Kazan Regiment on either side of their position – which were supposed to have swept the redcoats back into the river – were withdrawing now, their columns shredded by that terrible Minié fire. The Russian artillery were an élite corps, and being an élite carries terrible responsibilities. To lose a gun was the ultimate disgrace – captured guns were visible proof of victory. To lose a gun would greatly displease the Tsar. Paranoia about losing guns was a commonplace of nineteenth-century warfare; it would, in just over a month's time, launch the most famous cavalry charge in history. Now it affected the Russians.

After one final discharge, the fire from the battery ceased. The men of the Light Division, breathlessly scrambling towards the earthwork, heard through the smoke the jingle of harness. The Russian guns were limbering up. From the advancing British line there was a cry of: 'Stole Away!'

From the left flank, where his Green Jackets were pouring a flanking fire into the position, Norcott saw: 'The enemy guns, seeing their columns in full retreat ... were off; but not until the 32-pounder – there was no mistaking the demon shriek of this gun – had been discharged when I was within 30 yards of its muzzle. It made the earth shake and one's flesh quiver.

'The enemy's columns, however, showed again at the Redoubt. It was touch and go. Sir George Brown was riding fearlessly at the head of the Brigade urging them on. I drew my sword, more to make my encouragement conspicuous to the men, and galloping forward, called, "Come on, my hearties," rode right up to within five yards of the Battery.

'The enemy had jut turned to retire, and General Codrington, cantering up and pressing on, went into the Redoubt to show no one was there. Young Campbell of ours, his ADC, and I went in. But I do record it here, that the first man up to the embrasures of the Battery was a Green Jacket.'

Others would (and do, to this day) dispute the honour. The fact was that from three sides and with a ringing cheer the British infantry — Green Jackets, Green Howards, Fusiliers Welch and Royal, Dukes and Derbies, swarmed over the parapet and through the embrasures into the Great Redoubt.

Ensign Anstruther of the 23rd — a youth barely out of school — climbed onto the parapet holding the Queen's Colour of the Royal Welch. He was shot dead, but no sooner had the fallen silk shrouded the boy than it was raised again by Private William Evans. It was passed on to Corporal Soulbey, then to Sergeant Luke O'Connor who, though wounded, refused to relinquish it for the rest of the day.

The Russian guns were clearing out of the back of the redoubt as the British infantry were clambering in at the front and sides, but the Russian skirmishers, who had fought in the position too, were withdrawing more slowly, firing as they went. There was more hard fighting before the redoubt was secure. Two guns were caught in the mêlée — Captain Heyland and a group of the 95th fought the Russian gunners for possession of one of them. This was the Heyland who, the night before, had told Ensign Boothby that he'd rather lose an arm than a leg. As the last of the Russians fled or were bayoneted, Heyland, fainting from a wound, just had time to scratch 95 on his prize. His wound cost him his left arm; Ensign Boothby had already lost his right leg.

The other gun was taken by Captain Bell of the 23rd — but before he could secure it Lord George Brown rode up and angrily told him to rejoin his company. Private James Ryan, a Grenadier of the 19th, then took a hand. From outside the redoubt, Private Kirwin of the

19th saw him emerge. He wrote: 'Private James Ryan of the Grenadier Company, with his comrade, came out of the battery with horse gun and carriage. When the Russians saw them coming out with the gun they fired a cross-fire and one was wounded – Ryan's comrade. When the Regiment saw them, they cheered them and opened out in sub-divisions to let them pass.'

The confusion of the advance was even greater now as the men of six regiments crowded into the redoubt, some cheering, some mounting the parapet and waving their Colours, some dying, some fainting from wounds, some too weary to do anything but slump down and catch their breath.

There was no time, however, for resting on laurels. If the Russian guns had withdrawn, their infantry, some 10,000 strong and much of it still uncommitted, were close at hand. The Light Division, which had begun the advance with a frontage of a mile, were now for the most part crammed into the hundred and fifty yards of the Great Redoubt, much reduced by casualties, exhausted and in great confusion. The redoubt, designed to withstand attack from the south – the way the British had come – was wide open to the north – the direction of any Russian counter-attack. The earthwork, which gave good protection to troops attacked from below, gave little or none to those attacked from above. Already Sir William Codrington and some regimental officers were trying to deploy men on the top of the parapet, taking advantage of what cover there was, with their rifles pointing up the hill – in the direction of any Russian counter-attack.

That counter-attack was not long in coming. Above and behind the Great Redoubt, deployed in one massive column, stood the four battalions of the Vladimir Regiment. Above them were four more battalions of the Uglitz and away to the left, two more of the Kazan and four of the Sousdal, while over on the right, the remainder of the Kazan stilled traded volleys with the 7th Fusiliers. More Russian guns higher up the Kourgane were already pitching shell into the redoubt – one killed five officers of the 23rd who stood conferring about what to do next. Almost at the same moment, with that 'long sorrowful wailing sound' that was the Russian cheer, the Vladimir Regiment began to tramp down the hill to evict the redcoats from what they had taken at such cost.

*

A unit is never more vulnerable than when it has just carried out a successful attack. Quite apart from the inevitable confusion, there is a psychological reaction. Men who have summoned up the courage to advance into the enemy's fire, have overcome their greatest fear, have seen friends fall at either hand, have stormed an enemy position and fought and killed other men at close quarters because their blood was up, suddenly find that blood turns cold.

It was a fact well-known to older soldiers – it was the reason hills, villages – earthworks – had often changed hands several times in the course of a single battle. It was the reason attacking troops had supports – fresh troops close behind to follow-up, consolidate, push on through. Already as the Light Division were pouring into the Great Redoubt, some officers were looking over their shoulders for the men of the Support Line, for the bearskins of the Guards and the feather bonnets of the Highlanders. By now they should have been halfway up the hill, or, at the very least, emerging from the river bed – but they were nowhere to be seen. The Light Division were on their own.

The only other possible source of support were the two battalions of the division, which had so far hardly seen a shot fired. These were the two battalions of Buller's Brigade, of which the 19th – who had been in the thick of the fighting at the redoubt – was the third. On the extreme left of the entire British army, Buller's Brigade, the 77th, the 19th Green Howards and the 88th (the famous Connaught Rangers) had had an easier crossing than most of the army. Once across the river the 19th had veered into the centre to attack the redoubt, as had the 95th on the right. Buller, with his two remaining battalions, had been minded to do the same. Henry Clifford, on Buller's Staff, and a fellow staff officer had tried to marshal these two battalions at the river's edge.

Clifford explained, 'Glyn and myself did all we could to get the 77th and 88th into their places to advance in line. The 77th soon did so, but the 88th with whom we have always had the greatest trouble did not reform as well, but were in sufficient order to advance in good order against infantry. I reported this to General Buller and as he asked my advice, said I thought we had better advance at once.

'He sent me with the order to Colonel Egerton of the 77th. Colonel Egerton pointed out a strong Battalion of Infantry threatening our left and said he would take it upon himself to remain where he was and explain his reason for doing so to General Buller.

'As I was returning to General Buller a body of cavalry was pointed out to me in movement on our left, and I immediately reported it to General B. who was advancing with the 88th in a good line. He, fearing that the cavalry might charge the 88th in line, gave orders to form square.'

There they remained while the Light Division stormed up the hill and into the redoubt, and there they remained now as the Vladimir Regiment began its counter-attack. Buller was to come in for much criticism for his failure to support the rest of the division, but somewhere out on the Russians' right flank were upwards of 3,600 Russian cavalry. Such a force appearing on the British left flank at any time in the battle could have rolled the entire British infantry up from left to right. Buller would later have the pleasure of explaining this – or rather, *trying* to explain it – to an irate Sir George Brown.

In any case the real task of supporting the Light Division fell to the 1st Division – those missing Guards and Highlanders. Where were they?

While the Assault Line had advanced, fought through the vineyards and garden enclosures, crossed the river and assaulted the redoubt, the 1st Division had followed up slowly – *very* slowly. The division was commanded by HRH The Duke of Cambridge. The Duke was neither unintelligent, nor lacking in physical courage, but he owed his command to his royal blood and – perhaps in unconscious recognition of that fact – lacked confidence in his own judgement. As a result, his advance had been overcautious.

Also, as the Guards had followed up the assaulting divisions, they had suffered the same pressures from the right that had crowded and confused the regiments of the 2nd and Light Divisions. The 3rd Division, crowded from the right by the French, had imposed upon the right of the 1st Division – or rather, they had tried to. Her Majesty's Guards, however, took their dressing seriously and had no intention of sharing space with anyone: they had crowded right back, spreading out in a luxurious double line which had forced the 3rd Division to fall back behind them. The effect of this was that the 1st Division, instead of being the left half of the Support Line, now *were* the Support Line, with the 3rd Division in reserve. If Lord

Raglan was even aware of this, he didn't see fit to interfere; then as ever, the Guards were a law unto themselves.

All of this had taken up time, with the result that by the time the Lights were storming the Great Redoubt, the Guards had not even got their boots – or the Highlanders their spats – wet. The Duke had hesitated to disorder his division's splendid line by taking them through the vineyards and enclosures. Lord Raglan's order had been that he should *support the Light Division*; could he really mean Her Majesty's Guards to degenerate into a swarm of skirmishers, which was how the Light Division appeared as they charged up the hill to the Great Redoubt? Sir George Brown, at the head of his men attacking the redoubt, was in no position to make a personal appeal for support. It was only after repeated urgings, firstly from General Airey, Lord Raglan's Adjutant-General, and secondly from – of all people – de Lacy Evans, who, while embroiled in his own fight on the far bank, could see over his left shoulder the Light Division's predicament, that the Duke took his division down to the river.

Here they ran into the same problems as the Light Division. Although the guns of the Great Redoubt had been withdrawn, other batteries higher up were still active. Captain Wilson described crossing with the Coldstream: 'At first our progress forward was not seriously meddled with; the Muscovite being busy with Brown and Evans in advance; but suddenly – just as we reached the gardens bordering the Alma – a murderous storm of round-shot and shell broke upon us; with the view of allowing the first bitterness of the outburst to expend itself, the troops crouched, for a few moments, behind the embankments of the vineyard, and the blackened ruins of the village; but the virulence of that diabolic artillery was no short-lived spurt; so, onwards, through thick and thin. Right through the tangled shrubs tear the glorious battalions, they plunge into the river, they sprawl up the slippery banks on the other side, they are floundering through another vineyard, interspersed with fruit trees, and intersected with deep dry ditches; all the while, the air swarms thicker and thicker with projectiles. We are in a very hell, nothing to be heard, save the humming of the shells, the whiz of roundshot, the rattle of grape and canister. The trees crash, and split around, the ground is torn up under our feet, our comrades are beaten down.'

Here the Guards, by now as disordered as the Assault Line

divisions had been stopped to order their ranks – there was to be no 'Come on anyhow' with the Guards. The Duke, once across the river, dithered again, riding over to General Buller, still watching the open left flank with his two battalions.

Clifford, who was with Buller when the Duke rode up, described the scene. 'The Guards in the meantime had crossed the river and having us in their front, formed a perfect line under our protection, and out of fire of the enemy under the Bank.

'The Duke of Cambridge rode up to General Buller and said "What am I to do, Buller?"

' "Why, your Royal Highness I am in a little confusion here – you had better advance I think." '

As the Duke rode back to his division, busy reforming between the river's edge and the earth bank, above him the Light Division were facing the Russian counter-attack. The fire from the Russian batteries higher up the hill had already driven many of the men out of the interior of the redoubt, and the remainder were now confronted by the steadily advancing column of the Vladimir Regiment who, Sergeant Charlie Usherwood of the 19th observed, 'did not deploy into line but opened fire as they stood in column, the two leading ranks firing from the hip, throwing into us a heavy fire of musketry.'

As the men of the Light Division 'made a front' to face this attack, there occurred one of those confusions that can turn the tide of a battle.

Lieutenant Lidwill, also of the 19th, told the story. 'Our men kept firing and as I was telling them to fire low I distinctly heard the bugle call "Cease firing" in its monotonous tone. "Not one shot more, not one shot more". It was obeyed and I dropped to the rear again, utterly dumbfounded to try and find out the origin of this most unfortunate occurrence.'

The bugle call was taken up by buglers of every regiment, and there was a pause in the firing on the British side.

Lidwill soon found the source of the order: 'I had hardly joined the supernumerary rank when a mounted officer rode almost at me, shouting, "Sir, you are firing at the French." I had no words to convey to this distracted-looking maniac. My astonishment was so great at his utterance. He then went off full tilt to our left along the rear, to where I saw Warden sitting wounded on the ground, to whom he repeated that we had been firing on the French. This was the man who originated the cease firing, but strange to say from that day to this, I never could obtain the name of this distinguishing officer . . . The unfortunate bugler was interrogated, but all he could say was that he only obeyed the order this staff officer gave him.'

A veteran of the Peninsula, Sir George Brown knew a Frenchman when he saw one. Private Kirwin was standing close by. 'General Brown, detecting the mistake with his quick eye – for he kept his glasses to his eye – said that if he knew the officer that gave that word of command, he would blow his brains out on the field. "Take a deliberate aim, boys," said he; "they are foes, not friends." The men obeyed, and I believe every shot told.'

The damage, however, was done. The oncoming Vladimir soldiers had been given a brief respite, and on the British side the confusion caused was catching.

Moments later, another mounted officer – maybe even the same one – gave another bugler the order to blow "Retire". Again, others took it up. Soon the whole line was falling back. Casualties mounted: Colonel Chester of the 23rd and the bulk of his officers fell in a hail of bullets. Norcott of the Rifles saw what followed. 'The loss at this moment was frightful. Manfully did the mass stand up; such as were in front, firing. Here Chester fell and the better part of his officers and men. It was too much, and the mass, like a partially loosened cliff, began to slide down and down; now slowly, now more rapidly. The enemy pushed on, regained the redoubt and lined it.'

Major Champion of the 95th was in the redoubt when the Russians counter-attacked. 'The slaughter on both sides was terrific; then we were also taken in flank by the Russian 32nd, and their cross-fire dealt destruction to the 23rd and ourselves. Several regiments were fighting to our right. At length they retired, and the 23rd and ourselves reluctantly and last retired also; but a strong relief of regiments in *echelon* on the left was coming to our relief. Hume seized a Colour and fronted, and every officer with us did what was in his power to rally the men. Some fifty fine fellows crowded round the Colours. We had five sergeants shot with them, and four officers wounded.'

'Here we lost a great number of our men,' said Corporal Timothy Gowing of the 7th, 'and, by overwhelming numbers we (the 23rd,

33rd, 95th and Rifles) were mobbed out of the battery and a part of the way down the hill again.'

Back down the hill went the Light Division, leaving 900 of their number dead, wounded or dying on the ground they had so hardly won. The Vladimir Regiment, having regained the redoubt, confined themselves to lining the embrasures and firing into the retreating redcoats. Their decision to halt was a strange one: if they had followed on down the hill, it is conceivable that they might have pitched what was left of the Light Division onto the heads of the Guards and Highlanders who were even now forming up on that same narrow shelf of land at the river's edge from which the Lights had erupted. As it was, the Light Division were allowed to break off contact, and as they fell back towards the river they began to see, emerging from the riverbank, first Colours, then bearskins, and finally redcoats in lines, as ordered as if on the Queen's Birthday. The Guards were coming.

To understand why the Russian infantry failed to follow up their advantage we need to retrace our steps and rejoin Lord Raglan. Since giving the two leading divisions the order to advance he had taken little further part in the running of the battle, preferring to leave that to his individual divisional commanders. So while Sir George Brown led his men against the Great Redoubt, de Lacy Evans led his in a slow, bloody attempt against the Pass, the Duke of Cambridge dithered and Sir Richard England allowed his 3rd division to be shunted back into reserve, Lord Raglan had been content to do little more than spectate. He was not alone.

According to Calthorpe, at the opening of the battle, 'Lord Raglan had placed himself, with his staff, in front of the troops, and I must tell you that by this time his staff had grown to three times its proper number; that is to say, every officer of the commissariat or medical department who had a quadruped chose to join the headquarter staff, as probably the best position for seeing the battle. I should think there could not have been less than fifty or sixty mounted officers. This great number began to be a nuisance, as it perpetually obstructed the view, and they crowded round the Commander-in-Chief in a manner that in any other service would have been thought highly impertinent and resented accordingly.

'Some one suggested to Lord Raglan that it would be as well to hint that those gentlemen not actually serving on the staff had better move off. However, Lord Raglan, with his usual good-nature said, "Let then stay;" and then added, "You know, directly we get under fire, those not obliged will depart, you may rely upon it."

'Lord Raglan was quite right. In two minutes the first shot against us was fired by the enemy. I looked at my watch; it was exactly 1 1/2 p.m. The shot, which was evidently fired at the staff (the only body of horsemen in sight and the most advanced), fell short and bounded over us with a whiz that made many duck their heads. You should have seen the hangers-on scattered in all directions. There was no more crowding about Lord Raglan.'

Whatever his limitations in other areas, His Lordship had seemingly endless reserves of physical courage and good humour. As the two Assault Divisions had crossed the river, Lord Raglan and his now reduced staff had forded the river themselves, close by the bridge at the junction of the two armies, and then ridden forward amongst French skirmishers of Prince Napoleon's Division.

Calthorpe continued the story. 'Directly we got into the river, and were crossing to the road on the opposite side, a very heavy enfilading fire was poured upon us, both from cannon and small-arms. In the river two of the staff were shot down; but Lord Raglan, whose presence of mind never left him for a moment, turned to one of his staff and said, "Ah! If they can enfilade us here, we can certainly enfilade them on the rising ground beyond. Order up Turner's battery!" He then went on, following the road, which turned away to the right. In a minute more we were among the French skirmishers, who looked not a little astonished to see the English Commander-in-Chief so far in advance. A sudden bend in the road again to the left brought us under the most infernal fire from some of the guns posted, as I before mentioned, in front of our line. We were in a sort of lane with high hedges on both sides, and the round-shot came down it in a manner I shall never forget.'

Raglan continued to canter forward towards a knoll, at height of about seventy feet, which had been recently vacated by some battalions of Russian infantry. Arrived at the top of this elevation Raglan was now in one of the most extraordinary positions ever taken up by a commander on a battlefield. Not only was he on the right of the Sebastopol road when the bulk of his army were over on the left, but he was far in advance of the French, and in the middle of the Russian position. The view must have been spectacular. Over to his left he could see – from a position directly in line with them – the Russian Causeway batteries that were holding up de Lacy Evan's advance. Beyond that he could see – from a position to its left rear – the Great Redoubt, towards which Sir George Brown's men were clambering. Those near to Raglan heard him exclaim: 'Now, if we had a couple of guns here!' Calthorpe reported, 'Lord Raglan at once saw the immense importance of getting guns up here, where they could enfilade all the Russian guns. One, two, three aides-de-camp were sent to know why Turner's battery did not arrive.'

Down at the river, Turner's battery were having problems. Captain Lysons, one of de Lacy Evans' staff, came upon them. 'I found the leading gun of Turner's battery trying to cross, but the horses would not face the water. I turned my old horse, Bob, at it, when to my surprise and annoyance he too refused. A cry of disapprobation burst from the drivers; I turned my horse at it again, put spurs to him and in he went. I then rode down the stream in front of the battery horses, and they followed me.'

Gunner and driver Cox was with Turner's battery. He recalled, 'The artillery had all their work to do to get the guns across the river, for they sank deeply in the mud, and we had to work like horses to get them out and into position on the other side.'

By the time two of the guns arrived at the knoll, the Light Division had been evicted from the Great Redoubt and the Guards were preparing to advance up from the river. Calthorpe explained, 'Lord Raglan had been looking on all this time, having arrived on the high ground before alluded to just as the Light Division advanced up the hill. When he saw the 1st Division coming up in support, he said, "Look how well the Guards and Highlanders advance!" An aide-de-camp came up at this moment, and reported the arrival of two guns of Turner's battery. Thank God, the guns at last! But they arrived at the spot where Lord Raglan was without any gunners (at least, I think there was only one bombardier besides the drivers). However, this was no time for delay, so the officers of General Strangeways' staff dismounted and served the guns themselves.'

Gunner Cox was one of the gun crews. 'Just after we commenced firing, No. 6 man, who was coming up in rear of the gun, with a shell under one arm and a cartridge under the other, was picked off with a musket ball. I took up what he had dropped, and we did as well as we could without him. It was a case of every man for himself, and we could have rendered him no assistance even if he had been alive ... General Strangeways, who was near us at the time, said to our officer, "We seldom saw a gunner fall in the Peninsula, but there are plenty falling here." '

Even manned by these scratch crews, their fire proved effective. Standing nearby, Calthorpe saw: 'The first shot fired fell too short; it was aimed at the Russian 18-gun battery, which was causing our 2nd Division in its immediate front, and the Light Division and brigade of Guards in its right front, great loss. Our guns were only 9-pounders, and the distance was considerable. The second shot, however, went through a Russian tumbrel, and killed two horses. Those two shots were sufficient: the Russian General, seeing that he was taken completely in flank, gave orders for his artillery to limber up. This they did admirably, but, during the time, our two guns kept playing on their retiring artillery, causing them great loss; and the gunners and two more guns of Turner's battery having now arrived, the firing went on rapidly.'

If Raglan took little other part in the battle, this – almost his only intervention – was crucial. The withdrawal of the Russian guns in front of de Lacy Evans removed the log-jam at the pass and enabled his 2nd Division to start putting real pressure on the Russian centre on the Sebastopol road. Having once achieved this, the gunners on Raglan's knoll raised their sights and – at extreme range – fired a few roundshot at the Great Redoubt, where the Vladimir Regiment were about to follow the retreating Light Division down the hill. There was little chance of inflicting severe casualties at such a range. The rounds thudded into the turf close by the advancing Russian battalions, but flanking fire can have a moral effect out of all proportion to its effectiveness.

The commanders of the Vladimir, unwilling to lead their men forward while enfiladed – mysteriously – from the left, halted and contented themselves with consolidating in and around the redoubt and harassing the retreating Lights with musketry.

So the nightmare scenario – of a defeated Light Division being pitched at bayonet-point onto the bearskins of the Guards, and the whole lot being routed back across the Alma – was averted by Lord Raglan's curious choice of viewpoint and two 9-pounders. The Royal Artillery are the unsung heroes of many British battles. Gunners rarely feature in songs and stories; the great battle paintings tend to concentrate on advancing redcoats or charging cavalry – where guns feature, they are usually being 'saved'. In fact, the arrival or withdrawal of guns – not for the first time in this campaign, and by no means for the last – had turned the tide of battle.

It may not have appeared that way for the Russians. Until the withdrawal of the Causeway guns, things were going rather well for them. On their left, the French had been stalled. Their centre held. On their right, the British infantry's astonishing feat of storming the Great Redoubt had been nullified by the Vladimir's counter-attack. What faced the Guards and Highlanders of the 1st Division after they crossed the river was a restored Russian position. Though the Light Division had drawn the teeth of the Great Redoubt – there were no manned guns there now – instead there were masses of infantry, supported by further batteries of guns higher up. In storming it the first time, the Light Division had achieved the well-nigh impossible.

Now it all had to be done again.

The Guards were emerging from the river, in ordered lines, but not as a brigade. First out onto the open ground were the Scots Fusilier Guards. Ahead of them they saw the mass of the Light Division. The adjutant of the Fusilier Guards was Captain Hugh Drummond. Writing to the adjutant of the 1st Battalion the next day he described what confronted his battalion as they formed on the open ground below the redoubt. 'We were scrambling out of the river under the bank, not yet quite formed, when to our astonishment, they, the Light Division, formed squares in front of us and began to retire, for just in front of us was such a battery as we none of us expected, about 500 yards off.'

The squares Drummond thought he saw testify to the disorder in which the Light Division was falling back.

It is interesting to note, too, that the redoubt came as much of a surprise to Drummond as it had to the Light Division as they came up from the river. Not content to wait for the Grenadiers or the Coldstream, and 'eager to be at 'em', the Fusilier Guards now advanced alone and unsupported to where they could see the men of the Light Division trying to make a front above them.

Drummond describes what followed. 'The Brigadier advanced us out at once to their support before the Grenadier and Coldstream were out of the river, and then began our part of the fun. We blazed into them with our Miniés and marched on straight to the entrenchment under such a fire. We got halfway up and in another minute would have been in ... when the remains of the 23rd, 7th, and 33rd (keep this private) retired ... right through our Battalion and regularly swept part of our right wing away with them and a part of our 5th, 8th and 6th Companies.'

Exactly how it happened remains a mystery. The bulk of the Light Division fell back slowly and sullenly, firing as they went. Just as the Fusilier Guards reached a group of the Light Division who were firing at the newly reoccupied earthwork, a number of Russians ran onto the earthwork and fired a volley into a body of the 23rd, who had already suffered terrible casualties. The cry went up: 'Fusiliers retire'. A number of Guardsmen were knocked over or swept away by the rush to the rear that this order – which was taken up by others of both regiments – produced.

In a few moments a great gap appeared in the centre of the British line as a mixed bag of Light Division men and Scots Fusilier Guards fell back to the river.

To the Grenadiers and Coldstream now coming up on either side, the sight of a body of the Scots Guards in retreat was nothing more than an excuse to indulge in inter-regimental banter. As they passed by, there were cries of 'Where are the Queen's pets now?'

The Queen's partiality for all things Scottish extended even to her Household regiments, and was known and resented by the other two. To this resentment may be attributed the slur that the Scots Fusilier Guards had 'run away' at the Alma, which was to dog the regiment for the next few weeks – until it had expunged it in its own, and the enemy's, blood.

Carrying the Colour of the Scots Guards that day was Ensign Robert Lindsay. Making no bones about it he wrote to his father: 'The men fairly ran down the hill. I was left alone with the Colours, standing on the hill. The noise of the firing was so great it was in vain to call to the men. I firmly planted the Colours and waved my bearskin. The staff of the Colours was shot in two in my hand – but I contrived to hold up the broken piece. I cannot say how long I remained alone, but it must have been full five minutes at the very least. Then the men began to rally round me – Thistlethwaite who carried the other Colour among them. The Colours were completely shot through. I suppose that standing as I did on the slope of the hill, the Russians on the rising ground above me – their fire must have passed over my head otherwise I could hardly have escaped untouched while the Colours received 27 shots. In my own case I neither drew my sword nor fired my revolver, my great object being to plant the standard on the Russian redoubt.'

The Duke of Cambridge watched Lindsay and later wrote to his father, 'At one moment I thought him gone, the Colours fell, and he disappeared under them, but presently he came out from below them, the flag staff had been cut, the Colours fell over him, but he reared them again and waved them over his head.'

Only a portion of the Scots Guards had been carried away, but the remainder suffered terribly. Near Lindsay in the centre was Lieutenant Hugh Annesley. He described how 'I prayed "O God! spare me!" and I really no more expected to return alive than if I had been tied to the cannon's mouth. Only fancy grape and canister being fired at us within thirty yards, besides a whole battalion letting drive as hard as they could into us. Both the other officers in my company were wounded. The colonel (Berkeley) had his leg broken. All the sergeants were wounded, and two killed; and I believe, at least twenty or thirty of our men.

'I was close to Lindesay when the Queen's Colours was smashed in his hand; there were twenty bullet holes in it, yet he was not touched.'

Annesley himself was not so lucky. 'We were above thirty paces then from the ditch, and the fire was so hot that you could hardly conceive it possible for anything the size of a rabbit not to be killed. I kept on shouting "Forward Guards!" to the few men that were not swept away ... when a ball came and stopped my mouth most unceremoniously; it entered the left cheek and went out at the mouth, taking away the front teeth. I instantly turned to the rear, feeling it was about a hundred to one against my ever getting there, as the bullets were whizzing round me like hail. I tripped, and thought it was all over with me. However, I got up again, with the loss of my sword and bearskin, and at last got into the river and out of the fire.'

It was a moment of crisis. The Guards now had a huge gap in their centre.

Glancing across as he carried an order for de Lacy Evans to the far right of 2nd Division, the Guards Brigade looked to Captain Lysons: 'like three sides of a hollow square. A feeling of depression came over me. I felt the tide of fortune was setting against us.'

To the left of the Guards, where the Highlanders, having crossed the river, were about to start their advance, one of Sir Colin Campbell's staff commented that the Guards must withdraw or they would surely be massacred.

Sir Colin, who added to his military skills a gift for the memorable phrase, answered: 'It is better, Sir, that every man of Her Majesty's Guards should lie dead upon the field than that they should now turn their back upon the enemy.'

Nor did they. The Guards continued their advance – not so much a brigade in line as three separate battalions, the Grenadiers on the right, the Coldstream on their left, with a large gap between them into which was hurrying the remnant of the badly mauled Scots Guards, followed by rallied elements of the Light Division. The Grenadiers and the Coldstream were too far apart to support each other, but in parade-ground order and, crucially, two-deep.

With the Coldstream was Captain Wilson. 'During those terrible moments, the conduct of the soldiers was wonderful; scarcely a man of them had ever seen a shotted musket fired before, except at a target, and yet, they looked in the conjuncture as cool, as self-possessed, as if "marking-time" in an English barrack yard . . . The tumble down of mess-mates only gave rise to the quiet observation, "There goes old Tom," "Our Dick's done for."'

As they advanced, they did so over ground littered with Light Division wounded. Wilson continued, 'Our way lies over the dead and dying of the 7th, 23rd and 33rd. Piteous murmurs for water or for help arise from mangled bleeding forms, but we may not notice them. Scattered remnants too, of that brilliant Light Division, come running through our ranks, but those few officers of theirs, whom the bullet had spared, immediately rally this debris in our rear. Confusion can be only momentary with such soldiers.'

The Coldstream now came face to face with the right-hand column of the Vladimir Regiment, whose commanders, having seen the gap torn in the centre of the British line, were preparing to charge. Now for the first time in this battle a Russian column encountered a fully deployed British battalion.

Wilson described the moment. 'A thick wedge of grey-coated

helmeted foot shows on the slope to the right of the grand battery; it waits an opportunity of hurling an overwhelming mass upon our thin line. Another round of deafening cheers, and file firing is commenced right into that close-grained column. Every soldier takes deliberate aim; the distance does not exceed sixty paces; hence the Minié has easy game and works miracles.'

And yet the deadly effect of this fire was nearly undone once more: 'The rifles had just got steadily into play, when an officer galloped down the rear of the line, shouting, "Cease firing, you're firing on the French." A short pause, during which the soldiers grumbled out savagely – "Are we to stand quietly to be knocked on the head, and not return a shot?" However, the companies' leaders arriving at the conclusion that, inasmuch as our Allies wear neither helmets nor grey watch-coats, —— must be in error respecting the identity of the corps that peppered us so freely, quickly sung out "Go on with your firing boys!" Like wild-fire the welcome direction ran from man to man; away "pinged" the Minié balls merrily as ever. Here was an infraction of orders, which, as may be supposed, none were called on to answer for.'

The French were far away to the right. This misconception arose so many times on this battlefield that one is tempted to suspect French-speaking Russian officers employing deliberate deception. Whatever the cause, this time it resulted in only the briefest pause in the withering Minié fire.

Over to the right the Grenadiers were advancing on the redoubt itself. As they did so, they were approached by a messenger from General Codrington. He had a few hundred men of the Light Division rallied round the Colours of the Royal Welch. Seeing that the Grenadiers were unsupported – and with a Guardsman's eye for the niceties – he now sent to the Grenadiers to ask if his scratch force might – just this once – form on the left of the Grenadiers? The Grenadiers didn't hesitate. No, came the reply, they might not. So the Grenadiers advanced alone, save for a party of the 95th, who had asked the same question of a lower-ranking officer and been graciously accepted.

Up ahead of the Grenadiers were the 19th, still firing back up at the column which had driven them out of the redoubt. Lieutenant Lidwill of the 19th and his men were among them. 'We had been stepping back firing some ten or fifteen yards as they came closing on us, but a sergeant calling me by name said, "Sir, the right of the line has halted," so I shouted, "Halt, halt!" and we were all steady again. Sergeant Owen then cried out "Here are the supports again!" and looking round I saw a battalion of Guards as if on parade ...

'I now set to work again, and kept up a warm fusillade on everything before me. We completely silenced the battery.'

Private Kirwin, one of Lidwill's company, saw a mounted Russian officer urging his men on. 'He was waving his sword for the men to come on. I said to Michael McNearney, John Tuckford and two other men of the Regiment, "Do you not see that big b— waving his sword? Let us have a slap at him." I happened to be spokesman on that occasion, although Michael McNearney was senior soldier to me by six years. We raised our slides to 600 yards and took deliberate aim on the knee, five comrades together, and fired. I happened to look up after the shot. "Mick," said I, "he is down. He will never wave his sword again."'

Meanwhile, behind Lieutenant Lidwill, the Grenadiers had arrived. 'The Grenadier Guards were now within 50 yards of my Company, their No. 1 was exactly in rear of my No. 6, when the Captain said "Form fours, Sir, and let my men pass through you!" Of course I could not exactly form fours, because we were not told off after passing the river, but we loosened files and through this grand battalion went, straight at the column which fronted our rather used-up line.'

As the Grenadiers passed through the Light Division, they were confronted by battalions of the Vladimir and Kazan Regiments. Captain George Higginson, the Grenadiers' adjutant, was on the right flank. 'Encouraged, no doubt, by the check they had effected on the advance of the Light Division, the Russians had formed a line in advance of their breast-work, and were thus able to resist our advance with vigour; but after a volley from our front rank, our Grenadiers began their slow and steady advance, the rear rank firing while the front rank loaded ...

'Before long the enemy began to fall back on their breast-work, a movement which encouraged us to press forward as rapidly as we could without losing our compact formation.'

The Grenadiers' disciplined Minié fire took a terrible toll on the Kazan, but seeing that the Grenadiers' left flank was unprotected, the Russian commander – Prince Gortschakoff – led the two battalions of the Vladimir into the gap, intending to turn the Grenadiers' flank. The Grenadiers' Commanding Officer, Colonel Hood, halted his battalion. The situation was dire. The Scots had not yet come up; the Coldstream were too far away to help. Codrington's Royal Welch might have been useful there, but on grounds of protocol they had been turned away. The Derbies who had attached themselves were too few. Just when things looked as bad as they could be, that dread figure – the 'unknown staff officer' – took a hand. A mysterious officer rode along the line calling 'Retire! Retire!'

Fortunately, the left-hand company commander, Henry Percy, a cousin of the Duke of Northumberland, chose to interpret this order according to what he knew should be done: 'Retire! What the devil do they mean? They must mean "dress back."'

Under Percy's command, the left wing of the battalion fell back at an oblique angle to the remainder of the line and at once poured a devastating fire into the Vladimir. One of the first rounds shot Prince Gortschakoff's horse from under him, leaving him stunned and concussed. Soon the centre and right of the Grenadiers wheeled to their left and added to the destruction. The Russian columns halted, wavered and began to melt away.

As yet another Russian column advanced, this time from the right of the redoubt, George Higginson, the Grenadiers' adjutant, encountered the Light Division's commander. 'I came upon Sir George Brown, sitting on his grey horse absolutely indifferent to the hail of musketry which filled the air, and watching the relief and support which we were giving to the detached fragments of his – the Light – Division,' he wrote. 'In a loud encouraging tone he exclaimed, "Go on! Press on! The day is yours!"'

'Halting for a moment by his side, I noticed a heavy column of the enemy moving rapidly down to reinforce the hesitating troops defending the breast-work, and pointed out our danger to the general, for the fold of the ground prevented our men from seeing the threatening danger. The general replied, "Don't you get excited young man. I tell you the day is yours; press on!" Sir George, being short of sight, had not seen the approaching column. Our apprehension, however, was speedily relieved, for Turner's troops of Horse Artillery galloped up on our right, wheeled half-left, and with their accustomed speed and accuracy, threw shot and shell into the advancing columns. I could see the Russian commanding officers waving their swords and encouraging their men, but to no purpose, the columns turned and fled.'

On the Russian side, Prince Gortschakoff, concussed, had handed over command in his sector to General Kvetzinski and staggered off up the hill. Kvetzinski's position was parlous. Left and right of the redoubt, his own infantry's counter-attacks had come to a halt, their columns, raked by the Guards' terrible Minié fire and by the British artillery. The Guards were closing on the Great Redoubt. At this point Kvetzinski was himself wounded, once in each leg and then in the side. Carried on a litter, he continued to command – all was not yet lost. On his far right he still had ten uncommitted battalions, in a position to threaten the whole left flank of this second British assault on the Great Redoubt.

All that was about to change, for even as the Guards and the Lights began their general advance in the centre, there began to appear – up from the river valley, directly below his last ten battalions – the feathered bonnets of the Highland Brigade.

It was not the whole brigade. The Highlanders' line had suffered as much as every other brigade's from passing through the vine-yards, the enclosures and the river.

At the head of his brigade was Sir Colin Campbell. 'They passed through in a very disorderly manner necessarily; but the left bank being high, I was enabled to collect my right regiment (the 42nd) in a goodly manner under its cover ... On gaining the summit I observed a large portion of the Light Division advancing to attack the redoubt, which was a good deal to the right of my right regiment ... I hastened the formation of my right regiment, for the other two were still struggling through the difficult bottom from which I had emerged.'

As a result of this disruption, the three regiments emerged onto the high ground in *echelon* – one after the other – from the right. First up were the 42nd, the Black Watch, oldest of the Highland Regiments. In their kilts and feathered bonnets, they presented the strangest sight the Russians had yet seen. As their two-deep line deployed and advanced to the right of the redoubt, a column of the Kazan Regiment, joined by a body of the Vladimir who had emerged from the back of the redoubt, bore down on them.

Sir Colin Campbell recalled: 'The men were too much blown to think of charging, so they opened fire while advancing in a line, at which they had been practised and drove with cheers and a terrible loss both masses and the fugitives from the redoubt in confusion before them. Before reaching the inner crest of these heights, another heavy mass of troops came forward against the 42nd, and these were disposed of in the same way.'

Firing while advancing was not in Army Regulations: the 42nd's commander, Colonel Cameron, had learned it from his father, who had commanded 'The Auld Forty Twa' in the Peninsula, where he had developed it as a system. Sir Colin Campbell had employed it in action in India, and the whole brigade had been practising it since landing at the Old Fort. As a result, the fire of the Highland Regiments was particularly effective.

Even as the first two columns fell back, however, a new threat appeared. A two-battalion column of the Sousdal Regiment – hitherto uncommitted – appeared out of the smoke, charging down on the left flank of the Black Watch line. A regiment in line attacked from a flank is in mortal danger – with no time to make a front it can be rolled up and slaughtered with the bayonet. But the Sousdal were balked of their prey.

To Sir Colin's relief: 'Just at that moment the 93rd showed itself coming over the table of the heights, and attacked these bodies, who did not yield readily.'

Before coming out to the Crimea, the 93rd had been made up to strength with drafts of volunteers from other regiments. This infusion of men especially eager to participate in the war, added to the natural ferocity of the Highland soldier, made the 93rd a fiery command. Seeing the Sousdal column – which had been about to fall on the flank of the Black Watch – now presenting its own vulnerable flank to them, their first instinct was to charge. Sir Colin galloped over and restrained their eagerness. The 93rd commenced volley-firing, the Sousdal column replied, and a hot fire-fight followed. Sir Colin's horse, shot through the heart, fell under him. Moments later his groom appeared, leading his second horse as calmly as though on the hunting field.

Touching his cap, the man excused his presence so far forward by explaining that at the rear the shot and shells were falling so thick that he thought it best for the horse to bring him to the front.

Remounted, Sir Colin led the 93rd forward, firing as they went.

Again, the Minié did its deadly work, again, a Russian column fell back before a British line.

But the Russians were not done yet. There were two more battalions of the Sousdal. Two more columns appeared from the left, out of the smoke – this time about to fall on the left flank of the 93rd.

In Sir Colin's words, 'The 93rd, whom I had great difficulty in restraining from following the enemy, had only time to inflict great loss, when two bodies of fresh infantry, with some cavalry, came boldly forward against the left flank of the 93rd, when thinking (as in the case of the flank attack on the 42nd) of the dispositions I should make to meet it, the 79th made its appearance over the hill, and went at these troops with cheers.'

Once again the outflankers were outflanked – this time it was the Cameron Highlanders – and once again a Sousdal column, about to roll up one British line, was itself taken in flank by another. To the Russians these skirted soldiers appeared as if by magic, at precisely the wrong moment.

The last of the Russian columns halted, endured for a while, wavered, and at last withdrew.

As the Highland Brigade on the left were disposing of the Russians' last reserve, the Guards and Lights were closing in on the Great Redoubt.

Sensing that this was the critical moment of the battle, Lord Raglan was riding down to join them. Riding with him, Calthorpe saw the conclusion of the fight. 'The whole Division sent in a withering volley, which perfectly staggered the Russians, literally knocking over every man in their two front ranks. The enemy stopped, fired a random volley, turned and fled, without another attempt at staying the victorious course of the British troops. The moment the Russians turned, down went the bayonets, and the whole division charged up the hill, dashing through the battery.'

'With a shout of joy,' wrote Captain Hugh Drummond of the Scots Guards, 'we sent the whole Brigade up the hill into the ditch and massacred them in crowds. They bolted pellmell and we poured in such volleys as astonished their weak minds killing and wounding hundreds.'

With the Grenadiers was George Higginson, who described: 'Our line advanced with firm and impressive regularity until it came within fifty yards of the breast-work. The word "Charge!" rang out; the line broke into a run, and bounding over the parapet, our Grenadiers flung themselves on the few Russians remaining inside. The guns had already been removed by the Russians; only one was left for a trophy. Our ranks were re-formed under the stern orders of our colonel, and in a few minutes we stood again in column, prepared for any further movement or adventure. But it was soon evident that our enemy had had enough.'

Captain Wilson charged in with the Coldstream. 'The "Ruskis" await not the shock, they face about and off at "the double", leaving on the ground, hundreds of dead and wounded. Forward! Friend and foe are trampled on alike; the very Colours of a regiment of Brown's, which had been smashed to bits by the *feu d'enfer*, when closing with its prey, are trodden under foot. Pell-mell the Grenadiers break into the "big battery", but with the exception of a gun or two it is empty. And now the summit of the height gleams with British bayonets ... The first, second and light divisions have won the English half of the victory.'

Watching the final triumph from down by the river, Surgeon Munro of the Highlanders had a strange encounter. 'I was standing watching the struggle near the great redoubt, when, to my surprise, a gentleman in plain clothes approached me. He was a stout and rather heavy man, with prominent features; his face, bronzed by exposure, was well-covered by a dark brown beard and whiskers. He was on foot, and appeared to suffer much from the heat and from exhaustion, but was very observant of what was taking place, and carried a note-book in his hand. He addressed me in the following words: "This is a splendid sight! One that I have been looking forward to very wearily for months; and now I am satisfied, and pleased to see it." He did not tell me who he was, and I never saw him again; but he was so observant that I concluded he was some enthusiastic Briton, who for his amusement was taking notes.'

By now the Russians were in full retreat across the whole front, not even attempting to defend the much higher but unfortified Kourgane Heights. The Russians guns, infantry and so far unused cavalry streamed over them and away towards Sebastopol. Some British guns mounted the Heights and managed to send a few rounds into the retreating Russians, but those who expected the cavalry to be sent off in pursuit were to be disappointed.

Lord Lucan had brought up the Horse Artillery and was waiting for his Cavalry Division to be launched at the Russians. A well-conducted pursuit after a battle could turn a retreating army into a mob. Murat's pursuit of the Prussians after the Battle of Jena in 1806 had ended with the destruction of the Prussian army. Now was the time, surely, to do the same to Menschikoff's army, seize Sebastopol by *coup de main* and end the campaign at a stroke.

More cautious counsels prevailed: the French, St Arnaud told Raglan, could spare no infantry, their artillery ammunition was exhausted and they had no cavalry. Raglan's 900 cavalry and the as yet unused 3rd Division were all there was available to pursue an army of some 30,000 men who, even if defeated, were retreating in good order.

So pursuit was abandoned – the army would bivouac on the ground it had won. Recriminations began almost at once.

On the Kourgane, Wilson of the Coldstreams watched the Russians make a clean break. 'The southern slopes of the blood-stained ridge, and the valley beneath, swarm with retreating masses – some brigades in confusion; others in square order, rough customers still. Those infernal guns, too, that have so mauled us, go clattering down the rugged paths at the heels of teams of Cossack horses. They escape us! They laugh at our beards! we have missed the chance of doing Menschikoff a crushing hurt. He has gained, aye, and ably gained, too long a start.'

For all that, there was rejoicing all around him. The Heights were now crowned by British infantry, cheering, as Calthorpe wrote, 'On the further heights, about a mile and a half from the Alma, the British troops ceased their pursuit. And then arose such a cheer! – a cheer from 2,000 victorious men! – even some of the poor wounded fellows joined in it. I shall never forget that cheer as long as I live; it was indeed thrilling; I almost pitied the fallen enemy, it must have been so galling to them, as I heard a man of the Guards say to a comrade, "I say, Bill, pleasant for them poor devils (pointing to some wounded Russians) hearing our chaps cheer so." '

It was almost as galling to the cavalry, denied their share of the glory. Trooper Mitchell had galloped up to the top of the heights with the 13th Light Dragoons. 'Our divisions were in line on the crest of the hill hurrahing, and throwing their caps in the air. We took up the cheer, and I shouted with the rest, when our troop leader, looking sternly at me, said, "What are you shouting for? We have done nothing to shout for yet." He said the same to several others, so we gave it up, and left the cheering for those who had won the victory.'

Among the Coldstream, Wilson remembers: 'Officers shook one another by the hand, with a warmer grasp than they had ever used before – or since, may be – and tender questions passed round, as to the wounded. "Is old B—— badly hurt?" Is dear young C—— in danger" It was a golden hour, as the sun set on our first battle-field!'

John Hume and his brother Robert, who had last seen their brother on board a frigate off the coast, came upon him again on the Kourgane, much to all their relief: 'We all were glad to halt when the heights were crowned, tired after the day's hard work. My brother Gustavus met us – the three brothers untouched. Great congratulations on all sides from those who had escaped the dangers of the day.'

Even the Commander-in-Chief temporarily overcame his distaste for public displays of enthusiasm. Calthorpe recalled how: 'Lord Raglan rode up and down the line of troops, the men cheering him vociferously. There was such a shaking of hands: one felt very choky about the throat, and very much inclined to cry, as one wrung the hand of a friend; and "God bless you old fellow – so glad to see you all right!" and like expressions, were heard on every side between brother officers. It was a touching sight to see the meeting between Lord Raglan and Sir Colin Campbell.'

Campbell himself described that meeting. 'When I approached him I observed his eyes to fill and his lips and countenance to quiver. He gave me a cordial shake of the hand, but could not speak. The men cheered very much. I told them I was going to ask the Commander-in-Chief a great favour – that he would permit me to have the honour of wearing the Highland bonnet during the rest of the campaign, which pleased them very much.'

Too overcome with emotion to reply, Raglan nodded his assent amid the cheers of the Highlanders.

Not everyone was happy. At the back of the redoubt, Sir George Brown rode up to General Buller, who – with two of Sir George's battalions – had guarded the left flank of the army against that Russian cavalry which had never appeared. Lidwill of the 19th saw the encounter. 'General Buller ... drew his sword and saluted Sir

George Brown, who returned it with such a selection of choice expressions and acclamations. "He'd know," he said, "why the 77th and 88th were not brought into action, and he'd be d—d if he wouldn't.".

Not everyone was cheering. Colonel Lacy Yea, the fierce disciplinarian who had stood all day in the thick of the hottest fire, now stood among the wreckage of his 7th Fusiliers. According to Timothy Gowing: 'Our poor Colonel exclaimed at the top of the hill, when he sounded the assembly, "A Colour gone! And where's my poor old Fusiliers? My God – my God!" And he cried like a child wringing his hands . . .'

The Colour was soon retrieved, pulled out from under a pile of dead, but hundreds of his Fusiliers were gone for good. Gowing himself 'obtained leave to go down the hill; I had lost my comrade and I was determined to find him if possible. I had no difficulty in tracing the way we had advanced, for the ground was covered with our poor fellows – in some places in sixes and sevens, at others tens and twelves, and at other places whole ranks were lying.'

Not everyone was horrified by the carnage, Henry Clifford's African servant Jacob, for one: 'The savage blood in his composition was rather excited and warmed by the field of battle at "Alma", "Ah Ha, Sir," said the young demon, as he ran up to me after the action, loaded with a Russian rifle, sword, helmet, &c., "this is 'alta moi' so plenty men dead, legs and arms all over the ground! All Sir's enemies." He wished his brother and father and all the Kaffirs could see as he had, the English soldiers walk up to the cannon mouth with big hearts that had no place for fear in them.'

Private Kirwin of the 19th, was also searching among the dead, looking for a new rifle to replace his own, which was damaged. Among the Russian dead and wounded he found the general at whom he and his four comrades had fired a volley.

'When he saw me he was frightened to see the firelock in my hand. When I saw the state he was in I made signs to him. I rubbed down his hair, in token that I was not going to touch him. As I could not understand him, nor he me, I made signs to him to let me know where he was wounded.

'I was going away when luckily I met a young doctor belonging to the Fusilier Guards. I asked him if he would be kind enough to come and see a Russian General. "I will my man," said he. I presented him to the General. The first thing the doctor did was to offer him a glass of liquor, but he shook his head and refused. I told the doctor that he pointed out his two legs to me, where he was wounded; with that the doctor ripped up the legs of his trousers. There were the five wounds, apparently the shots we five men had fired ... The doctor took bandages out of his bag and bandaged him up.

'I was retiring, but first I paid him that respect that I would my own General, although he was an enemy. He stretched out his hand to me and such a shake-hands I never remember receiving before. He squeezed the forefinger of my right hand; only for shame's sake I would have roared out, he hurted me so much. I suppose it was to show his gratitude for the kind turn I had shown him as a British soldier.'

Not all such encounters ended as happily – many Russians had already shown a willingness to fight to the death. Timothy Gowing, still searching for his friend, saw an example. 'A young officer of the 95th gave a wounded Russian a little brandy out of his flask and was turning to walk away when the fellow shot him mortally. I would have settled with him for his brutish conduct, but one of our men, who happened to be close to him, at once gave him his bayonet, and dispatched him. I went up to the young officer and, finding he was still alive, placed him in as comfortable position as I could, and then left him, to look for my comrade.'

Gowing concluded that: 'The Russian officers were gentlemen, but their men were perfect fiends.'

A little further down the hill he came upon his comrade. 'I found him close to the river, dead. He had been shot in the mouth and left breast, and death must have been instantaneous. He was now in the presence of his glorified Captain; he was as brave as a lion, but a faithful disciple. He could not have gone a hundred yards from the spot where he told me we should "have to shift those fellows with the bayonet".

'I sat down beside him and thought my heart would break as I recalled some of his sayings, particularly his talk to me at midnight of the 19th; this was about 6 p.m. on the 20th. I buried him with the assistance of two or three of our men; we laid him in his grave with nothing but an overcoat wrapped around him, and there I left him with a heavy heart.'

Riding close by, looking for his regiment's wounded, Captain

George Higginson of the Grenadier Guards, noted: 'The unnatural attitude of the dead and the contorted movements of the wounded gave rise to feelings which it needed all one's resolution to control. Almost the first among the dead whom I recognised was poor little Harry Anstruther, his red coat and shirt thrown back, disclosing the bullet wound which had struck him full on the heart. Only two days before he had found me lying prone on the grass writing a hurried letter to my people at home, and throwing himself down beside me, asked for a slip of paper on which to write a few lines. I have reason to know that the dear little lad expressed in those hurried lines the conviction that he should meet his death in the coming fight . . .'

As night fell across the battlefield an army, the majority of whom had had their first experience of battle, was now coming face to face with the reality of war. The inadequacy of the army's administration to cope with casualties on this scale, those shameful deficiencies which would mar the glory of this day and appal the nation, would be revealed in the cold light of dawn.

In the meantime, as the army lit their bivouac fires on ground the Russians had confidently expected would still be theirs at nightfall, the prevailing opinion was the one George Higginson himself heard expressed only a few minutes later: 'Before reaching the river bank I met another litter, also carrying to the shore a grievously wounded soldier whom I recognised by the cap which lay upon his prostrate form as a private in the Guards. As he turned his face towards me I saw his lips move, and in the belief that he had some message to his friends at home, I halted the bearers and bent over my saddle to listen. With a faint smile he simply said, "I think, sir, they'll say we did our duty today!"'

CHAPTER FOUR

The wounded passed a terrible night. Some four to five hundred men were brought into the field hospitals, but this was only a third of the total. The remainder lay out all night.

'No army ever took the field, or landed in a hostile country, with the prospect – nay, the certainty – of immediate battle, so unprepared and so imperfectly supplied with medical and surgical equipment as did our small but splendid Crimean army. The men that filled its ranks were the finest soldiers that I ever saw in stature, physique, and appearance. We have not had anything like them since, and never shall, I fear; and it is mournful even now to remember how rapidly those fine fellows disappeared, in a great measure because we did not understand how to take care of them, or to speak more plainly, because we failed to take care of them,' wrote the surgeon, George Munro of the 93rd Highlanders, years later. 'We had a large number of regimental medical officers, but no regimental hospitals, and there were no field hospitals, with proper staff of attendants. We had no ambulance with trained bearers to remove the wounded from the battle-field, and no supplies of nourishment for sick or wounded.

'On landing in the Crimea, the regimental hospital was represented by one bell tent, and the medical and surgical equipment by a pair of panniers containing a few medicines, a small supply of dressings, a tin or two of beef tea, and a little brandy, and these panniers were carried by a wretched pony woefully out of condition.

'The instruments were the private property of the surgeon, paid for out of his own pocket, as one of the conditions attached to promotion. The only means of carrying sick or wounded men consisted of ten hand-stretchers, entrusted to the band.

'In the event of battle, the transports were at hand, but these were not prepared for the reception of wounded, and we had no such thing as a hospital ship.'

The task of collecting the wounded – more than 1,600 men – on the field of the Alma rested with comrades, regimental bandsmen, drummers, and the few men of the ambulance corps, of whom Albert Mitchell wrote, 'These old pensioners had been sent out to act as an ambulance corps, but they turned out a complete failure. Poor old men, they had far better stayed at home and enjoyed their pensions, for most of them soon died. How could it be expected otherwise? Most of them with broken constitutions to enter on such a campaign as it proved to be.'

Even if some did make it to a field hospital, conditions were appalling. Lieutenant Annesley of the Scots Fusilier Guards, who was shot through the mouth in the Great Redoubt, had made his own way out of the fighting and eventually found some shelter.

'There were six or seven of our fellows there: one with five balls in him, another three, and a third with his leg broken. My servant got me some blankets, and then we got a stable, half burned down, cleaned out, and five of us lay there for the night, very wretched, as you may suppose, operations going on all round us. Some weak brandy and water and some tea were all we had. The shed we were in was a horrid thing – the heat, and dust, and flies intolerable,' he wrote.

Touring the field hospitals with Lord Raglan – who worked till late giving orders for the accommodation of the wounded – Somerset Calthorpe observed: 'Here might be seen the surgeons hard at work in their terrible but merciful duty, their arms covered with blood, the floors strewn with limbs just amputated, and slippery with gore. The enormous number of wounded quite overpowered the unceasing efforts of the medical officers.'

Surgeon Robinson of the Scots Fusilier Guards was 'occupied as long as the twilight permitted in tending the wounded, and afterwards as far as practicable by firelight, in the open air. Every few minutes, the parties in search came in with a fresh sufferer previously overlooked. We were ourselves faint and exhausted. I had been out on foot all day, and without any refreshment except from the stream, whose waters, if not mingled with blood, were certainly rendered turbid enough by the feet of men and horses, and by an occasional mouthful of spirit from an aide-de-camp's flask. I never appreciated tea so much in my life, as some I fortunately had, together with biscuit, in my haversack. For the means of making it, a teapot and hot water, I felt very grateful to a picquet of another regiment, who were sitting round the fire with the wounded.'

There were few lamps, few instruments, no operating tables, no bandages, no splints, and hardly any drugs – Chloroform, the one drug that might have alleviated the sufferings of men undergoing battlefield amputations, was officially frowned on. Pain was still considered an important part of the healing process. Dr John Hall, the Army's chief surgeon, was of the opinion that, 'The smart use of the knife is a powerful stimulant and it is better to hear a man bawl lustily under the knife than see him sink silently into the grave.'

Some practitioners ignored his memorandum forbidding its use, but one disobeyed Dr Hall at one's peril and most obeyed his rules.

For the unwounded, exhausted as they were, sleep was near impossible; Trooper Albert Mitchell, with the 13th Light Dragoons, found it so: 'We heard all around us the groans of the wounded and dying; some calling for the love of God for a drop of water. Others were praying most devoutly, well knowing this to be their last night in this life.'

Many, too excited or too traumatised by what they had seen, sat around fires for most of the night. C.T. Wilson listened to his Coldstreamers. 'It was pleasant to listen that night to the talk round the watch fires. The excited soldiers eagerly asked one another "What will they say in England about the battle?" "Nobody could complain as how we haven't done our duty anyhow." "Shall we get a medal?" And, then, the game cocks would crow of their personal feats. "How the rifles let daylight into that Rooshian column." "How no men in this world could stand up against English and French soldiers." "How poor old Bob got his last fall in that there garden, just as he was a plucking them grapes."'

But even sitting round the fire had its dangers, as Lord George Paget noted in his journal: 'It can hardly be believed, but so it is, that one source of danger ... was by the "popping" of the Russian loaded barrels, that our fellows, after breaking them off their stocks, make use of as a sort of grate over their fires; of course, when they get red-hot, off they go, and the balls come whistling about our ears most unpleasantly.'

Muskets, Paget noted, were still going off all over the battlefield: ' "Pops" are going off every minute, as our fellows wander about, and discharge the muskets near the wounded for safety, as they shoot at our fellows whenever they can.'

Not all of the battlefield wanderers were on missions of mercy. Albert Mitchell and his fellow Dragoons were going for water at first light. 'We saw parties making their way home to their camps who appeared to have been out all night, and who now had full haversacks. There was a little drummer-boy, I shall not say what regiment he belonged to, he had his haversack so full that a pair of officer's gold epaulettes were sticking out at the top. They were all making haste, evidently fearful of being reported absent at roll call. Besides these parties, there were plenty of camp followers who had been at the same work, some of whom looked as though they would not stand at trifles.'

In the cold light of day the battlefield presented a still more awful spectacle. Somerset Calthorpe too was out early. 'I was up at daybreak on the morning of the 21st, and, filling my flask and a bottle with weak brandy and water, I sallied out to walk over the field of battle. The poor wounded were far more quiet than the previous evening; many doubtless had died during the night, and many were too weak and exhausted to do more than moan. I found all glad of something to drink, and my little store was soon finished, and I then went back for more. Although it was only just light, numbers of our men were going about among the wounded, giving them drinks of water from their canteens. Many told me they had been doing so all the past night. God bless them for it!

'It was a horrible scene – death in every shape and form. I particularly observed that those shot through the heart or forehead appeared all to have died with a smile on their faces, generally speaking lying flat on their backs, with the arms spread out and the legs rather apart. Some looked so happy, poor fellows! that one felt comforted, and thought that they, at least, were now where no sorrow is. Those who appeared to have died in the greatest pain were those shot through the stomach; these had always their legs and arms bent, and with all expression of agony on their faces.'

Where the dead lay thickest Wilson of the Coldstream Guards came upon the remains of a Russian battalion. 'Men who had been shot through the heart, remained in the very attitudes in which they received their mortal hurts; thus, you had but to set one corpse on its legs again, to have a statue in clay of a soldier in the act of ramming down a cartridge; another body presented the posture of taking aim, and so on, through all the sections of the platoon exercise. But the most striking of the victims of instantaneous death, which I came across, was a young Russian rifleman – he could not have been more than sixteen years old at the outside – who appeared kneeling amid the havoc, with his hands clasped, and his great glassy blue eyes turned heavenward – the ball must have smitten the lad as he prayed! That rigid form, the sun beaming on his waxy brow, and round about, a ghastly huddle of defaced carcases, shivered arms, heavy shot shell splinters, all smeared with clotted gore, composed a picture that haunted me for many days.'

Only now did the inadequacy of the medical arrangements become clear. The wounded and the sick – there were another thousand new cholera cases – were carried, by comrades, band-boys, drummers, by parties of sailors, or by French ambulances, down to the coast to be ferried out to the 'hospital ships'. These were simply transports fitted with a few medicines and medical stores. Only one, the *Kangaroo*, remotely fitted the description and it, like all the others, was grievously overloaded: equipped to deal with 250 men, it received between 1,200 and 1,500. Once on board the men were laid on the bare planks of the deck, crammed together. Most of them were too weak to reach the sanitary conveniences, so it wasn't long before the men were covered in filth. A naval surgeon, James Peters of HMS *Vulcan*, reported that on the morning after the battle: 'a small steamer came alongside with 86 soldiers, in charge of an assistant surgeon of HMS *Agamemnon*; six of these had been wounded in the cavalry skirmish the night before the battle, and had suffered amputation. No document nor order about them was sent, and I considered that no others were coming, and proceeded to arrange them on the main deck ... about noon boat after boat came alongside with the sick and the wounded, and I was obliged to ask for a signal to be made for surgical assistance ...

'About 6 p.m., finding that there were nearly 500 on board, and that others were alongside, I requested the first lieutenant, in the absence of the commander, to prevent any others coming on board ... Of course with so large a number of men pushed on board so quickly, any arrangement was out of the question, and with the exception of those first placed on board, the sick and wounded were placed indiscriminately on the decks, to the great risk of the wounded, for with diseases such as cholera and dysentery extensively prevailing, the atmosphere becomes quickly tainted. But the marines and sailors of the vessel, albeit rough nurses, behaved in the kindest manner to the poor creatures. But great distress was experienced from want of urinals and bed pans, one only of each being on board; and from the want of these, many blankets were thrown overboard by my orders when they became foul.'

The officers' lot was slightly better; Hugh Annesley of the Scots Fusilier Guards, wrote home to his mother from the hot fly-blown hut near Bourliouk.

'I with two others am on board Her Majesty's ship *London* ... Poor B—— came to see me ... and burst into tears when he recognised me, I was so altered. Of course, one cannot have an ounce of lead through one without swelling, and my face is like a good-sized turnip, my mouth much larger than I have any desire to see it in the future. I do not suppose the ball could have hit me in any other part of the head where it would not have been attended with more danger – a most summary dentist the ball was, to take out all my teeth at one smash, except four grinders (there was a decayed one, which I hope has gone with its brethren, but I can't make out yet if it has or not). There is a good bit of tongue gone also, but the doctors say that it will not signify, and that I shall speak as plain as ever, or at most, only with a becoming lisp; so, altogether, I think even you must allow that I have every reason to be thankful.'

Not all were so fortunate. Captain Braybrooke of the 95th, who had been wounded at the Great Redoubt was, following the amputation of his arm on shore, one of the five hundred or so men taken on board the *Vulcan*. Laid on an iron bedstead with only a single blanket to protect his mutilated frame, he lay unattended for eight hours as the medical ship's surgeon tried to cope with the horrors on deck; by nine o'clock that evening Braybrooke was dead.

The hospital ships sailed on the morning of 23 September. The wounded men rolled about on the decks with the ships' motion, crying out in pain as they collided with each other. They were bound for the Barrack Hospital at Scutari – a converted Turkish artillery barracks facing Constantinople on the Asiatic side of the

Bosphorus – which the senior Medical Officer, Dr John Hall, would shortly declare to be 'on a very creditable footing ... nothing is missing.'

That this was almost the exact opposite of the truth was a fact that would soon shock the British nation to the core. To some of the older campaigners among the higher ranks, those younger officers who were already complaining about the inadequate arrangements for the care of the sick and wounded must have appeared to be mere *croakers* – after all, the medical arrangements were much the same as they had been in the Peninsula forty years earlier, so what was so different now? One thing that *was* different was the presence with the Army of William Howard Russell, first and greatest of the war correspondents. Billy Russell, as he was known, was a charming affable Irishman with a gift for making friends. He was *The Times* correspondent with the Army of the East. Although *The Times*, under its editor John T. Delane, was a Radical newspaper, and regarded with suspicion by most army officers – 'By God, sir, I'd as soon see the Devil' was General Pennefather's greeting to Russell – it wielded enormous influence. What Russell wrote would be on the hundred most influential breakfast tables in England within days. What Russell had seen of the officers and men who stormed the Great Redoubt had moved and impressed him; what he had seen of Lord Raglan had not. What he saw on the beaches and in the field hospitals appalled him.

A political storm was brewing which would burst over the heads of the Government when his latest dispatch was published on 9 October, and set in train the process whereby that well-bred young lady named Florence would hit the Army's complacent medical establishment like a blast of grapeshot.

The job of clearing the battlefield and burying the dead took place on 21 and 22 September. Timothy Gowing, newly promoted sergeant in his badly depleted 7th Fusiliers, was on burial detail, and described the scene. 'The dead were buried in large pits – and a very mournful and ghastly sight it was, for many had been literally cut in pieces. It was a difficult matter really to find out what had killed some of them.'

Gowing was not the only man whose conduct on the day of battle had been noticed by his superiors. The morning after the battle,

Captain Morgan of the 95th, who had held aloft the Colours at a moment of crisis, and personally shot a Russian sharpshooter, was summoned before his senior officer, when the following conversation took place:

'Morgan, do you think you were justified in shooting that Russian yesterday?'

'I think I was, sir.'

'I think you were not; it is not the duty of an officer. You should have told one of the men to shoot him.'

Lord George Paget toured the battlefield with Colonel Lacy Yea, hearing his account of the 7th Fusiliers' battle. 'In my rounds I came upon Lord Raglan, just sitting down to dinner (in the open air), and he desired me to get off and sit down. After having shaken him by the hand, and offered my congratulations, I was moving down to another end of the table, when he said, "Oh George, come here and sit next to me. I have been hard at work all day, and now I should like to have a little small talk."'

Paget, who was generally regarded as something of a character, had, of course, been known to Lord Raglan since his infancy. When Paget took the opportunity to hint to Lord Raglan about the cavalry's frustration, Raglan made a joking reference to Paget's young wife: 'I asked him whether the cavalry might not have been of more use (in reply, by the bye, to a joking remark he made to me, "Well George, you see I thought about Agnes in the battle") when he said that if our cavalry had been up, they could not have taken a gun, or done anything, and his object all along had been to – what he called – "shut them up" (those were his words), the enemy's cavalry being so superior in numbers.'

That same day news of the battle had reached another anxious wife, Fanny Duberly, still on board the ship off Eupatoria. She wrote, 'Was awoke from a restless sleep by the entrance of my maid – a soldier's wife – with her apron over her eyes. I naturally asked what was the matter. "Oh, ma'am! Captain Tatham has sent to say he received despatches, which will oblige him to leave Eupatoria today. And there has been a dreadful battle – 500 English killed, and 5,000 Russians; and all our poor cavalry fellows are all killed; and, the Lord be good to us, we're all widows."

'God, and he only, knows how the next hour was passed – until the blessed words, "O thou of little faith", rang in my heart.

'At breakfast I asked Captain Fraser for the particulars of the message; but he, from a feeling of kindly wishing to save me anxiety, assured me he had heard nothing about the battle, and did not believe a word of it. However, at two o'clock, I went ashore to see the Governor, and ascertain the words of the despatch. He told me that there had been a severe battle at the River Alma, but no official particulars had yet reached him.'

It was not until the following day that Fanny learned, to her intense relief, that the cavalry had not been engaged; by then the army was on the move.

The Allied armies resumed their march on Sebastopol on the morning of 23 September, in the same order as before, British on the left, French and Turks on the right. The advance was over grassy plains, which reminded Somerset Calthorpe, riding at the head of the column with Lord Raglan's staff – of Sussex downland. They were following the same route the Russians had taken, and there were already signs that they were not beaten yet.

Calthorpe observed, 'The Russian retreat must have been made in better order than most had imagined, for there were not many traces of a beaten army. A good many helmets and knapsacks were to be met with, and occasionally a ghastly corpse, but altogether it did not give one the impression of a disorganised force.'

The Russian retreat *was* conducted in far better order than had at first appeared on the evening of the battle of the Alma. Pursuit after defeat is always the most dangerous time for an army, and the Russians, thanks in equal measure to their own skill and all the Allied delays, had managed to make a clean break.

Sickness was still affecting both Allied armies, and many fell out on the march. Surgeon Munro of the 93rd Highlanders came across an old friend.

'As I walked in the rear of my regiment, I observed four soldiers carrying a stretcher on their shoulders, on which a sick man lay. They were moving slowly and carefully, so as to disturb the sufferer as little as possible; but when they saw me approaching they gently laid their burden on the ground and asked me to do something for their officer. On stooping down I saw that the poor fellow was in the last stage of cholera, beyond help or even hope. He was so emaciated and so changed that I did not recognise an old friend; but he knew me, and addressing me by name, implored me in a feeble whisper to do something to alleviate his sufferings. Poor fellow, when we last met, in a gay ballroom in England, he was a powerful handsome man, a picture of strength, but before me lay a shrunken helpless form, still alive and breathing, but his breath was icy-cold, too certain a sign that the end was near.

'There was nothing in my power to do for him; I had not even a drop of water to moisten his parched lips. So the soldiers raised their dying captain on their shoulders once again and moved slowly on, while I walked beside them, as even my presence appeared to afford comfort to my poor friend. He died within half an hour after I saw him, by the road-side, and the only friends near him were the four soldiers of his own company and myself.

'It was evident that the men were much attached to their officer. They were stalwart, rough-looking fellows, but walked so carefully, handled him so gently, spoke so tenderly, and, when all was over covered the dead face so respectfully that I could not help expressing my thanks. But they said, "Oh! no, sir, we do not deserve any thanks. We would have done anything for him, for we have served in his company for years, and he was always good and kind to us, and there was no braver man."

'I do not know any class of men amongst whom there is less selfishness and more brotherly kindness than amongst the soldiers of the British army.'

The next river line reached was the Katcha, where the heights had offered the enemy another strong defensive position. The Russians had chosen not to make a stand here, but if any still believed that the Russians were about to fold after the licking they had received on the Alma, news from the fleet soon disabused them. That evening, bivouacked in the village of Eskel, Calthorpe wrote to a friend, 'I have just heard that Lord Raglan has received a despatch from Sir Edmund Lyons, brought up to headquarters from the *Agamemnon* by Lieutenant Maxse, informing him that the Russians have sunk five line-of-battle ships and two frigates across the entrance of the harbour of Sebastopol! That looks like a desperate defence.'

Sebastopol's main, or outer, harbour lies roughly east-west, with its mouth – opening out into the Black Sea – at its western end. It was this harbour mouth that was now blocked by the sunken Russian vessels. Admiral Korniloff, the commander of the Russian fleet, had considered taking his ships out to engage the Allied fleets in one big all-or-nothing battle, but had been talked out of it by his naval captains. Though Prince Menschikoff, the overall commander, had shown scant tactical ability at the Alma, he now displayed sound strategic sense. After ordering the blocking of the harbour mouth, he decided to march the bulk of his troops out of Sebastopol and into open country. There they could maintain communications with the rest of Russia and, when reinforced, launch an offensive against the besieging Allies. In the meantime the defence of Sebastopol would be left in the hands of Korniloff, assisted by Colonel Todtleben, a military engineer of German origin, who was to emerge as the Russian hero of the siege.

Meanwhile, the Allied commanders had been considering the question of an immediate assault on the city's north side. On the northern shore of the main harbour, apart from a few storehouses and a factory, the only buildings were forts. Most of these were designed to protect the harbour mouth against attack from the sea, but one, the Star Fort, was placed on the high ground above the northern shore to defend the city from just such a landward attack. By 23 September this fort, armed with 47 heavy-artillery pieces, had been augmented by trenches and supporting batteries on either flank. More than this, it could also call on the supporting fire of the Russian fleet in the harbour below.

In the unlikely event of a successful storm – at inevitable huge and bloody cost – the Allies would have gained nothing other than a foothold which left every useful part of Sebastopol in Russian hands on the far side of a 1200-yard-wide harbour. In effect, it would be a complete waste of men and time, and General Sir John Burgoyne, the army's chief engineer, had already advised Lord Raglan against such a venture. He preferred the option of a flank march right round Sebastopol with a view to attacking it on the south side.

While the commanders pondered these matters, the army had more immediate concerns. As Calthorpe wrote to his friend, 'Here are the most beautiful vineyards and fruit-gardens I ever saw. It is much to be feared that the men will make themselves ill, they eat such an amount of fruit . . . It is useless remonstrating with them. I told several that it was the surest way of getting cholera. It had no effect, they would go on eating just as one used to do at school. There had been an attempt to put sentries round some of the gardens; however the men manage to evade them, and carry away their havresacks full of fruit.'

It wasn't only fruit; the whole village was comprehensively looted. Wilson of the Coldstream described the types he saw filling the street: 'an "honourable and gallant MP" portentously bearded, and so besmirched as to his comely features, that the acute porter of the "Rag" might have failed to recognise him ... a big-kneed red-headed "laddie", bending under a huge basketful of *kail* destined for the use of the mess (the sly bottle peeping out of his haversac, being for private consumption) ... a broth of a boy of the "ould Rangers" shouldering a vast feather bed ... a Zouave – always visible wherever fighting or plunder are to be had – with a slaughtered kid dangling under one arm, and an inlaid work-box secured under t'other ... a brace of Ensigns loaded with an innocent booty of grapes and Jerusalem artichokes ... and lastly a "fatigue party" of the "Queen's Own", hurrying homeward with a miscellaneous collection of chairs, benches, bed-posts – in fact, legs and wings of all kinds of domestic furniture – "just to get up a bit of a blaze till the company fall in to-morrow yer honour", the corporal in command informed me.'

Further down the street he found a gentleman's seat, 'like a Twickenham cottage': 'chock full of English, French and Turkish soldiers, who, disappointed in the expectation of finding money or silver spoons, ... were playing the deuce with everything that fell in their way. One stupid fellow amused himself with smashing a handsome pier-glass with a poker; another stabbed away at the silken window curtains with his bayonet; a third danced an Irish jig upon the grand piano-forte; a fourth ... was elaborately expunging the Calmuck eyes and noses of the stolid family portraits.'

The next day the army – reinforced now by the 57th Foot and the Scots Greys – resumed its march. Across the Belbeck the nature of the country changed to hills covered with thick vegetation. The cavalry and artillery suffered here from the lack of water and forage for the horses.

That afternoon, Lord Raglan visited the French commander,

Marshal St Arnaud, to discuss the options. An assault on the north side of the city – assuming it was ever seriously considered – was now finally rejected. It was agreed that the south side offered better prospects for an Allied assault and, crucially, two harbours – Kamiesch and Balaklava – that could be used as supply bases. Accordingly, both armies would, the following day, march round Sebastopol and invest it from the south. Throughout the conference St Arnaud had sat bolt upright in his chair, barely able to speak. He was too ill to attend a second conference the following morning, to finalise the details of the day's march. Later that day he handed over command to Marshal Canrobert.

The British advanced with the cavalry in front, followed by the artillery of the Light and 1st Divisions. Behind them, in column of regiments, came the infantry of the Light and 1st Divisions, then the 2nd and then the 3rd. As the army got itself into motion Lord Raglan's staff rode forward to take a first view of the objective of the expedition: Sebastopol. Calthorpe was among them.

'The first glimpse we had of the town from the land was certainly very striking: there appeared a great number of stately buildings, some of a large size, probably barracks. Then there were several handsome churches, and many large private houses with green roofs to them. All the buildings were of white stone, and, with the sun on them, quite dazzling. The harbour looked beautiful – very extensive; the water so quiet and so blue; the remainder of the fleet which had not been sunk riding at anchor with the Russian ensign flying from their peaks. There seemed little movement either in the town or harbour; and although our staff must have been conspicuous, and were within easy reach of their heavy guns, they took no notice of us.'

Meanwhile, the infantry, forbidden to use the road, which was reserved for the artillery, were struggling through the bush which covered the plateau. Wilson of the Coldstream described the going. 'Everybody who has seen "beaters" pushing their way through a thick cover may form a faint idea of the difficulties which beset, and the obstacles which retarded, our progress. The heat was overpowering – not a breath of air percolated the dense vegetation . . . You scrambled on with arms uplifted to protect the face against the swinging back-handers dealt by the boughs; now, your shakoe was dashed off – now, the briers laid tenacious hold on your haversac, or on the tails of your coatee. It was as much as you could do to see the soldiers immediately on your right and left. For the time, military order was an impossibility – brigades and regiments got intermixed. Guardsmen, Rifles, Highlanders, straggled blindly forward, all in a ruck. There was much suffering, and some stout soldiers dropped involuntarily to the rear, to be heard of no more.'

The cavalry were kept busy screening the army's advance, scouting and protecting the flanks – this was bread-and-butter cavalry work, though most officers and not a few of the men longed for that ultimate moment of the cavalryman's life, the charge. It was a moment that seemed destined to elude them – a situation that didn't improve the tempers of the Cavalry commander, Lord Lucan, or his brother-in-law and subordinate, Lord Cardigan. Lord George Paget, on rearguard duty with his 4th Light Dragoons, wrote in his journal that evening: 'Cardigan has just ridden in from the cavalry (three miles off) and describes a dreadful night they had of it, having got into a narrow pass, in which he says one battalion might have annihilated them, but then he added, "Mind Lord Lucan was in command." which accounts in his mind for it, and perhaps for his colouring of it.'

For Paget, bringing up the rear of the army with Sir George Cathcart's 4th Division was even grimmer. 'We are much disgusted at being attached to the Fourth Division, which is the last coming out; but when reflecting that such a man as Cathcart was placed in a similar position – that of forming the reserve – I did not feel justified in remonstrating, mine being the last regiment out, as his is the last division. But yesterday the Scots Greys joined the army, having come out from England after us, and I certainly anticipated that they would take our place. Judge then of our disappointment this morning to find that they are gone on to the front, leaving us still as camel-drivers, and always humbugged by being told that the rear would be attacked.'

Of course, Paget noted, there were compensations. 'Personally I have been a gainer, as it has made me independent of the "two generals of cavalry"; but it is natural that the regiment should grumble, particularly as we have had much more trying and harassing work than all the cavalry put together, without the chance of honour and glory, of which however, as luck would have it, they have as yet had no more than themselves.'

The British army was not the only army toiling through the woods. Prince Menschikoff – assuming that the Allies were about to attack the north side of Sebastopol – was moving his army into the interior, just as Raglan – assuming that the Russians were fortifying themselves in Sebastopol – was moving his army round to the south. Both armies were in ignorance of each others' whereabouts. Both were about to be enlightened.

The thick vegetation made co-ordination difficult. It was not long before the different units of the advance guard lost touch with each other, and the whole British advance on Sebastopol was being led by a troop of horse artillery, unsupported by the Riflemen or cavalry it had set off with. Before long, Lord Raglan and his staff cantered up to join the gunners: the Commander-in-Chief was now literally at the head of his army. Where was the cavalry? Raglan sent General Airey on down the track look for them – seconds later, he came spurring back. There was a Russian column on a track ahead of them, at right angles to the British line of march. Raglan's escort deployed in skirmish order, the guns were readied, the cavalry were ordered up.

'Just at the same moment,' said Calthorpe, 'the Russians got the alarm and began to run . . . so the cavalry that had arrived were sent in pursuit, and a troop of horse artillery. The guns opened from some rising ground on some fugitives, causing them some loss. One party of Russians rallied for a moment, and gave Captain Chetwode's troops a volley; but as every bullet went over their heads, they must have been too frightened to take the least aim. The Russians abandoned all their wagons, and fled into the woods on either side of the road, where many were followed by our men, and killed or taken prisoners.'

Among the cavalry ordered up was Trooper Albert Mitchell of the 13th Light Dragoons, he who had been silenced by his troop leader after cheering on the heights of Alma.

'At this time I felt very unwell, with every symptom of cholera. I lay down, and after a little while fell asleep. Suddenly I was awakened by the orders "Mount," and then "Gallop". At the same time we heard the report of firearms in our front, apparently very close. In a few moments we came out upon an open space of perhaps two acres. On the left-hand side of the road stood a long low building, perhaps thirty yards long, with outbuildings in rear. Along the road, and out on the green were a number of wagons all loaded. Horses were loose and galloping about, and a party of Russian infantry were just escaping into the brushwood. We went straight on past the house as fast as we could go. We had not gone far when we came across a dead Russian Hussar laying in the middle of the road, and a little further on an overturned wagon and a dead horse. There were plenty of clothing and provisions scattered along the road. Large black loaves and some dried fish. One of our men picked up a new Hussar officer's superfine cloth jacket ... By this time all the symptoms of cholera had left me, and I felt quite well again, so leaving my horse with my comrade for a few minutes, I went round to the back yard where I found another of our men. We caught a large black pig; it was lean but we did not mind that. We soon cut his throat in spite of his cries, and soon he was dead. I took one of the hind legs and hung it in front of my saddle intending to have a pork supper that night. It hardly looked fit for a dog to eat, yet I felt proud of my prize.'

Among the prisoners, Somerset Calthorpe found: 'A Russian officer, a captain of artillery, who was found seated on a baggage wagon quite drunk. He had a champagne bottle in his hands, which he offered to us, only unfortunately it was empty.'

After the commissariat and artillery had relieved the wagons of anything of military value, the troops were allowed to pillage them. Calthorpe watched. 'In a few minutes the ground was strewed with every sort of thing – handsome Hussar uniforms, rich fur cloaks, every kind of undergarment, male and female. Several wigs I saw being offered for sale, amidst the laughter of the men. French books and novels of an improper kind were not unfrequently met with in the baggage of the Russian officers. All these were offered for sale and disposed of to the highest bidder. A gold Hussar pelisse would sell for about 30s or £2.'

Not everyone cared for the Hussar pelisses. Trooper Mitchell described them. 'They were sky-blue, with yellow lace, the number (12) being on the buttons, showed they belonged to the 12th Hussars. They were of a very coarse cloth, nearly as coarse as a blanket.'

Others were not so choosy. Lieutenant Lidwill of the 19th helped himself to 'A splendid Hussar dolman, similar to our 7th Hussars' winter dress. Brown fur collar and cuffs and, as its owner was a large man, it fitted me nicely and loosely over my coatee.'

In the baking heat of Sebastopol's Indian summer, a heavy fur dolman appeared superfluous, but those who picked them up would be glad of them in the months to come.

The clash had come as a surprise to both sides: the head of the British army, marching towards Sebastopol, had collided with the tail of the Russian army marching away from it. Calthorpe, and the rest of Raglan's staff, now saw the rest of the force of which this had been the remnant.

'Looking into the plain below us, we saw a very large force of infantry and artillery: it was variously stated at from 20,000 to 30,000 men. It appeared afterwards from the prisoners that this was the army under Prince Menschikoff, whom we had beaten at Alma, now on their retreat to Batchi-Serai and Simpheropol, having left Sevastopol at 3 o'clock that morning.'

It was not the last they were to see of that army.

The British army assembled round Mackenzie's Farm – its owner was a local worthy of Scottish origin – and then descended from the Mackenzie Heights to where the Traktir Bridge crossed the Tchernaya River. Ahead of them, across a wide plain bisected by two valleys – the northernmost of which was soon to become the most famous valley in military history – lay the port of Balaklava.

The following morning, by 7 a.m., the army was on the march once more. By 10.30 they were at the village of Kadikoi, perched on a small plateau above Balaklava. The seizure of this port was essential to provide a base for the fleet, for the landing of supplies, reinforcements and the Siege Train. The fleet had already sailed down from the Katcha, past Sebastopol, and has waiting just outside the harbour for the army to take possession of the port. At first they thought the town was undefended, but as Lord Raglan and his staff rode forward, a shell, flying from the old Genoese fort that topped the eastern heights above the harbour mouth, landed among them. Soon Riflemen from the Light Division were skirmishing up the hill, while shells from the British flagship *Agamemnon* slammed into the fort.

Watching the assault were men of the 1st Division, Captain Wilson among them. 'The Rifles climbed the eastern (embattled) height; the 7th and 33rd rushed perspiring up its western neighbour. "In another five minutes the 'sweeps' will be into 'em, 'bayonets fixed'."

"So they will, but no need of cold steel, – for see, there's the white flag!" Such were the observations current among us in support.'

Somerset Calthorpe, among the staff – none of whom were wounded by the fire of the fort's solitary 18-pounder – observed, 'a small white flag ... flying from the end of the musket, held by a Russian soldier close to the Genoese fort. On this signal of surrender all firing ceased on both sides, and our Rifles were to be seen entering the castle in triumph.'

The fort had been manned by the town's commandant and 80 Greek militia. According to Wilson, the commandant 'declared that, on the first appearance of the British, he had hung out a cambric handkerchief in token of surrender; but no notice being taken of the rag (it was not perceived) and a shell having sung unpleasantly close to his ears, he valorously determined to stand to his guns; however the increasing fury of the ships' fire, and the advancing clouds of riflemen, suggested the propriety of again trying the effect of the peace-ensign, and having, this time, selected a more demonstrative article of his wardrobe (one of his best linen shirts) ... hostilities were suspended and Balaclava became ours – without costing one drop of blood!'

With Balaklava in British hands there now followed a debate between Lord Raglan and Marshal Canrobert. In theory, since the French had so far taken the right of the line of the Allied armies, Balaklava should be allotted to the French as a supply base. When the armies swung round and faced north to attack the south side of Sebastopol, the French army would be on the right and the British on the left, next to the sea. In such a case the French would need Balaklava as their supply base, and the British would use the two westerly ports of Kamiesch and Kazatch. However, the British Admiral, Sir Edward Lyons, had already represented most strongly to Lord Raglan that Balaklava was by far the better base, and that since it was in British hands, it should remain so.

Canrobert, new to command and no doubt keen to maintain good relations, announced himself willing to cede the right of the line to the British, so in the forthcoming siege of Sebastopol the French would take the left, with Kamiesch as their base, and the British the right, with Balaklava as theirs. It was a fateful decision. The French would have their left flank guarded by the sea and their right flank by the British. The British, on the other hand, had an open right flank, and so would constantly be torn between prosecuting the siege and protecting their right flank from Menschikoff's army. The consequences of this decision became clear very quickly.

The armies now moved into the positions that, with minor alterations, they were to occupy for the remainder of the war. To someone viewing it from the high ground to the south, the harbours of Sebastopol might simply be described as forming a 'T' shape, the bar of the 'T' the main harbour, the upright, projecting southwards towards the viewer, the Man of War Harbour.* It is around this southern projection, the Man of War Harbour, that the city, the naval buildings, the barracks and the dockyards were clustered, and it is this harbour that was to be the focus of the Allied siege. The bare, treeless plateau, known as the Upland, rises to about 3,000 feet and completely surrounds the city. The highest part of the crest is 500 feet above the valley of the Tchernaya River, which flows into Sebastopol Bay. This Upland extends roughly eight miles from north to south and eight miles across, and it was here that the Allies now encamped, surrounding the Man of War Harbour, with the French on the left facing the town and the British on the right, facing Karabelnaya, a suburb, and the dockyards.

Prince Menschikoff had left the city, narrowly missing a collision with the head of the British column, and leaving its defence in the hands of Vice-Admiral Korniloff and Colonel Todtleben. To defend the city against the Allied armies they had six militia battalions – a total of 5,700 men – 18,500 sailors, 4,500 marines, the Taroutine Battalion of Menschikoff's army, and 5,000 workmen: a grand total of 35,800 men. Russian sailors were routinely trained as soldiers, and could provide an almost limitless supply of crews for the heavy guns provided by the fleet and armouries. The dock workers, as well as receiving military training, were especially skilled in handling heavy machinery, mounting guns and fortification work.

Todtleben had already begun a line of defences extending from the main harbour – the bar of the 'T' – southwards around the Man of War Harbour – the upright of the 'T' – and up the other side to rejoin the main harbour. These defences, a rough 'U' shape in which the 'T' sat, were composed mostly of earthworks based on the classic

* See Map 3.

pattern pioneered by Vauban in the seventeenth century, with low silhouettes and smooth angled sides to deflect incoming roundshot. Packed earth made a better defence against artillery than stone walls: an officer in the Peninsula described pitching roundshot into an earthwork 'like firing plums into a pudding'.

The defence lines consisted of a series of bastions – large artillery platforms – linked by loopholed walls of stone and earth. The most significant of these bastions, and the two identified early on as 'the keys to Sebastopol', faced the British. These were the Malakoff, a twenty-eight-foot-high semi-circular tower of stone, five feet thick and thirty in diameter, with five heavy guns on top, and the Great Redan, a similar 'V'-shaped construction further south. Flanking the Redan was the so-called Barrack Battery, and facing the French was the Bastion du Mat, known by the British as the Flagstaff Bastion.

These bastions dominate the story of the siege, and the rest of the war. They were sited to be mutually supporting: men attacking any of them could be fired upon in flank from the others. These defence lines had been traced many years earlier, and Todtleben, fresh from the Russian siege of Silistria, was improving them day by day. By 26 September, the lines of Sebastopol mounted 172 guns, most of them heavy artillery.

Even so, as the Allies took up their positions on the high ground overlooking these defences, some were for an immediate assault, to carry the city by *coup de main*, General Cathcart for one, who was eager to live up to his reputation by some spectacular act,

'We are now in sight of Sebastopol,' wrote Lord George Paget, from the heights on the evening of 27 September. 'Up here, indeed, there is a beautiful view of it. I rode up with Cathcart. As we emerged on the heights, we soon came to a stone quarry, with heaps of stone slabs squared, and the very barrows and working tools left on the ground as if we had disturbed them in their work. When our men had got a little settled, I walked with him and his staff a little more to the front, and as we lay on the ground with our telescopes out, he said, "I could get in there tonight with my division, if they would let me. I have tried hard, but am not allowed to make the attempt."'

Sir George was soon to learn that the Russians were on the *qui vive*. When Calthorpe visited Cathcart later that evening, he saw:

'He and his staff were partaking of dinner. All at once they heard "Whiz – whiz – whiz – WHIZ, BANG!" and a shell exploded a few feet from them, to their intense disgust and the discomfiture of their dinner arrangements. On this being repeated a second time, they thought it more prudent to shift their dining-place to a spot less attractive to Russian shot and shell. Sir George Cathcart is all anxiety to assault the town, and I believe, thinks he could take it with his division alone. I fear he is somewhat rash, and appears to wish to cut out a line of his own.'

These were prophetic words. Cathcart was later to change his mind about the practicability of such an assault, but his desire for urgent, independent action remained.

The next day the Allies began landing their siege artillery. The British train consisted of twenty 8-inch guns and thirty 24-pounders, each with 500 rounds per gun, as well as ten 15-inch mortars with 300 rounds per mortar. In addition, fifty large-calibre naval guns were also landed, with 1000 sailors to man them. Of the 8-inch guns, four were the so-called Lancaster guns, constructed on the latest principles with rifled barrels – the first rifled artillery used in warfare – and an oval bore. Unlike the spherical shells fired by other guns, the Lancasters' ammunition was of conical shape, 18 inches long, containing an explosive charge of 12 pounds of gunpowder. Great things were expected of these mighty new guns.

If the artillery for the siege looked forward to the twentieth century, the methods of its prosecution had not changed since the days of Marlborough. First, great fortifications would be dug for the big siege guns. Once these had been dragged into place, the Allies would approach the defences of Sebastopol by digging a series of parallels, long lines of trenches running parallel to the enemy's lines. Once the first parallel had been dug, a series of 'saps' – communication trenches – would be pushed forward, zig-zagging so as not to be enfiladed – that is, fired down lengthways by the enemy. These saps (which give the name Sappers to the Royal Engineers) would be the starting point for the next parallel, which would come out to right and left. Slowly and painfully, the series of parallels – all linked to each other by zig-zagging saps – would be dug, until the last parallel (usually the fourth or fifth) was close enough under the enemy's walls for infantry to attack without having to cross too much open ground.

When the big siege guns had done enough damage to the enemy's entrenchments, and silenced the enemy's guns, so the plan went, the infantry would leap out of the last parallel and rush towards the enemy's lines to carry them at bayonet point. Supporting troops would wait in the first, second and third parallels and, once the first wave had gained a foothold, push on over the walls and into the heart of the enemy town.

The high ground surrounding Sebastopol is divided by a series of ravines. One of the largest of these, the Woronzov Ravine, down which the Woronzov Road runs into the heart of the city, split the British siege lines in two, so the British approaches to the enemy's lines were divided into what became known as the Left and Right attacks.

On the left a battery was to be erected, known as Chapman's Battery after the engineer officer in charge. From there a series of parallels would be pushed forward. On the right of the Woronzov Ravine Gordon's Battery was to be erected and a second series of parallels would be pushed forward from there. On the far right of the British position was to be another battery, the Victoria Battery or, because of its armament, the Lancaster Battery.

On the Allied left the French were following a similar procedure, erecting batteries and pushing parallels forward towards the Flag-staff Battery.

This siege was never, in truth, a siege in the classic sense of the word. Sebastopol was not surrounded, nor was it blockaded. The besieged garrison could enter and leave the city freely, either across the harbour to the north, or out of the Karabelnaya suburb at the extreme north end of the British line, where the British-held part of the Upland ended, overlooking the ruined village of Inkerman. Russian convoys passed in and out of the city here, and the garrison could communicate freely with Menschikoff's field army, which was hovering on the Allies open flank, awaiting an opportunity to strike.

On 30 September Hugh Clifford wrote in his journal, 'Bodies of Russian troops moved into Sebastopol yesterday and about a Division is now moving in. Our force is not large enough to invest the place on the right – which is open and guarded by a strong force of Russians who are not molested by us as we wish to get our siege pieces in position without being disturbed.'

This weakness on the right was to have dire effects in the weeks to come. In the meantime, that, together with the rocky nature of the ground on the British side, meant that the British batteries would not come as close to the enemy as the French ones. This would be partly compensated for by the greater size of the British siege artillery.

Cholera continued to take its toll, and it was no respecter of persons. On 29 September, Calthorpe had been with Lord Raglan. He wrote, 'early in the morning to take leave of Marshal St Arnaud, who that day started for the Bosphorus, on board the *Berthollet* French steam frigate. He found the Marshal very ill and weak, and able to speak only in a whisper a few words of thanks for his visit. Lord Raglan was much touched with the interview, and tears stood in his eyes as he turned away from the sick room. The doctor in attendance on the Marshal told Lord Raglan that he did not think he would live through the day, or, at any rate, would never survive to reach the Bosphorus.'

Marshal St Arnaud died before reaching the Dardanelles.

Four days later, in the camp of the Light Division, Hugh Clifford, taking an order to the Colonel of the 77th, 'Stumbled over the body of a poor fellow just dead of cholera, rolled up in his greatcoat, outside the hospital tents. The Doctor saw me and asked me to look in. Four men in their blankets lay on the ground vomiting and groaning. All ill with cholera, "no hope for them", and as the Doctor had only a little opium and rum to give them, they must die. This sad sight was lighted up by some of the (ration) fat of the pork, in a pot in the middle of the tent, with a bit of rag lighted in the centre of it.'

That same day, in Wilson's regiment, the Coldstream Guards, 'Captain Jolliffe died of cholera, after a few hours' agony. Captain Jolliffe was one of those unhappy beings who felt what is called a presentiment of approaching death; this mysterious, but not uncommon, feeling seems to have gotten hold of his mind shortly after our arrival at Varna, for about that time a remarkable change took place in his manner and way of life. From being a more than ordinarily cheerful man, he at once grew silent, melancholy, and earnestly religious. Poor fellow, sweetly resigned and full of confidence in his Redeemer, he obeyed the last order like a good soldier of Christ. There were moist eyes among us as we stood round our comrade's grave, and more than one rough "private" muttered "God bless him," when the first spade full of dust fell upon the uncoffined corpse ... Without venturing to enter on the question of the "presentiment", I may mention that, during the earlier portion of the late war, five intimate friends of mine were impressed with an unshakeable persuasion of their impending fate; and the issue proved that they had thought rightly; every one of them perished by the sword or pestilence!'

By now the British army was losing men to sickness at a rate of one hundred a day. Three thousand were in the hospital in Scutari, and losses among the regiments who had been in the forefront at the Alma were still rising. Daniel Lysons of the 23rd, who guided the gun teams across the Alma, had been appointed Commanding Officer of his Regiment that evening, replacing Colonel Chester, killed at the Great Redoubt. Now he wrote to his mother, 'The command is no easy work at present. I have no adjutant, my old sergeant-major was shot, my drum-major has died of cholera, my assistant sergeant-major was wounded, a junior captain is doing duty as major, and my companies are all commanded by young lieutenants, two of whom do not belong to the regiment.'

The relative strengths of the Allied armies had changed: when they had first landed in the Crimea they had roughly equal numbers. The French now mustered 35,000 men, to a British infantry strength of 16,000. In the light of this disparity, which was to worsen as the campaign continued, it was agreed that General Bosquet and two Divisions would be detached as a Corps of Observation to help guard the heights on the exposed British right.

Now the Allied armies got to work, with one of the soldiers' most effective – and least popular – weapons: the shovel. The difficulties of the ground were felt immediately by the British. Calthorpe noted in a letter home, 'The French broke ground on the evening of the 9th, and had made a trench upwards of 1000 yards long by daylight the next morning; this parallel is, on average, at a distance of 1200 yards from the Russian works. The enemy never discovered that they were at work, so they were unmolested, and consequently the trench was admirably constructed; the soil was well adapted for the purpose, being a rich loam, so it was easily put into any form and stood at a good angle. Our ground is very different, being (when not rocky) very loose and crumbling, and therefore cannot be made to stand at a proper angle without an extra amount of gabions, fascines and sandbags.'

Fascines were bundles of brushwood, used to fill ditches; gabions were large, cylindrical wickerwork containers which, when filled with earth, provided good cover from bullets, shot and shell. That same night Wilson's men were placing them out in front of the British lines. Wilson described the scene. 'Oct 9 – A great day in the journal of a siege. At last we have broken ground before the place! The night happening to be clear, and very cold, a good deal of anxiety was felt about the working parties. We feared lest the Russians might either see or hear our men, and in consequence harass them, ere they had time to fill their gabions – in other words before they had thrown up (with the aid of gabions) a bank high enough to cover them, as they laboured, from the enemy's "look-out". In this instance, however, the icy wind was our friend-in-need; blowing sharply from the NW, it whirled the clatter of the pickaxes to our rear, instead of to our front; hence the besieged remained in ignorance of British proceedings, till the work had made considerable progress.'

At the same time the batteries were being prepared and the trench lines were being opened up, the siege guns had to be dragged up from Balaklava to the heights. As usual, lack of adequate transport was a problem: it had dogged the British since their first landing and would continue to do so throughout the whole campaign. The few local carts which had so far been assembled were too small to be of much use in shifting the great siege guns up on to the heights, and the wagons of the field artillery had to be stripped down to assist.

The Navy hauled their own guns up. In Balaklava, hunting for provisions, Hugh Clifford witnessed this: 'Saw the sailors pulling the guns that have been landed from the fleet, about 30 men to each gun. They are fine fellows and work with such good will. A piper was sitting crossleg on the first gun and all the men singing and keeping time to his tune.'

Among the sailors was Midshipman Evelyn Wood, who had watched the battle of the Alma from the topmast of his ship and was now delighted to be serving ashore with the Naval Brigade: 'The Artillery lent us travelling carriages for the 68-pounder guns, but they could not lend us enough for the 32-pounders, and nearly all these we hauled up the hill, and later down into the battery, on the little solid wheels called "trucks" on which they were worked on board ship. We had fifty men divided between the drag ropes, and a fifer or fiddler on the gun, and if neither was available, a Bluejacket with a voice and ear for music was mounted on the gun to sing the solo of a chorus song, to the tune of which we hauled the guns. I have never seen men work so hard continuously for so many days.'

The sailors impressed everybody. A few days later Fanny Duberly, now living in Balaklava Harbour, on board the *Star of the South*, wrote: 'Lord Cardigan very kindly lent me a horse, and Mr Cator and I rode up to the front. Here we saw Captain Hillyar, of the Naval Brigade, who is working hard to get his guns into position. These seamen appear to work with the greatest energy and good-will. One meets a gang of them harnessed to a gun, and drawing with all their might and main; or digging at entrenchments, singing, laughing, and working heartily and cheerily. But their experience of camp-life is short indeed in comparison with that of our poor soldiers, with whom they contrast so gaily.'

There was concern among the 'Jack Tars' that the 'Lobsters', as they called the redcoats, should get all the glory. Henry Clifford commented, 'Armed with pistols and cutlasses, if ordered, they would rush on the walls of Sebastopol as soon as look at them. They all wish they had the Minié rifles. I'm glad they have not, I am sure they would shoot as many friends as foes. Like all of us they wish to be at it, and are tired of waiting to open the ball.'

Corporal Timothy Gowing of the 7th, last seen at the Alma burying his dead comrade, found it: 'no child's play dragging heavy siege-guns up from Balaclava; it was a long pull, and a strong pull, up to our ankles in mud which stuck like glue. Often on arrival in camp we found but little to eat, hardly sufficient to keep body and soul together; then off again to help get the guns and mortars into their respective batteries, exposed all the time to the enemy's fire, and they were no ways sparing of shot and shell.

'We would have strong parties in front of us, as covering parties and working parties; often the pick and shovel would have to be thrown down and the rifle brought to the front. Sometimes we would dig and guard in turn – we could keep ourselves warm, digging and making trenches and batteries, although often up to our ankles in muddy water.'

Though there was mud, there was little water for washing. John Hume, of the 55th, reported, 'At this time we all, from the general of division down to the smallest drummer-boy began to be troubled with one of the plagues of Egypt – the cause, want of water, and having no change of clothes.'

Even the Guards were soiled, mud-stained and 'aboriginal' of appearance, with one exception, as Wilson noted: '"Toby", of whose valiant gambolling at the Alma, I have already spoken. While all else were of the earth, most offensively earthy, he played about, unsmutty, and taintless, sparkling his eye, silky his coat, joyous his shrill bark. For this dainty aspect, the pretty beast was indebted to his owners, the drummers, who, I verily believe, stinted themselves in soap and water, that the little chap might be, as they expressed it, "a credit to the battalion".'

For the British soldier, trench-digging was not congenial work. Wilson explained. 'Strange as it may appear to many, English soldiers (with the exception of the Guards, who are almost entirely village-born, with an infusion of that most magnificent of physical elements – "the navvy") are, to a certain extent, poor hands with the "pick and shovel", simply because one-half of the men composing our line regiments are town-bred – lads of loom and spinning-jenny – who possibly never set eyes on a ploughed field before they "listed".

'Our allies, conceiving the art of throwing up earth-works to be nearly as important a branch of the military trade as the act of loading and discharging a musket, train all their young soldiers to the use of the pick and shovel.'

It was beginning to dawn on many British officers that the French army was a much more professional organisation than their own.

Throughout these preparations the Russians gunners proved alert, skilful and – at this stage of the siege – plentifully supplied with ammunition. On the afternoon of 12 October, Calthorpe carried a message down the trenches of the Left Attack.

'It was anything but pleasant work, as the last two hundred yards before you get into the trenches are quite exposed, so, directly I made my appearance, some five roundshot were sent at me, and I had to keep my eyes open to get out of their way. It has been observed that if an officer makes his appearance the enemy fires directly, but a private will probably be left alone; they must have good telescopes to be able to make out which is which at that distance.'

By 16 October both Chapman's and Gordon's Batteries – on the Left and Right Attack – were completed, manned with a total of 67 guns. A further six, including the Lancasters, were sited in the Victoria and One-gun Batteries, making a total of 73 guns. Against the enemy's works to their front the French had concentrated a further 53.

At a council of war on the evening of 16 October it was agreed that the Allied batteries would commence the bombardment of the city the following morning, with both fleets joining in. Troops were to be in place for an infantry assault, should the bombardment prove even more successful than anticipated.

Despite all the hardships, morale was high. Most now expected an early end to the campaign, and 'home in time for the pheasant shooting'. Not everyone, however, found this a pleasing prospect: General Cathcart, with that Dormant Commission burning a hole in his pocket and great deeds yet to perform; the cavalry, who viewed with dismay the prospect of a return home with the infantry and artillery decked with laurels and they – the élite of the army – forever remembered as the 'look-ons'.

Lord George Paget noted in his journal: 'We hear that Cathcart is very angry at the way things are going on, and at his being never consulted. What a thing war is, and what wrangling and jealousies does it engender! There are Lucan and Cardigan again hard at it, because they can't agree, and it is found desirable to separate them. Cardigan must needs be ordered up here to command the 4th and 11th, both of which are usefully placed, with their respective divisional generals, and all this must needs be upset to part these two spoilt children.'

Reflecting on his decision, before war broke out, to quit the army, Paget concluded: 'No, the ploughshare is the thing to look forward to.'

It had been confidently expected that the Russians would collapse after the Alma, now it was confidently expected that the defences of Sebastopol would disappear under the fire of such a concentration of heavy artillery. A mood of anticipation prevailed.

On the night of 11 October, Fanny Duberly and her husband took a moonlit ride to the extreme right of the British lines to view the city: 'I could not but feel a high degree of excitement, and I think it was not unnatural. We were standing on the brow of a hill, backed by our magnificent troops, and fronting the enemy; the doomed city beneath our feet, and the pale moon above: it was indeed a moment worth a hundred years of every-day existence. I have often prayed that I might *"wear out my life, and not rust it out,"* and it may be that my dreams and aspirations will be realised.'

A few days later Henry Clifford noted, 'All Artillery Officers – French, English and Naval – say ... after a fire of 48 hours, little will be seen of Sebastopol but a heap of ruins.'

According to Midshipman Wood: 'On the 16th October the betting in our camp was long odds that the fortress would fall in a few hours. Some of the older and more prudent officers estimated that the Russians might hold out for forty-eight hours, but this was the extreme opinion. A soldier offered me a watch, Paris made, which he had taken off a Russian officer killed at the Alma, for which he asked 20s. My messmates would not allow me to buy it, saying that gold watches would be cheaper in 48 hours.'

At dawn on 17 October the Russians began a sporadic fire on the Allied batteries. At 6.30 a.m. the Allied bombardment began with 72 British and 53 French guns. The Russians replied all along their defence lines.

Thus began the greatest artillery battle the world had ever seen. Lord Raglan watched from the quarries in front of the Third Division camp from which he hoped, if the bombardment was successful, to lead his troops to the assault that afternoon.

Calthorpe watched with him. 'The roaring and whistling of the shot, as they flew through the air on their course of destruction, surpassed anything ever heard before. In a few moments everything was enveloped in smoke, so that we could only sit and guess and hope we were doing well. About half an hour after we commenced "pounding" a breeze sprang up and cleared the smoke away for a short time; we had then an opportunity of seeing what we had done. The first thing observed was the Malakoff tower quite silent, and the top of it all knocked to pieces. This had been done entirely by the fire of the four heavy guns (68-pounders) in our detached battery on the right of the right attack; in the course of the day it became a complete ruin. Here and there also a gun had been silenced, but for

the most part, no great advantage had been gained by either party
... the French appeared to fire somewhat slower, but this was
accounted for by the fact that most of their guns were of brass, and
consequently cannot bear quick firing after a certain time.'

Reduced to the role of spectator for the moment, Wilson described
the scene in the batteries. 'The air is alive with the boom, the hiss,
the whiz of projectiles. A little beyond, or, a little short of our works,
the earth is ploughed with bounding shot, or indented with deep
holes, dug by the bursting of shells. Dense clouds of smoke hang
about the town, and so fill the batteries that the artillery-men work
in the dark, almost pointing their pieces by guess. Ever and anon, a
roundshot, striking the angle of an embrasure, rips out gabions, kills
a gunner or two, perhaps dismounts a gun. Tumult and confusion
all embroiled, shouting, and blood, groans and death.'

Midshipman Wood was down in the Naval Brigade camp when a
message came from Captain Peel's battery for every available man to
take powder up to the battery. Wood took four carts full of powder
and a party of men from his own ship up to Peel's Battery. 'Having
placed the men under cover, I went towards the eastern end, the
guns of which were manned by detachments of the *Diamond* and
the *Queen*, that part of the battery being called from Captain Peel's
ship, the "Koh-i-noor". Two guns in the Redan enfiladed the left-
hand guns of the right (or eastern) face of the 21-gun battery, and
as I passed them a shell close over my head made me stoop, till I felt
my foot was on something soft, and another hasty step repeated the
sensation. Looking down, I saw I was treading on the stomachs of
two dead men, who had been fighting their guns stripped to the
waist when killed, and whose bodies had been placed together. I
was not only startled but shocked, and the feeling made me hold
my head up when in danger.'

Watching Captain Peel that day, young Wood's admiration for
the man grew. 'Before the first bombardment, Captain Peel asked
Lieutenant Ridge and Midshipman Daniels of HMS *Diamond*, and
Lieutenant Douglas and Midshipman Wood of the *Queen* to disregard fire in the battery, by always walking with head up and
shoulders back and without undue haste. He himself was a splendid
example. I know he felt acutely every shot which passed over him,
but the only visible effect was to make him throw up his head and
square his shoulders. His nervous system was so highly strung,

however, that eight months later a mere flesh wound incapacitated him for many months. He was a most tender-hearted man towards his fellow-creatures and animals; and in 1851, when he was crossing the Nubian desert from Korosko to Abu Hamed, he dismounted from his camel in order to give a small dying bird some water.'

Over in the French batteries, which – since their guns were of a lighter calibre – had been placed six hundred yards closer to the enemy, Russian fire soon began to tell. At 9 a.m. disaster struck. Wilson watched as '. . . a shell burst on the powder magazine of No. 4. French Battery; the magazine blew up, and nearly fifty corpses, headless, legless, blackened, burnt, mangled, littered the ground, intermingled with fainting wounded, broken gabions, trenching tools, ammunition boxes, spare guns, accoutrements and arms.'

Shortly afterwards, according to Somerset Calthorpe, in Lord Raglan's trench: 'General Canrobert sent word to Lord Raglan that it was of no importance, as it was *not* one of their magazines that had blown up, but a new sort of shell (!) which the Russians had thrown into their trenches. General Rose and one of General Canrobert's aides-de-camp brought this monstrous piece of information, and appeared quite astonished when we all said we did not believe such a humbug, and that we had not the smallest doubt that it was a magazine . . . half an hour later the aide-de-camp came back with an apology from General Canrobert for having misinformed Lord Raglan, and begged to say that he had received the report from the General in the trenches, and that it had since been ascertained that it was their principle magazine which had exploded, all of which we knew perfectly well before.'

The Russians now redoubled their fire against the other French batteries, which, partly enfiladed and out-gunned, were soon silenced.

'Soon after eleven o'clock General Rose came again to Lord Raglan from General Canrobert, to say that it was quite impossible for them (the French) to continue their fire, as two batteries on their right were altogether silenced, and one on their extreme left (Fort Genois) was in a very bad state, and the cannonade from the enemy since the explosion had almost ruined the remainder of their works.'

At 12.30 p.m. the French fleet, which had been delayed by contrary winds, came into position and began bombarding Fort Alexander and the Quarantine Fort on the south side of the harbour mouth. Half an hour later the British fleet opened fire on Fort Constantine at the northern mouth.

'The noise of the cannonade' said Wilson, 'deafening before, is absolutely stunning, now that the ships' broadsides are pelting away at the granite. So dense is the smoke, that we can make nothing of the naval tactics; but the bare fact of the "bluejackets" being at work, raises expectation of smash, downfall, triumph.'

At about the same time Calthorpe went to visit the One-gun Battery, containing a solo Lancaster gun, also manned by blue-jackets. 'The object it was firing at, a Russian liner in the Man of War Creek, was at a distance of 3,400 yards. When the Russians found this out they moved the ship a few yards further on, and in such a way as we could only bring this gun to bear on her stern, and on about three ports on her broadside . . . The practice made by this Lancaster was not as successful as had been anticipated . . . every shot went either a little too much to the right or left, or too high or too low. I think near thirty of these shells were fired before one took effect, but that one was supposed to have exploded in her, and, if it did, it must have much discomposed the crew.

'Considering that each of these shells cost near £25, it was rather expensive work.'

Later, in the 5-gun battery, Calthorpe saw the effect of Russian fire from warships in the harbour. Here, the British casualties of the day were highest.

'They were occasioned chiefly by the fire from two steamers in the harbour, that steamed round and round in a circle, and in that manner fired both their broadsides . . . in the course of the day, one of them was disabled by our shot and had to sheer off. It was most amusing to see the sailors who manned the guns in this battery; there were two reliefs of them and, as soon as one had done its turn of duty, you heard the officer say "Now then, second relief, fall in; you others can go and sky-lark." A nice place in which to sky-lark, with 68-pound shot, and 13-inch shell dropping in amongst you every moment! However the bluejackets did not mind, and took the permission given them quite literally; and in a minute ever so many of them had jumped on the parapet to see "them b——y Rushions"; then some fellow would cry, "Look out, shot!" and down they all jumped, and after the iron messenger had passed over, or exploded, as the case might be, they were all up again, talking at such a rate, and making the drollest remarks, giving their private opinions as to the siege, and how the place ought to be taken.'

Bombarded now by land and sea, the Russians still gave as good as they got.

'The *Muscov* never flinches,' observed Wilson with grudging respect, 'he stands like a man to his guns, both landward and seaward. He must be liberally supplied with cannon, for if we dismount one of his pieces, its embrasure is silent only for a few minutes, and then blazes away hotly as ever – a fresh heavy-pounder at work.'

In fact, the Russians had spare cannon buried near every gun position, so that knocked-out pieces could be replaced in short order.

At 3 p.m. the British guns scored a major success. Wilson saw: 'a fearful explosion . . . in the core of the Russian works. It was distinctly audible above the din of the conflict – it was visible also – a prodigious black pillar shooting up through the smoke that shrouded town, batteries, ships, sea, everything. It was a sublime moment! The allies shouted with one accord, and some men screamed "The day's ours! the city's in ruins!" Not so. Those Russians must be chained to their cannon, for with them there is no relenting. The Redan spits furiously as before; nor is the heavy metal, about the basement of that dilapidated white tower, one jot less troublesome.'

At this point, Lord Raglan later wrote, the Redan had never been, nor ever would be again, so vulnerable. With the Malakoff in ruins, an assault might have been practicable, but for one thing: with the French batteries out of action, any assault would have to made through a terrible flanking fire. It was not possible. Once the French batteries closed down, there was never any serious prospect of an assault.

At 4.30 the Russians attempted a sortie against the batteries on the extreme left of the French line. Two hundred Russian infantry charged out to within fifty yards of the guns, but were driven back by rifle-fire from the trenches, leaving many dead and wounded in no man's land.

At 5.30 the Allied fleets withdrew to their former anchorages.

'Soon after, as it began to get dusk,' Calthorpe recalled, 'the firing on both sides sensibly diminished. Lord Raglan then returned to Head-quarters, and sent orders to our batteries that they were only to answer the fire of the enemy, gun for gun, during the night. General Canrobert sent to Lord Raglan to say that he hoped to open fire again on the Russian works the following morning. Nobody, however, believed him!'

By the end of the first day's bombardment the Russians had suffered some 1,100 casualties, largely through the need to keep large bodies of troops massed close behind the bastions to meet the expected assault. The Naval commander, Vice-Admiral Korniloff, was killed by roundshot near the Malakoff early in the day. The Redan had been demolished and 33 of its 38 guns dismounted. Todtleben shared Lord Raglan's opinion that this had been the Redan's most vulnerable moment.

The following morning the bombardment began again: this time the British, acting alone, had to bear the full brunt of the Russian response, and the Russians had not wasted the hours of darkness. The Redan, a smoking ruin at last light, appeared at dawn to be stronger than ever. Unserviceable guns had been removed, platforms relaid, new embrasures created and 38 new guns – of heavier calibre – hauled into place.

As the artillery duel continued, Captain Peel treated Evelyn Wood to another exhibition of *sang froid*: 'A shell weighting 42lbs penetrating the parapet, rolled into the centre of a gun's crew, who threw themselves on the ground. This would not, however, have saved them, for there were several cases of powder being passed into the magazine on the spot, but Peel stooping down lifted the shell, and resting it against his chest carried it back to the parapet, and, stepping on to the ledge of earth termed Banquette, rolled it over the Superior crest, on which it immediately burst.'

On the 19 October the French re-opened their bombardment, silencing many of the batteries opposed to them, but again – overnight – the enemy repaired the damage and dragged new guns into place. The Russians were showing that resilience in defence so characteristic of their military history.

There was now no hiding a sense of profound disappointment. Wilson wrote: 'The siege – or more properly, the bootless discharge of much cannon at mud banks – rubs on. It is manifest we do not make way – it is manifest that the Russians have more than 200 guns well served, admirably constructed batteries, and probably the ablest engineer in the world ... The war has produced no greater man than Todleben.'

As the days wore on, the supply of ammunition started to become an anxiety. The prospects of an early end to the campaign receded. Fanny Duberly's diary charted the fading hopes.

'Thursday, 19th – We thought Sebastopol was to stand, *perhaps*, a three days' siege – more likely a single day's; while some, more arrogant still, allowed it eight hours to resist the fury of the Allies!'

'Friday, 20th – There is a *talk* of storming the town tomorrow. I fancy if it was intended, it would not be talked about beforehand'

'Saturday, 21st – All appear to concur in thinking that the Crimea will be our winter quarters.'

The Allied gambit – overwhelming bombardment, immediate assault – had failed; it was now the Russians' turn to make a move. That move was not long in coming. On the evening of 21 October, Calthorpe wrote: 'The Russians made a strong reconnaissance of our position before Balaklava.'

CHAPTER FIVE

While the Allies had been bombarding the city, Prince Menschikoff had not been idle. The field army he had taken out of Sebastopol had been reinforced: the 22,000 infantry, 3,400 cavalry and 78 guns were now based at Tchorgun, within striking distance of the British lines of communication. Every reinforcement and all supplies for the British army besieging Sebastopol had to be dragged on pitifully inadequate transport from Balaklava, on the coast, across the plain separating that port from the plateau on which were the British and French siege lines. If Menschikoff's army, under Lieutenant General Liprandi, could seize Balaklava, the British position on the plateau would be untenable. The Allies would be left with two options. The first would be a counter-attack to try to re-take the port – a risky venture against such a force as Liprandi had in hand, with the garrison of the still-untaken Sebastopol ready to sally out in their rear at a moment's notice. The second option would be an evacuation by sea via the French base at Kamiesch, a venture which was likely to prove costly, possibly even catastrophic, for both armies. At a strike the Allied siege of Sebastopol could be lifted.

Given the nature of this threat, and the presence of Liprandi's army just beyond the Tchernaya, the defences of Balaklava looked inadequate – until one considered the general weakness of the British forces. The approach march of any Russian move on Balaklava would be similar to the route the British had taken a month earlier, across the Tchernaya River and down the great plain, following the line of that same Woronzov Road which split the British siege lines* when it climbed up onto the plateau.

The plain is split by a long ridge-line, down which the Woronzov Road runs. It is known as the Causeway Heights. Viewed from the

* See Map 3.

137

plateau, these heights are not easy to discern, but down below they clearly divide the plain into two valleys, the north valley between the road and the heights, and the south valley between the road and Balaklava. As an outer defence for Balaklava a series of six redoubts had been established, running roughly east to west down the Causeway Heights. The first, near the village of Kamara, was on Canrobert's Hill – named by the British in honour of the French commander. Redoubts 2 and 3 were on the Causeway Heights themselves; the remaining three ran in a line to the foot of the plateau. Together, these formed a protective shield for the village of Kadikoi, which commanded the gorge running down into the port of Balaklava itself. The importance of Kadikoi – the key to Balaklava – was reflected in its garrison: the 93rd Highlanders, under the command of Sir Colin Campbell, to whom the defence of the port was entrusted. Encamped close by, within the ring of redoubts, was the cavalry division under Lord Lucan, placed so to threaten the flank of any force moving on Balaklava. Lastly, the eastern heights overlooking the gorge and the port itself were defended by a battery of artillery manned by the Royal Marines.

In the event of a Russian assault, Sir Colin could rely on the support of the infantry divisions on the plateau, but until they descended, the defence of the vital harbour depended on the cavalry, his one battalion of Highlanders and the garrisons of the redoubts. The British were already seriously overstretched – the French had provided two divisions under Bosquet to man the edge of the plateau – but the defence of the garrison was left in the hands of the Turks, who had been formidable on the Danube, driving the Russians off Turkish soil before the Allies could take a hand.

On 23 October, Somerset Calthorpe wrote home. 'The redoubts before Balaklava are so far finished as to be each garrisoned by some four companies of Turks, with eight or nine guns of position,' he said. 'These works are not strong, yet are capable of holding in check any sudden attack on Balaklava, if properly defended. I am sorry to say these Turks don't seem worth very much; they are very idle, and there is the greatest difficulty in getting them to work, even though it is for their own security and comfort. But we must hope for the best.'

The cavalry were kept busy patrolling the no man's land between the Balaklava defences and the Tchernaya River. Lord George Paget, who had been out one evening, fell in with Sir Colin Campbell.

'We walked down the hill in our front some way together,' he said, 'and then lay down, occasionally putting our ears to the ground, to listen; and a very pleasant hour I had with him . . .

'On our return from our walk in front, we of course had to make our way through the Turks, who seeing us coming up in the dark from the front, tremulously whispered, "Johnny," and on our giving the *lingua franca* countersign of "Buono Johnny," they seemed highly delighted, and we heard them muttering to each other, "Ah Johnny, buono Johnny, buono, buono." '

This constant patrolling and occasional skirmishing was very far from the glory that the young officers of the cavalry had imagined would be theirs in this war. The infantry and guns had done all the fighting at the Alma; now they – and the Navy – were getting all the glory up on the plateau. The cavalry's role so far had been that of spectators, earning the men their hated nickname of the 'look-ons'. Frustration was mounting; it may have been a pun on their commander's name, but it was still derisive. There was a lot of wild talk about 'having a brush at them' down by the river, or even beyond. It was starting to annoy Sir Colin, and when Paget called on him later that evening, he railed, 'those young officers of cavalry, who would fall out from their regiment, and come to the front and give their opinions on matters they knew nothing about, instead of attending to their squadron, as I would make them do . . . These young gentlemen talk a great deal of nonsense . . . I am not here to fight a battle or gain a victory; my orders are to defend Balaclava, which is the key to all our operations, my lord, and I am not going to be tempted out of it.'

Sir Colin, of course, had made his name; the young bloods of the Light Brigade had yet to make theirs. Their chance was coming – and sooner than they thought.

An hour before daybreak the Cavalry Division – the Light and Heavy Brigades – had been 'standing at their horses', as they did every morning. Lord Lucan and his staff had ridden forward in the direction of the redoubts to observe the enemy as they did every morning. Lord George Paget had joined Lord William Paulet and Major MacMahon, two of his friends on Lucan's staff. As they rode forward, some fifty yards behind Lord Lucan, it was just like any other morning since the cavalry had encamped down here on the plain; soon they would be stood down to water their horses and cook breakfast. As Paget and his friends approached to within three hundred yards of the Turkish redoubts they saw: '. . . that from the flag-staff, which had, I believe, only the day before been erected on the redoubt flew two flags, only just discernible in the grey twilight.

'The conversation which ensued will ever be vividly impressed on my memory. "Holloa," said Lord William "there are two flags flying; what does that mean?"

' "Why, *that* surely is the signal that the enemy is approaching," said Major MacMahon.

' "Are you quite sure?" we replied. We were not long kept in doubt! Hardly were the words out of MacMahon's mouth, when *bang* went a cannon from the redoubt in question, fired on the advancing masses of the enemy.'

Messages were sent at once to Lord Raglan and Sir Colin Campbell, who immediately turned out all the troops under his command. The Royal Marines manned the guns on the eastern heights and the 93rd and a company from the Invalid Battalion occupied some rising ground in front of the village of Kadikoi. General Canrobert was informed, stood Bosquet's Corps to arms and, with his staff, hurried to join Lord Raglan.

Orders were sent to the 1st Division and Sir George Cathcart's 4th, to descend onto the plain. The Duke of Cambridge might have been slow to get his Guardsmen and Highlanders on the move, but Sir George Cathcart – who had been chafing at being kept out of action for weeks – at first refused to move at all.

'Quite impossible sir,' he told the staff officer who arrived with the message, 'It is impossible for my men to move, as the greater portion of the men have just come in from the trenches. The best thing you can do, sir, is to sit down and have some breakfast.'

Pressed by the staff officer, who reiterated the urgency of the situation, Cathcart eventually agreed to consult with his staff officers 'and see if anything can be done'. Cathcart was feeling increasingly left out of things, and was clearly in no great hurry to co-operate with his commander-in-chief. It was some time before the 4th Division began to move slowly down towards Balaklava.

Cathcart's delay was to leave Lord Raglan short of infantry at a critical moment later in the day.

Down in Balaklava, Fanny Duberly was feeling unwell, and had decided to spend the day quietly in her cabin. 'But on looking through my stern cabin windows,' she wrote, 'I saw my horse saddled and waiting on the beach, in charge of our soldier-servant on the pony. A note was put in my hands from Henry a moment after. It ran thus: "The battle of Balaklava has begun, and promises to be a hot one. I send you the horse. Lose no time, but come up as quickly as you can; do not wait for breakfast."

'Words full of meaning! I dressed in all haste, went ashore without delay, and mounting my horse "Bob", started as fast as the narrow and crowded streets would permit.'

Upon the plateau, Lord Raglan and his staff had ridden to the edge of the escarpment known as the Sapoune Heights. From here the whole of the coming battlefield lay spread out several hundred feet below him like a huge map. It was not a view calculated to cheer. Among Raglan's staff, Somerset Calthorpe watched.

'The Russians established a battery of field artillery close to the village of Kamara, and opened fore on No. 1 redoubt (that on Canrobert's hill); at the same time a column of infantry (some 1200 men) advanced up to it, the Turkish garrison firing on them in a desultory sort of way with small arms, but without attempting to use their heavy guns. To our intense disgust, in a few moments, we saw a little stream of men issue from the rear of the redoubt and run down the hill-side towards our lines; these were immediately followed by a regular cloud of fugitives, and the Russians entered the fort to find it garrisoned by dead and wounded men. In this way they captured four iron guns of position which we had lent the Turks.'

Those guns, though manned by Turks, were British, and though a British Royal Artillery NCO in command of them had spiked the guns, they were now in Russian hands. Worse was to follow.

Calthorpe, watching with his fellow staff officers described what happened. 'The garrison of No. 2 redoubt, when they saw the Russians enter No. 1, immediately bethought themselves of flight, instead of attempting to hold it for a moment against the enemy, and, to the indignation of all, we saw these miserables coming out of the work laden with their baggage, &c., and deliberately marching to the rear.'

They didn't march deliberately for very long, Calthorpe said. 'Large parties of the enemy's cavalry, consisting chiefly of the

Cossacks and the Don ... let loose on the runaway Turks. The yells of these wild horsemen could be distinctly heard where we were as they galloped after these unhappy Moslems, numbers of whom were killed by their lances.'

Within minutes, the Russians had brought up infantry and guns and begun firing into No. 3 redoubt. This too was evacuated, this time with hardly a shot being fired. As the redoubts had fallen, the cavalry had been steadily withdrawn, with no artillery to reply with; all they could do was watch helplessly as the Turks fled.

Trooper Michell of the 13th Light Dragoons noticed, 'They were very careful of their kettles and pans, for they rattled and clattered as they ran past us. Our men called out, "No Buono Johnny," but that made no impression on them, for soon they were off as fast as they could go towards Balaklava.'

They weren't all Turks. As a Russian officer hauled down the Turkish flag in No. 3 redoubt and waved his sword tauntingly at Mitchell and his comrades, Mitchell said, 'An English artilleryman came down from the redoubt past us. He complained bitterly of the manner in which the Turks had left him. He said he had the greatest difficulty in persuading them to fight the guns at all, and after firing a few rounds, and seeing the enemy draw near, they one and all bolted leaving him alone in the redoubt. However, he added, "They won't fire the guns on you from this redoubt, for I spiked them both before I left." '

No. 4 redoubt was soon abandoned too, but though more than a thousand Turks now streamed down towards Balaklava, harried by marauding Cossacks, the Cossacks did not have it their own way. From his new position by the cavalry camp, Trooper Mitchell saw: 'Two Cossacks came over the ridge together. One of them lanced a Turk in the back, who uttered a loud scream and fell. Another Turk being a short distance ahead, they both made for him, but before they could reach him, Johnny who had his piece loaded and bayonet fixed, turned suddenly and fired at the foremost knocking him off his horse. The other coming up, made a point, but whether it touched the Turk or not I cannot say, but in an instant he had bayoneted the Cossack in the body, and he also fell from his horse. Johnny resumed his journey at a walk for by this time the Cossacks, who now saw us advancing, turned about and made their way over the ridge. Now this exploit was witnessed by many of our men, who cheered Johnny lustily.'

The fleeing Turks passed across the front of the Light Brigade, where Lord George Paget rather acidly noted their actions. 'The Turks who thus abandoned these redoubts ... did not *run* – there was no need for that, as they had taken time by the forelock – but drawled slowly by us in twos and threes, laden with their blankets and kits, which they had given themselves time to collect, their cry being "Ship, ship", a name by which they were for some time known, alternately with that of "Buono Johnny," '

Fanny Duberly riding up from Balaklava as she had been ordered, was almost caught up in the confusion of this retreat. 'I was hardly clear of the town, before I met a commissariat officer, who told me that the Turks had abandoned all their batteries, and were running towards the town. He begged me to keep as much to the *left* as possible, and, of all things, to lose no time in getting amongst our men, as the Russian force was pouring on us; adding, "For God's sake, ride fast, or you may not reach the camp alive." Captain Howard, whom I met a moment after, assured me I might proceed; but added, "Lose no time." Turning off into a short cut of grass, and stretching into his stride, the old horse laid himself out to his work, and soon reaching the main road, we clattered on towards the camp. The road was almost blocked up with flying Turks, some running hard, vociferating "Ship Johnny! Ship Johnny!" while others came along laden with pots, kettles, arms, and plunder of every description, chiefly old bottles, for which the Turks appear to have a great appreciation.'

The first round had gone to the Russians: the outer ring of Balaklava's defences and nine British guns were now in the enemy's hands. Calthorpe said this was, 'Through the confounded cowardice of the Turks.'

Lord George Paget took a more charitable view. 'The bravest troops in the world never should have been placed in charge of those redoubts, en l'air, and unsupported as they were, or rather at such a distance from all supports.'

Either way, Balaklava – and thus the entire British position in the Crimea – was now under threat. As the Russian infantry had stormed the three redoubts on the Causeway Heights, the Russian cavalry, under General Rhyzov, had moved up behind them along the north valley. Now Rhyzov took his command over the heights and into the south valley.

All that stood between this large body of cavalry and Balaklava was the 93rd Highlanders, supported by a few stray Turks, some Invalids and one field battery.

The British cavalry had initially been placed to one side, in position to threaten the flank of any advance on Balaklava. Later, the Light Brigade had been moved – on Raglan's orders – almost to the foot of the plateau, to await the arrival of the infantry. The Heavy Brigade were following when Raglan – with his chessboard-like view – saw this new threat to his supply base. At once he sent an order to Lord Lucan to send the Heavies back to the south valley to support Campbell.

Rhyzov had already detached four squadrons of Hussars – roughly 400 men – from his main body to attack the Highlanders' position at Kadikoi. Now wheeling left, they descended the heights and advanced towards the low ridge before the village where Sir Colin Campbell had placed his Highlanders.

Fanny Duberly had been salvaging what she could of their possessions from the now-abandoned Light Brigade camp. She wrote that she was 'superintending the striking of our tent and the packing of our valuables. Henry flung me on the old horse; and seizing a pair of laden saddle-bags, a great coat, and a few other loose packages, I made the best of my way over a ditch into a vineyard, and awaited the event. For a moment I lost sight of our pony, "Whisker", who was being loaded; but Henry joined me just in time to ride a little to the left, to get clear of the shots, which now began to fly towards us. Presently came the Russian cavalry charging, over the hill-side and across the valley, right against the little line of Highlanders. Ah, what a moment! Charging and surging onward, what could that little wall of men do against such numbers and such speed?'

The traditional formation for infantry facing cavalry was the square, as formed imperfectly by the 77th and 88th at the Alma. Sir Colin Campbell, firm advocate for and practitioner of disciplined rifle fire – had seen at the Alma what the Minié could do. Behind the ridge, where they had been sheltering from the Russian artillery on the newly captured redoubts, he formed the men two-deep. To Russell, *The Times* correspondent watching on the plateau, they looked like 'a thin red streak tipped with a line of steel' – a line that has been misquoted to this day.

As the Russian cavalry approached, the guns on the eastern

heights opened up on them. Sir Colin described the scene: 'During this period our batteries on the heights manned by the Royal Artillerymen and Royal Marines, made excellent practice on the enemy's cavalry which came over the hill in our front.'

Standing with the men of the 93rd, watching the approaching cavalry, was Surgeon Munro. 'While they were approaching, Sir Colin ordered the 93rd and Turks to re-form line on the crest of the hill; and, as we were doing so, the two companies of the regiment, which had been detached, under the command of Major Gordon, arrived, and took up their positions in the line. Thus we stood for a few seconds, while the cavalry was rapidly nearing us; but the Turkish battalions on our flanks began to get unsteady, and at last fairly turned, broke, and bolted.'

The Turks ran down through the Highland camp, where they came under attack from an unexpected quarter. 'A stalwart Scottish wife,' wrote Munro, 'was employed at the time washing some articles of clothing beside a little stream that flowed through a vineyard at the base of the hill, on the crest of which the 93rd stood in line, apparently, and really, I believe, quite unconcerned about the battle, and unmoved by the sound of roundshot which passed over her head. When she saw the Turks rushing down the hill and amongst the tents, she thought that they were bent on plunder, and watched them for a minute with suspicious eye; but when they swept past her, and trampled on things which, being washed she had spread out to dry, she broke out into a towering rage, and seizing a large stick that lay on the ground near her, laid about her right and left in protection of her property. When she understood that the Turks were bolting from the battle, and had deserted her own regiment, which she saw standing firm upon the hill above, she laughed in scorn, and again plied her stick, striking heavily, at the same time using her tongue, a sharp weapon at times, she abused the flying "Johnnies" roundly in braid Scotch, to the great amusement of the men of her own regiment, who encouraged by applauding her.'

On their own now, the Highlanders awaited the onset of the Russian cavalry.

'It was at this moment,' said Munro, 'that Sir Colin rode along the front of the 93rd, telling the regiment to be "steady"; for if necessary every man should have "to die where he stood". He was answered by a universal and cheery response, "Ay, ay, Sir Colin; we'll do that."

'I do not think there was a single soldier standing in the line who had an anxious thought as to our isolated and critical position or who for a moment felt the least inclination to flinch before the charge of the advancing cavalry. On the contrary, they appeared to have settled themselves firmly where they stood to receive the expected shock, and to be pleased that everything depended on themselves in what they expected to be a regular hand-to-hand struggle.'

As it had in the Peninsula, where Sir Colin learned his trade, the sudden appearance of a steady line of redcoats, as if sprung from the earth, caused the enemy to falter. As they did so, at 1,000 yards, they gave the Russians their first volley.

Munro recounted what followed. 'When Sir Colin thought that our Minié rifles might reach the enemy he ordered the line to fire a volley; but when the smoke from this had blown aside, we saw that the cavalry were still advancing straight for the line. A second volley rang forth, and then we observed that there was a little confusion in the enemy's ranks and that they were swerving to our right.'

As the Russians did so, the Highlanders, living up to their reputation as 'the wild 93rd', showed signs of wanting to rush down off the ridge and tear into the enemy ranks.

Surgeon Munro took up the story.

'The men of the 93rd at that moment became a little, just a little restive, and brought their rifles to the charge, manifesting an inclination to advance, and meet the cavalry halfway with the bayonet. But old Sir Colin brought them sharply back to discipline. He could be angry, could Sir Colin, and when in an angry mood spoke sharp and quick.'

Those words, sharp and quick, entered our language: *Ninety-Third! Ninety-Third! Damn all that eagerness!*

Munro went on, 'The men were quiet and steady in a moment; and then the grenadiers, under my old friend Ross, were ordered to change front and fire a volley. This third volley was at much nearer range than the previous ones and caught the cavalry in flank as they were approaching, apparently with the intention of passing by our right. It shook them visibly, and caused them to bend away to their own left until they had completely wheeled, when they rode back to their own army, followed by a burst of wild cheering from the ranks of the 93rd . . .

'The Highlanders were a good deal elated and proud to think that under their old chief and in sight of three armies they had stood in line only two-deep to receive the charge of European cavalry.'

Proud as they were of their achievement, there was some surprise at the small number of casualties the Minié rifle had apparently inflicted. Two years later, in Simferopol, Munro met a Russian Hussar officer with a severe limp, who told him he had been present at that charge.

When Munro asked him why the Russian cavalry hadn't charged home, the Russian replied: 'In the first place, we did not know that you were lying down behind the hill close to the guns which were keeping up a galling fire on our columns, and which it was our object to capture, until, when we were at the gallop, you started from the ground and fired a volley at us. In the next place, we were unable to rein up, or slacken speed, or swerve to our left before we received your second volley, by which almost every man and horse in our ranks was wounded. Again, when we were inclining to our left to wheel, as we thought, a wing of your regiment changed front, and fired a volley into our flank, which also took effect amongst us, one of your bullets breaking my thigh and making me the cripple that you see. But you know, of course, that a mounted man, though severely, or even mortally wounded, can retain his seat in the saddle long enough to ride out of danger." '

Thanks to the 93rd's stand, the immediate threat to Balaklava had been removed, but the main body of Rhyzov's cavalry still remained: the Ingermanland Regiment in the first line, the Kiev Regiment behind them, Cossacks on either flank, and an Uhlan Regiment and more Cossacks in support. This force of some 2,000 men had crested the Causeway Heights and were now dropping into the south valley. As they did so, they saw before them and moving across their front, the Heavy Brigade, riding back to support Campbell.

The commander of the Heavy Brigade, General Scarlett, was short-sighted – almost a requirement for high command in this army, or so it appeared. At first he didn't notice the horsemen massing on the crest to his left, but once they were pointed out to him, he did not hesitate, ordering, 'Left wheel into line!'

The ground the Heavy Brigade were on was difficult for cavalry. Scarlett's leading elements, two squadrons of the Inniskilling Drag-oons, were about to enter the now-empty camp of the Light Brigade. Behind them the Scots Greys were just emerging from a ruined vineyard through which, behind *them*, the 5th Dragoons were picking their way. The *wheel into line* was delayed by the need for the Inniskillings and the Greys to dress to their right to make room for the 5th Dragoons to deploy. A further complication was the arrival of Lord Lucan – shouting orders and ordering his divisional trumpeter to sound – which the squadrons ignored.

It was a critical moment. The 300 men Scarlett had under hand were now about to be charged by 2,000 Russian cavalry attacking downhill. Facing their squadrons and with their backs to the enemy, the officers of the Heavy Brigade unhurriedly attended to their men's dressing. Satisfied at last, Scarlett ordered his trumpeter to sound the Charge. Out in front of his brigade, accompanied only by one ADC, his trumpeter and his orderly, Trooper Shegog, General Scarlett then rode straight at the enemy without a backwards glance – British cavalry officers did not look behind to see if their men were following; it was assumed they would be.

From the Light Brigade's position, Lord George Paget watched what followed. 'The dense mass of Russian cavalry, animated and encouraged doubtless by the successes of the morning (for the poor slaves had been told that the Turkish redoubts had been taken from the English) – advancing at a rapid pace over ground the most favourable, and appearing as if they must *annihilate* and *swallow* up all before them; on the other hand, the handfull of redcoats, *floundering* in the vineyard, on their way to meet them. Suddenly within twenty yards of the dry ditch, the Russians halt, look bewildered, as if they were at a loss what to do! the impression of which appearance of bewilderment is forcibly engraven in my mind on this occasion, as well as later in the day.'

Whether the Russians halted because of the sight of this outnumbered enemy charging uphill at them, or because Rhyzov wanted to extend his line to match Scarlett's, has never been established. Whatever the cause, the effect was, for the Russians, disastrous. The effectiveness of cavalry depended on shock action and impetus. Cavalry caught standing were in trouble. Encumbered by the rough ground over which they were passing and the slope up which they were charging, it was nevertheless the Heavies who had impetus. There was a spattering fire of pistols and carbines from the Russian ranks, then, several horses' lengths ahead of his brigade, Scarlett and his three companions charged alone into the enemy's mass. They had already cut their way several ranks deep before the Scots Greys and the Inniskillings – slowed to a trot by the tangled vines, ditches and tent ropes – crashed into the enemy's front rank, the Inniskillings with a wild Irish yell, the Greys with a cheer.

Paget and his men watched. 'The Heavies struggle – flounder over the ditch and trot into them! There followed anxious moments! "red spirits and grey", green coats and blue! all intermingled in one confused mass.'

The Greys and Inniskillings all but disappeared as the Russians' flanking squadrons folded round to envelop them. At that moment, from the left rear of the Greys, the 5th Dragoon Guards hit the Russians, catching some in flank, some even with their backs turned. Trooper Mitchell, a spectator with the 13th Light Dragoons, said, 'For a few seconds we could see little else but dust and smoke (for the Russians fire their pistols when they charge, and then use the sword) but on the smoke clearing away we could plainly see our red jackets had gone clean through their leading squadrons and were engaged with the next.'

Charging with the 5th Dragoons Guards was Sergeant Major Henry Franks. He recalled, 'When the charge sounded, the Brigade made a rush, and the men gave what I suppose was intended for a cheer, but was really a yell of defiance. Some of the Russians seemed to be rather astonished at the way our men used their swords. It was rather hot work for a few minutes; there was no time to look about you. We soon became a struggling mass of half frenzied and desperate men, doing our level best to kill each other.'

A corporal in the same regiment wrote to his parents: 'Such cutting and slashing for about a minute was dreadful to see. The rally sounded but it was no use, none of us would come away until the enemy retreated, then our fellows cheered as loudly as they could. When we were in the midst of them my horse was shot; he fell and got up again, but I was entangled in the saddle, my head and one leg on the ground; he tried to gallop on with the rest, but fell again, when I managed to get loose. While I was in that predicament, a Russian lancer was about to run me through, but Macnamara came up at the time, and nearly severed his head from his body; so thank God, I did not get a scratch.

'I got up and ran to where we saw a lot of loose horses, taking one belonging to the Enniskillens, and was soon with the regiment again. When I first remounted, I saw a Russian who had strayed from the rest; he rode up and tried to stop me, I took a pistol from the holster-pipe and shot him in the arm, he dropped his sword, I then ran him through and the poor fellow dropped to the ground.'

An officer of the Inniskillings later described his feelings as his squadron charged home. 'I never in all my life experienced such a sublime sensation as in the moment of the charge. Some fellows speak of it as "demoniac". I know this, that it was such as made me a match for any two ordinary men ... Forward – dash – bang – clank – and there we were in the midst of such smoke, cheer and clatter, as never before stunned a mortal ear. It was glorious! I could not pause. It was all push, wheel, frenzy strike, and down, down, down they went!'

In the ruck the opposing horsemen were packed so tightly that many could scarcely raise their sword arms. Unable to swing their heavy cavalry sabres, many were reduced to using their basket hilts like knuckle-dusters, or clawing the enemy out of the saddle. The Heavies were, as their name implied, big men on big horses, and many simply bowled their opponents over, or barged their way through.

Where there *was* room for swordplay, the fighting was brutal and bloody. Franks saw: 'Private Harry Herbert . . . a fine dashing young fellow, attacked by three Cossack Lancers at the same time. He disabled one of them by a terrible cut across the back of the neck, and the second one scampered off. Herbert made a point at the third man's breast, but his sword blade broke off about three inches from the hilt, yet Harry was not to be foiled by this mishap. He threw the heavy sword hilt at the Russian, which hit him in the face, and the Cossack dropped to the ground; he was not dead, but it spoiled his visage. Herbert also spoiled the appearance of two or three more of them after that.'

In the mêlée, Franks saw Cornet the Hon Grey Neville unhorsed. 'Mr Nevill was making his way on foot in the midst of the yelling and struggling men, when he was surrounded by four or five Cossacks, and before anyone could get near to assist him he had received two or three lance wounds, and had fallen to the ground. Two of our men rushed to his assistance, but he being on the ground there was the danger of the horses tramping him under their feet. One young fellow, with great presence of mind, saw the danger, and in a moment he dismounted, and stood across the prostrate Officer's body. With his left hand he held his horse's bridle, and with his sword he parried the assaults of the Cossacks for a few moments until two more men dashed in. Three of the Russians were killed.'

In the frenzy of battle many abandoned lessons of swordsmanship learned over many years, preferring instead the Irish pubfighter's principle: if you see a head, hit it! It was the same on both sides. One trooper, explaining his head wound to the surgeon, explained: 'I had just cut five [a regulation "body cut"] at a Russian, and the damned fool never guarded at all, but hit me over the head!'

As the Greys, Inniskillings and 5th Dragoon Guards slashed, punched, clawed and barged their way through the Russian cavalry, the 4th Dragoon Guards arrived on the scene, delivering their charge into the Russians' right flank. Moments later the 1st Royal Dragoons arrived. The dispersal of the Heavy Brigade caused by its rapid counter-march and the nature of the ground over which it travelled meant that instead of arriving *en masse*, its regiments arrived one after the other, delivering to the Russians a succession of body-blows.

Lord Paget, an onlooker like the rest of the Light Brigade, described the result: 'The clatter of the swords against the helmets, the trampling of the horses, the shouts! – in short the din of battle (how expressive the term) still ring in one's ears. One body must give way. The heaving mass must be borne one way or the other. Alas, one has but faint hopes! for how can such a handful resist, much less make head through such a legion? Their huge flanks lap round that handful, and almost hide them from our view. They are surrounded and must be annihilated! One can hardly breathe! . . . One pants for breath – one general shout bursts from us all! It is over! They give way! the heaving mass rolls to the left! They fly!'

All of a sudden, the Russians gave way. From the plateau, Lord Raglan and his staff saw, in Calthorpe's words, '. . . the entire body of men and horses move back a little; and after a minute or two the whole making a rush to the rear, our dragoons cutting and slashing about them with an energy and force which must have been deeply felt on the heads and shoulders of the fugitive Russians.'

Sergeant Major Franks recalled what happened next. 'The trumpeter sounded for us to rally and form up again for another charge. Several of the enemy had retired already, and the remainder seemed to give us a wide berth ... by the time the Troops were again in line and ready for another advance, the whole of the Russians had disappeared round No. 1 Redoubt, and retreated to their main body.'

In just over eight minutes, Scarlett's 700 men had put to flight a Russian force of 2,000. As the Heavies reformed, they could hear the 93rd Highlanders cheering them from their ridge.

A few moments later, Sir Colin Campbell himself rode up to the Scots Greys, crying, 'Greys! Gallant Greys! I am sixty-one years old, and if I were young again I should be proud to be in your ranks.'

More restrained, but equally heartfelt, was Lord Raglan's message to General Scarlett, delivered by an ADC. Sergeant Major Franks said, 'We were now ordered to "sit at ease", and await the next move. A few minutes later an officer of the staff galloped up to General Scarlett, and said to him, "I am ordered by Lord Raglan to say, Well done Scarlett!" and the grand old soldier replied, "Thank his Lordship." At this instant a murmur ran along the ranks, which became dangerous near to being a cheer, but one or two of the officers gave the caution, "steady, men," and this prevented what I believe would have been an outburst.'

Well might they have cheered. Between them, the Heavy Brigade and the 93rd Highlanders had transformed the situation. The inner defences of Balaklava had held, the Russian cavalry were now pulling back into the north valley. The second round had gone to the British.

There was a brief respite to tend to the wounded. Private Abbott, the 5th Dragoon Guard who had stood over Cornet Neville protecting him from Cossack lances, now carried him to the doctors but, as Franks wrote, 'His case was hopeless from the first; and he only lived a few minutes. His dying wish was that his father would take care of Abbott. Lord Braybrook afterwards made Abbott a grant of twenty pounds for life, and he also received a medal for distinguished conduct.'

Casualties in the charge were surprisingly light. The Heavies reported 10 killed and 98 wounded that evening, many of those injuries suffered later in the day. They had inflicted roughly 270 on the enemy. Heavy Russian greatcoats and thick shakoes had proved resistant to sabre cuts – and the Russian sabres were equally ineffective. Like many others', General Scarlett's brass helmet had been badly dented, but he was unharmed. His ADC, Captain Elliott, suffered fourteen sabre cuts, few of them more than skin-deep; the worst had been inflicted by a trooper of the Greys slashing wildly in all directions.

Where the sabre did cut home, it inflicted terrible wounds. Surgeon Robinson of the Scots Fusilier Guards noted: 'Some of the wounds inflicted by our heavy cavalry, whose charge was greatly admired, showed the physical powers of the men. I dressed a poor wretch, the muscles of whose neck behind, were completely divided down to the spine, by a back stroke of a sabre: yet he was staggering about the field, it might almost be said, holding his head on. The cool air had prevented bleeding to any extent. Another man was seen (not by me), a portion of whose skull is said to be cleanly sliced off.'

Throughout the Heavy Brigade's action the Light Brigade, although only five hundred yards away, had remained inactive; some of the men had even dismounted. Here was yet more frustration for the officers and men of the Light Brigade. Just as the war seemed to be settling down to a regular siege, with little further use for cavalry, the Russians had brought on a set-piece battle. At last cavalry had had a chance to proved their worth, and had done so – and throughout it all, the Light Brigade had looked on.

As the Russian cavalry withdrew, exposing their flank to the Light Brigade, another opportunity presented itself. This, surely, was the Light cavalry's moment – practically what they were designed for.

At least one officer thought so too: Captain Morris, the 'pocket Hercules' of the British cavalry commanding the 17th Lancers, rode up to Lord Cardigan to urge such a course upon him. Witnesses heard the following exchange.

'My Lord, are you not going to charge the flying enemy?'

'No. We have orders to remain here.'

'But my Lord, it is our positive duty to follow up this advantage.'

'No. We must remain here.'

'Do, my Lord, do allow me to charge them with the 17th. Sir, my Lord, they are in disorder.'

'No, no, sir. We must not stir from here.'

Convinced that his orders from Lucan required him to remain strictly on the defensive, and never a man open to persuasion, least of all from an 'Indian' officer – Morris had seen action in the Sikh Wars – Cardigan and his brigade stood and watched as the Russians rode off towards the north valley.

The frustration was felt by both men. Morris slapped his leg and shouted, 'My God, my God, what a chance we are losing!'

Cardigan muttered to himself, 'Damn those Heavies. They have had the laugh of us this day.'

The Light Brigade's inaction at this potentially critical point generated controversy for years to come, with Cardigan and Lucan blaming each other, and Cardigan denying outright that Morris had made any representations to him about charging the retreating Russians. Whatever Cardigan's orders had been, it was generally held in the army that he would have been justified in seizing the initiative.

Wilson of the Coldstream thought so, quoting the regulations for the Austrian Order of Maria Theresa:

> If a superior officer act on his own responsibility *without* orders from his chief, and, by so doing, turn the tide of war in favour of the flag, under which he serves, he, on the strength of the evidence given by his fellows, receives the commander's cross.

Had the Light Brigade charged at this point, they might have destroyed the Russian cavalry force for relatively little loss, and put the seal on a great British victory. Instead they were forced to stand idly by yet again, and watch what must have looked like their last chance of glory fade away. To all intents, the battle of Balaklava was over.

Up on the Sapoune, Lord Raglan and his staff watched as the British infantry at last began to descend into the plain to support the forces protecting Balaklava. The 1st Division were the first to arrive, taking up a position near Sir Colin Campbell's ridge with the Guards in front and the Highlanders in support. Half an hour later Cathcart's 4th Division began to appear. Called up by General Canrobert, two squadrons of Chasseurs d'Afrique and the French 1st Division were placed in reserve at the foot of the escarpment directly below Raglan's position. There was now no prospect of a renewed Russian attempt on the British supply base.

At 11 o'clock, Somerset Calthorpe watched as the Russians began to withdraw. 'Lord Raglan from the place that he occupied, commanding as it did so extensive a view of the whole of the valley of Balaklava and the position of the Russian forces, thought that he perceived a retrograde movement on the part of the enemy. Upon a closer examination with our glasses it appeared pretty evident that the Russians were removing our guns which they had captured in the forts.'

The Russians were cutting their losses. If the morning's advance had been an attempt to capture Balaklava – Prince Menschikoff later said in self-justification that it was merely a reconnaissance in force – it had failed. The Russian cavalry had refused at an impenetrable hedge of Highlanders, and been turned back by the big men and big horses of the Heavy Brigade. All they had now were the redoubts, and with the steady build-up of British and French forces in the plain, their hold on these was under threat. They did, however, have the guns – nine British 6-pounders were still in Russian hands.

Wellington had never lost a gun, or so it was believed. Raglan, who was rarely far from the Great Duke's side, must have known better, but myth can be more potent than reality. The prospect of British guns being paraded in Sebastopol – possibly even St Petersburg – as tokens of victory was unbearable. At once Raglan sent an order to Lord Lucan: the cavalry were to seize any opportunity to retake the Heights. An order was sent to Sir George Cathcart to hurry forward and support the cavalry.

For a man who had been itching to get into action since he had landed in the Crimea, Cathcart's movements had been painfully slow. His 4th Division were still in no position to assist Lucan in any way. Lucan, having been kept on a tight leash since the start of the campaign, could not believe that Lord Raglan wished him to act alone, with just the cavalry, against infantry and guns in fortified positions. For a further half hour, he did nothing while, up on the plateau, Raglan became more and more agitated. At length, increasingly alarmed about the fate of the captured British guns, he dictated a further order: probably the most famous – or infamous – order ever issued by a British commander in field:

'Lord Raglan wishes the cavalry to advance rapidly to the front –

follow the enemy and try to prevent the enemy carrying away the guns. Troop Horse Artillery may accompany. French cavalry is on your left. Immediate.'

ADCs were lined up behind Lord Raglan like cabs at a rank, but instead of taking the next in line, Raglan chose Captain Louis Nolan. Nolan, 'the finest horseman in the army', was the man who could take the order down the escarpment at the break-neck speed the situation required – for that he was the ideal choice. In other respects, he was far from ideal: hot-headed, frustrated, an advocate of the almost limitless possibilities of light cavalry, he was im-bued with a deep and abiding contempt for the two cavalry generals he was about to encounter, 'the Noble yachtsman' and 'Lord Look-on' – the cautious ass and the dangerous ass.

Lord Lucan was in a quandary. The order delivered to him by a breathless Nolan didn't make sense. Lord Raglan's chess-board view of the battlefield had its drawbacks. What was clear to a watcher up on the plateau was less clear down on the ground. If Lucan turned and looked due east he could see, to his right, the Causeway Heights were he knew the Russians were in possession of the redoubts for-merly held by the Turks. To the left of those heights he could see the north valley, down which the defeated Russian cavalry had retreated three-quarters of an hour before, and where he knew the bulk of Lip-randi's force now stood. To the left of the valley was a range of long low hills on which, during the morning, the Russians had established a battery of artillery. To Lucan, the order to attack made no sense. There were plenty of guns around – at the end of the valley, on the Causeway Heights to the right, and on the Fediukine to the left – but these were all Russian artillery batteries supported by infantry.

Even if Raglan's order had been clearer and specified the captured *British* guns on the Causeway Heights, it is difficult to see what unsupported cavalry could do uphill against the Russian infantry and guns in and around the redoubts. As it was, the order was not clear – and the one man who could clarify it was in no mood to do so. Part of an ADC's job time was to interpret the order for the benefit of the recipient, and clear up any ambiguities, but Nolan was too wrought-up to bandy words with a man he despised. In the little drama that ensued, each man appeared subconsciously aware that he was speaking for the benefit of posterity.

Lord Lucan asked, 'Attack, Sir, attack what? What guns, Sir?'

With a wave of is arm in the direction of the Causeway Heights and the North Valley, Nolan replied, 'There my, Lord, is your enemy, there are your guns.'

From this it was clear to Lucan that the Light Brigade was to attack the Russians in the valley. Offended by Nolan's manner, and unwilling to lay himself open to further insolence, Lucan rode over to his brother-in-law, Cardigan, at the head of the Light Brigade, and conveyed what he thought to be the meaning of Raglan's order.

Cardigan responded, 'Certainly, sir, but allow me to point out that the Russians have a battery in the valley to our front, and batteries and riflemen to each flank.'

To this Lucan replied, 'I know it, but Lord Raglan will have it. We have no choice but to obey.'

To point out the lunacy of taking the Light Brigade into a three-way artillery cross-fire might have been the sensible course. To a man of honour – which Cardigan certainly was – it was unthinkable. Cardigan rode off in search of his second-in-command, Lord George Paget.

Lord George was with his regiment, the 4th Light Dragoons, in the Brigade's second line. As the senior officer after Cardigan he was in command of the second line and, therefore, second-in-command of the Light Brigade. At that moment he was oblivious of the conference taking place at the head of the first line some two hundred yards away.

He wrote, 'We remained on the ground we were occupying in two lines . . . dismounted, and employing our time in the interchange of the commodities of life (of which we were in much need not having broken our fast), consisting of biscuits, hard-boiled eggs and the like; the more provident sharing of flasks of rum with those who took no thought of the morrow, while others were consoling themselves with that universal panacea for soldiers in war, as well indeed as in peace the "tobacco leaf".'

While he was thus employed, Lord Cardigan rode up. The relationship between the two men had always been uneasy; the conversation that ensued did nothing to improve matters.

'The first intimation I received of our intended attack was conveyed by Lord Cardigan riding up and saying, "Lord George, we are ordered to make an attack to the front. You will take command of the second line, and I expect your best support, *mind, your best support*", this last sentence being repeated more than once, and perhaps with a rather marked emphasis, as I thought it was probably more the result of excitement than anything else. But it caused me to answer with equal emphasis, "Of course, my Lord, you shall have my best support." '

Cardigan returned to the head of the Brigade, which was formed up with, from left to right, the 11th Hussars, the 17th Lancers and the 13th Light Dragoons in the front line with, one hundred yards behind, the 4th Light Dragoons and the 8th Hussars as the second line. Each regiment was in extended line, two deep.

Lord George Paget was still enjoying his cigar when he saw an incident to his right.

'After we had mounted, and just before we commenced our advance, Colonel Shewell, commanding the 8th Hussars, happened to rest his eye on one of his men with a pipe in his mouth, which so excited his military ire that he halloaed to him that "he was disgracing his regiment by smoking in the presence of the enemy".'

He was not the only one, for as a trooper of the 8th records, Shewell continued, ' "What's this? What's this? — one, two, four, six, seven men smoking! — Swords drawn, and seven men smoking! — Why the thing is inconceivable! Sergeant — Sergeant Pickworth", he calls out. And the truth is, we were warming our noses each with a short black pipe, and thinking no harm of the matter. "I never heard of such a thing," the Colonel said, "and no regiment except an 'Irish' regiment would be guilty of it." '

Listening to this tirade, Paget thought it, 'a grave view of the question which certainly I (his commanding officer) did not, or at least had not, up to that time reciprocated, inasmuch as I at that very moment was enjoying a remarkably good cigar.

'The question then rose in my mind, "Am I to set this bad example? (in the Colonel's opinion at least) or should I throw away a good cigar?" — no such common article in these days, be it remembered. Well, the cigar carried the day, and it lasted me till we got to the guns — with shame do I say it.'

Cardigan, at the head of the brigade, was unaware of this commotion as he ordered the advance, and the brigade moved off at a walk. As they did so the 11th Hussars on the left of the first line held back — as their colonel, Douglas, had been personally ordered to by Lord Lucan – to form an intermediate line between the first line and Lord George Paget's second. The Brigade advanced as follows:

17th Lancers   13th Light Dragoons
11th Hussars
4th Light Dragoons   8th Hussars

As the first line broke into a trot, down something of an incline, Paget brought the second line on, slightly slower, to maintain the regulation distance of one hundred yards. It was at this point that Nolan, who had obtained permission to ride with the 17th Lancers, commanded by his friend Captain Morris, galloped forward waving his sword and shouting.

Morris called to him, 'That won't do Nolan! We've a long way to go and must be steady!'

To Cardigan's outrage, Nolan overtook him. Nolan was still shouting when almost the first shell fired by the Russian battery on the left exploded above him. A splinter pierced his chest, his body convulsed, his horse turned and bore him, uttering an unearthly shriek, through the ranks of the 13th Light Dragoons. Whether Nolan had realised his mistake and was trying to put it right in those last moments of his life, or if he was merely carried away by the excitement of the moment, or if he was attempting to increase the brigade's pace will never be known, but what *is* certain is that Nolan was, ironically, the first Light Brigade casualty. There would be many more within seconds if the Light Brigade continued their advance.

They had just entered the killing ground of the left-hand battery, Fediukine. As they crossed the front of this battery they would be subjected to an enfilade fire – fire from a flank, which with round-shot can mow down a whole line of men and horses – for the best part of four minutes. As they moved out of that battery's arc of fire they would come within range of the Don Cossack battery, lined up across the bottom end of the valley, whose fire would continue to inflict casualties unless the Light Brigade's horseman could reach their guns and sabre the gunners. In the last minute before they did so they would pass under the guns of the right-hand battery, Causeway Heights, where another eight guns would enfilade them, this time, from the right flank.

The watchers on the plateau, British and French and Russians, could hardly believe that so small a force – scarcely more than a regiment's sabre strength – could be about to push on down the valley and attack the main body of Liprandi's force, guns of infantry backed by a large force of cavalry.

Up on the heights, Calthorpe was among his uncle's staff, watching, 'To the horror of all of us on the heights above, we saw our handful of light cavalry advance down towards the Russian batteries. We all saw at once that a lamentable mistake had been made – by whose fault it was impossible then to say.'

Also watching from the plateau was Henry Clifford, visiting the staff of a French general of Bosquet's Corps. 'From the commanding position in which I stood by the side of General Brite we saw the Light Brigade of Cavalry moving forward at a trot, in face of the Russian Army. "Mon Dieu!!" said the fine old French General, "Que vont-ils faire?" They went steadily on, as Englishmen go only under heavy fire, artillery in front, on the right and left.'

Even some of the men – especially those in the front line – could hardly credit what was about to happen. Riding in the ranks of the 11th Hussars was Trooper Edward Woodham.

He described, 'The man next to me was named Wootton, an unsophisticated West-countryman, and when the order was given to move, he says to me, "Ted, old fellow, I know we shall charge." I recollect looking round and replying, "Oh nonsense! Look at the strength in front of us. We're never going to charge there." Presently we got into a gallop, and then all was excitement. I remember looking at Wootton, and saying, "Yes, we're going to charge, and with a vengeance, too." . . . poor fellow; he was shot down almost instantly, and I had the melancholy duty of reporting his death to his bereaved widow and family.'

By now the Russian guns were firing from the left and straight ahead, scything down men and horses. Trooper Thomas Wroots, was with the 11th Hussars. 'The charge was a regular "Derby" – I was near a man called Morton at one time. He was wounded in the right arm, and the pain was so great that he shrieked out fearfully. He asked me to undo his sword-knot, so as to pull his sword off and thus get his arm clear; but something, I can't tell exactly what, just then happened, and I had to ride on, for there was death all round. Another man near me was shot in the left side, and I should think he rode fifty yards, then all at once he tumbled to his left and came down on the ground like a lump of clay – just like a lump of clay, that is the only description I can give of it.'

As roundshot and shells tore gaps in the ranks, men closed in to the centre to maintain the line. Trooper Wroots had fallen back and was trying to push forward again.

He said, 'I was right in the centre of the Squadron. Just after we started I got pushed out – that is, me and my mare got pushed out of the line. I cried out, "Let me come up! Let me come up!" Just then the Russians commenced firing, and in half a second there was room for an omnibus to come up.'

In the same regiment was Sergeant Seth Bond. He recalled the smoke and confusion in the ranks. 'The reports from the guns and the bursting shells were deafening. The smoke too was almost blinding. Horses and men were falling in every direction, and the horses that were not hurt were so upset that we could not keep them in a straight line for a time. A man named Allread who was riding on my left fell from his horse like a stone. I looked back and saw the poor fellow lying on his back, his right temple being cut away and his brain partly on the ground. After moving on a short distance, Lieutenant Trevellyn, of ours, was shot through the foot and was in great agony. I begged him not to fall out, if so he would be done for, and so he kept with us.'

On the right of the front line, with the 13th Light Dragoons, was Trooper Albert Mitchell. 'I rode near the right of the line. A corporal who rode on the right was struck by a shot or shell full in the face, completely smashing it, his blood and brains besmattering us who rode near. His horse still went on with us ... Oaths and imprecations might still be heard between the report of the guns and the bursting of the shells, as the men crowded and jostled each other in their endeavour to close to the centre. This was unavoidable at times, especially when a shell burst in the ranks, sometimes bringing down three or four men and horses, which made it difficult to avoid an unpleasant crush in the ranks.'

Trooper Wightman of the 17th Lancers saw Sergeant Talbot hit. '... He had his head clean carried off by a round shot, yet for about thirty yards further the headless body kept the saddle, the lance at the charge, firmly gripped under the right arm.

Also with the 17th Lancers Corporal Thomas Morley observed,

'The Russian gunners were well-drilled. There was none of that crackling sound . . . where one gun goes a little ahead and the others follow, having the effect of a bunch of fire-crackers popping in quick succession.

'In such case the smoke of the first gun obscures the aim of the rest. The Russian Artillery at Balaclava went off at the word of command all together. One tremendous volley was heard with flashes of flame through the rolling smoke. While they reloaded the smoke lifted so that they could see to take aim again . . . If we had been moving over uneven ground we should have had some slight protection in the necessary uncertainty of aim of the guns, but moving as we did in compact bodies on the smooth ground directly in range, the gunners had an admirable target and every volley came with terrible effect.

'There is a natural instinct to dodge cannon balls. In such a fire as we were under it is changed into an impulse to hurry.'

Without orders, the whole brigade began to accelerate, realising instinctively that the only way to stop the fire of the guns was to get among them.

Cornet George Wombwell, also of the 17th Lancers, was acting as an ADC to Lord Cardigan. 'We broke into a gallop, every man feeling convinced that the quicker we rode through awful showers of grape shot, musketry, and shells, which they poured into our flanks as we passed, the better chance we should have of escaping unhurt.'

Wombwell was only yards behind Lord Cardigan himself, still riding alone at the head of his brigade, erect, immaculate sword at the slope.

Cardigan's conduct during the charge – like almost every other aspect of his life – was to become mired in controversy. To Wombwell he was at this moment: 'The very incarnation of bravery. He kept his eyes firmly fixed on the distant guns in front.'

Even Captain Morris of the 17th, who had no reason to love Cardigan, said he led the brigade 'Just as it ought to be – in short, like a gentleman.' There has been much criticism of Lord Cardigan over the years, most of it justified, but this too should be remembered: if you wanted a man to ride head-on at an enemy gun battery, James Brudenell 7th Earl of Cardigan was the man to do it, and the officers and men of the Light Brigade were the men to follow him.

Commanding the second line, 100 yards behind, Lord George

Paget said he '... found it necessary to increase the pace, to keep up with what appeared to me to be the increasing pace of the first line, and after the first 300 yards my whole energies were exerted in their directions, my shouts of "Keep up; come on", being rendered the more necessary by the stoical coolness (which made such an impression on me at the time) of my two squadron leaders, Major Low and Captain Brown, whose shouts still ring in my ears of "Close in to your centre; back the right flank; keep up, Private So-and-so. Left squadron keep back; look to your dressing."'

Private Connor of Lord George's 4th Light Dragoons remembered, 'Lord George led our line gallantly. There was no sign of flinching; but he made us laugh as he kept drawling out in his own peculiar tone, "Now then men, come on." I saw Gowers' horse shot. The animal staggered, turned round two or three times and fell.'

Before the second line entered the killing ground, Connor said, there was laughter and banter among the troopers. 'One would tell another "that he would lose the number of his mess that day", meaning that he would be shot; others said "Here goes for victory!" whilst others declared they would have Russian biscuits for dinner.'

Within less than a minute they too came under fire as the Fediukine battery which had raked the first-line regiments now opened up on the 4th Light Dragoons and the 8th Hussars.

Private Grant of the 4th Light Dragoons said, 'A shot came over a hill and dropped on the neck of a horse belonging to a man called Gowers. The shot cut the horse's head off as cleanly as if it had been done with a knife. The horse stood for a moment then dropped. Gowers got onto a spare horse, and in a few moments afterwards this horse's head was also shot clear away.'

Within seconds the second line were riding through the carnage of the first line. Falling horses and wounded men presented another hazard. Private Joseph Grigg of the 4th Light Dragoons said, 'The lines were about a hundred yards apart, so that when a man went down with his horse, the man behind him had time to turn his horse on one side or jump him over the obstacle. Every man had his work to do to look before him, and there were not many chances to watch the dreadful work of the shots, shells, and bullets, which were showered on us from all directions ... the man on my right hand went down with a crash, and soon afterwards the man on my left went down also.'

Riderless horses from the first line came careering back down the valley. Lord George Paget observed, 'Ere we had advanced half our distance, bewildered horses from the first line, riderless, rushed in upon our ranks, in every state of mutilation, intermingled soon with riders who had been unhorsed, some with a limping gait, that told too truly of their state. Anon, one was guiding one's own horse ... so as to avoid trampling on the bleeding objects in one's path – sometimes a man, sometimes a horse – and so we went on "Right flank, keep up. Close in to your centre". The smoke, the noise, the cheers, the "*ping ping*" whizzing past one's head; the "*whirr*" of the fragments of shells; the well-known "*slush*" of that unwelcome intruder on one's ears! – what a sublime confusion it was!'

Paget noted that terrified and wounded horses sought out the company of their own kind. 'One incident struck me forcibly about this time – the bearing of riderless horses in such circumstances. I was of course riding by myself and clear of the line, and for that reason was a marked object for the poor dumb brutes, who were by this time galloping about in numbers, like mad wild beasts.

'They consequently made dashes at me, some advancing with me a considerable distance, at one time as many as five on my right and two on my left, cringing in on me, and positively squeezing me, as the round shot came bounding by them, tearing up the earth under their noses, my overalls being a mass of blood from their gory flanks (they nearly upset me several times, and I had several times to use my sword to rid myself of them).'

Paget's right-hand regiment, the 8th Hussars, were taking casualties too.

Lieutenant Edward Seager wrote to his wife the following day, 'The fire was tremendous, shells bursting among us. Cannon balls tearing the earth up and Minié balls coming like hail, still on we went never altering our pace or breaking us up in the least. We passed through the whole of this fire without a check, our men behaved nobly, poor Fitzgibbon was shot through the body and fell.

'Up to this time I was riding in front of the men on the right of the line of officers and Clutterbuck, who was on my left, got wounded on the right foot by a piece of shell that must have passed me, and Captain Tomkinson, who commanded the squadron, had his horse shot. I then took command of the squadron and placed myself in the centre. Malta had just previously got a ball through her neck just above the windpipe, but she went bravely on.'

Some men uttered prayers, some curses. Seager placed his faith in his personal talismans, as listed to his wife: '. . . your's and the darling children's picture, my dear mother's present (prayer book and Testament) . . . your letter containing dear little Emily's hair . . . the dear locket you gave me in Exeter . . .'

At the Alma the commanders had huge difficulty directing lines of infantry in the noise, smoke and confusion of battle. How much greater the difficulty when the line was of galloping horsemen.

Lord George Paget was fully occupied in keeping his own regiment's dressing. 'And so, on we went through this scene of carnage, wondering each moment which would be our last. "Keep back, private So-and-so. Left squadron, close in to your centre." (It required, bye the bye, a deal of closing in, by this time to fill up the vacant gaps.)'

Already he was losing touch with his right-hand regiment. 'After we had continued our advance some 300 or 400 yards' distance, I began to observe that the 8th were inclining away from us, and consequently losing their interval. At the top of my voice I kept shouting, "8th Hussars, close in to your left. Colonel Shewell, you are losing your interval," etc.; but all to no purpose. Gradually – my attention being equally occupied with what was going on in my front ("*Mind your best support, my Lord*," being ever present in my mind) – I lost sight of the 8th . . .'

In fact the 8th Hussars were veering to the right in a direction that meant that they would miss the line of guns at the end of the valley. The wind was blowing down the valley, in the same direction as the charging horsemen, so that the Don Cossack battery was shrouded in its own smoke. The 8th Hussars' straying to the right was to be of crucial importance in a few minutes' time.

Seeing that the 11th Hussars had slackened their pace in accordance with Lucan's order, Lord George brought his 4th Lights up alongside them.

The first line were approaching the guns. As the Russian gunners sponged, loaded, rammed and fired as fast as they could, the unthinkable looked about to happen. That double line of horsemen – Lancers and Light Dragoons – its ranks thinned, its front contracting moment by moment as men closed into the centre, instead of turning back, kept coming on, ever faster.

Trooper Albert Mitchell recalled: 'As we drew nearer, the guns in our front supplied us liberally with grape and canister, which brought down men and horses in heaps. Up to this time I was going on all right, but missed my left hand man from my side, and thinking it might soon be my turn, I offered up a short prayer; "O Lord protect me, and watch over my poor mother." We were now very close to the guns for we were entering the smoke which hung in clouds in front.

'I could see some of the gunners running from the guns to the rear, when just at that moment a shell from the battery on the right struck my horse, carrying away the shoulder and part of the chest, and exploding a few yards off. Fortunately I was on the ground when it exploded, or some of the fragments would most likely have reached me. On my recovery from the shock, I found my horse was lying on his near side, my left leg was beneath him, and my right above him. I tried to move, but just at that moment I heard the second line come galloping on towards where I lay, and fully expecting to be trampled on, I looked up and saw it was the 4th Light Dragoons quite close. I called out, "For God's sake don't ride over me." '

The guns' last salvo blew Lieutenant Wombwell's horse from under him – he was right behind Cardigan at the time and as he fell, he saw Cardigan's own horse falter and then lurch forward, carrying His Lordship between two guns – the first man through.

Corporal Morley of the 17th Lancers also survived that final blast. 'The flame the smoke the roar were in our faces. It is not an exaggeration to compare the sensation to that of riding into the mouth of a volcano, but those who did not fall were through the guns in an instant and full of fight.'

In seconds, what remained of the first line – 17th Lancers and 13th Light Dragoons – were in amongst the gunners who had punished them so cruelly for the last seven minutes. Repeatedly denied the chance of action, held back, mocked as useless peacock bastards and finally exposed to a murderous fire to which they had no reply, the men of the Light Brigade were in no mood to offer quarter. Some gunners scrambled under the guns and limbers; others tried to remove their guns.

Corporal Morley said, 'Our arrival at the battery silenced it instantly, and the gunners began to try to move the cannon away. The gospel of Russian fighting was always to save the guns . . .

'My first thought after we were through the line was to look for
an officer to see what we were to do. I saw Lord Cardigan at first but
I had no impulse to join him. I think no British soldier ever had. He
led 670 and none relied on him. I saw troopers riding past him to
the right and left.'

Eventually Morley saw Lieutenant Jarvis of the 13th Light
Dragoons. 'He was about 200 yards to my left front, riding to his
right towards a cannon that was retreating to the rear. I galloped up
to him and informed him that Lord Cardigan was above, pointing
with my sword to the place, my lance having been shot away at the
last volley as we charged the guns. He replied, "Never mind, let's
capture that gun!" We raced towards it. He said, "Cut down the
gunners!" He shot one of the horses in the head bringing it to a
sudden stop. The gunners disappeared between the horses and gun-
carriage as we slashed at them. We both dismounted and took out
the dead horse while more of the Brigade gathered about to assist
us.'

Having turned the carriage around, they tried to race it back to
the British lines: 'We started back off the field at a gallop with the
mounted cannon, and were near the place where I had seen Lord
Cardigan, when a large body of Cossacks charged, who appeared
from behind a hill and surrounded our group. I was riding on the
right of the gun in the direction in which the Cossacks attacked us.
In the mêlée I got through the wrong end and had to ride back again
down the valley. I was pursued by seven of them until they fairly
chased me into a body of Russian cavalry with its back to me. There
was no alternative but to ride through or surrender to the Cossacks.
I put spurs to my horse and bolted into the line. I got through
with a knock on the head from a Russian officer, that would have
wounded me but for my dress cap, which I eventually lost . . . More
members of the Light Brigade were riding about – some of them
wounded – fighting as best they could.'

The momentum of the charging cavalrymen had carried them
swiftly past the guns and into the ranks of the Russian cavalry
drawn up in rear of the gun line. By now the ranks of the two
leading regiments were disordered as they fought it out with the
Russian horsemen in ones and twos.

Meanwhile, the supports – the 11th Hussars and 4th Light
Dragoons under Lord George Paget – were themselves approaching

the gun line. As at the Alma, little information was passed down the chain of command. Here, because of the dust and smoke, the very presence of this battery at the end of the valley came as a surprise to Paget.

He said, 'A line of field artillery was formed up across the plain in our front, consisting of at least twelve guns. This battery, owing to the dust and confusion that reigned, had not been perceived by us (by me at least) until we got close upon it, though we had of course been suffering from its fire on our onward course. The first objects that caught my eyes were some of these guns in the act of endeavouring to get away from us, who had by this time got close upon them. They had, I fancy ceased to fire on our near approach, and the men were dragging them away, by lassoo harness, but others with their horses still attached. Then came a "View Halloa!" and a sort of simultaneous rush upon them by the remnants of the 4th and cut and thrust was the order of the day.'

Riding in the ranks of Paget's regiment was Trooper Grigg. 'I remember, as we neared the guns, Captain Brown, who was in command of our squadron, called out to the men in the second line, who were getting too near to the front, "Steady, men, steady! you shall have to go in directly."

'Just before we got to the guns, we gave three loud cheers, and then in a moment, we were in among the enemy . . .'

One of his comrades, Private Herbert, found himself recalling the words of his divisional commander. 'We knew what was expected of us, for two or three days before the charge Lord Lucan addressed us, saying, "Keep your horses well in hand, men, and obey your officers; but when you get in amongst the Russians skiver them well!" As he spoke he gave us with his own sword a demonstration of what he meant which was pointing and cutting with the weapon.'

They skivered them now as, with the 11th Hussars slightly in the lead, the support line crashed through the gun line. Not all the gunners were trying to remove their guns: one crew at least fired off another shot.

Private Grigg said, 'As I passed the wheel of the gun-carriage the gun was fired, and I suppose some of the 8th Hussars got that shot, or shell, or whatever it was. The wind was blowing from behind us, and the smoke from the guns prevented us from seeing very well what work there was for us to do.

'The first man I noticed was a mounted driver. He cut me across the eyes with his whip, which almost blinded me, but as my horse flew past him, I made a cut at him and caught him in the mouth, so that his teeth all rattled together as he fell from his horse. As he fell I cut at him again; and then I made for another driver, and cut him across the back of his neck, and gave him a second cut as he fell. A few gunners stood in a group with their rifles, and we cut at them as we went rushing by.'

Over to Grigg's left was Trooper Woodham of the 11th Hussars. 'as soon as we reached the guns the men began dodging by getting under them, and for a time defended themselves with rammers; but it was no contest – they had no chance with us and we cut them down like ninepins.'

Unaffected by the blood-lust that had seized his men, Paget saw, 'A Lancer ... prodding away at a dismounted Russian officer, apparently unarmed. I holloa to him to let him alone, which he obeys, though reluctantly (for their monkeys are up by this time), and the act, while it was not very graciously acknowledged by the officer in question, was begrudged by some who saw it.'

Paget tried the same trick with his own orderly, with less success. Private Herbert saw what happened: 'Many of our men were fighting dismounted, their horses having been killed by fire or steel. Some of them performed prodigies of valour, amongst them being Sam Parkes, a private of my own regiment. When we were mixed up with the guns Parkes was on foot, his horse having been killed. He was surrounded by Russians and fought like a demon. In a curious way he got level with his officer, for he disobeyed an order. He was going for a Russian, and for some reason the officer shouted: "Spare him Sam!" But Parkes was far too busy looking after his own skin, so the Russian had to go.'

One of Paget's troopers, Robert Grant, performed a rare act of mercy. 'I saw two or three old Russians on horses ... They were quite old men. They appeared to be paralysed, and they did not seem pleased and they did not look sorry. They were quiet and still. I put my sword against one of their faces and said, "What do you want here, you old fools?" I would not touch them ... They were poor harmless fellows, who as I thought, were obliged to be there. They were not volunteers, but old men who would have given all they had in the world to be somewhere else. They were not the right men in the right place, so I left them and turned my horse on to the young and strong, who were using their swords most vigorously. There were too many likelier sort of fellows about to touch without attacking those poor old cripples.'

Paget saw: '... some fierce hand-to-hand encounters and our fellows in the excitement of the moment, lost sight, I fear, of the chief power of their sabres, and for the *point* (the great efficacy of which was amply exemplified on this day) substituted the muscle of their arms, in the indiscriminate appliance of the cut, which generally fell harmlessly on the thick greatcoats of the Russians.

'Well, the work of destruction went on, of which, I, however was a passive observer, conceiving it more within the province of my duty to observe and endeavour to direct than to occupy myself with the immediate destruction of the foe.'

Paget's immediate concern was the enemy guns: 'The four or five guns to which I have alluded as being more immediately in our front, were soon disabled, one of them ... having been overturned. While the 4th were thus engaged, I observed twenty or thirty yards ahead two or three of the guns scrambling away, drawn by horses with lassoo-harness, which it was evident had thus been attacked, so that they might be dragged away at the very last moment, on which I said to Captain Brown, who was close to me, "There are some guns getting away, take some of your men to stop them," which order, I need not say was promptly and effectually obeyed.'

Some men dismounted and tried to disable the guns by spiking them − hammering a nail in the vent to prevent it being fired. Trooper Woodham was one. 'Each man had spikes in his pouch. All the cavalry regiments were supplied with gun spikes whenever there was any likelihood of a battle. We had no hammers, but drove the spikes in with the hilt of our swords or our hands in any way we could.'

Trooper Connor was another. 'I was one of those who tried to cut the traces of the Russian guns. I used my pocket knife. But I found that within the leather were chains of steel. Our officers did more service with their revolvers than we could with our carbines. They fired five shots to our one, and that seemed to alarm the Russians.'

By now the bulk of the second line were involved in the cavalry mêlée with the Cossacks. According to Trooper Buckton of the 11th Hussars, 'We were all higgledy-piggledy, but fighting more like devils than men. We were being cut up in a dreadful way and we could not stand it.'

Trooper Grigg of the 4th Lights said, 'Beyond the guns the Russian cavalry, who should have come out to prevent our getting near the gunners, were coming down upon us howling wildly, and we went at them with a rush. I selected a mounted Cossack, who was making for me with his lance pointed at my breast. I knocked it upwards with my sword, pulled up quickly, and cut him down across the face. I tried to get hold of his lance but he dropped it. As he was falling I noticed that he was strapped on to the saddle, so that he did not come to the ground, and the horse rushed away with him. His lance, like all the others used by the Cossacks, had a black tuft of hair, about three inches from the blade, to hide a hook having a sharp edge, with which the reins of their enemies are cut when the lance is withdrawn after a thrust.'

In the thick of the fighting, Paget had lost his orderly. 'It was about this time that my orderly, Private Parkes, a fine specimen of an Englishman, about six feet two inches high, who had lost sight of me in the mêlée, came rushing past me, his sword up in the air, and halloaing out, "Where's my chief?" to which I answered, "Here I am my boy, all right," – the last I saw of him, for he had his horse shot under him, was himself wounded, and afterwards taken prisoner.'

Robert Grant, of Paget's regiment, noted the effectiveness of pistols in cavalry combat. 'Our officers had revolvers, and they did great execution with them. The privates had not revolvers. Those revolvers did great service. In fact the officers altogether did a great deal more service than the men, because of the revolvers. Many of the Cossacks got shot foolishly like, for after one exchange they thought it was all over, but the revolver had several barrels. Those Cossacks were all for plunder and they tried to surround our officers but they got knocked down with the shots. I gave one man a nick between his shako and the top of his jacket. He fell, but I do not know whether I killed him. I can't remember whether he sang out at all, but he did not trouble me again.'

However, Paget never even drew his pistol. 'Oddly enough, the possession of a revolver never entered my head, and the only act of mine, on this day, as regards immediate destruction was that of saving an officer's life, and happy for me has since been the reflection of this, for doubtless the revolver would have been a tempting weapon more than once, had I thought of it.'

Paget had more important concerns than 'immediate destruction', for unknown to him, he was now commanding what was left of the Light Brigade.

Lord Cardigan's conduct during the charge, until he passed between the guns, was beyond reproach. Having, in his own words, 'received the order to attack from my superior officer in front of the troops', he had led those troops from the front (and without looking back), straight at the enemy. He had been the first man through the Russian guns. There, finding himself alone, and having being slightly wounded and almost captured by Cossacks, he appears to have decided that his work was done. Having led his men into the cauldron, he felt it no part of his duty to bring them out. Looking back up the valley, he saw numbers of the first line – those who, for one reason or another, had never reached the guns – straggling back towards the British lines and, turning his horse's head round, set off back up the valley himself.

This conduct, on the part of a man with a talent for making enemies, was open to misinterpretation. Somerset Calthorpe wrote in his journal that Cardigan's horse: 'took fright – swerved round – and galloped off with him to the rear, passing on the way by the 4th Light Dragoons and 8th Hussars before they got up to the battery.'

These words were to lead later to a long and acrimonious lawsuit. Cardigan justified his actions, claiming, 'It is quite sufficient for a general of brigade to return with as well as lead the attack of the front line, unless he should by chance come in contact with his supports, in which case he would remain with them.'

Cardigan claimed not to have seen the supports, though men of both the 4th Light Dragoons and the 8th Hussars claimed to have seen *him*. Assuming that the stragglers that he could see were all that was left of his first line, Cardigan rode after them.

Among the wounded men and horses who had strewn the ground in front of the guns across which Cardigan rode was Trooper Albert Mitchell, who came from a tavern in Portchester nearly into the cannon's mouth, then was pinned under his horse, calling to Lord Paget's 4th Lights not to ride over him.

'Whether they heard me or not I shall never know. But one thing

I do know, He, in whose name I called out to them, did hear, and most mercifully answered my prayer, for He guided them over me so not a hoof touched a hair of my head. To Him alone be all honour and praise for His manifold mercies to me.

'After they passed I tried to extricate my leg, which after a short time I succeeded in doing and stood upright, finding myself unhurt, except my leg, which was a little painful from the crush. I still had my sword in my hand, and soon found there were numberless bullets flying around me which came from the infantry on the flank of their battery, who fired at any of us who were dismounted. Just at this time a man of my regiment named Pollard came to me, and throwing himself down beside the carcase of my horse for shelter from the bullets, called to me saying: "Come here Mitchell, this is good cover." I said "No, we had better make our way back as quick as possible, or we shall soon be taken prisoners, if not killed, if we remain here." Upon this he jumped up, and we both started to get back, but had not gone many yards when a poor fellow called to us to help him. He was in a similar position to mine, and he belonged to our regiment. I took him beneath the arms, and Pollard raised the horse's forepart a little so that I managed to draw his leg from under the horse, but his thigh was broken, and, besides, he had a severe wound on his head, which covered him with blood. On seeing his injuries, we laid him gently down. He said, "You can do no more for me, I thought my thigh was broken before you pulled me out. Look out for yourselves." '

A little further down the valley Mitchell became separated from Pollard. 'Just then Lord Cardigan came galloping up from the direction of the guns, passing me at a short distance, when he turned about again, and meeting me, pulled up, and said: "Where is your horse?" I answered: "Killed my lord." He then said in his usually stern hoarse voice: "You had better make the best of your way back as fast as you can, or you will be made prisoner." I needed no telling for I was doing so as fast as I was able. He then rode a little farther down, and in a few moments returned past me at a gallop.'

Was this a last attempt on Cardigan's part to look for the remains of his brigade? If so, he then concluded that they had already gone back down the valley, and turned to follow them.

In fact, the bulk of the Light Brigade were still far beyond the Russian guns, fighting it out with Russian cavalry. Most assumed that they were being supported. It soon became clear that this was not the case.

Lord Lucan, declaring, 'They have sacrificed the Light Brigade, they shall not have the Heavy', had halted the Heavy Brigade at the extreme range of the Russian guns, though not before they had taken casualties. Cathcart's infantry were still far behind. Still believing that the rest of the British army was close on their heels, some regimental commanders pushed on.

Colonel Douglas of the 11th Hussars was 'impressed with the idea that we were being supported, and that shortly, both fresh infantry and cavalry would come up'. He had charged on, with just 40 of his men, almost to the Tchernaya River at the very end of the valley, and was now entangled with large numbers of Russian cavalry.

Captain Morris, the 'pocket Hercules' of the 17th Lancers, was also under the delusion that they were merely the vanguard of a general British advance. He had passed through the guns and, seeing Russian Hussars ahead, had led his men at them. Behind the guns, the 13th and 4th Light Dragoons were involved in another cavalry mêlée, and to the right, Colonel Shewell and his Irish Hussars had missed the guns and were consequently the only formed body left in the brigade. The bulk of the Light Brigade were now scattered in small groups all over the end of the valley, fighting individual battles with groups of Russian gunners, drivers, cavalry and Cossacks.

As Lord George Paget had noticed, the men's blood was up – some of them had worked themselves into a berserker blood-lust.

Corporal Morley of the 17th Lancers, last seen trying to gallop off the field with a Russian gun, now found himself one of a mixed crowd of troopers. Confronted by a formed body of Russian Hussars, 'I ordered Private Clifford of my own troop to halt, instead of which he charged into the solid column and was cut and pierced to death in front of my eyes.' Morley could see that unless they were rallied all the men would be cut up piecemeal.

'I turned back to my scattered comrades, who were riding about like myself in all directions, not seeing which way to go. I raised my sword and shouted to them to fall in.'

Among them was Trooper Wightman. 'We heard the familiar voice of Corporal Morley, of our regiment, a great, rough, bellowing man from Nottingham. He had lost his lance hat, and his long hair was flying out in the wind as he roared, "Coom 'ere! Coom 'ere! Fall in, lads, fall in!" Well, with shouts and oaths he had collected some twenty troops of various regiments. We fell in with the handful this man of the hour had rallied to him, and there joined us also under his leadership Sergeant Major Ransom and Private John Penn of the 17th. Penn, a tough old warrior who had served with the 3rd Light in the Sikh war, had killed a Russian officer, dismounted, and with great deliberation accoutred himself with the belt and sword of the defunct, in which he made a great show.'

A second body of Russian cavalry were between Morley's band and the way home.

'Morley,' said Wrightman, 'roaring Nottingham oaths by way of encouragement, led us straight at them, and we went through and out the other side as if they had been made of tinsel paper.'

Paget now found himself faced with Morley's problem on a larger scale. Russian numbers were beginning to tell. Captain Morris and his Lancers had been badly cut up, and he was wounded and made prisoner. Colonel Douglas and his men of the 11th were being driven back up the valley towards the Russian gun line.

Lord George saw that: 'Masses of the enemy's cavalry were pursuing the latter, the more forward of them (who were advancing in far from an orderly manner, and evincing that same air of surprise, hesitation and bewilderment that I had remarked against the Heavy Brigade in the morning – *appearing not to know what to do*).'

It is at this moment that languid, cigar-smoking, disillusioned Lord George Paget became one of the true heroes of the Charge. He recalled something his father – Wellington's cavalry commander at Waterloo – had told him: 'I remember with what force occurred to my mind an expression I had often heard from the lips of Lord Anglesey: "Cavalry are the bravest fellows possible in an advance, but once get into a scrape, and get their backs turned, and it is a difficult matter to stop or rally them."'

Paget set about rallying his men: 'I shouted at the top of my voice, "Halt, front, if you don't front my boys we are done!" and this they did, and for a few minutes both regiments showed a front to the advancing enemy.

'Hardly, however, had we thus rallied, when a cry arose, "They are attacking us, my Lord, in our rear!"

'I turned round, and on looking in that direction saw there, plainly enough, a large body of Russian Lancers formed up, some

500 yards behind us, in the direct line whence we had originally come, and on the direct line of our retreat!'

Trooper Grigg, of Paget's own regiment, was one of those who had rallied to his cry. 'I heard Lord Paget call out, "Rally on me!" I turned and saw him holding up his sword, and we all turned our horses towards where he had taken up a position in front of the guns. On arriving there, we noticed a regiment of Polish Lancers, which had come out from an opening in the hills behind us and was preparing to charge our rear ...

'It seemed to me then, in the terrible din, confusion, and excitement, that all the gunners and drivers were on the ground, either dead or wounded.'

The Russian – or Polish – Lancers had been up on the Causeway Heights; they had watched the Light Brigade charge through the guns and had then descended into the valley to cut off their retreat. Looking back up the valley, the way they had charged, Paget and his command (for his it now was) could see first the Russian gun-line, shrewn with dead and wounded gunners, drivers, horses and troopers, and beyond that a line of Russian Lancers blocking the way home.

'On the impulse of the moment,' wrote Lord Paget, 'I then holloaed out, "Threes about" – adding, "We must do the best we can for ourselves."

'But by that time, and indeed long previously all order and regularity of formation had been lost; but still there was sort of nucleus left whereon a fresh "rally" might be made to encounter our new foes, and this was to a certain extent effected by the individual exertions of the officers ... with their swords held in mid-air, to the cry of "Rally, rally!" when some few stragglers from the first line (which had long ago been broke up) joined us.'

During the charge, the 8th Hussars had lost speed and veered to the right, leaving Lord George Paget to hit the guns with only his own regiment and the 11th Hussars. Now, unlike the other regiments of the brigade, the 8th were still a formed body. Seeing the trap that had closed behind the brigade, Colonel Shewell gave his Irishmen the word "Right about wheel!" and led them straight at the Russian Lancers.

Lieutenant Edward Seager of the 8th wrote to his wife, 'We immediately wheeled about to show fight and we advanced upon them. The Colonel and Major got through them somehow . . . I kept with the Squadron, Clutterbuck the left troop, and Philips the right, me in front of the Squadron, leading. The men kept well together and bravely seconded us. We dashed at them. They were three deep with lances levelled. I parried the first fellow's lance, the one behind him I cut over the head which no doubt he will remember for some time, and as I was recovering my sword I found the third fellow making a tremendous point at my body, I had just time to receive his lance point with the hilt of my sword, it got through the bars, knocked off the skin of the top knuckle of my second finger, and the point, entered between the second and top joint of my little finger, coming out at the other side. I shall most likely be returned wounded in the Gazette but you see I have only got a slight scratch that might look interesting in a drawing room.'

Where the 8th Hussars led, men of the other regiments followed. The men rallied by Lord George Paget went: 'Helter skelter . . . at these Lancers as fast as our poor tired horses could carry us, rear rank of course in front (as far as anything could by this time be called a "front"), the officers of course in the rear, for it must be remembered that we still had our pursuers behind us . . .

'. . . as we neared them, down they came upon us at a sort of trot (their advance not being more than twenty or thirty yards), they stopped ("halted" is hardly the word) and evinced that same air of bewilderment (I know of no other word) that I had twice before remarked on this day.'

As well as bewilderment, this particular regiment showed a strange lack of belligerence. Paget said, 'A few of the men on the right flank of their leading squadrons . . . came into momentary collision with the right flank of our fellows, but beyond this they did nothing, and actually allowed us to shuffle, to edge away, by them, at a distance of hardly a horse's length.

'Well, we got by them without, I believe the loss of a single man. How, I know not! It is a mystery to me! Had that force been composed of English *ladies*, I don't think one of us could have escaped.'

Some put the poor performance of the Lancers down to their being a Polish regiment – conscripts with little sympathy for their Russian masters. Certainly there had been a steady trickle of Polish deserters since the siege began. Others put it down to cowardice, and saw it as another example of the inferiority of Russian cavalry.

Trooper Buckton of the 11th Hussars put it down to horsemanship and the famous British cheer: 'Our poor fellows – the mere handfull that were left of them – hurrahed and hallooed as loudly as they could and that apparently had an effect upon the Polish horsemen, for it was evident their horses had not, like ours, been trained to withstand the noise and din of battle; and when they heard the British "hurrahs" and saw our fellows rushing towards them at such a mad pace, they became restless and turned round and about, and before they could form again in any kind of way our men had bobbed through their ranks and were scampering up the hill before them.'

Trooper Wroots of the same regiment put it down to sympathy and 'friendly fire': 'I saw the Captain of the Lancers quite plain. He said something to his men, and they all turned threes right and took up their places. It was then that their own artillery fired into them. We got past them, and my belief is they took pity on us, and let us pass them without touching us.'

Not everyone got through unscathed, as Wroots saw. 'I saw one fellow, however, run up behind one of our sergeants – I think his name was Hudson – and catch him right in the middle of his back with his lance. He was not killed then; the ambulance brought him in afterwards, but he soon died.'

Once through the Lancers it was every man for himself back up the valley, through the same storm of fire which had decimated them on the way down.

'What a scene of havoc was this last mile,' wrote Lord George Paget, 'strewn with the dead and dying, and all friends! some running, some limping, some crawling; horses in every position of agony, struggling to get up, then floundering again on their mutilated riders!

'Mine was an unenviable position, for I had had a "bad start", and my wounded horse at every step got more jaded, and I therefore saw those in my front gradually increasing the distance between us, and I made more use of my sword in this return ride than I had done in the whole affair. However, with the continual application of the flat of it against my horse's flank and the liberal use of both spurs, I at last got home.'

Trooper Woodham of the 11th had his horse shot under him and, like Albert Mitchell, he was pinned by the animal.

'A Corporal of the 13th Light Dragoons rode up and commenced pulling at my horse's head, thinking it was not dead. And so it proved, for the animal gave a bit of a struggle, which I took advantage of, and so regained my feet. All then was smoke and confusion, and all our men that I could see were cutting right and left, and making their way back to camp . . .

'I began running as hard as I could, when a soldier belonging to the 8th Hussars, who was lying under his horse, shouted to me, "For God's sake man, don't leave me here." At this time the firing from the guns was so incessant – indeed it was murderous; still I returned and strove hard to release him, but without effect, the horse being dead. The enemy at this time were coming up the valley and killing the wounded on their march: so I said to the man "It's no use my stopping here; we shall both be killed." The poor fellow said something in reply, but I don't recollect it now. I then reluctantly left him to his fate, and joined three or four of my comrades who, like myself, had been unhorsed and were trying to escape on foot. To facilitate our retreat we threw everything away that in the least encumbered us; even our "busbies" we pitched on one side; in fact, we retained nothing except our sword-blades and those we carried for our defence . . . the enemy, seeing us together concentrated a heavy fire upon us; and in order that the gunners might direct their attention to something else, we lay flat down, and they did not pursue us further. Shortly afterwards I espied a riderless horse belonging to the 17th Lancers, which I succeeded in capturing by seizing hold of its bridle; and mounting it, I rode at full gallop to the top of the valley, when I handed it over to the regiment to which it belonged.'

Fire from the guns and the infantry were not the only danger. Some Russian Lancers and Cossacks pursued the remnants of the brigade down the valley, finishing off stragglers and wounded.

Sergeant Seth Bond, of the 11th Hussars, remembered, 'A young man named James Elder (my servant who turned me out in the morning) fell from his horse, no doubt shot by some of the rifles pursuing us from the bottom of the valley. I looked back for a moment and saw three Lancers in the act of piercing him, and heard him cry "Oh! Oh! Oh!" as the lances entered his body. I dare not look again, as at that moment I heard a voice, which proved to be Captain Dunn's, say, "Look out, Bond, or that villain will cut you down." I turned my head at once to my left, and had no sooner done so than I received a tremendous blow from a sword on my left arm. The blow quite benumbed my whole arm, and I thought at first that it was off. It cut through my tunic, and also cut my arm a good deal, but after a short time I was able to use my fingers sufficiently to handle the reins. Almost immediately afterwards I received two more sword cuts on the same arm, one below the elbow and another near the wrist. About the same time I received a heavy blow on the head, cutting through the bear skin and lining of my busby, but only bruising my head so as to raise a large lump. I also had several cuts on my back ... I had been all the time looking to my right for danger, not knowing that those [Russian] Hussars were attacking us on our left until Captain Dunn called out to me.'

Further down the valley, Bond was joined by a riderless horse, which ran alongside his own. 'By this time we had got back to the battery taken from the Turks, and as we passed it the Russian cavalry left us to the mercy of the guns and the Russian rifles, the latter running down in front of the battery and firing at anyone they saw. Just then I heard a voice call out, "Stop that horse." I looked back and saw a horse galloping close after me. I pulled up and caught it, and found it was a Sergeant of the 8th Hussars who had called to me to stop it. The moment I had done so, one of our own men comes running up and says, "Let me have the horse, Sergeant." I told him I had stopped it for the Sergeant behind. He said he had lost his horse as well, and meant having it. He was mounted when the Sergeant who called to me first came up. The Sergeant said it was not quite fair, as he had asked me to stop it. I said in reply that I could not refuse one of our own regiment, to which the sergeant replied "Ah well, I suppose all is fair in war, so let me have hold of each of your stirrups, and I'll run: the sooner we get out of this the better." We were then under fire, so the Sergeant ran between the horses, holding on by the stirrups until we were out of danger.'

Many of the wounded were beyond help. Trooper Sheridan of the 8th Hussars passed Lord Fitzgibbon, who had been shot through the body on the way down the valley. 'I saw Lord Fitzgibbon, who was mortally wounded, pull out his purse and offer it to anyone of us who would dismount and accept it, as his Lordship did not like it to get into the hands of the Russians; but Lord! we did not think

TOP: Parade of the Scots Fusiliers *Courtesy of the Director, National Army Museum, London*

BOTTOM: The Grand Charge, Alma *Courtesy of the Director, National Army Museum, London*

LEFT: Alma. Forward Forty-Second! *Courtesy of the Director, National Army Museum, London*

BOTTOM LEFT: View of Sevastopol *Courtesy of the Director, National Army Museum, London*

BELOW: A Hot Day in the Batteries *Courtesy of the Director, National Army Museum, London*

TOP: A Quiet Day in the Battery. The central figure is Captain William Peel *Courtesy of the Director, National Army Museum, London*

BOTTOM: Charge of the Heavy Brigade *Courtesy of the Director, National Army Museum, London*

TOP: Charge of the Light Brigade. Caton Woodville *Courtesy of the Director, National Army Museum, London*

BOTTOM: Relief of the Light Brigade *Courtesy of the Director, National Army Museum, London*

TOP: Second Charge, Inkermann *Courtesy of the Director, National Army Museum, London*

BOTTOM: The Battle of Inkermann (death of General Cathcart) *Courtesy of the Director, National Army Museum, London*

TOP: The Roll Call: Calling the Roll after an Engagement, Crimea. Lady Elizabeth Thompson Butler *The Royal Collection © 2005, Her Majesty Queen Elizabeth II*

BOTTOM: Attack on the Malakoff *Courtesy of the Director, National Army Museum, London*

TOP: The Storming of the Great Redan (in the right background is General Windham) *Courtesy of the Director, National Army Museum, London*

BOTTOM: The Fall of Sebastopol *Courtesy of the Director, National Army Museum, London*

of money at such a moment as that. Life and honour were more precious to us than money, so I suppose the Russians got the English gold after all.'

After his encounter with Lord Cardigan, Albert Mitchell was making his way back on foot. 'The mounted were making their way back as fast as they could, some singly, and some in parties of two or three, but whenever the battery on our left could see anything like a party together, they would be sure to send a shell at them. In this way many men were killed on their return.

'There were several riderless horses galloping about the plain. I tried very hard to get one but could not. I saw two officers' horses belonging to my own regiment. I could tell them by the binding of the sheepskins on the saddles. They appeared almost mad. I would have given a trifle just then to have had my legs across one of them, for I was getting tired . . . Presently a Captain of ours came running past me, and shortly after he got up behind a mounted man of ours, and they both rode back together on one horse.

'I could now see some Cossacks showing themselves in swarms on our right, thinking to cut some of us dismounted men off. As soon as I saw them approaching, I bore more away to my left front, and a party of Chasseurs de Afrique . . . These having showed themselves menacingly it had the desired effect of turning the Cossacks from their purpose.'

The French Chasseurs d'Afrique – colonial cavalry – had been sent to the foot of the escarpment by General Canrobert early in the day; they were the French cavalry mentioned in Raglan's fateful order. While the Light Brigade had charged down the valley, 150 of these men under Major Abdelal had carried out a gallant and skilful attack against the Fediukine battery which had so mauled the brigade from the left during its advance.

In Lord Lucan's opinion, the silencing of this battery prevented the destruction of the Heavy Brigade, who had also taken casualties as they advanced in support of the Light. It also ensured that the returning remnants of the Light Brigade were only fired on from one flank, although most of the Light Brigade were unaware of this at the time.

Lord George Paget saw the Chasseurs, 'Appearing as if they had just been turned out of so many bandboxes, advancing towards us at a walk at the head of the valley, with a line of skirmishers in their front, and forming a strange contrast to our dusty and tired soldiers.

'I thought to myself as I gazed on them, "You are very pretty to look at, but you might as well have taken a turn with us, and then perhaps you would not look as spruce as you do." But I little knew the good service they had been rendering us during our absence.'

In ones and two, mounted or on foot, wounded or dying, the Light Brigade straggled back. Watching from the Sapoune, the normally stoical Henry Clifford was overcome with emotion. 'The tears ran down my face, and the din of musketry pouring in their murderous fire on the brave gallant fellows rang in my ears. "Pauvre garcon," said the old French General, patting me on the shoulder. "Je suis vieux, j'ai vue des battailles, mai ceci est trop." Then the smoke cleared away, and I saw hundreds of our poor fellows lying on the ground, the Cossacks and Russian Cavalry running them through as they lay, with their swords and lances.'

Below the escarpment, Fanny Duberly, peering down the valley into the smoke and dust, had lost sight of the brigade. 'Presently come a few horsemen, straggling galloping back. What can those *skirmishers* be doing? See, they form up together again. Good God! It is the Light Brigade!'

Among the survivors were Corporal Morley's band, much reduced by a point-blank volley from Russian infantry, a group led by Sergeant O'Hara of the 17th, and another by Lieutenant-Colonel Mayow, the Brigade Major. The regimental butcher of the 17th Lancers who, hearing that a fight was in progress, had abandoned his shambles, grabbed a horse and charged with his regiment brandishing his pole-axe also emerged unscathed, as did two Sardinian officers, Major Govone and Lieutenant Landirani, who were attached to the brigade as observers, but decided to charge with them. "Jemmy", a Jack Russell belonging to the Officers' Mess of the 8th Hussars, had followed the regiment, yapping at the horses' heels, all the way down the valley; he now returned with only a minor neck wound.

By the time those still on horseback had reached the ground from which they had started, Albert Mitchell, on foot, had reached ground formerly occupied by the Heavy Brigade. Here they had stood waiting to support the Lights until pulled back out of range of the Russian guns by Lord Lucan.

'On my arrival at the spot whereon the Greys had been formed,' Mitchell wrote, 'there was a man standing by himself whom they had left behind. As I came along he heard me, and calling out, said: "Is that an Englishman?" I answered, "Yes," and going to him found he had been wounded by a piece of shell just between the eyes, which had blinded him. He had bled very much and was still bleeding. I had a handkerchief in my breast, which I bound round his wound, and taking him by the arm, led him along. We had not gone many yards when we fell in with the man who had ridden on my left. He was lying on his back with arms extended, and labouring very hard for breath. Each breath he drew brought up a quantity of blood, which, as he lay on his back, he could not clear from his mouth, and was almost choking. I could see death in his countenance, but turned him over and placed his arm under his forehead, thinking he would be better able to relieve himself of the blood than by lying on his back. It was a good bit lower down the valley where I had first missed him from my side, so it is likely his horse was shot, and he, afterwards, in trying to make his way back dismounted.'

A little further up the valley, Mitchell made contact with some of Cathcart's infantry, '. . . coming near No. 4 redoubt, which the enemy had left and which was now held by our 68th Light Infantry. The men were lying down in the ditch, and the poor Scotch Grey whom I was leading, saying he felt faint from loss of blood, I led him up to the ditch of the redoubt, and coming to an officer first, I said: "Have you got a drop of water sir, if you please, you can give this man, he is very faint from loss of blood?" He answered: "Yes my lads, you shall have something better than water;" upon which he filled a tin pint cup, half with rum, and the remainder with water. The wounded man drank a good half, and his moustache and mouth being covered with blood, had dipped into it, but that did not matter then, I emptied the cup, and thanking the officer for his kindness we made another start.

'We had not gone but a little farther when we met our commissary officer, Mr Cruickshank, mounted on a pony with saddle-bags filled with bottles of rum. He was making his way to meet any men returning from the charge. He very kindly gave us a good drop each, which helped us along nicely.'

Mitchell took the man to a dressing station and left him in the care of the doctors there. 'I have heard that he was discharged blind, and was allowed a shilling a day pension, and some time after again recovered his eyesight.'

As Lord Cardigan rode past the Heavies he was greeted with a cheer. General Scarlet rode out to meet him. Characteristically, Cardigan's first words damned Captain Nolan, who had brought him the order: 'What do you think, General, of the aide-de-camp, after such an order being brought to us which has destroyed the Light Brigade, riding to the rear and screaming like a woman?'

Equally characteristic was Scarlett's reply: 'Say no more, My Lord, for I have just ridden over his dead body.'

Cardigan then rode over to the re-forming regiments of his Brigade, where he was also cheered. 'Men!' he declared, 'it is a mad-brained trick, but it is no fault of mine.'

To which some men replied, 'Never, mind My Lord! We are ready to go again.'

Not all of the reunions were so cordial. Lord George Paget, mindful perhaps of the implied criticism in Cardigan's words earlier in the day ('Mind, your best support') and feeling that His Lordship had abandoned them at the guns, could not resist a jibe at his expense:

'The involuntary exclamation escaped me, "Holloa, Lord Cardigan! were you not there?" to which he answered, "Oh, wasn't I though? Here Jenyns, did not you see me at the guns?"'

Thus began one of the two controversies about this action that continue to this day: Lord Cardigan's conduct, and the question of who was to blame. The first was to run for years in messes and clubs, in print and journals, and eventually in the libel courts, and ended to no one's satisfaction.

The second began almost immediately.

'What did you mean, sir,' asked Lord Raglan when Cardigan reported to him, 'by attacking a battery in front, contrary to all the usages of warfare and the customs of the service?'

To which Cardigan replied, reasonably enough, 'My, Lord I hope you will not blame me, for I received the order to attack from my superior officer in front of the troops.'

Later that evening, taxed by Raglan with not exercising his discretion and preventing the charge, Lucan's response was, 'I gave the order to charge under what I considered a most imperious necessity, and I will not bear one particle of the blame.'

This controversy has already occupied enough volumes to fill a sizeable bookcase. Suffice it to say that an unclear order, written in haste in a fluid situation and conveyed by an over-excited, insubordinate staff officer to two unimaginative commanders who were hardly on speaking terms is as good a recipe for disaster as anyone can conceive.

Disaster is no exaggeration. The Light Brigade lost 113 officers and men killed, 134 wounded and 45 made prisoner out of the 661 who took part in the charge: almost half of the brigade. More damaging still was the loss of 362 horses. Cardigan's command could now muster only 195 men mounted and fit for duty. The Light Brigade effectively ceased to exist.

'All those who were able at once formed,' wrote Trooper Woodham of the 11th Hussars, 'and it was a dreadful sight to see the havoc that had been made. Soon afterwards I met trumpeter Smith, one of the survivors, whose horse I had to attend to. I asked him where his horse was, when he told me that it had been killed. I replied, "Well, it is not such a bad field, after all; it was the first I was ever in where there was no horse to clean." This was not said as a joke . . . there was nothing to joke about then.'

The worst of it was that this sacrifice achieved nothing that had not already been achieved by 11 a.m. – before the Light Brigade had moved off the ground they had occupied for most of the day. The Russians remained in possession of the redoubts they had captured early that morning and succeeded in towing away the guns they contained – the guns that Raglan had hoped the Light Brigade could save. Liprandi had failed to capture Balaklava, but his occupation of the redoubts did at least deny the British the use of the Woronzov Road. Russell of *The Times*, and many writers since, have pointed to the Russians' control of this, the only metalled road from Balaklava to the Upland, as the cause of much of the army's sufferings in the coming winter. In fact the road was only reachable from Balaklava over a very poor track, and in any case the Russians abandoned the redoubts in December, leaving the situation exactly as it had been if the battle of Balaklava had never been fought.

The Light Brigade's action and that of their comrades, the Heavies, was to give the Russians an exaggerated respect for British cavalry for the remainder of the campaign. Some of the prisoners from the Light Brigade were taken before General Liprandi. Among them was Paget's orderly, the formidable Sam Parkes: 'If you're a Light Dragoon,' Liprandi asked him, 'what sort of men are your Heavy Dragoons?'

He assumed that the men had been drunk, and took some convincing that they were not. 'By God, General,' an Irishman said to him, 'if we'd had anything to drink we should have had half Russia by this time.'

At which Liprandi laughed and said, 'Well, my man, if they were all like you, I believe you would!'

The Light Brigade had contributed something, too, to the British army's – and the British nation's – self-belief. Within weeks Tennyson would immortalise them in a poem which ensured that their action would become the world's abiding memory of the Crimean War, and the most famous cavalry action in history. The Light Brigade's iron discipline under fire, and the fact that they had, incredibly, captured an artillery battery by frontal attack and overthrown a superior cavalry force drawn up behind it, had confirmed the reputation already gained by those thin red lines at the Alma, by the Heavies' uphill charge against superior numbers, and the 93rd's stand before Kadikoi. Whatever the blunders of the higher commanders, it was now believed, the officers and men would carry the day.

Let the last word – and a final qualification – go to Lieutenant Edward Seager of the 8th Hussars, in his letter to his wife: 'British soldiers, if ordered, ride up to the cannon's mouth, but it is a shame to sacrifice such men.'

CHAPTER SIX

On the morning after the Battle of Balaklava, John Hume and his brother went down to the plain to examine the battlefield. In the afternoon they returned to their camp – the 2nd Division's camp – on the heights. Not being on duty, they took themselves onto the breastwork on the ridge above the camp to look down at the besieged city.

'Some of us were looking at Sebastopol from the stone breastwork near our camp, when we heard heavy firing from our picquets. Soon after we saw some Russian artillery come galloping over the crest of the height near Shell Hill, followed by columns of infantry. "Green guns, by Jove!" said Daubeney; and off we ran as hard as we could to camp.'

Colonel Daubeney, 55th Regiment, was right: the pea-green painting of the guns and limbers proclaimed them to be Russian.

'We found the division turning out,' continued Hume, 'and in a very short time we were ready for any amount of Russians.'

It was just as well, for coming at them was Colonel Federoff, out of the Sebastopol garrison, with six battalions, about 4,300 men, and four guns. On his right, coming up out of a great ravine – the Careenage Ravine – which led up from the city, another column protected his right flank. Just when it might have been assumed that the Russians had had enough, here they were, coming back for more.

The ground over which this action was about to be fought, on the right of the Allied siege lines, was to have a great bearing on the events of the next eleven days, and of the campaign as a whole. It had no name, but was known by the allies as Mount Inkerman. It was at the extreme right of the British siege lines, on the heights above the Tchernaya Valley. These heights, and the steep slopes running down to the valley were (and still are) thickly covered with scrub. The undulating ground here is dominated by two features: Shell Hill (also known as Cossack Hill and also, as it was the most forward of the British positions, Funk Point), almost in the centre of the heights, and the slightly higher Home Ridge further south, behind which lay the 2nd Division camp, and down which the Hume brothers ran.

Forward of Home Ridge was a lower ridge known as Fore Ridge.*

Two great ravines scar the Upland here: the Careenage Ravine, which drops down into Sebastopol, and the Quarry Ravine, which drops down into the Tchernaya Valley. Both these ravines offered the Russians covered approaches up onto the Upland. Up the Quarry Ravine ran the Post Road, which, coming from the Crimean interior in the north, crossed the marshes at the head of the harbour by means of a causeway, and then wound up the heights towards Home Ridge. Another road ran up out of Sebastopol itself via the Careenage Ravine, crossed that ravine and brought the traveller ascending from the city to a point slightly to the east of the Light Division camp. Once up on the heights, the plateau – between the Careenage Ravine on one side, and the steep slopes leading down to the plain over which the battle of Balaklava had been fought – was about fourteen hundred yards across.

The defence of this ground, vital to the security of the Allies' right flank, was entrusted to the 2nd Division, which had been the right-hand Division of the assault line at Alma. These were the men who, under their commander de Lacy Evans, had been split by the burning village of Bourliouk. Men of the left-hand brigade, the 95th Derbies, had swung left and assaulted the Great Redoubt. Others of the 55th, the Westmoreland Reaping Hooks (nicknamed after the shape of the numbers in their title), including Captain John Hume and his brother, had attached themselves to Colonel Lacy Yea's Fusiliers. The bulk of this division, including the 30th and the Fiery Forties – the 41st, 47th and 49th Regiments – had battled their bloody way towards the Causeway Battery on the main road to Sebastopol. They had distinguished themselves at the Alma and paid the price in casualties.

Now, understrength but their morale firm, their day-to-day business was to defend the British right flank. While the 3rd and 4th

* See Map 5.

Divisions and half of the Light Division manned the trenches in front of Sebastopol, it was the task of the remainder – the 2nd Division, the other half of the Light Division, the Guards, and the Highlanders down at Balaklava – to maintain a chain of outposts to guard the army's vulnerable flank and their lines of communication to Balaklava.

To do this, the 2nd Division had established a chain of picquets – standing patrols, in modern parlance – as a forward line of defence. In the event of a Russian attack from Sebastopol or the Tchernaya Valley, these picquets would fall back on the division's main position on Home Ridge. If the attack proved too strong for the 2nd Division alone to hold it, they could expect French reinforcements from Bosquet's Corps of Observation, stretched out along the Sapoune, from the Guards a mile and a half to their rear, and from the other British divisions.

Despite the importance of the Mount Inkerman position to the British, little had been done to fortify it. Where the Post Road merges with another track coming from the bottom of the Quarry Ravine the British had erected a low earth bank called the Barrier. Over to the (British) right of the Barrier, on a spur known as the Kitspur, the British had erected a two-gun battery. This battery – also known as the Sandbag Battery – had been briefly occupied by two guns in response to a Russian gun which had been firing on British positions from across the Tchernaya. When the Russians had removed their gun, the British had removed theirs. The battery now stood deserted. Of no tactical value, it was used by the picquets on the British right as a rallying point and shelter. Apart from this, the position was largely unfortified. The British 2nd Division was fully occupied picqueting and patrolling this ground – other divisions were too busy in the trenches and batteries around the city. No one thought of using the 6,000 Turks: after Balaklava, no one trusted them even to dig.

This defensive plan was now to be tested. The first picquet engaged was Lieutenant John Connolly's of the 49th Regiment. Connolly spread his men out into skirmish order and opened fire on the advancing Russians. Soon Connolly and his men were engaged hand-to-hand with the Russians, and Connolly, having broken his sword killing one Russian, continued to lash about him with his telescope.

Eventually, as the ammunition ran low, Connolly and his men began to fall back on the main position.

To Connolly's right, at the Barrier, was Major Champion of the 95th (Derbyshire), whom we last saw in the Great Redoubt at the Alma. To support Connolly, Champion called together his 95th picquets and aligned them on either side of the Barrier. Soon they too were under attack.

'They masked their approach by attacking the 49th picquet in front of me by a few skirmishers, who retreated and drew off the 49th. I had taken up position to support the 49th, so was quite ready; but you may judge of my astonishment when I saw the guns and a large body of men dividing to turn my two flanks. Colonel Herbert, who had just left, had told me, in case of the 49th being driven in, to hold the position as long as possible.

'We met the enemy boldly, pitching into his artillery until it was sufficiently advanced to play upon us; then I retired the picquets behind the crest, and fought their foot soldiers until the artillery could be brought up, by which time all my picquets were concentrating towards me, and we made a general rush to the barrier of our main picquet.'

Colonel Herbert, in overall command of the picquets, was already sending requests back to de Lacy Evans, the divisional commander, for reinforcements, but got the dusty answer: 'Not a man!'

Having drawn his division up on Home Ridge, Evans intended to fight his battle there, not further forward. All he wanted the picquets to do was fall back – until they did so, they were masking his guns. On the ridge he had eighteen 9-pounders ready to fire which couldn't, for fear of hitting their own men.

Forward, at the Barrier, Champion was now hotly engaged by much greater numbers. 'We defended ourselves vigorously against the swarms of Russians now appearing everywhere except in our rear; and we stood with artillery and rifles until all our ammunition was at the last ebb. I knew that succour must come shortly, and sent to say how we were hard pressed. Then I told the men that supports were coming up to us, and I made them cheer and fix bayonets, which daunted the Russians, who had nearly driven us out by turning one flank. I tried to get up a charge, but it was too much for human nature, and the few men I had with me; but they advanced a little, firing a few shots, and the Russians fell back.'

Champion, known in the regiment as a deeply religious man, strode amongst his men in the thick of this fire-fight shouting, 'Slate 'em boys!' at the top of his voice. At length, frustrated at his picquets' refusal to fall back as they were supposed to do, Evans sent two companies forward. As they advanced, his 18 guns opened up on the Russian reserve columns on Shell Hill. Under this punishment the columns melted away and Federoff ordered a retreat.

Champion heard: 'The cheering sound of our guns crowning the hill behind us, and pouring showers of grape. The division all formed in battle order, came up, and the retreat of the Russians was an accomplished fact. They were forced back with very great loss, the light company driving them along to the very walls of Sebastopol.'

As the Russians withdrew, Federoff was wounded. The Russian columns began to degenerate into a mob and only the covering fire of Russian steamers in Sebastopol Harbour enabled them to make a clean break and stopped the retreat becoming a rout.

The flanking column which had shadowed Federoff's advance had no better luck. This 800-strong column was made up of sailors from the garrison, Russian sailors being routinely trained to fight on land. The ravine was guarded on the British side by a small picquet from the Guards under Captain Goodlake of the Coldstream. Goodlake was something of a dare-devil, and for some time had been carrying out a policy of aggressive patrolling against Russian outposts. A few days earlier he and his sergeant, Ashton, had raided a Russian picquet and taken an officer and several men prisoner. Hearing the fighting going on on the heights, Goodlake was on the alert for just such a surprise attack as the one that these Russian sailors were now attempting. With Sergeant Ashton he crept forward down the ravine, leaving his picquet of sixty men manning an improvised barricade round the corner higher up.

As the two men took shelter in a cave further down the ravine they suddenly found the column passing before them only feet away, heading uphill. Suddenly spotted, they were fired on at close range, but neither man was hit.

Ashton said to Goodlake, 'They would kill us over that picquet job.' Both men, realising that surrender was not an option, decided to sell their lives dearly. Goodlake and Ashton both fired into the column – it is interesting to note that Goodlake was carrying a rifle – and then dashed in amongst them, striking out with their rifle butts.

It should have been the end for both of them, but so thickly packed was the column and so similarly dressed were the Guardsmen – in their grey greatcoats and forage caps – to the men they were attacking that once they had penetrated into the midst of the column all fighting ceased and the two men were swept along in the column's headlong advance. No doubt the sailors were expecting the enemy to be redcoated, and clearly the men in the middle of the column had not seen the fracas at its edges.

Goodlake and Ashton now found themselves in the midst of a Russian column advancing against their own men. Turning the bend, the head of the column, confronted by Goodlake's men, halted. In the brief confusion that followed, Goodlake and Ashton were able to break free and rejoin their own side. A lengthy fire-fight followed.

It was vital that the sailors were prevented from reaching the top of the ravine, from which they could have fallen on the rear of Evans' guns, now punishing the Russians on Shell Hill. Despite the gallant attempts of their commander, the sailors could not be induced to run into the storm of Minié fire with which Goodlake and his men met every advance on their part. As the sounds of battle died away above, the sailors retreated sullenly back down to Sebastopol.

Up on the heights the 2nd Division had reason to be pleased with themselves. Evans' plan had worked, and the enemy sent packing for a loss of 12 killed and 72 wounded. What was not realised – or even considered – was that Russians had achieved something too: they had had a good look at the ground on Mount Inkerman, they had seen how weakly it was defended and, more importantly, they had seen how slow the Allies had been in bringing up reinforcements.

'The lesson read to us on the 26th of October,' wrote Captain Wilson of the Coldstream, 'left only a faint impress on official memories. The right flank of the Allied positions remained unguarded except by a few hundred bayonets of the 2nd Division ... The forewarned are not always fore-armed.'

Of course hindsight is a wonderful thing, and there were few indications that anything bigger was brewing, other than the arrival with the Russian armies of the Tsar's two sons: the Bear Cubs, Grand Dukes Michael and Nicholas. Besides, the Russians made elaborate diversions beyond the Tchernaya, seeming to threaten another attempt against Balaklava. Above all, the 2nd Division seemed to have shown itself perfectly capable of holding the Inkerman Heights on its own and without any further fortification.

John Hume wrote, 'no-one thought that the Russians, after their experience on the 26th of October, would attack again on the same ground.'

What the Allies had considered as just another sortie was merely a curtain raiser for something much bigger. Prince Menschikoff was under pressure from St Petersburg, where the Tsar was growing alarmed at the progress of the Allied trenches and the resumption of the bombardment. He feared that an assault on Sebastopol would not be long in coming – in fact, Raglan and Canrobert were preparing plans for such an assault, timed for 7 November. Knowing that French reinforcements were on the way – it is ironic that the Allies could reinforce their armies more quickly by sea than the Russians, fighting on home ground, could by land – the Tsar was now putting pressure on Menschikoff to take action that would either lift the siege altogether, or at least impose a delay on the Allies, until winter set in. The attempt on Balaklava had been Menschikoff's first attempt; the sortie onto Mount Inkerman the following day was the prelude to the second.

The plan Menschikoff came up with was based on that vulnerability of the Allied right flank, which had been a feature ever since the siege lines were established. If the Russians could establish themselves, with artillery batteries, on Mount Inkerman, the British siege batteries would find themselves under fire from behind. The British end of the Allied siege lines would thus become untenable and the Allies would be forced either to try and recapture the ground they had lost, or abandoned the siege altogether.

Either course would be costly; the latter, under the noses of the Sebastopol garrison and the Russian field army, could be catastrophic.

On 3 or 4 November, two divisions – the 10th and 11th – of Dannenburg's 4th Corps were due to arrive from Bessarabia. This would, for the first time in this campaign, give him superiority in numbers. Menschikoff's plan was for General Soimonoff, with 19,000 men and 38 guns, to issue out of Sebastopol, from the Karbalnaya suburb, cross the Careenage Ravine and ascend the heights to Shell Hill, while General Pauloff, with 16,000 men and 96 guns, was to cross the Tchernaya by the causeway and ascend from there. Once on the heights, the two forces were to rendezvous at Shell Hill (which Soimonoff would by now have captured) and unite under the command of General Dannenburg (who would march with Pauloff's contingent). The combined guns of both forces, in massed batteries on Shell Hill, would dominate the whole of the Mount Inkerman feature, enabling Dannenburg to drive the British off it. Measures were to be taken to prevent the British being reinforced, as they had been on 26 October.

In order to pin Bosquet's Corps and prevent him coming to the aid of the British, Liprandi's army, which had attacked Balaklava a few days earlier, was now, under Gortschakoff, to threaten Bosquet's position on the Sapoune.

Once the main attack had been successful they too would assault up the steep slopes onto the Upland. At the same time the guns of Sebastopol and the men-of-war in the harbour were to support Soimonoff on the Russian right flank, the Sebastopol garrison were to be ready to sally out if there was any sign of confusion in the Allied trenches, and a diversionary sortie was to be launched against the left of the French siege lines, near the sea.* If all went according to plan, the understrength British 2nd Division, denied reinforcements, would be confronted with 35,000 Russian troops attacking from two directions with overwhelming artillery support.

In essence, it was a sound plan, but it suffered from a number of flaws. It demanded a degree of co-ordination between units which, in the age before radio communications, would be near-impossible. The operation was to be carried out by troops, many of whom were unfamiliar with the ground and who, as they had been re-organised by Menschikoff, would be fighting under commanders they did not know.

The plan also called for a change of commander under fire in the middle of a battle, with all the potential for disaster that entailed. Nor was Dannenburg the kind of forceful commander needed at such a moment – he had already requested a 24-hour delay to the execution of the plan. Ostensibly this was to give his men time to rest after their long marches – and certainly his fresh troops were

* See Map 3.

not in the best of condition. In fact, Dannenburg was reluctant to send his men into action on the first anniversary of their defeat by the Turks at Oltenitza. On the night before the action he issued a set of marching orders to Soimonoff which completely altered the plan. Soimonoff ignored these, but the incident does betray Dannenburg's lack of confidence in the venture. Dannenburg's proposed alterations, sending Soimonoff up the west side of the Careenage Ravine, at least show that he was alive to one of the plan's other flaws: that a force of 35,000 men and 134 guns were to deploy on an area with barely room for half that number. Finally, there had been far too little time for adequate planning, reconnaissance or the issuing of orders.

Even so, given his superiority in numbers, especially in guns, and the advantage of surprise – always something of a speciality with the Russians – Menschikoff had grounds for optimism.

The battle of Inkerman – the sortie of 26 October is generally referred to as Little Inkerman – is more easily understood if it is viewed as two battles fought on either side of an imaginary line drawn from the centre of Home Ridge to the centre of Shell Hill. Although the fighting on each of the two halves of the battlefield (Left and Right, viewed from the British perspective, looking north) affected the other, the participants in either battle remained largely in ignorance of what was happening there. The nature of the ground and the poor visibility ensured that this was the 'soldier's battle' *par excellence*.

Dawn came at 6 a.m. on the morning of 5 November with a watery sun serving only to lighten the fog. A steady drizzle was falling. The picquets of the 2nd Division – four each of the 55th on the right and two each of the 41st and 47th on the left – moved out to relieve the night picquets. The most forward of these was on Shell Hill where, due to the bad weather, the officer in command had moved his men down to a more sheltered position at the base of the hill.

James Hume of the 55th was not with the 55th's picquets, but the whole party was commanded by his brother. Hume said, 'They had great difficulty in making out the positions of the old picquets, especially as that of Shell Hill, the most advanced of all, had been changed during the night, and retired from its forward position, on the crest of the hill, to some distance below and behind it on our side, which was unfortunate in its results, for it seems impossible that the preparations of the enemy for their attack could have been unnoticed had the picquet remained in its old position. The officer in command of the old picquet, having reported to the officer commanding the reliefs that all was quiet in front, began to retire his men in the usual manner.'

In fact, said Hume, there had been some intimations of unusual activity. 'Sergeant-Major Francis Williams, of the 55th ... who had gone out at midnight amongst and beyond the outlying picquets, heard unusual noises and movements in the direction of Sebastopol, and was quite certain that he heard the rumbling of heavy wagons or artillery, either caused by supplies entering the city or by guns coming out towards the Inkerman valley. Thinking it might be the latter, he made a report to the officer commanding the headquarter picquet. He, not thinking there was anything unusual going on, did not take much notice of the report.'

Sergeant-Major Williams was not the only man to hear noises. Private Bloomfield of the 95th Derbyshire, last seen advancing up the heights of Alma, had been on the night picquet at the Barrier.

'All went well until about 12 p.m., when some of our sentries reported wheels and noise like the unloading of shot and shell, but the Field officer on duty took no further notice of it. All the night from about 9 o'clock in the evening the bells were ringing and the bands were playing and a great noise was all over the town.'

So did Bloomfield's commander, Lieutenant Carmichael of the 95th, who was trying to sleep huddled in his cloak on the wet ground while the picquet Field Commander Major Grant took a turn on watch.

'I remember hearing the clang of the church bells in the town, and the rumble of wheels in the valley, but the latter noise raised no suspicions in my mind, as it was a nightly occurrence, and had been reported previously, and it was well known to all that enemy used the road during the night.'

In fact what Lieutenant Carmichael and Private Bloomfield were hearing were not the wheels of supply wagons, but the guns and limbers of Pauloff's artillery moving up to attack their position.

Bloomfield continued, 'This night there was a great fog, so much that we could not see a man 10 yards away from us, and nearly all the night there was a great drizzly rain falling, so by the morning we were all very wet and so cold that we could not handle our arms properly. We stood to our arms an hour before daybreak, and remained so until the day was breaking. We then got ready to go home as the new picquet had arrived.'

Such was the condition of the men that Carmichael and his command were dismissed early: 'On the morning of the 5th November (Sunday) the new picquets under Colonel Carpenter 41st Regt came down to the Barrier to relieve us at the usual time, an hour before daylight, and were drawn up on the road behind the picquet wall – after waiting, perhaps a little less than the usual hour Col. Carpenter told Major Grant that he would not keep the old picquets any longer, and that if the enemy attacked that morning he was ready to receive them – He was killed, I was told subsequently, a little later in the morning, almost on the spot where he then stood just by the "Barrier". His picquets then moved off to relieve the old ones, mine being the nearest, and smallest in number, were the first collected, and as we had been exposed to the wet all night and it was still raining and foggy, Grant told me to take my men back to camp at once, without waiting for those on the right to come in, which was customary. On my return to camp, I found that the 2nd Division, which was always under arms for an hour before daylight had been dismissed and the wood and water parties had been sent out.'

Grateful to be off duty at last, Carmichael went into his tent where his servant, Thomas Smith, brought him a hot cup of ship's cocoa. To all appearances, yet another Sunday of dreary camp routine was starting.

Out on the left, at Shell Hill, also known as Cossack Hill, the new picquet – composed of the Grenadier company of the 41st Foot (The Welch Regiment) commanded by Captain Hugh Rowlands – were taking up their positions.

'On the morning of the 5th, Rowlands wrote later, 'I and the company were for outlying picquet. Colonel Haly of the 47th was Field Officer of the day and he gave me my choice. I selected Cossack Hill (alias Funk Point). When I passed through the night picquet you cannot imagine a more cheerless aspect. Day had scarcely commenced breaking in the East, and a damp cold mist clung to the ground, making objects indistinct or rather imperceptible at a few yards distance. On arriving at Cossack Hill, I halted the company about half way up and went out to plant sentries 150 yards over the hill. Having done so, I returned to the company which had just piled arms and ordered the men to take off packs, when the sentries commenced firing in a most determined way.

'I ran up to enquire the cause when one shouted out that there were columns of Russians close to them. I stood to my arms and advanced in extended order, thinking it was a sortie something like that of the 26th. On getting to the top of the hill I found myself close upon, very truly, thousands of Russians.'

Soimonoff had arrived on the heights, and was launching his attack on Shell Hill. Throwing out 300 riflemen as skirmishers, he advanced with 6,000 men in his first line – packed into the usual columns of attack – with a further 3,300 in reserve. Behind them came his 22 heavy guns, followed by a further 9,000 infantry.

Rowlands said he '... immediately gave an order to retire, which was done for about 200 yards, when I halted on the next bit of high ground and lay down quietly waiting for them. Fitzroy who was in support of me then came up with the Light Company. His men I likewise extended to reinforce my own.

'When we retired the Russians came on with the most fiendish yells you can imagine. We commenced firing. To my dismay I found that half the firelocks missed fire, which dispirited the men. At this period the Russian columns opened with their field pieces, pouring in grape and shell.'

The reason for the British rifles misfiring was the constant drizzle, which soaked the charges. The only remedy was the repeated firing off of percussion caps. This affected most British units engaged on this day and served, for a time, to neutralise the advantage conferred by the Minié rifle.

In the 2nd Division camp the sound of firing had not at first occasioned any alarm – nervous sentries often fired at suspicious sights or sounds, or even the occasional Russian patrol. Lieutenant Carmichael and his servant were just dismissing the noise as another such incident when the firing became heavier and extended along the front.

'I then came out of the tent, being still accoutred, with the intention of falling in my recently dismissed picquet, and proceeding with it to reinforce the outposts, but the order was given at once for the whole regiment to stand to their arms by Major Champion ... and for the tents to be struck, and my duty was then of course to fall in with my own Corps. The men fell in quickly, on their usual parade ground, already under fire of shot and shell, and the tents were struck by the men detailed for that duty – there was of course a good deal of hurry and confusion. A number of loose baggage animals frightened by the firing came galloping through and in front of the camp, and the men who had been away on different duties came running in to join the ranks.'

Another man who had just come off duty was Private Edward Hyde of the 49th. 'As soon as belts came off in the morning, we were all busy lighting fires, where possible, and getting breakfast ... I had been lighting a fire to make some water hot in a three-legged iron pot, which had been brought up from Balaklava. The weather was raw, cold, and terribly foggy, so that we could not see three yards before us. As usual, we stood to arms about half-past five to unbelt and dismiss, when suddenly the bells of Sebastopol began to peal merrily. I should think all the bells they had were ringing, and, before the order was given to dismiss, grape and canister began to fall all around us.'

Within seconds the night picquets who had shrugged off their equipment, water and wood-gathering and fatigue parties were falling in in their companies – under heavy artillery fire now – and being rushed forward to reinforce the picquet line.

At the picquet line, Captain Rowlands was still falling back, heavily engaged with Soimonoff's oncoming columns. 'We then got some reinforcements from the 55th and the 30th but were gradually obliged to retire. I begged and entreated Colonel Haly to allow me to charge, which he did. After a little hand-to-hand work we turned them and drove them back about 500 yards, when we were met by a fresh column and compelled to retire.'

During this hand-to-hand work which Rowlands mentions so laconically Colonel Haly was wounded, dragged from his horse and set upon by a group of Russian infantrymen. Rowlands and a private soldier from the 47th dashed in among them, rescued the colonel and fought their way out. Rowlands was wounded in the arm and evacuated from the field. For this action, both Rowlands and the private who assisted him would eventually be awarded a new decoration, which was now only in the planning stage.

For ever after Rowlands was known in his regiment as 'the man who started the battle of Inkerman'.

*

A few days after Little Inkerman, de Lacy Evans had been injured by a fall from his horse, and command of the division had passed to General Pennefather. Although at this stage the Russian offensive looked like a repeat of Federoff's attack of 26 October, Pennefather intended to fight a very different battle from Evans'. Instead of allowing the picquets to fall back, and basing his defence on Home Ridge, Pennefather intended to fight as far forward as possible – using his picquets to contest every inch of ground – until reinforcements could arrive. To this end he continued to feed the picquets, sending men forward to thicken the skirmishing line.

It was a high-risk strategy: if the Russians broke through his forward line there was little or nothing to stop them overrunning the entire Inkerman position. Pennefather's hope was that the thick brushwood and the thick fog would conceal his lack of numbers from the enemy.

At the Alma, most British officers had not realised the tactical implications of their main infantry weapon. Now the broken nature of the ground effectively forced the correct tactics upon them. Over much of the battlefield this was virtually bush fighting – it was impossible to maintain lines, or march shoulder-to-shoulder. Loose skirmish lines were the only tactics possible. Though these conditions affected both sides equally, they favoured the British.

Once it was working properly, the Minié rifle once again gave the British the advantage in fire-fights; in the poor visibility at Inkerman its much greater range may have been nullified, but at closer ranges it was still much the more accurate weapon. At the Battle of Vittoria in 1813 the Brown Bess musket – similar to the weapon the Russians were still using in 1854 – inflicted a casualty with one round out of 459; at the Alma the Minié took effect with one round out of 16.

The fighting on the British right had not gone unnoticed elsewhere in the camps of the other divisions. Three-quarters of a mile to the rear of the 2nd Division camp was that of the Guards.

Here, Captain Wilson of the Coldstream had been hoping to enjoy a Sunday morning lie-in. 'On the morning in question, the tent of which I owned a sixth part was occupied by only two officers beside myself, the rest of our tenants being on picquet in Canrobert's redoubt. All at once we three were aroused by the bellowing of artillery; we thought nothing of it – "It's only a little fire in the front." With a yawn and a stretch we again disposed ourselves to sleep; but just as our eye-lids dropped, the twittering of Miniés fell upon the ear – "Hang it, the sentries at their old game, blazing at Will o' the Wisp." Sleep no more; every moment the cannon spoke louder and louder – every moment the rifles cracked sharper and sharper. There could no mistake as to something being in the wind, so we arose, and commenced to pull on boots and begird ourselves with swords and revolvers, in order to be prepared for a "fall in" nor did the summons tarry. As cloak and hairy cap were huddled on, cries, hoarse and hurried, electrified the camp, "STAND TO YOUR ARMS! STAND TO YOUR ARMS!"'

In a nearby tent was Captain Tower with three brother officers. 'We hurried on our arms, as we always slept in our clothes, and found the Battalion falling in. Vesey Dawson was in command, on a chestnut horse; Granville Eliot, Adjutant, on his old grey Arab, Bashi-Bazouk. It rained a great deal during the night, and that memorable Sunday morning dawned a nasty damp foggy day; the mist was rising from the ground and the brushwood was quite wet; we could only see a few yards before us, but we could hear the pattering of musketry, and the firing had been going on fully half an hour before we came on the scene of action. We left the camp in column of fours, but before we got to the Second Division tents one or two round shot came right through our ranks, and we began to have an idea how close the enemy was, and of the serious nature of the business.'

In the Light Division camp men were also buckling on their equipment and setting out for the fight. Sergeant Timothy Gowing of the 7th Fusiliers wrote, 'The ever-memorable battle was raging on our right rear, and (by the shouts of the combatants and the tremendous firing) we knew that something very serious was going on; so as many of us as the General could spare were ordered to march as fast as our legs could carry us to the assistance of our comrades, then at the dreadful fight raging at Inkerman. As we had just drubbed the enemy terribly, our blood was up; but we were hungry – many of us had had nothing to eat for twenty-four hours – and were wet through to the skin. They say an Englishman will not fight unless his belly is full; that's all bosh – let him once be roused, and you will see whether he will or not.'

The Light Division's route took them up via the windmill on the Post Road, a mile in the rear of Home Ridge. Awaiting orders, Lieutenant George Lidwill of the 19th, last seen picking up a Russian Hussar dolman on the road to Sebastopol, saw: 'A scene such as I shall ever remember. From all directions, battalions and detachments were hurrying by the shortest routes towards the Windmill. The excitement and energy of the army on its march to Inkerman was surprising. Guns and tumbrils at a canter passed along the road where I stood. As far as I could see, across the open plains were batteries upon batteries speeding on the same errand.'

It says much for the spirit of this army – wet, cold, half-starved, ravaged by disease and having been subjected to a baptism of fire at the Alma that would have broken many – that the first instinct of its men at this moment of crisis was to grab their weapons and equipment and rush, often without waiting for orders, towards the sound of fighting.

By now this was the situation on Mount Inkerman: Pennefather's 2nd Division were now stood to arms on Home Ridge which, like their camp just behind it, was under a heavy bombardment from the 38 guns on Shell Hill. General Pennefather continued his policy of feeding troops forward in penny packets to thicken up his picquet line. The 95th were deployed forward of Home Ridge. Wishing to reinforce the Barrier, Pennefather sent forward the left wing of the regiment under Major Hume.

Before they went, Lieutenant Carmichael, with the right wing, saw them acquire a new – or rather, old – recruit. 'Just previous to the advance of the Left Wing, an old soldier of the Ambulance Corps, and wearing their uniform came up and asked permission of Brown to fall in with his Company. His bearing was very plucky and good, he said he had served in the Sikh wars, and would show us how they used to fight in India – a rifle was given to him, and he advanced with the left wing. I heard after the battle that he was wounded a few minutes later.'

The result of Pennefather's policy of splitting battalions was that before long, with the exception of a small remnant of the 55th and some companies of the 47th, his entire division was fighting forward, in small bodies, separated from each other or any possibility of control from Headquarters by thick fog and swirling smoke. They were supported by just two British field batteries, Pennycuik's and

Turner's, to the right and left of the Post Road. This was a battle fought, for the most part, in thick fog, with visibility at times no more than ten feet – the two batteries were firing at where they knew the Russian guns to be.

Lieutenant Carmichael, now at the head of his – the 3rd – company of the 95th, to the rear of these guns, watched as the gunners fired. 'I should judge, at the flashes of the enemy's guns on Shell Hill, and drew soon a heavy fire on themselves in return – some of these men fell, and we also suffered, although we had been ordered to lie down to obtain what shelter we could from the ridge. One round shot, I remember, tore into my company severing the left arm and both legs of a man in the front rank and killed the rear rank man without any perceptible wound. Other casualties were also occurring in other companies, as when I called to some bandsmen to carry the poor fellow who had been so mutilated away . . . they were as I saw, and they said, too busy with other wounded, and could not attend to this one . . . The guns . . . came into action short-handed and were firing as fast as they could load, and each successive discharge and recoil brought them closer to our line . . . we assisted the gunners to run the guns into their first position, and some men also aided in carrying ammunition.'

Although the guns were virtually firing blind, the important thing at this stage was to show a front to slow the onrush of Soimon-off's men. This they achieved, but at a heavy cost to themselves, although it was clear that they must soon be overpowered by the weight of fire coming from Shell Hill.

At 7 a.m., Lord Raglan and his staff, Somerset Calthorpe among them, arrived at the 2nd Division camp, into which Soimonoff's artillery on Shell Hill was pouring a destructive fire.

'Already the cannon-balls came tearing through the camp of the 2nd Division by dozens at a time,' Calthorpe wrote. 'Tents were every moment being knocked over by shot, or blown to pieces by exploding shell. I saw several baggage-horses tethered in a line, killed by one shot, which passed through them. The scene of con-fusion which the camp exhibited was frightful. Many bodies were lying about of men who had never even seen the enemy – possibly were hardly aware of their vicinity. The first one I observed was that of an officer lying flat on his back, with a cloak covering his face. I asked a servant who was near, and he told me it was Captain

Allix (aide-de-camp to Sir de Lacy Evans) who had been killed by one of the earliest round shots from the enemy. I had been talking to him the night before.'

Having discussed his conduct of the battle with General Penne-father, His Lordship saw no reason to intervene further except in one point. This – similar in nature to his sole intervention at the Alma – was to prove decisive. Seeing that the weight of Russian artillery on Shell Hill was proving critical, Lord Raglan gave orders for two 18-pounder guns belonging to the siege train to be brought up to redress the balance. After an initial error in transmitting the order, it was conveyed to Colonel Gambier down at the Siege Park. Gambier had no draught horses, but assembling 150 men and bring-ing out man-harness he and whatever officers he could muster began the painful task of dragging the guns up towards Home Ridge. The big guns were on their way – it was now a question of whether the 2nd Division's picquets and whatever reinforcements they received could hold on till they arrived.

Perhaps Soimonoff intended to act alone without waiting for Pauloff's men, or maybe he was sucked into the battle like a man with his sleeve caught in machinery. His decision to act alone, while Pauloff's men, and his commander, Dannenburg, were still toiling up the steep slopes from the Tchernaya Valley, might have been provoked by the action of a party of the 49th under their com-mander, Major Thornton Grant. A battalion of Soimonoff's men, probing the British left via the Mikriakoff Glen, suddenly con-fronted Grant and his two hundred or so men. The surprise as these two forces – hitherto hidden from each other by thick mist – appeared to each other only yards apart must have been mutual, but Grant was the first to act, crying, 'Give them a volley and charge!'

Grant's men delivered their volley, lowered their bayonets to the charge and ran at the Russians cheering wildly. The speed and shock-effect of their reaction unnerved the Russians, who fell back in some disorder almost to the foot of Shell Hill. Almost immediately, Grant's party were pushed back by a strong Russian counter-attack. They fell back slowly, bringing with them a number of prisoners. Their rifles, which had initially suffered from the damp like all those of the 2nd Division, were now working perfectly and inflicting casualties every step of the way. Even so, the situation was critical;

this attempted right hook by Soimonoff could punch into the left rear of the 2nd Division's position, behind Shell Hill.

At this very moment over to the east, the British were just beginning to discover that this was no mere repeat of 26 October, and that Soimonoff's columns were not all they had to contend with. The lead columns of Pauloff's force were emerging out of the mist before the Barrier. The British position on Inkerman, it was now clear, was under attack from a giant pincer.

The immediate threat – and the only one those on the British left half of the battlefield were even aware of – was from Soimonoff's columns. Pennefather's position was in grave danger, with Soimonoff's infantry driving on from the front and working their way round his flank.

The arrival of the first men of the Light Division – four companies of the 88th Connaught Rangers – could not have been more timely. The Irishmen, turned out in a hurry and packed off towards the fight before they had even been able to fill their cartridge pouches, appeared at the head of the Mikriakoff Glen and almost collided with a large Russian column. After firing a volley, the Russians charged in such strength that the Rangers' line – already disordered by the thick brushwood – was split in two. The right half – the Grenadier and No. 5 Companies – were driven back one hundred and fifty yards before they could rally. The left – the Light and 7th Companies – after firing a volley, drove the Russians facing them back uphill to a position almost level with Shell Hill. The retreating Russians took shelter behind a high wall, beyond which were Soimonoff's remaining nine battalions.

Sixteen of the more enthusiastic Rangers vaulted over this wall in pursuit – their bayoneted bodies were found the next day, the furthest advanced of the British dead.

The remainder of the Rangers fell back. As they did so, Captain Crosse found himself alone. Captain Steevens, who had the story from Crosse that evening, described what followed.

'When the Light company and No. 7 retired, he found himself surrounded by a knot of Russians, who advanced to attack him; having just taken out his revolver, to save one of the men (Lance-Corporal M'Donough, No. 7 company), he was luckily ready for this sudden onslaught, and shot four of the enemy; a fifth bayoneted Captain C. in the leg, and fell over him, bending the bayonet in the wound, and at the same time pulling Captain C. on top of him; a sixth then charged him, but, with his sword, he was enabled to cut along the Russian's firelock onto his hands, compelling him to turn back. Captain C. at once got up and made off, but was again attacked by the Russian whom he had just encountered, and again drove him back; he then fell in with his colour-sergeant (Cooney), Privates Samuel Price and John Gascoigne, and Pat Daly of the grenadier company and another man who had come to look for Captain C.; as there was no officer with the company, Sergeant Cooney was sent to rejoin, but Privates Price, Gascoigne, and Daly retired with Captain C., and defended him against the continued attacks of Russians; they then met some bandsmen of the 49th Regiment with a stretcher, who carried Captain C. to the camp, the three privates of the 88th, rejoining their companies.'

The right half of the Connaughts, who had been forced back, had now been joined by three guns of Townshend's battery under Lieutenant Miller RA. Now, without limbers, they were overrun by that portion of the Russian column which had continued its advance. Miller's men fought round their guns with swords, rammers, sponge-staves and even their bare hands – one man described as a Clitheroe bruiser felled Russian after Russian with his fists – but in the end, they were driven off, and the guns remained in Russian hands.

The Rangers had administered a check to part of Soimonoff's right hook, but the bulk of his columns rolled on towards Home Ridge. Just as his right-hand column, which had come up the Careenage Ravine, was about to fall on the left rear of the 2nd Division's camp, however, out of the mist came more Light Division reinforcements: General Buller and four companies of the 77th, under their commander, Colonel Thomas Egerton.

With Buller, as ever, was Henry Clifford. 'On reaching the left brow of the hill, I saw the enemy in great numbers in our front, and about 15 yards from us; it was a moment or two before I could make General Buller believe that they were Russians. "In God's name," I said, "fix bayonets and charge." He gave the order and in another moment we were hand to hand with them.'

As Egerton's men drove the Russians before them, Clifford noticed that the left of the 77th's line was overlapped by another part of the Russian column, previously unnoticed in the fog.

'Our line was not long enough to prevent the Russians outflanking our left, which was unperceived by the 77th, who rushed on, with the exception of about a dozen, who, struck by the force on our left and who saw me taking out my revolver, halted with me. Come on," I said, "my lads!" and the brave fellows dashed in amongst the astonished Russians, bayoneting them in every direction. One of the bullets in my revolver had partly come out and prevented it revolving and I could not get it off. The Russians fired their pieces off within a few yards of my head, but none touched me. I drew my sword and cut off one man's arm who was in the act of bayoneting me and a second seeing it, turned round and was in the act of running out of my way, when I hit him over the back of the neck and laid him dead at my feet. About 15 of them threw down their arms and gave themselves up and the remainder ran back and fell into the hands of the 77th returning from the splendid charge they had made and were killed or taken prisoners.'

Again the shock effect of a small body of determined men charging out of the fog had checked a much larger force and thrown them back in confusion. This fighting on the British left flank at the start of the day typifies the fighting right across the battlefield of Inkerman: Russian columns would emerge onto the heights, appear out of the fog and be driven back by small groups of British infantry by a combination of Minié fire and bayonet charges. The Russian columns would rally and counter-attack, or else a new column would appear and drive the British back. British reinforcements would arrive – often in company strength or less, often from a different regiment – and drive back these newcomers, only to be pushed back in their turn. Almost superhuman courage would be shown by both sides; there was little or no scope for generalship.

As Captain Wilson of the Coldstream Guards, now hurrying up to reinforce the British right, put it, 'One might as well attempt to describe the manoeuvres of a faction fight in Tipperary, as to narrate the details of this death struggle.'

The force that Egerton's 77th had charged was the head of a column that had come up the Careenage Ravine. The main body of this column now found itself stalled in the ravine as its lead elements fell back. To complete their confusion, they now came under a vicious flanking fire from an outlying picquet of the Guards under Prince Edward of Saxe-Weimar. Choosing his ground with care, he had deployed his men in skirmishing order and held their fire until he saw the head of the column giving way before Clifford's charge. As they did so, the Guardsmen poured a punishing fire into the column massed in the ravine below. In a few moments the Russians began to fall back down the ravine, Prince Edward and his Guardsmen pursuing them with fire all the way.

At the extreme right of Soimonoff's right hook, one of his battalion columns was stopped in its tracks by a small band of the 47th under Major Fordyce of that regiment, in a classic line-versus-column battle, isolated by the fog from all the other combats going on around it. Fordyce pursued the retreating Russians almost to the foot of Shell Hill. To Fordyce's right now appeared Egerton's men of the 77th, Brigadier Buller at their head, with Henry Clifford at his side. Almost immediately they were confronted by two more Russian columns pushing forward from the foot of Shell Hill. As usual, the Russian column halted, the men looking about them with an air of men waiting for instructions.

Turning to Buller who rode beside him, Egerton asked: 'There are the Russians, General, what shall we do?'

Buller replied: 'Charge them!'

The 77th's line overlapped the more numerous enemy on both sides. After a volley the 77th swept forward, bayoneting, butt-stroking and clubbing the Russians, driving this column almost to the foot of Shell Hill as well. It was noticed here that a number of Russians who 'fell' during the initial charge rose up again after the British passed over them. These men – nicknamed resurrection men by the British – showed no inclination to fight, and were too numerous to be made prisoner. By tacit agreement they were allowed to slip back to their own lines unmolested by the returning British.

Observing this repulse, and the jubilant redcoats hunting their comrades through the brushwood, those battalions of Soimonoff's force who had earlier driven back a wing of the Connaughts and captured Miller's three guns, now fell back to Shell Hill. Unable to drag away the captured guns, they abandoned them.

If Soimonoff's infantry were everywhere falling back now, his guns on Shell Hill were still dominating the battlefield, blasting out roundshot, grape and canister as fast as his gunners could sponge, ram and load.

Charging with the 77th, General Buller was hit. Henry Clifford was with him. 'Shortly after the cannon opened on us, General

Buller's horse was struck with round shot in the chest. I rode off to Camp and got his other horse, which he mounted under a tremendous fire of shell, cannon and grape shot; he was hardly in the saddle when I saw a cannon ball strike some yards in front of him. I called out, but he could not see it and fortunately did not move, for the cannon ball struck his horse in the chest, a little higher up than the first, and remained in the poor animal's side, giving the General a severe contusion upon the left knee.

'Glyn put the poor animals out of their misery, and I got the General on my horse and took him off the field, and when I had given him over to the care of his servant, seeing he was not much hurt, returned to the fight and put myself under the orders of General Pennefather.'

Buller wasn't the only general hit in that sector of the battlefield. It had been observed by the British that Russian officers were mostly unmounted. This inability to get round the battlefield swiftly may account for the command and control problems that gave the Russian columns a lack of dash – hesitation at crucial moments that many observed that day, but no one ascribed to lack of courage.

There had been one mounted officer, on a dark-coloured charger, who had been seen urging on his men as the 77th charged. As the Russian column withdrew back up Shell Hill this officer – who had been a target for the 77th's marksmen during the fight – was seen to fall, or dismount hurriedly, from his horse.

It is not known whether this was Soimonoff himself; what *is* known it that it was at about this time that Soimonoff was mortally wounded. Whatever one thinks about Soimonoff's decision to push on with his attack without waiting for the arrival of Pauloff's columns, there can be no doubting his courage and his inspirational leadership on the ground.

With his death the spirit went out of the Russian right pincer. The last of his front-line battalions fell back gravely mauled by British artillery fire, and his reserve battalions waited to link up with Pauloff. The battle for the British left was over.

As the last of Soimonoff's front-line columns were falling back, to play no further part in the battle, the threat shifted to the British centre and right. Pauloff's columns were starting to appear. The first eight battalions of this force, emerging from the Quarry Ravine, picked up one of Soimonoff's stray battalions and now fell on the

British right. This extended from the Barrier on the Post Road to the Sandbag Battery out on the extreme right. The Barrier was held by one wing – about 200 men – of the 30th Foot under Colonel Mauleverer. Seeing the enemy columns approaching, the men of the 30th opened fire, only to discover that their rifles, like those of many of the picquets, misfired. Mauleverer, a strong athletic man – one of his Mess-night tricks was to vault over a billiard table – leapt over the Barrier, followed by his Adjutant, and led his men in a downhill bayonet charge which pushed the lead Russian battalions back on their supports, disordering them both, and finally sweeping them from the field – some back to Shell Hill, some back down the Quarry Ravine.

Out on the right, Pauloff's first onset met with more success. The Sandbag Battery was held by a small picquet of the 55th under Lieutenant Barnston.

John Hume of that Regiment described what happened.

'He did not occupy the battery, but a small hill a few paces from it overlooking it, sending six of his men to the end of a spur on the left front of the battery. After he had been in his position about twenty minutes he heard firing in his front and, being anxious for the safety of his six men, ran down to look after them. To his dismay he found that they had been forced to retire by superior numbers, and the Russians were looting things they had left behind them. He retired at once to the rest of his men, and, charging down upon the enemy, drove them off for the moment; then, seeing that he was greatly outnumbered, he retired his party slowly, keeping up a heavy fire until he joined the main body of the picquet. It was during this retreat, and while cheering on his men, he saw a Russian officer on a pony leading his men most gallantly. Lieut. Branston pointed him out to Private Bell, 55th Regiment, who knocked him over with the first shot.'

The 55th picquet fell back, leaving a Russian battalion in possession of the Sandbag Battery. Believing that they had secured a real foothold on the heights, the Russians were exultant. For the rest of the day – despite its having almost no tactical significance – the Sandbag Battery was to become a magnet for fresh troops arriving from all three armies in the battle. This was merely the opening round of a bloody struggle which would see the Battery change hands time after time for the rest of the day.

*

Round Two was about to begin. Brigadier Adams planned a counter-attack with the 525 men of the 41st Regiment. Approaching from Fore Ridge, the regiment opened fire on the 4,000 or so Russians before them. Attacked in front by a line that they, like many Russians that day, assumed to be the head of a huge British column, the Russians fell back. Adams' men pursued the Russians and regained the Sandbag Battery, but they resisted the temptation to follow the Russians downhill, halting at the edge of the Heights. Moments after this attack, Adams was wounded in the foot and carried from the field. He later died of this wound, one of many men in this battle to die of apparently minor injuries.

It was now 7.30, and although it must have appeared to the British that the battle was won, the worst was yet to come. All of Pauloff's battalions were now deployed on Mount Inkerman, his guns had joined Soimonoff's on Shell Hill and with those, plus Soimonoff's reserve battalions, Dannenburg, the new commander, now had a total of 19,000 men and 90 guns. The bulk of these, 10,000 or so, were massed in or around the Quarry Ravine and, as the Russian guns on Shell Hill began to switch fire onto the British centre and right, these began their advance.

They fell first on Adams' men of the 49th and 41st Regiments at the Sandbag Battery. Five Russian battalions, numbering about 4,000 men, advanced on Adams' 700. These Russian battalions, who had come with Dannenburg from the Danube, were made of sterner stuff than Soimonoff's columns, many of whom had already had a taste of the Minié at the Alma. This time, although the British skirmishing fire took its toll, the columns rolled relentlessly on.

Private Edward Hyde of the 49th was in the battery with Adams. 'The Russian infantry got right up to it, and clambered up the front and sides of it, and we had a hard job to keep them out. Directly we saw their heads above the parapet, or looking into the embrasures, we fired at them or bayoneted them as fast as we could. They came on like ants; no sooner was one knocked backwards than another clambered over the dead bodies to take his place, all of them yelling and shouting. We in the battery were not quiet, you may be sure, and what with cheering and shouting, the thud of blows, the clash of bayonets and swords, the ping of the bullets, the whistling of the shells, the foggy atmosphere, and the smell of the powder and blood, the scene inside the battery where we were was beyond the power of man to imagine or describe.'

Eventually Russian numbers told, and Adams and his men fell steadily back to Home Ridge. The Sandbag had changed hands once more.

It was at this moment that British reinforcements arrived on the scene – the Grenadier Guards had been the first to leave the 1st Division camp and now, under the command of the Duke of Cambridge, they arrived in front of the Sandbag. Again ignoring its uselessness as a position, the Duke decided to retake it: national pride demanded its recapture. The Grenadiers descended the forward slope of Fore Ridge towards the 7,000 Russians spread in a vast arc around the Sandbag. Their commanding officer, Colonel Reynardson, gave the order for a volley, but most of the rifles misfired; there was no time to correct the fault and the Guardsmen charged with levelled bayonets.

With the Grenadiers was their Adjutant, George Higginson. 'On forming our line on the ridge of the Second Division, and seeing beneath us the grey coats of the huge advancing column of the enemy, our Brigadier-General Bentinck, by whose side I was riding gave the order to "charge", and I witnessed the rush of the line . . . down the rugged slope, full upon the advancing host. The exulting cheer which foretold the brilliant result of the charge confirmed my dread that our gallant fellows would soon get out of hand; and in fact, except for one short period during the long day when we contrived to make some kind of regular formation, the contest was maintained by groups under company officers, who were unable, owing to the mist and smoke of musketry fire, to preserve any definite touch.'

The Grenadiers drove the Russians before them out of the Sandbag Battery and over the steep edge of the Heights down towards the Tchernaya Valley far below. Like Adams' men before them they didn't get out of hand, but halted, resisting the temptation to follow the fleeing enemy and thus lose the advantage these Heights gave them. Close behind them came the Scots Fusilier Guards. Ordered to form on the Grenadiers' left, Colonel Walker suddenly became aware of two fresh Russian columns coming out of the St Clement's Ravine, a lesser ravine to the south of the Quarry. As he moved to oppose them, the Duke of Cambridge angrily ordered him to obey his initial orders. Reluctant to disobey his divisional commander, Walker wheeled his men across the advancing enemy's front. Moments later in the mist he met Bentinck, his brigade commander, who angrily ordered him to resume his former position. The Scots Guards were now counter-marched to the head of the St Clement's Ravine, by which time the Russian column was only fifty yards away. At such a short range the Guards' volley was devastating. Once again the Russian columns melted away.

By now, though, in the broken ground and mist, another band of Russians had slipped past the Grenadiers' flank and re-occupied the Sandbag Battery; now it was the Scots' turn to take it at the point of the bayonet. All around the Battery the fight ebbed and flowed, with column after column of Russians coming up out of the St Clement's Ravine in front and the Quarry Ravine to the left. For their part, the Guards were taking casualties and running low on ammunition.

The Sandbag fell yet again, to a fresh Russian force who drove out the mixed bag of Grenadiers and Scots Fusilier Guards who held it. As they rallied about thirty yards to the rear, preparing to counter-charge once more, the Coldstream arrived, hurrying up from the rear. Not willing to have *their* prize recaptured for them by their fellow Guardsmen, the Grenadiers charged once more, driving into the Battery where the Russians were now so tightly packed that many were unable to escape over the parapet and were bayoneted where they stood. Again the Grenadiers – a dwindling band now – drove the Russians to the edge of the Heights; again, the Russians counter-attacked, forcing the Grenadiers back to the Battery. By now, the Coldstream had formed up on their right, just in time to receive the Russians' next charge.

With them was Captain Wilson. 'No sooner were we in line than an unlooked-for perilous difficulty showed itself. Many of the Miniés, at least in my neighbourhood, missed fire. The failure is easily accounted for. Throughout the rainy night, the loaded rifles had, according to custom, been piled outside the tents; consequently locks, stocks, and barrels were very wet. However, so excellent was the workmanship of the arm, that after a fruitless expenditure of several caps on each damp nipple – one soldier told me he had used sixteen caps before he discharged his piece – we were cheered with bangs, denoting "all right".'

It sometimes happens in war that a position acquires a symbolic value out of all proportion to its tactical importance: the Sandbag Battery was one. It had become the bloody arena for a test of wills as, oblivious to the battle raging elsewhere, Russians and British charged and counter-charged.

Wilson described the fighting. 'Matchless "private soldiership" was all-in-all ... The hill was immersed in vapour; a man could scarcely see the length of his own company; no man could tell with precision what was going on fifty paces on either side of him. The ground on which we stood was rough, and sprinkled with bushes. Below us, on the right, was the valley of the Tchernaia, a very sea of mist. On the left yawned a deep ravine, separating us from where the 2nd Division struggled. With their dismal "regulation" howls, the enemy surged up the slopes, front, right, and left. One column attacking the sand-bag battery – which being without a *banquette* or step, whereupon the defenders might stand to fire over the parapet, was indefensible according to ordinary rules; but this outrageous, abnormal emergency admitted of no rules, so we regarded the miserable work as a very citadel, and clung to it, tooth and nail – other columns at the same time assailing both flanks. Owing to the thickness of the fog, the Russians could approach within thirty paces of us without being clearly perceived. This was no disadvantage to the English; for at such close quarters, the Minié played with terrific effect on the serried masses, blasting them like flashes of lightning ... After a minute or two of sharp firing, the columns would get troubled; waver a little; and then, to the right about, and retire; nevertheless, we were not left unmolested for an instant; no sooner had one corps made off, than its supporting battalion started up before our view, with the same dull stereotyped yells, the same obstinate but soulless action.'

It was brutal, close-quarter fighting, Wilson said; 'Amid a dense fog raged wholesale murder; the mortal strife was hand to hand, foot to foot, muzzle to muzzle, butt-end to butt-end. It must not be supposed that we always stood rooted to the ground, that we never budged. No, the fight rested not steadfast for an instant. It was now backward, now forward, now sideways.'

Of the men who had stood-to with Wilson a couple of hours earlier many were already dead. 'Scarcely had we fallen to, before I saw the Coldstream Adjutant, Elliott, than whom no man was ever more deservedly beloved, stretched dead, and the favourite "grey" – poor little Bashi-Bazouk – standing bleeding by his master's side. As my company took ground to a flank, the colour-sergeant was felled with a bullet through the side. Never can I forget the look that the dying man cast upward at me as I passed on: it was horrible in its intensity. Every moment, on every side, comrades were dashed down.'

Captain Tower, also of the Coldstream, wrote in his diary, 'Our men were getting very few and far between; our poor company, No. 1, suffered terribly, but we yelled and screamed and fired at the columns we saw in our front; they were immensely superior to us in numbers, ten to one at least, and they seemed now to stand their ground very well; they pressed us *hard*. But determination and dogged courage kept them back, and not a yard would we yield. The numbers in front of us increased every second, and we were really hand to hand with them; the bushes were full of English and Russians mixed up together. The groans of the wounded, officers yelling and screaming at their men, the soldiers shouting at one another, and (I have no doubt) using their favourite expressions, and the firing almost deafened one.'

Lacking a fire-step, as Captain Wilson had noted, the Battery was difficult to defend, but as the dead piled up, Wilson wrote, men could climb over them to get a shot off over the parapet.

'The Guards, occupying the redoubt, by standing on the carcasses of the slain, were enabled to fire over the parapet at the enemy fermenting underneath; or as cartridges grew scarce, to smash out their brains with musket butts, and to heave big stones down upon them. The Russian officers behaved like true soldiers. They were ever in front of their less adventurous rank and file, urging them on with voice and uplifted sword; nay, they rushed freely on certain death, with the view of inflaming the sluggish spirit of their fol-lowers. I saw one glorious fellow leap with an hurrah from the parapet of the battery into the midst of a *chevaux de frise* of bayonets. A private soldier followed; while one would wink, the two were dead, pierced to the backbone in twenty places.'

Realising that his fast diminishing thin line of 1300 Guardsmen could not hold out much longer without reinforcements of Duke of Cambridge had ridden off in search of some. The first person he met was Sir George Cathcart, who had brought up six companies of his

4th Division from the trenches in front of Sebastopol. The Duke urged Cathcart to move up and reinforce his left. To the left of the Guards' position at the Sandbag the open ground – which came to be known as the Gap – was unoccupied. This Gap was some four hundred yards, and it constituted a dangerous breach between the Guards and the small number of British troops still hanging on at the Barrier. Through this breach Russian columns from the Quarry Ravine might pour at any minute, rolling up the Guards from the left or storming unopposed to the very slopes of Home Ridge*. Though no great tactician, the Duke had rightly seen where the British were most vulnerable, but Cathcart had his own ideas. His gaze was focused on the far right, where he could see a Russian column working their way round to the right of the Sandbag Battery, which was once again exerting its terrible pull. Cathcart was driven by other factors besides; this was the rising star of the army, of whom great things had been expected, but Cathcart had been late for the Alma, late for Balaklava, and, though carrying his Dormant Commission which made him Raglan's acknowledged successor, had nevertheless been sidelined and ignored. Now was his hour. Now, with one telling, battle-winning stroke, he would vindicate himself and make his name. Eyes fixed on that distant column, he led his men off to the right. Sir George Cathcart had an appointment with destiny.

General Pennefather was more forthcoming: he could spare the Duke one wing of the 95th, half a battalion of the Rifles and a wing of the 20th, who had just arrived exhausted after a night in the trenches. If the Duke thought he had neutralised the threat to his left flank, he soon had cause to think again. Colonel Horsford's Riflemen, it is true, spread out and partly plugged the Gap, but the 20th and the 95th took one look at the battle raging round the Sandbag Battery . . . and headed straight for it. The right wing of the 95th – the left had been sent off to the left under Major Hume – was commanded by Major Champion, last seen urging his men to 'Slate 'em' at the Barrier on 26 October.

'Owing to various circumstances I had only the Grenadiers and two other companies at the time, and we were firing into the enemy when I was ordered up to the battery to help the Guards, very much

* See Map 5.

pressed. Thus we had Russians both in front and rear – I found great slaughter; 41st, 95th, Grenadier Guards, and Scots Fusilier Guards all fighting mixed up together lining the battery,' he wrote.

Commanding Company No. 3 in Champion's wing was Lieutenant Carmichael. 'An order was brought to Champion to advance the right wing to the support of the Guards in the two-gun battery (the Sandbag). We wheeled in open columns to the right, and as we approached it, we could hear the cheering and hurrahing of the Russians over the din of the fight . . . an exclamation from one of my men drew my attention to my left, and turning round, I saw through the mist and smoke a line of the enemy's skirmishers close to my left flank. I wheeled my company at once to the left, and opened fire – at this moment the Duke of Cambridge rode up to me and not having, I suppose, noticed the enemy's skirmishers told me to take care, or that I should fire into the Guards. I pointed out who we had got in front of us, and he then rode on towards the left. Our fire drove the skirmishers, who were quite close to us, back, and some of the men including Private Timothy Abbott began to follow them with the bayonet but I got them back, and we went into the Battery, as having both Colours with me, I felt anxious for their safety.'

Even in the carnage of the Battery, there was time for the social niceties: 'Directly we got to the Battery we formed to the assistance of the Guards who were hotly pressed on all sides – my men showed front chiefly to the left of the battery and the Sergeant with the colours stood close to where those of the Guards were standing, carried by two young officers, to one of whom I was speaking for a few moments. I think . . . that he was at Harrow with me, although some years my junior.'

Again, damp rifles were a problem. 'The rifles of many of the men, who had been out the previous night would not at first go off from their damp condition, but the rifles of fallen men were to be had. My Colour Sergeant, Sexton (subsequently commissioned) was one of those in this predicament, but I passed him one thrown down by a gigantic Guardsman, who was shot through the mouth by my side and who reeled off to the rear, choking with blood.'

The men of the different regiments were soon intermingled. Carmichael said he 'went backwards and forwards between the flanks of the Battery several times, as at one moment one would be implored to bring assistance to the right, at another time it was the left that was pressed, and could not hold out any longer without help. The men behaved with great pluck and tenacity – I saw no flinching, although we were several times outflanked. At one time, I thought we must be driven out, as they penetrated into the battery as far as the left Embrasure, but the leading men were shot down, and the others drew back. At this time I fought with a rifle, as many other officers did during the day,' Gentlemanly objections to officers shooting enemy skirmishers had been left at the Alma.

Fighting not far from Carmichael, among his Coldstreamers, Captain Wilson made this assessment of officers' weapons. 'As these isolated engagements took effect beard to beard, officers had occasionally opportunities of testing the sort of stuff out of which their swords had been forged. Wilkinson's cutlery stood the trial well – not so the handiwork of less careful armourers. At any rate, I can assert that my recreant blade, which had been bought of the tailor who rigged me out on appointment, bent like a thing of pewter over the thick skull of an unpleasantly forward Calmuck.'

As at the Charge of the Light Brigade, officers' revolvers proved useful close-quarter weapons, but they had their limitations.

'The "Colts" which were either decently capped, or had escaped the malign influence of the wet night, did their owners faithful service; but such pistols as had suffered from damp, or were furnished with miserable American caps, bought at Constantinople, could not be depended on. Out of my five barrels I could only persuade one to do its duty; from that one, however, went a lucky, but not mortal ball.'

Wilson was one of those officers who found himself commanding men of different regiments. 'I saw many linesmen fighting intermixed with Guardsmen. On one occasion, being hard pressed on a flank, I ran to another band of our fellows to obtain help. Among those I appealed to was a soldier of the 20th Regiment; to my shout "Fall in there my good fellow," the honest man under the impression that he was being ordered away altogether, replied – "O yer honour, don't be after sending me off, I'd like to go on fightin wid the Guards."

The man was killed with the Guards just minutes later.

Still the Russians kept coming. Captain Tower of the Coldstream wrote, 'Column after column kept pouring up the hill . . . The parapet in front of us was too high to fire over, and the enemy kept climbing into the embrasures and up the exterior slope of the parapet; but one after another they fell, shot by our men as they showed ... We could see lines of bayonets outside the parapet, and could hear them howling and cheering one another on; it was now *fearfully* exciting ... they kept getting nearer and our men fell very thick ... Our ammunition was beginning to fail, some of the men had not had a round of their own for a long time; the dead furnished the living; but now that even began to fail, and the men in their excitement threw stones, lumps of earth, anything they could see, over the parapet among the Russians, and they came back among us with interest.'

This was the kind of fighting that the Russians had sought all along and been mostly been denied, driven back by British rifle-fire before they could close with the bayonet. If they had thought that the British were long-range marksmen with no stomach for cold steel, they were learning better.

'Tactics,' wrote Wilson, 'there were none. The exigency out-stripped art; brute valour and moral constancy were the sole arguments applicable to the situation. Front, right and left, every Englishmen saw, or felt a foe. This foe must be kept at arm's length, or all was lost, and under the remarkable circumstances of the case, he could only be withstood by individual exertion, by an exhibition almost superhuman of Anglo-Saxon "pluck", and by the shattering bullet of the Minié. Therefore wherever danger was, British soldiers stood, clustered in sparse knots, fighting each on his own hook – so many lions at bay.'

Casualties among the Guards were mounting. Looking around him, Wilson saw, 'Three officers of my acquaintance, stretched side by side almost. Two, Butler and Neville had done forever with human misery; the third, Pakenham of the Grenadiers, lived still; I heard him faintly beg for a stretcher, heard him murmur how he had been basely stabbed after his fall. I looked about me for the drummers, whose duty it was to succour the wounded, but a sudden press carried me off, and I saw that brave soldier no more.'

The Neville Wilson referred to, Henry Neville, was brother to Grey Neville, who had been unhorsed at the Charge of the Heavy Brigade and had lain there, mortally wounded, while Trooper Abbot stood astride his body fending off Cossacks. Lord Braybrook had now lost two sons in the Crimea. Pakenham of the Grenadiers was Lord Pakenham, the Earl of Longford's grandson.

Surgeon Robinson of the Scots Fusilier Guards came upon him shortly afterwards. 'I saw Colonel Pakenham of the Grenadiers in a sinking state from several severe wounds: I gave him a drink from my flask. He attempted to convey some wish to me, but owing chiefly, I think, to an impediment in his speech (a lisp), I was unable, after many painful efforts in his part, to catch the purport. A man of my battalion, severely hurt, was urgent in his cries for assistance and removal to hospital. His wound, I found, must soon terminate fatally. Removal was alike, at the time, impracticable, dangerous, and useless, for he was shot through the intestines, the contents of which were escaping. He was alternately supplicating help, and uttering imprecations on the enemy, who had given him the fatal wound, it would seem, when he was lying injured and defenceless from a comparatively trifling hurt. I thought it my duty to tell him how short a time he had to live, and to suggest his occupying the brief interval in prayer. I had the satisfaction of witnessing him doing so, for I was necessarily lying for some time by his side; but in his ejaculatory petitions he could not avoid recurring to and execrating the brutality of the enemy every now and then. Some hours after, when riding by, I saw him in a sitting posture, and believed him to be quite dead.'

The wounds suffered by one anonymous soldier of the Fusilier Guards testify to the intensity of the fighting around the Battery. 'We had fought about an hour upon the high ground when I was struck. My front rank was shot dead. I took his place and was firing away as fast as ever. In a few minutes a musket ball went through my right arm. It was just like a pin touching me at the time. I continued firing about five minutes; then I got a ball in the left breast. I never fell; but thank God, the ball passed quick as lightning through my back, just below my shoulder. The wound is three or four inches higher before than it is behind because the enemy were higher than we, they firing in a slanting direction. I thought at this time the ball was in my chest. I fired thrice after this – then I reeled like a drunken man. I could scarcely stand for the want of blood . . . I threw my firelock from me. I had my blanket and greatcoat on my back; I pitched them off. I was staggering down the hill as well as I could, when I was soon struck on the arm with a bit of shell. I had not time to say a word till another ball went through my left thigh. I got about twenty yards further down and then fell on my face. I never got timorous till then. The balls were flying over wholesale. I tried to get up, and, with the help of God, I got to my feet once more. I was not one minute on my feet till a ball struck me on the first joint of the middle finger of my left hand, and broke it. I still kept my feet, and got to the bottom of the hill, where I fell, and lay for four hours before I was carried away.'

The shell which hit the Guardsman may well have come from Sebastopol Harbour. Sergeant John Palmer of the 20th remembers: 'A ship called the *Twelve Apostles*, which had been sunk across the harbour to prevent our ships entering, and whose deck was nevertheless above water, could clear the fort with her shells, and whenever we were in possession of that redoubt they made it too hot to hold us, but when the Russians regained possession the ship ceased firing. We could never understand how this was managed.'

Palmer continued: 'The struggle round this little redoubt was terrible; we charged the enemy again and again. Just as I was making a point at a Russian, my foot slipped, and instead of giving a wound I received one in my thigh. It was, however, only slight, for my comrade, poor old Jesse Patient, shot the man dead; and away we went again, charging over the redoubt and down the ravine some distance. When we fell back Jesse got captured, and as he had always said he wouldn't be taken alive, I suppose he had a good fight for liberty, for after the fight some of our men found his body dreadfully cut about, and they buried him with the others.'

In the thick of this fight was Timothy Gowing. He and some of his comrades from the 7th Fusiliers had been rushed up by their divisional commander, Sir George Brown, and, in the way of this battle, been fed in wherever they were needed.

'One of our majors, Sir Thomas Troubridge, was the admiration of all, for, though terribly wounded, he would not allow himself to be removed from the ground until victory had declared itself, but remained, with the bravest fortitude, encouraging his men to "fight it out". He would now and then call out: "Fire away, my lads! Give them the steel if you get a chance! Stick to them, my men!" It was a sergeant named Laws (a Norwich man) who ran for a doctor to attend upon him; but his resolute spirit did not forsake him. No, he would rather die on the field at his post with the Fusiliers than be carried to safety . . . At the Alma his conduct was the admiration of all who could see him, for he was often in front of us, encouraging him; but he escaped that fiery ordeal without a scratch, to fall, with both feet gone, on a more glorious field. When he was lying, apparently bleeding to death, with both his stumps resting upon a gun-carriage, he called upon us to "shift those fellows with the bayonet", animating us by voice and gesture; although the poor man could not lead us, he could cheer us on. And on we went with an irresistible rush and routed them then and there. On one occasion after he was wounded he called upon us not to forget our bayonets, adding "They don't like cold steel, men!"

'Neither did I; it was here that I received two bayonet wounds — one in each thigh — and would most likely have been dispatched, but that help was close at hand. The fellows who wounded me fell at once to the same description of weapon — but not to rise again and write or talk about it.

'Revolvers and bayonets told heavily that foggy morn; and when our men were short of ammunition, they pitched stones at the enemy. My legs were quickly bandaged, and after giving the enemy a few parting shots at close quarters (which must have told upon their crowded ranks) I managed to hobble off the field, using my rifle, and another I picked up, as crutches. We could spare none to look after the wounded; it was every man for himself. After hobbling some distance out of the range of our fire, I lay down, for I could get no further without a little rest.'

Up to this point, as the tide of battle washed back and forth over the Battery, the British had been content — when it flowed in their favour — to halt at the edge of the Heights and merely harass the Russians with fire as they fell back down the steep, brush-covered slopes to the Tchernaya Valley below. It was almost more than flesh and blood could stand not to plunge down after them in headlong pursuit, and finally one group of soldiers, a party under Captain Wilson, now did.

'The group, with which I was connected, had forced a superior number of Russians into hurried flight down the hill's side into the valley. With this good fortune the brave fellows ought to have been content. Not so, however. Immediately the "Muscov" showed their heels, I saw several soldiers break away from the right of my party and pursue the fugitives. It was plain that, unless the hunters were quickly halted, they hastened to destruction. Therefore, shouting "halt! halt!" I ran after them ... Down the steep we went: the dogs of war hot upon the trail, I calling them off with impotent vehemence. We reached the valley in disorder.'

By abandoning their position on the Heights, Wilson's men had forfeited their greatest advantage. Down on the valley floor they were greatly outnumbered and vulnerable.

'Scarcely had our feet touched the plain, before some of Liprandi's riflemen sprang up from among the bushes, and blazed full in our faces. A few men dropped.'

Worse was to follow. Sir George Cathcart had hurried to the extreme right of the position with six companies of the 46th and 68th Regiments under their Brigadier, General Torrens. He had refused the Duke of Cambridge's request that he fill the gap on the Duke's left. Shortly afterwards General Airey, Raglan's principal Staff Officer, had ridden up with orders to the same effect – to occupy the Gap. Cathcart appeared in good humour, merely replying with a hunting metaphor – that he had *so good a pack* he didn't need to be cautioned. But once Airey had gone, Cathcart pressed ahead with his own plan. Beyond the Battery he could see a Russian column moving round to its right – the head of the same column that Wilson's men had attacked. It posed nothing like the threat that Cathcart imagined, but he, valuing his own tactical judgement far more than the Duke of Cambridge's or Lord Raglan's, decided *this* was the key to the battle.

Cathcart ordered General Torrens to attack. The men of the 46th and 68th – all of whom, having missed out on the action at the Alma and Balaklava, were spoiling for a fight – shook out into a long thin line and advanced firing. Having shed their greatcoats, they were practically the only redcoated troops on the field that day – both sides being dressed in grey greatcoats had already caused some confusion earlier in the day, and would again. With the 46th on the left and the 68th on the right, General Torrens in the centre and Cathcart and his staff close behind, the line advanced on the Russian column at the edge of the Heights.

Riding beside General Torrens was his son, Captain Torrens of the 23rd, who was acting as his ADC. 'At the moment our charge was made a desperate fight was going on between the Guards and the enemy along the ridge ... and especially at the small unarmed and unfinished earthwork at its crest; dense columns were crowding up the hill and keeping up an almost incessant fire. They were almost concealed by the smoke, and the thick bush which at that time covered the heights, and it was only now and then as the smoke occasionally cleared away that we could discern the dark mass of long brown and grey great coats, flat caps and cold blue steel approaching us. We charged and drove them back before they reached the top of the hill, charging down the hill so as to meet them and taking them partly in flank.'

Cathcart's men were still using the old smooth-bore musket, but though their firepower was not as devastating as the Minié, there were fewer misfires.

With the 46th was Lieutenant Frederick Dallas, who wrote, 'The fire was very heavy. At last the enemy began to waver, and we took advantage of it and made a most splendid headlong Charge on them, pushing them down the steep side of the mountain in utter confusion. The slaughter of them here was immense, for we charged right at them, and every man had shot away his 60 rounds (or nearly so) before we could get them to pull up.'

Control of these overexcited troops was almost impossible, made worse by the fact that a number of officers were hit as the line advanced. Among them was General Torrens, described by his son, Captain Torrens.

'Both General Torrens' horse and my own were shot during the charge . . . he received his wound while on foot, striving to stop the men, who were too eager and were following the repulsed enemy down the hill.'

As Torrens lay wounded, Cathcart rode up to him, crying, 'Torrens, well and gallantly done!'

Cathcart probably thought, seeing the Russians fleeing before his men, that he had won the battle. He was soon to be disabused. If he, like pretty much everyone else that day, had simply plunged into the carnage round the Battery, he would at least have reinforced the men fighting there. As it was, his headlong charge down into the valley started a general movement which imperilled the whole of the British right.

Back up on the Heights, the troops around the Battery having seen first Wilson's men and then Cathcart's pursuing down the slopes, decided to follow suit. Captain Burnaby of the Grenadiers had already led a party of Grenadiers out into the thick of a party of Russians threatening the Battery.

Private Bancroft of the Grenadiers, who was with Burnaby, wrote, 'I bayoneted the first Russian in the chest; he fell dead. I was then stabbed in the mouth with great force, which caused me to stagger back, where I shot this second Russian and ran a third through. A fourth and fifth came at me and ran me through the right side. I fell but managed to run one through and brought him down. I stunned him by kicking him, whilst I was engaging my bayonet with another. Sergeant-Major Algar called out to me not to kick the man that was down, but not being dead he was very troublesome to my legs; I was fighting the other over his body. I returned to the Battery and spat out my teeth; I found only two.'

In the Battery, Major Champion of the 95th described how he: 'proposed to some of the Guards that our men should mount and charge over the battery, which they did in style.'

As Champion led some men over the parapet of the Battery, Lieutenant Carmichael led a party out of the left side. Everywhere the cry *Charge!* was taken up.

'The enemy turned at once, several of those overtaken threw away their arms, and knelt down asking for mercy mentioning the name of Christ (Christos),' wrote Carmichael. 'These were taken prisoner and taken to the rear, but the pursuit was continued down the hill and into the ravine – I thought the battle was won, and the men were also exultant.'

The frustration that caused this headlong charge was born of the incredible persistence of the Russians in attacking again and again, up steep slopes into the teeth of a gale of Minié fire. Every time the British thought they had seen them off once and for all, up would come a new column, or an old one re-formed. The British wanted to be done with this battle.

As his men pursued the Russians into the ravine, Carmichael remembered, 'A fine young soldier of the 95th, Lance-Corporal Purcell, came up to me saying, "We are driving them again, Sir", alluding to the repulse of the sortie of the 26th October, and at the same time was about to run his bayonet into a Russian's back whom we were overtaking. I cried out "Don't kill him!" and he instead seized him by the belt behind and flung him to the ground, and took his weapon off him.'

Most men now thought the battle was won: all the Russian columns they could see were falling back down off the Heights, but Champion himself was beginning to have his doubts. He could see the danger that already faced Wilson and his men down below: once on level ground, the Russians would stop, rally and turn, and the British, widely dispersed, would be surrounded and destroyed. Unable to ride his horse down the steep slope, he dismounted to follow his men on foot and, as Wilson had done, try and call them back.

As he did so he was hit by a musket ball. Champion started to describe the situation in his own words. 'Finding they were going too far, and would be surrounded on return, I got off Highflyer, and went down the hill to recall—'

Champion's account, in a letter to his brother written five days later, ended abruptly, because the doctors would not let him write more. He died some two weeks later, on 30 November.

Now there was no stopping the stampede down the hill after the Russians. Only the Duke of Cambridge managed to hold back 100 or so men, mostly Grenadiers, including their Colour Party. He could see what few others could: that while some Russian columns were fleeing down the slopes, others were still advancing up them. Six battalion columns had climbed out of the Quarry Ravine and, just as the Duke and Lord Raglan had feared, advanced into the Gap. There was no one there to stop them. The 95th, the 20th and all of Cathcart's men who had been supposed to fill the Gap were now halfway down into the Tchernaya Valley, hunting fugitive Russians through the brush. These six new Russian columns bore down on the Duke of Cambridge and his hundred men left in the Sandbag Battery.

After Major Champion was wounded, his Adjutant, Major Macdonald of the 95th, hearing a cry from above warning about the new threat from the Gap, returned up the hill. Chief of the Macdonalds of Glencoe, he was hit by a spent bullet at the Alma; it had lodged in his belt ornament. Now, as he rode back up towards the Battery, he saw in front of him a skirmishing line of grey-coated men.

'I am very near-sighted and did not recognize the party until very close and I suddenly turned round and made off as fast as I could, intending to pass them on one of their flanks, but close upon this I met a very small party ... returning and with Russians pursuing. I returned with them having the enemy both front and rear and very shortly afterwards on our right also ... I was standing in my stirrups looking round to see where we could charge through them with the best chances when I received a ball through my right knee which gave under me and I fell from my horse.'

Close by Macdonald when he was hit was Sergeant Pat Murphy of the 95th. Murphy was: 'very ill with dysentery at the time, and I came off the trenches that morning; my big coat was almost as heavy as myself for it rained all that Saturday ... Mr Macdonald got wounded in the left thigh and was pitched about four yards off to the left of his horse. I ran to him and lifted his head and asked him where he was wounded: he pointed to his thigh. I then saw for myself the blood oozing through his trousers ... I made several attempts to get him up on my back ... I told him I could not leave him in such an exposed position, for the enemy would surely kill him if they came across him, and they were looking and firing at us at the same time ... leaving my rifle on the ground while stooping to get him on my back, he said, "For God's sake, Murphy, let me down!" I let him down when I saw some Russians coming up at the charge. I made a grab for my musket and he told me not to fire: he fired with his revolver, and then I fired: when we could see there were two or three on the ground and the other were retiring ... I told him I might never show myself in the regiment again if I left him. He told me to go, and I if I lived to tell the Colonel what had happened: when I found there was no use persuading him I left him ...'

As Murphy left Macdonald, the Russians approached, fired several shots then, despite his indicating that he was wounded, beat him with musket-butts and bayoneted him a total of twenty times. Astonishingly, Macdonald survived to recount the experience. He said he did not recall feeling any pain, but he learned the truth of the term 'cold steel'. The Russians moved on, leaving him for dead.

In the valley below, the truth was finally dawning on Sir George Cathcart. His command was now scattered and blown. The Russians they had been pursuing had halted and were re-forming. A scattered fire-fight had begun with these when Cathcart's men found themselves being fired at from above – by one of those six battalions that had plunged through the Gap and was now lining the edge of the

Heights, on the positions the British had abandoned.

Sending for the remainder of his 46th and 68th men to follow, Cathcart collected the 50 or so men he had under hand and tried to counter-attack back up the Heights. Lieutenant Dallas of the 46th was among them.

'The men came up gaily, and we formed as we could, and with a mere handful returned the enemy's fire, as long as our ammunition lasted. We were placed, I should say 50 of us, with most of the staff of the Division, on a small sort of natural platform, about 10 yards from the Russian Infantry Regiment which had outflanked us and had come round to the summit of this fatal hill, to receive us on our return from the Charge. How many of us escaped I can form no idea (few indeed did). We were so close to the enemy that they threw stones, and clods of earth in our faces.'

Dallas saw Cathcart leading the way. 'As I was coming up the hill he was just in front of me. As I passed him he recognised me and said, "There is nothing for us but the bayonet, Dallas!" Noble-hearted old Hero! I shall never forget him sitting there quite calmly on his horse, certainly not 12 yards from the front rank of the Enemy.'

Lieutenant-Colonel Colin Campbell of the 46th (no relation to Campbell of the Highland Brigade) took up the story. 'Dallas took the five men next to him and attempted as he described "to boil up a little charge". But when he got within about ten yards of the Russians, finding himself totally unsupported, he ran back again as fast as he came; extraordinary to say, he got back untouched, although he says that every man in the Russian line seemed to be firing point-blank. Three out of his five men were killed.'

All morning the Russians had toiled up these steep, almost vertical, slopes and the British had fired down on them from above. Now the boot was on the other foot. Seeing they could make no headway against the 800 men above them, Cathcart was heard to mutter: 'I fear we are in a mess.'

They were almost his last words. As a staff officer rode up, bringing the bad news that the rest of his command were out of ammunition and could not attack, a bullet struck Cathcart in the breast, killing him instantly. Most of his staff died in that same hail of bullets.

Cathcart's heroic death went part of the way to redeeming him in the eyes of his colleagues; the spot where he fell was known for the rest of the siege as Cathcart's Hill, and his death was described in letters home, and even in the press, in the most romantic terms.

The worst Henry Clifford, who had served under him in South Africa, could say was: 'Poor Sir George Cathcart was too rash, he took the Guards and others of our brave army too far from any support, and much increased our loss. He is indeed a very great loss to us – tho' he has always been thought *too brave!* which is a fault that has cost him his life. We often thought at the Cape he would fall, for he would not take the precaution every General officer ought to take of a valuable life, if not for his own sake, for that of his Division.'

By his rashness and tactical misjudgement, Cathcart had almost snatched defeat from the jaws of victory. The men who had followed him, and those elsewhere on the Heights who had followed his example, now found themselves scattered on the valley floor, surrounded, outnumbered, low on ammunition and with the superb position they had held on the Heights now occupied by the enemy. They were left to make their own way back up, in small bodies, the best way they could. Some, including Dallas, eventually made it back to Home Ridge. Many did not.

Captain Wilson of the Coldstream Guards and his men were almost in the marshes of the Tchernaya Valley, under fire from Russian skirmishers. As they tried to make their way back onto the Heights, they were joined by some of these stragglers.

'Several soldiers of the 46th and 68th – remnants of Torrens' crushed brigade – joined us: we all turned and began to re-ascend the hill. The rise was precipitous, the ground slippery; distant field pieces let fly grape at us, without, however doing much hurt; *tirailleurs* kept peppering our backs; not a round left in our pouches. Every minute guardsmen or "liners" rolled over, some struck with lead, others done for through sheer exhaustion,' Wilson wrote.

When they were halfway up the hill, Wilson and his men found themselves being fired at by the troops they could see above them, whose grey greatcoats looked much like their own.

'The soldiers around me cried out, "Why our own chaps are firing on us; we be mistaken for Rooshians." Looking upward, I beheld through the vapour which still hung on the plateau, a black line of infantry, which I also took for our countrymen; and so, with one accord we roared, "Hold hard, for God's sake; we are English!" The louder we shouted, the heavier rained the balls about our ears. Dismal predicament: a set of panting wretches clambering up a mountain, between two fires! We still toiled upward, and now it became plain that the troops shooting at us from above were Russian, that by some mishap had gotten possession of our old position on the ridge.'

Organising his men into a single file he led them off to the left, hoping to contour round the side of the hill and work his way gradually up to the summit. On another, equally precipitous slope, Lieutenant Carmichael of the 95th, who had been so sure the battle was won less than half an hour earlier, was making his way back up at the end of a similar file of men of all regiments.

His experience had been similar to Wilson's. 'Their skirmishers saw the false position we were in, and pushed on, some of those also who had been faltering turned again. With greatcoats on and pretty well blown, and impeded by the stiff oak brushwood, we made but slow progress back. My first idea was to climb up the side of the hill on the base of which we were standing to pass in front of the Battery, and to get in by its right . . . but the brushwood was so thick and the hill so steep, that I gave it up, and determined to follow those who were making for the left of the Battery by a narrow winding little footpath . . . up this we travelled in single file. I believe I was the last of this string, the man just in front of me being a Guardsman, who I thought went very slow.'

What had happened back at the Sandbag Battery? The Duke of Cambridge had been holding it with his hundred men, with six Russian battalion columns advancing against it. Among the Grenadiers in the Battery was Captain Higginson, their Adjutant. He had stepped out the back of the Battery when he was approached by a man who stood out among the grey-coated Guardsmen.

'It was at that moment that I saw a figure in naval uniform, rendered more distinctive by a tall glazed hat, coming towards me. The new arrival proved to be Captain Peel of the *Diamond*, one of the most adventurous and daring of that Naval Brigade that had been landed to take part in the siege operations. On my expressing astonishment as seeing him amongst us at such a moment, he simply remarked, "Oh there was nothing going on at my little battery on the hill behind; and as I heard you fellows had plenty to do, I thought I would come and look at you." I replied with some gravity of manner that we were in a tight place awaiting supply of ammunition and long expected support. While this conversation was going on, I felt a bullet pass from behind through my bearskin cap, causing me for the moment, to stoop forward. I exclaimed, "This is rather hard lines! here are our own fellows mistaking us for the enemy, and firing upon us, instead of coming to our relief." He turned his field-glass in the direction I pointed, and said in a subdued voice, "No, by heaven! it is the enemy getting round our rear." '

It was lucky that Peel, having nothing to do in his battery in front of Sebastopol, had wandered up on to the heights looking for a fight. If the Russian columns had approached any closer without being identified, two terrible – unthinkable – things might have happened. There was an imminent danger that the Queen's cousin would fall into the hands of the enemy, and that the Colours of her First Regiment of Guards would be thrown at the feet of the Tsar.

Though the Duke of Cambridge's instincts were to make a stand by the Colours, his staff officers were insistent he remove himself at once, saying, 'Sir, you will be taken!' They hustled him away towards Home Ridge.

Rallying his few men round the Colours, Higginson began a fighting retreat to Home Ridge. 'Clustered round the Colours, with scarcely a round of ammunition left, the men pressed slowly backwards, keeping their front full towards the enemy, their bayonets ready at the "charge". As a comrade fell, wounded or dead, his fellow took his place, and maintained the compactness of the gradually diminishing group, that held on with unflinching stubbornness in protecting the flags. More than once from the lips of this devoted band of non-commissioned officers and rank-and-file came the shout, "Hold up the Colours!" fearing, no doubt, that in the mist and smoke they might lose sight or touch of those honoured emblems, which they were determined to preserve, or in their defence die.'

As the triumphant Russians now regained once more the butcher's yard that was the Sandbag Battery, Higginson and his men edged back towards Home Ridge, holding the Colours aloft.

'The two young officers, Verschoyle and Turner, raised them well above their heads, half unfurled, and in this order we moved slowly back, exposed to a fire, fortunately desultory and ill-aimed, from front, rear, and left flank. Happily the ground on our right was so precipitous as to deter the enemy from attempting to outflank us on that side. As from time to time some Russian soldiers, more adventurous than their fellows, sprang forward towards our compact group, two or three of our Grenadiers would dash out with the bayonet and compel steady retreat. Nevertheless, our position was critical. By the time, however, we had traversed half the distance to the breastwork of the Second Division (which I proved by subsequent measurements to be 700 yards distant from the Sandbag Battery), the pressure on our rear, and left was relaxed . . .

'Free at last to rejoin our main body, we hastened our pace, and soon decried the Duke of Cambridge and the rest of our Brigade on the crest of the ridge. I shall never forget the cheer with which the returning colours were welcomed by all ranks, HRH being almost moved to tears, for, as they all said, "We had given you up for lost." '

Captain Wilson, edging up the side of the hill not far from where Higginson and the Colour Party were conducting their fighting retreat, explained what made the Russians who had been about to overwhelm the Colour Party fall back so unexpectedly.

'At length, my little band – it had dwindled to next to nothing – topped the ridge. The fog has passed away, there is broad daylight now. But where are the English? Gone: and in their stead large bodies of the enemy. A bad look out, we're in for it!' he wrote.

Wilson and his band had reconciled themselves to death or capture when all of a sudden, 'Hark, the *pas de charge!* the roll of fifty drums! the bray of fifty clarions! We're saved! We're saved! See, clouds of Zouaves and Algeriens! Bosquet's Light infantry! As they come bounding towards us, we flourish our muskets with rapture in the air. We cry "Thank God!" We cheer – how we cheer – "*Wive Francais*" (Such was the unscholarly pronunciation of the benediction). The French reply with equal heart, "*Vivent les Anglais! Les Anglais sont les plus braves soldats du monde!*" and on every side, hot Zouave hands are stretched forth to clasp ours. We mix with the glorious ranks, and now the grand, the ecstatic moment of a life – VICTORY! TRIUMPH!'

Wilson and his men were not the only men cheering at that moment. The French, for all what Lord Raglan described as 'their infernal toot-tooting', had never been more welcome.

Minutes earlier, Timothy Gowing, lying bayoneted through both thighs, also saw them coming up. 'The Zouaves passed me with a ringing cheer of *"Bon Anglais"* and *"Vive l'Empereur"* repeated over and over again.

'A mounted officer of rank, who was with them, stopped and asked me a number of questions in good English. He turned and spoke to his men, and they cheered me in a most lusty manner. The officer kindly gave me a drink out of his flask, which revived me considerably, and then, with a hearty shake of the hand, bade me good-bye, and passed on into action, shouting out something about the enemy walking over his body before he would surrender.'

Welcome as they were, why had the French been so long in coming? Bosquet's very purpose on the Sapoune had been to reinforce the British right flank, and yet the battle on Mount Inkerman had raged for over an hour before his first battalions arrived. Gortschakoff's force in the valley – the army which had fought at Balaklava eleven days earlier – had been ordered to demonstrate against Bosquet's position, to pin him down and prevent him aiding the British. In this they had been successful. Bosquet remained convinced that the threat to his front was real, that at any moment Gortschakoff's troops would start assaulting up the Heights towards him, and that to send men away to help the British in his left rear would fatally weaken his own position.

At about the same time that the Duke of Cambridge was scouting round for reinforcements to plug the Gap, Bosquet did bring two battalions up to aid the British, but en route, he encountered Sir George Brown and the ill-fated Sir George Cathcart, who breezily informed him that they were not needed. Their motives for this extraordinary claim (other than xenophobia; both men were Napoleonic veterans) were unfathomable. Cathcart might not have wanted the French to come in and share the glorious victory he thought he was about to achieve. Bosquet was an experienced soldier, with a deal of campaigning in North Africa under his belt. Some time later, recognising a crisis when he heard one, even at a distance, he brought more troops of Bourbaki's Brigade – troops that Wilson had encountered, led by Bosquet himself.

With great élan, Bosquet's men swept forward, overrunning the Sandbag Battery and driving its latest Russian occupants out and away down the St Clement's Ravine. Then, victims of their own success, they swept onto the long curving spur to the Quarry Ravine where, unable to manoeuvre, they began to take casualties from Russian fire across the ravine. If the Russian troops still on the Heights in that sector had been quicker off the mark, they might have bottled Bosquet and his command up on that spur – from which the only way out was the way they had entered – and either destroyed them by artillery fire or forced them to surrender. As it was, Bosquet was able to extricate his units and bring them back intact to Home Ridge.

The arrival of the French was the first sign that the tide might be turning in favour of the Allies. The second sign was the arrival of the 18-pounders, the two siege guns ordered up by Lord Raglan almost at the start of the battle. After a certain amount of initial confusion, 150 gunners and assorted volunteers painfully dragged them up from the Siege Park. Colonel Gambier, who had started the guns on their long, slow journey up to the Heights, had been wounded, and they were then put under the command of Colonel Collingwood Dickson.

Dickson commandeered some draught horses which were bringing disabled guns out of the battle and arrived at Home Ridge at about 9.30. The guns were immediately sited pointing northwest towards Shell Hill and brought into action. The Russians now had nearly 100 guns on Shell Hill, including 12-pound field guns and 32-pound howitzers, so it might appear strange that the arrival of two British 18-pounders should be identified by so many who were there as the turning point of the battle. But the difference between the guns was more than just a matter of weight of shot: these British siege guns were long iron monsters weighting forty-two hundredweight, firing a big charge and throwing their 18-pound balls with great power and accuracy.

The second round fired ripped into a Russian battery, beginning what eye-witnesses described as a tyranny over the Russian artillery. Within minutes the Russian batteries, who had dominated the battlefield so far, were being forced to limber up and shift position as roundshot after roundshot tore into them. The slackening of the Russian fire from Shell Hill and the steady picking off of their guns affected everything that followed.

Gathered round the 18-pounders were many men who had seen

the hardest of the day's fighting. Drawn up in support behind the guns were the remnant of the Duke of Cambridge's Guardsmen. Nearby, sheltering under the parapet, among a crowd of officers and men of all regiments who had drifted in from all over the battlefield to the only rallying point they knew of, was Lieutenant Carmichael of the 95th, who climbed back up the Heights and skirted the then Russian-occupied Sandbag Battery.

'I met Major Patullo of the 30th Regt. He like me had no following whatsoever, and had just come up from the left, and was, he said, almost tired out – he proposed that we should go back to the breastwork in front of the 2nd Division camp – which we did. Behind this breastwork we found seated a good many officers and men of all regiments. The two 18-pounders were hard at work firing and the gun detachments not at work were also seated about the guns. We found it difficult to get places, but some officers made space for us. A shell fell close to Patullo just after he sat down but exploded without injuring him or anyone else so far as I saw. The enemy's fire tho' heavy was not I think generally well directed, most of it passed over the breastwork. The gunners worked splendidly,' he wrote.

Stung by the fire of the 18-pounders, the Russians redoubled their own fire on Home Ridge. Of the siege guns' crew, seventeen men fell in the first few minutes, but as soon as one fell, another from the 150 who had dragged the guns up to the Heights sprang into his place. This was an artillery duel the Russians could not win.

In the words of Colonel Dickson, 'I had only two 18-pounders with me, but as these were of heavier metal and superior calibre to the guns of the Russian field artillery, we were enabled not only to cope with them and to keep down their fire, but to overwhelm them wherever we directed their fire along their lines of batteries, and the superior range of our guns was such that they could not retire to any distance to keep out of the range of the 18-pounders without losing the power of returning our fire, and so we eventually compelled the Russians to withdraw their artillery from the field.'

The Russians were not finished yet. Pauloff still had 6,000 men in hand and, in eight battalion columns with four in reserve, they advanced along the line of the Post Road against the British centre, supported by the guns on Shell Hill. Pennefather had little left to throw at them – about 200 men forward in a ragged skirmish line and 800 men on Home Ridge itself, mostly on the flanks; the only reinforcements he had received in the centre were the 63rd (West Suffolk) Regiment and a wing of the 21st (North British) Fusiliers, who were now approaching from the southwest.

As the Russian columns came on, a confused fire-fight developed between Russian and British skirmishers – Pennefather was still following his policy of fighting the battle well forward. Some Russian columns in the centre managed to bypass the knots of skirmishers and, taking advantage of the fog and the ground, pushed on to the lower slopes of Home Ridge.

On the left a Russian column appeared out of the mist and overran three British guns of Turner's battery. The gunners, unsupported, fought with their swords – one of the sergeants was seen with one arm protectively round the barrel of his gun, slashing out in all directions. His body was later found to have nearly fifty bayonet wounds. Once the gunners were killed or driven off, the Russians tried unsuccessfully to spike the guns. As they did so, in the confused way of this battle, a unit of stray Zouaves appeared as if out of nowhere and drove them off.

A little further to the east a party of the 55th were surprised and bundled away from another British gun – suddenly there were Russian troops on Home Ridge. Before these Russians and below them was the 2nd Division camp; beyond that, the Post Road. The Russians had finally penetrated into the heart of the British position. All that stood before them was one French regiment, the 7th Léger.

Somerset Calthorpe, who was, as usual, at Lord Raglan's side in the 2nd Division camp, saw what followed.

'The French advanced up towards the ridge in good order, presenting a broad front and formed in a line four deep. The moment they reached the crest of the hill they came under the direct fire of the Russian guns and lost in the first minute a number of men. This threw them partially into confusion; they were seized with a panic, and the large majority retired down the hill, in spite of the bugles sounding and the drums beating the *pas de charge*.'

Despite the entreaties and threats of their officers, the French fell back down the ridge, the Russian fire was particularly severe and had already killed a number of their own, Russians who were crowding the ridge. Most of the British army was lying down at the time. Only moments earlier, Calthorpe had seen General Strangeways –

who had helped manhandle the two guns into position on the knoll at the Alma – hit by a roundshot which took off his leg below the knee.

'He turned round and asked in a calm voice for someone to help him off his horse. Major Adye had already dismounted and went to his assistance. He placed the poor old General on the ground, and then hurried off to procure a stretcher to carry him off to the rear. Almost at the same moment that General Strangeways was mortally wounded, a shell entered Colonel Somerset's horse just behind the saddle, and burst inside, covering him (Colonel Somerset) with blood, and splashing several of the staff around. Wonderful to say, Colonel Somerset escaped unhurt, except for a slight bruise.'

General Strangeways, who had survived Waterloo and the Alma, was carried off asking to be allowed to die among his gunners. In all this carnage, Calthorpe noted, Lord Raglan never once lost his composure.

'Although a man of the kindest heart and warmest sympathies, Lord Raglan in action never allows his attention to be taken off by the casualties around him, and therefore, though in the midst of this great slaughter, neither his voice nor his manner was apparently changed. Indeed, to such an extent is this indifference carried, that it is a common saying among his staff, that, "My Lord rather likes being under fire than otherwise." '

Rallied once more by their officers, and spurred on by two British staff officers reminding them – in their best schoolboy French – of the achievements of their forebears, the French attacked again. This time, assisted by the remnants of the 55th, they took the ridge, driving the Russians before them at the point of the bayonet. As the 55th mounted the breastwork at the top of the ridge, John Hume said, 'Colonel Daubeney was engaged with the officer leading the Russians when a soldier of the Rifle Brigade came up and shouting, "There you are, sir!" ran the officer through with his bayonet.'

Minutes later the Russians were back and the French – with the 57th diehards to their left and Egerton's 77th in support – found themselves preparing to receive the charge of 2,000 infantry, but just as this Russian column looked unstoppable – in spite of the French rifle bullets ripping through their ranks – and about to close with the bayonet, it stopped. The men in the front ranks were seen to look about them in confusion: something had gone wrong.

Several times during this battle a relatively small counter-attack, delivered at the right psychological moment, had an effect out of all proportion to the numbers involved. Now, urged on by General Pennefather, Colonel Daubeney of the 55th did the same.

John Hume described how Daubeney: 'took about thirty non-commissioned officers and then, passing out at the flank of the breastwork, charged the flank of the 2nd Battalion of the Russian column, and he and his men managed to get right through the battalion, destroying its formation . . . Sergeant Walker, 55th, a fine, powerful man distinguished himself greatly in the charge on the Russian column, using the butt-end of his rifle with great effect.'

As the 55th burst out of the eastern side of the column, Dickson's 18-pounders opened up on the columns, mowing great lanes through them at a range of less than a hundred yards.

At the same moment a cry went up from the French 7th Léger: 'Avancez les tambours!'

The massed drums began the terrible, hypnotic *pas de charge* and the French tramped forward, bayonets levelled, driving the Russians back to head of the Quarry Ravine.

To the left of this battle, another column was met by the 63rd (West Suffolk) and a wing of the 21st (Royal North British) under Colonel Ainslie. These men had come up from the trenches in front of Sebastopol following a cold and weary night. When they arrived on the Heights, Ainslie sent a party under Major C.R. Sackville, Lord West, off to the left, where they would play a crucial part in the battle.

Ainslie and his men now advanced, with the 63rd (West Suffolk) on their right. Seeing what must have been the main column assaulting Home Ridge to their right, Ainslie was about to attack it when another column appeared out of the mist on their left. Turning to his second-in-command, Major Haines, Ainslie remarked, 'Damn it, we must go in at these fellows first.'

He then gave the word: 'Fusiliers prepare to charge.'

It was generally felt by the officers in the regiment that Ainslie was over-fond of the parade ground, and that this rigidity might affect the men in battle. Ainslie must have felt vindicated by what followed. As Haines said, 'I have never seen troops behave better.'

The men advanced in perfect order volleying as they went. With the 63rd on the right flank they drove the enemy northeast towards the Post Road.

In the moment of victory, Ainslie was wounded, probably by a shell fragment. He wrote to his brother the next day, 'I am not ... hit either dangerously or severely but as it is in the lower part of my back it obliges me to keep my bed in a particular position which prevents me from writing.'

He died on board ship in Scutari Harbour nine days later.

Elsewhere on the field, Marshal Canrobert had arrived, and consolidated on the right flank with 8,700 men and 24 guns. Pennefather – whose blood was well and truly up – announced to Lord Raglan that if reinforced, he would advance and 'Lick them to the Devil!' But there were no reinforcements, and in the absence of extra men, Canrobert would not co-operate in a general advance. He was later much criticised for this – and nicknamed *Robert Can't* by some British officers – but as the French had reinforced the British as agreed, and their arrival had turned the tide, there was little Raglan could do but give in.

For their part, the Russians, who had clearly hoped to consolidate on Shell Hill, bringing up sapper equipment and gabions, were growing anxious about their guns. The two British 18-pounders, which had switched fire to the advancing Russian columns, now began to exert their tyranny on the Russian gun-line once more. At the same time, Lord West's party of 21st Fusiliers and another of the 77th began working forward through the brush towards Shell Hill, firing on the Russian guns as they did. To the horror of the 18-pound balls smashing guns and limbers and ploughing through men and horses was now added a steady hail of Minié fire, dropping gunners and drivers.

Once again paranoia about guns set in. The removal of one or two guns from one of the batteries – probably only intended as a tactical move – set in train a general withdrawal. All around Shell Hill the Russian artillery began limbering up and pulling out. General Dannenburg, most of his staff officers dead or wounded, most of his columns shattered, and many thousands of his own dead littering the ground between him and Home Ridge, ordered a general withdrawal. To cover the withdrawal, the Vladimir Regiment, regarded by the Russians as the heroes of the Alma for their counter-attack at the Great Redoubt, advanced down the forward slope of Shell

Hill. For their efforts they were rewarded with the attentions of the 18-pounders, which inflicted terrible casualties on their massed ranks. They stood it manfully for a few minutes before retiring – in good order – back over the hill.

By this time the whole Russian army was in full retreat. There was an angry conference behind Shell Hill between Dannenburg and Prince Menschikoff, who had waited five hundred yards to the rear with the two Grand Dukes. Menschikoff wanted to halt the withdrawal.

Dannenburg replied, 'Highness, to stop the troops here would be to let them be destroyed to the last man. If your Highness thinks otherwise, have the goodness to give the orders yourself, and take from me the command.'

Menschikoff rode from the field. Under the covering fire of the two steamers *Chersonese* and *Vladimir* in Sebastopol Harbour, the Russians abandoned Mount Inkerman. In British accounts of the fighting, the Russians are generally seen as a formless mass, usually fleeing, scattering, surrendering or bayoneting the wounded, but the duration, ferocity and high butcher's bill of this battle show that this was not the whole story. In the smoke and fog and broken ground there was opportunity for men to behave well or badly, as cowards, brutes or heroes, and often as all three in turn. No one who has walked the field of Inkerman can fail to come away impressed by the courage and patriotism of the grey-coated soldiers of the Tsar.

'Our loss has been a sad one and we are but ill able to stand such "Victories",' said Henry Clifford; he spoke the truth. There was none of the cheering heard at the Alma, or even Balaklava; relief and exhaustion were what most men felt. An army already weary, wet and hungry before the battle had even started had fought a brave and determined enemy to a bloody standstill. They had given the Russians, in the words of General Pennefather, 'A hell of a towelling', but they had done so at an appalling cost.

'The aspect of the field was awful,' wrote Timothy Gowing, 'dead and dying mutilated bodies in all directions. Many of our men had been wounded frequently with shot and bayonet; others were cut limb from limb, and yet a spark of life remained. Many had perished by the bayonet, and it was noticed that but few had fallen with one thrust. In and around the Two-Gun Battery the sights were sickening. Our Guardsmen, and 41st, 47th and 49th, lay locked in the arms of the foe with their bayonets through each other – dead. Some of our officers and men were found dead with no fewer than twelve or fifteen bayonet wounds; the appearance of the poor fellows who had been thus tortured was painful. To describe the scene would be impossible – the result of eight hours' hand-to-hand conflict – it was horrible to look upon. Scarcely did any field in the whole Peninsular War present, as a result of conflict, such a murderous spectacle as the terrible sights that now lay before us. There were literally piles of dead, lying in every posture one could imagine; I may say that there were acres of defaced humanity – ghastly wounds from sword, bayonet, grape and round shot; poor fellows literally shattered, and yet with life still in them. Others lay as if they had been asleep – friend and foe mixed together. In some parts of the field our men lay in ranks as they had stood; and the enemy in columns, one on top of the other.

'The Russian Guardsmen lay thick all over the field; upwards of 2,000 dead were found belonging to the enemy. Just outside the Two-Gun Battery the wounded were numerous and their groans were pitiful, while cries of despair burst from the lips of some as they lay, thinking perhaps of wives and helpless little ones far away.'

Nearly 11,000 Russians had fallen – most of them killed – including 256 officers and six generals. British losses were 2,357, of whom 597 were killed. Of the ten British generals who had taken the field that morning, all were dead or wounded, as well as five of their successors, and 130 British officers were wounded and 39 were dead or dying. The French had lost 786 men. The dead and wounded strewed the ground – little more than a square mile – over which 56,000 men had fought, from Shell Hill in the north to Home Ridge in the south, from the Careenage Ravine in the west to the Sandbag Battery in the east. It was there, at the Sandbag Battery, that Marshal Canrobert rode up, looked at the thickly piled dead of three nations and declared, 'Quel abbatoir!'

CHAPTER SEVEN

On the morning after the Battle of Inkerman, Fanny Duberly and Henry rode from Balaklava up to the front, intending to tour the battlefield. At the last minute Fanny, by now accustomed to the sight of dead and wounded, turned back, because of the reports already coming down from those who had been there.

'I could not go. The thought of it made me shudder and turn sick. On his return, Henry told me that the field of Alma was child's play to this!' she wrote.

Others, like Midshipman Evelyn Wood, had more practical motives for visiting the field. 'My light sailor's shoes were worn out within a week, in carrying messages for our Commander while he and my shipmates were at meals. I could not have gone on working but that John Handcock, the Marine who had looked after me on board, and who was stationed on Balaklava Heights, hearing of my shoeless state, sent me down a pair of his own boots. These were also worn out, for although I rode my pony down to Balaklava, it was necessary for me to walk up, as it could not carry me and the things I brought for the Mess. I did not like the idea, however of despoiling a dead man, so I took a Bluejacket with me, to whom I promised half a sovereign for a satisfactory fit. These he soon produced, and I had reason to praise the good workmanship of the Russian boot contractors.'

Riding the battlefield, Henry Clifford encountered one of the men he had fought with. 'This morning as I passed the Russians, prisoners and wounded, a man amongst them ran up and called out to me and pointed to his shoulder bound up. It was the poor fellow whose arm I had cut off yesterday; he laughed and said "Bono Johnny". I took his hand and shook it heartily and the tears came in my eyes. I had not a shilling in my pocket; had I a bag of gold he should have had it. I enquired if he had been cared for and the Doctor told me he had and was doing well.'

Clifford reflected on his actions the day before. 'The excitement certainly was tremendous while it lasted, and it is well perhaps it is so, for I am sure in cold blood I never could strike at a man as I did then and if I had not, in all probability, those with me would not have charged and we should have lost our lives.'

The work of collecting the wounded and burying the dead went on; it was not always clear which were which. Captain Macdonald of the 95th, bayoneted twenty times by the Russians after he had ordered Sergeant Pat Murphy to leave him, was found by a group of men of his own regiment who did not recognise him, so covered in mud was he. Unsure whether he was alive or dead, they followed the standard army procedure in such cases: they picked him up to chest height and dropped him, to see if he grunted. Realising, perhaps from his voice, that he was their adjutant they carried him off the field. Astonishingly, Captain Macdonald lived, and died peacefully in his bed in 1876.

Behind Home Ridge, officers and men of the 2nd Division were surveying the wreckage of their camp. John Hume said he: 'found a dead artilleryman seated in our stone shelter where we used to sit in fine weather. He had evidently gone there to have a quiet smoke under cover. A round shot or piece of shell took the top of his head off, leaving him sitting up leaning against the wall as if asleep. Two of the occupants of our tent, my brother and Barnston, being severely wounded, did not return to camp.'

Many of the small comforts they had managed to scrape together had been destroyed. According to Hume, Daubeney, their commanding officer, who had led the gallant 30-man charge into a Russian column, had come back to a severe disappointment.

'After the fight Lieutenant-Colonel Daubeney sent his servant for a bottle of beer; he had got two small casks containing bottled beer and porter a day or two before. The servant found that a round shot had passed through the casks, which were placed end to end. Only one bottle was unbroken. This was a serious loss, as beer was a great luxury at the time.'

The beer wasn't the only loss. 'The whole of the band instruments of the 55th were destroyed during the battle; they had always been placed in a tent by themselves for safety. The tents were all struck, by order of General Pennefather, when the battle began. The English artillery galloped over the tents, and all our instruments were smashed – a serious matter for the officers, who had to replace them after the war at a cost of upwards of £500.'

At a time when regiments, who were often in remote locations for long periods, depended on their bands for entertainment, this was a very serious loss.

At Lord Raglan's Headquarters that morning, Somerset Calthorpe said stable doors were being shut.

'It was resolved to occupy all ground on which the battle of Inkerman had been fought, and to construct a system of redoubts for the better protection of this part of the position. These works will take considerable time and labour to make. In the meanwhile a strong brigade of 4,000 French troops are to camp in the immediate vicinity of our 2nd Division . . .

'It was also decided at this council of war that a letter should be addressed to Prince Menschikoff by the Allied Generals, complaining of the Russian soldiers stabbing our wounded men when lying on the ground.'

Menschikoff's reply, as recorded by Henry Clifford, was reasonable enough in the circumstances:

'The answer made to Lord Raglan's remonstrances touching the brutal treatment of our wounded met with on the ground at Inkerman, was to this effect, "the General Menschikoff was sorry for it, but if men would come and fight an ignorant people without provocation in their own Country they must expect it."'

At a second Allied council-of-war on 7 November, Calthorpe heard more urgent matters discussed.

'It had been, as you may remember, the intention to have assaulted the town on the morning of this day, and indeed Lord Raglan was still anxious for it to be carried out. General Canrobert, however, was strongly opposed to it, and maintained that it would be utterly impracticable to attempt to storm the place with our present small force, while the enemy had so large an army in the field, and which at any moment might again attack us at any point in our rear. He therefore counselled that we should wait for reinforcements which are shortly to be expected; and that in the meantime we should not make any offensive movement against the enemy, but confine ourselves to acting on the defensive, holding our present works without making any absolute advance. For the better protection of the right of our position, he (General Canrobert) engaged that the French troops should construct the greater portion of the new works to be erected there, and also that they should occupy the same. Lord Raglan, although utterly opposed in every way to the first part of this scheme, had no alternative but to accept it, as the English Army was now reduced to little more than 16,000 bayonets.'

The battle of Inkerman had had two immediate results, both of which were brought home at this conference. Firstly, there was now no chance of an immediate storm of Sebastopol until the spring. Some British generals at the conference, including de Lacy Evans, even urged that the Crimea be evacuated for the winter. Raglan rejected this, realising that an embarkation under the enemy's noses would be fraught with danger and that it would be considered an admission of defeat – and if they went, it would be unlikely that they would ever to able to return.

The second result was that from now on in this enterprise, the French were the senior partners.

'The siege is I fear only nominal,' wrote Henry Clifford a few days later. 'We are I believe, only keeping up appearances. Our force is much weakened by sickness and fighting, and can only hold the ground of our position and batteries till more *men* are sent out. The French receive reinforcements daily, and will have 50,000 men before long. I try to believe we have 12,000 fighting men, but we could not bring more than 10,000 into the field in case of a row, if that. Strong letters were written from the right place to the Duke of Newcastle after the battle of the Inkerman, in which I don't think any very pleasing prospects were pointed out, and *men! men!* called for even more than shot and shell, medicine for the sick, or warm clothing for the winter.'

The conference agreed that the army should be 'hutted', and preparations were set in hand for overwintering before Sebastopol. Just how effective these measures were would soon become clear.

For their part, the Russians, despite the mauling they had received at Inkerman, had some cause for optimism. The battle had achieved one of its subsidiary aims: it had delayed the enemy's assault on Sebastopol. From now on their policy was decided. The battle had shown that the Russian army could not defeat the Allies on the open battlefield. The fire of the Minié was too devastating, and their columns were too clumsy, slow-moving and ill-co-ordinated. Indeed, many Russian junior offices had come to the conclusion that they were simply not trained to engage in modern warfare. However, if conditions inside Sebastopol were hard, and likely to get harder as the year drew to a close, on the Upland they would be a great deal worse. For the time being, there would be no more offensives; in Tsar Nicholas's words, it was time to employ two of Russia's oldest and most reliable generals: Generals Janvier and Fevrier.

The Russians did not have to wait that long. In the early hours of 14 November, Midshipman Evelyn Wood was lying in his tent in the Naval Brigade camp. Like many men on the Heights, Wood was suffering from chronic diarrhoea brought on by a steady diet of salt pork, often uncooked, and the effects of constant cold and wet. Ill and half asleep, Wood nevertheless retained his sailor's ear for the weather.

'It was blowing steadily in gusts at 4 a.m. when the battery Relief marched off, and sheets of rain beating on the tent made me congratulate myself I been excused duty. At about 5 a.m. the tent pole was bending so ominously that the two Lieutenants in the tent with me, having put on all the clothes they possessed, held the pole by turns. At six o'clock, however, while the pole still held intact, a heavier blast of wind, lifting the tent right up in the air, carried it away. I was certainly uncomfortable with the rain beating down on me, and yet my sufferings were as nothing in comparison with hundreds of our soldier-comrades, some of whom wounded, and many sick, lay for hours exposed to the fury of the elements; for the hospital marquees, owing to their great spread of canvas, offered so much resistance to the wind that they were the first to fall.'

It was the beginning of one of the worst hurricanes ever recorded in the Black Sea. The scene was the same in all of the camps.

Henry Clifford wrote, 'General Buller's Bell tent went down about the first. The pole broke, and I found him floundering about like a rabbit in a net, the tent on top of him; and when we got the door open and let him out, he was not in the best of humours. He would not come into Glyn's and my tent, which we managed to keep standing through it all, and would go and sit out in the open, under a small mud bank, built to protect his horses . . .

At 10 o'clock the storm abated sufficiently to allow us to get his tent up again, and we got him into it, but so cold he could not stand.

I got him into bed, and with the help of a stiff glass of rum and water, got him warm in the course of a few hours. It was sad to see the poor old gentleman in such a state, turned out of his frail dwelling in such weather.'

John Hume of the 55th was on picquet at the Barrier. 'It was almost impossible to stand, and we often had to move about on our hands and knees. I got under shelter as much as I could, and sat on a very hard stone. A number of things were blown from the camp as far as my picquet; amongst other articles an air-cushion came sailing down. One of my men caught it and gave it to me. I found it a great luxury, as I could not move about much, and the stone was growing harder ... My servant, Hartley, with great difficulty brought me my breakfast – some capital Irish stew. He gave a dismal account of the state of the camp. All the tents were down, and the sick and others were exposed to the storm and rain.'

Back at the Naval Brigade camp, Evelyn Wood was one of them. 'When the tent blew away, my two companions took shelter under a low wall of stones which we had built round the powder magazine about a hundred yards from where our tent had stood, and when the storm had moderated a little more, more rain falling, I tried to join them; but the wind knocked me down, and I travelled the intervening distance on my hands and knees. Even in this fashion, however, the wind was too much for my remaining strength, and I should not have got to the wall but that our Gunnery Lieutenant and two Bluejackets going down on their knees, and joining hands, stretched out to intercept me. When I got under the shelter of the wall my comrades did all they could to help me, giving me the most sheltered spot.

'As we looked around, we could not see more than two or three tents in any of the camps still standing, and these were protected by stone walls. We lay huddled together, thinking what might have happened to the ships.'

It was worst of all for the ships, even in the harbour. Fanny Duberly was in her quarters aboard the *Star of the South*. 'At seven o'clock, when I looked through the stern cabin windows, the harbour was seething and covered with foam, and the ships swinging terribly. By nine it had increased to a frightful extent, and I could hardly, even when clinging to the ship, keep my footing on deck,' she wrote. 'The spray, dashing over the cliffs many hundred feet, fell like heavy rain into the harbour. Ships were crushing and crowding, all adrift, all breaking and grinding each other to pieces. The stern work of the *Star of the South* was being ground away by the huge sides of the *Medway*, which was perpetually heaving against her.'

It was catastrophic for ships anchored outside the harbour, some of whose masters had complained only days before about not being admitted to its shelter. Determined as ever not to miss anything – her nickname among the troops was The Vulture – Fanny managed to struggle ashore and headed for a viewpoint on the rocks.

'Captain Sayer, Mr Rochfort, and Captain Frain started for the rocks to try if by any means they could save life,' she said. 'The next tidings were that the *Prince* and the *Resolute*, the *Rip van Winkle*, the *Wanderer*, the *Progress*, and a foreign barque, had all gone down, and out of the whole, not a dozen people saved. At two o'clock, in spite of wind and weather, I managed to scramble from ship to ship, and went ashore to see this most disastrous sight . . . At the moment after my arrival, the devoted and beautiful little clipper ship *Wild Wave* was riding to her death. Her captain and crew – all but three small boys – had deserted her at nine o'clock; and she was now, with all her masts standing, and her helpless freight on board, drifting with her graceful outlines and her heart of oak, straight to her doom. She is under our feet. God have mercy on those children now!

'Captain Frain, Captain Liddell, and some seamen heave a rope downwards, at which one boy springs, but the huge wave is rolling backwards, and he is never seen again.

'A second time they hurl it down to the boy standing on the stern frame, but the ship surging down upon the ruthless rocks, the deck parts beneath his feet, and he is torn, mangled and helpless; but clinging still, until a wave springs towards him eagerly, and claims him for the sea.

'The third and last survivor catches at the friendly rope, and swooning with exhaustion and fear, he is laid upon the rock; while in a moment, with one single bound, the little ship springs upwards, as though she, too, was imploring aid and falls back a scattered mass, covering the sea with splinters, masts, cargo, hay, bread, and ropes.'

In the afternoon Somerset Calthorpe went out to assess the

damage. 'Out of all the camps, both English and French, consisting of many thousands of tents, I don't think a dozen had stood during the gale. Everywhere the hospital marquees had been blown down ... Our poor sick and wounded soldiers were consequently exposed to the weather, and I fear many deaths were hastened, and all had their sufferings increased by this sad catastrophe. The light cavalry camp on the heights presented the most melancholy aspect; the unfortunate horses looked like drowned rats; a quantity of the saddlery and accoutrements had been blown to the winds, no one knew where. Several of the horses were dying, if not already dead; the forage was destroyed, so that nothing could be given to the unhappy animals to eat.'

By the evening the storm had abated. The extent of the disaster outside the harbour became clear by morning, which dawned bright and still. A total of twenty-one ships had gone down, mostly with all hands. Even more disastrous for the British than the loss of life was the loss of stores for the winter. The steamer *Prince* went down with 160 souls. She had also been carrying 2,700 tons of supplies, including warm clothing and medical stores.

The storm of 14 November was followed, briefly, by milder weather – the sun even appeared now and then – but it did not last. By early December, heavy rains had given way to hail, snow and biting winds coming off the sea. Occasional thaws would leave the Upland and the roads to Balaklava a sea of mud; they were invariably followed by hard frosts, then rain, hail, and more snow.

Thus began the slow death of the army of the Alma, Balaklava and Inkerman. It died of starvation and exposure, from lack of winter clothing, fuel and food. The problem was not the extreme weather conditions – Evelyn Wood thought the weather no worse than could be expected in the north of England in a bad winter, and many of these officers and men had served in Canada – but the total inadequacy of the army's administration to cope with them.

The public at home had been made aware, by Russell of *The Times* and others, of the army's atrocious medical and supply arrangements. Over the next four months they would face – and fail – their severest test. The Commissariat, run by Commissary-General Filder with, in his own words, three incompetent clerks, was staffed at the lower levels by men ill-paid, despised for not being gentlemen, and unwilling to put their careers at risk by shouldering any kind of responsibility. These men were dependent on their meagre salaries to live, and likely to be held personally responsible for any money spent or supplies issued without proper authorisation.

The system of forms, authorisations, requisitions and dockets, all of them, naturally, in triplicate, baffled even those with a lifetime's experience in the Service. As often as not the problem was not the lack of supplies as the inability to get them to those who needed them.

General von Manteuffel once said that any reasonably competent officer could command a panzer division, but that it took a genius to supply one. Lord Raglan had no such genius at his disposal; there was no one who could cut the Gordian knot of red tape and get what supplies there were moving.

In contrast with the French, who had a hutted town of one hundred acres for their Commissariat, plus a further fifty acres of shops, there was no officer with overall responsibility among the British, and no administrative chain of command. In Balaklava itself, chaos reigned supreme. A shipload of lime-juice sat in the harbour while, nine miles away, men's teeth fell out from scurvy. Bales of hay rotted, or were used as makeshift jetties while, in the Light Brigade camp, as Henry Clifford wrote home: 'The cavalry horses are so hard put to it that they have eaten each other's tails off, *this will make you laugh, but not us who see it and the cause.*'

Boxes of ammunition, rations, clothing, medicines, surgical equipment, engineer stores, building materials, all lay about in great profusion but total disorder. Ships arrived unexpectedly and were either unloaded – their cargoes left to rot or decay on the quays or in the streets – or were sent back to Constantinople, only to repeat the journey days later. The town itself horrified those who visited, whether arriving by sea, or coming down from the siege lines.

Fanny Duberly, who lived amongst it by day and spent nights aboard ship, described it. 'If any body should ever wish to erect a "Model Balaklava" in England, I will tell him the ingredients necessary. Take a village of ruined houses and hovels in the extremest state of all imaginable dirt; allow the rain to pour into and outside them, until the whole place is a swamp of filth ankle-deep, catch about, on an average, 1000 sick Turks with the plague, and cram them into the houses indiscriminately; kill about 100 a-day, and bury them so as to be scarcely covered with earth, leaving them to rot at leisure – taking care to keep up the supply. On to one part of the beach drive all the exhausted bat ponies, dying bullocks, and worn-out camels, and leave them to die of starvation. They will generally do so in about three days, when they will soon begin to rot, and smell accordingly. Collect together from the water of the harbour all the offal of the animals slaughtered for the use of the occupants of above 100 ships, to say nothing of the inhabitants of the town – which together with an occasional floating human body, whole or in parts, and the driftwood of the wrecks, pretty well covers the water – and stew them all up together in a narrow harbour, and you will have a tolerable imitation of the real essence of Balaklava. If this is not *piquante* enough, let some men be instructed to sit and smoke on the powder barrels landing on the quay; which I myself saw two men doing today, on the Ordnance Wharf.'

Henry Clifford wrote home after a trip to the harbour hunting for provisions, 'I was from early this morning until now, 6 o'clock, going 8 miles and getting through the streets (if they may be called so) on horseback. In every direction horses and oxen are to be seen dead or dying in the mud and our men working more like beasts of burden than Christians are floundering about up to their knees in mud. Three horses in every Cavalry Regiment die on average every night of cold and hunger. Siege guns, mule carts, ox and artillery wagons, broken or upset, corn sacks full of corn, bales of hay, sacks of spoiled biscuits are tumbled together in wonderful confusion and the number of men carried on stretchers, French, English and Turks, tell the tale of misery, suffering, illness, death, the consequence of war.'

What supplies did move up onto the Heights went by the single unmetalled track via the Col, climbing six hundred feet over nine miles. The only road – the Woronzov – could be reached only by another equally bad track. Work that should have been done on these tracks while the weather allowed was neglected: British troops were too busy on the trenches and batteries, and the 11,000 Turks now dying by degrees in and around Balaklava had been employed only briefly. So every bullet, every blanket, every biscuit, had to be painfully man-packed up the Heights by soldiers already worn out from long wet nights in the trenches, bad diet and inadequate shelter from wind, rain, snow and frosts.

Midshipman Evelyn Wood, of the Naval Brigade, watched the soldiers' plight with horror. 'The troops at Balaklava in December and in January carried on their heads 7000 loads of siege materials from the harbour to the Engineer Parks, and 145 tons of biscuits to the Army Headquarters; if they had not done so, not a man in the Front could have existed. The half-starved, insufficiently clad, overworked, but uncomplaining Old soldier serving at the Front, was generally in the trenches four or five nights, and in one recorded instance for six nights, in a week; those on sentry duty, 300 yards in advance of our works, having to stand motionless for two hours at a time. When they got back to camp they had but the shelter of a worn-out tent, through which the rain beating, collected in puddles; the feeblest fell asleep, completely exhausted, to awake shivering, and carried to a hospital tent but little better than the company tent, and two or three days later to a grave. The stronger men went out with picks when available, and dug up roots of stunted oak and vines for fuel, and then roasting the green coffee berry in the lid of the canteen, pounded it in a shell fragment, and boiled it. The greater number, however, unequal to so much effort for so little result, consuming their biscuit and rum, slept, generally in a wet greatcoat or blanket, until required to carry a load of ammunition or biscuit. These loads were limited to 40lbs; but the exertion was great, for the men on the Balaklava track waded through mud.'

Incredibly for an Empire founded partly on the tea trade, the soldiers were mostly issued with green coffee berries, instead of tea, making the simple production of a hot drink too laborious and time-consuming for many to bother with. It was not until well into December that the army followed the navy's example, and centralised the cooking of rations.

The Highlanders guarding the lines of communication were spared trench work, but they were allotted the task of carrying artillery ammunition up to the batteries. Surgeon Munro described how it was done.

'So many loose shot or shell were placed in a field blanket, and two or four men, grasping the blanket by the corners, swung the load along between them. Many of the men preferred slinging the loads over their backs, and staggering along under the weight of two or more shot. To carry heavy loads over a good road would have been severe labour of itself, but to flounder under them through deep, tenacious mud, into which at every step the men sank halfway up to the knee, and out of which it required a considerable amount of muscular effort to drag their feet, made the labour ten times more severe. It was too much to require from men exhausted by starvation and by previous disease, from which many had barely recovered, and from existing disease, from which many suffered, but of which they made no complaint, until they were unable to drag one leg after another.

'The parties generally returned to camp, after performing this duty, perfectly done up, their greatcoats soaked through by the rain or sleet, their underclothes saturated by the profuse perspiration caused by the violent exertion of carrying heavy loads over such ground as I have described, and their well-worn boots and trews thickly coated with mud. They had no change of clothes, no dry things to put on instead of their wet ones, and were obliged to sit or lie down in their wet things on the damp ground within their tents, and shiver from cold until the next issue of grog.'

Fatigue was exacerbated by bad diet. Munro described the consequences. 'We came to loathe our daily dole of salt beef or pork, and as we moved through our camp, and looked into the soldiers' tents, their ration meat might be seen piled up in heaps within, untouched for days, because they would not or could not eat, or had no fuel, or even did not know how to cook, so as to make it palatable. Indeed this necessary article (fuel) was so scarce at times that we had barely sufficient to boil the water for our tea, in which we soaked the hard dry biscuit, the only process by which many who were not blessed with good teeth could make it eatable, and which, often for days together, was the only nourishment many of us had. The consequence was that numbers of the men became scorbutic, and many of them died of scorbutic dysentery.'

Disease racked the army. All the sicknesses that had beset the army in the summer and autumn now attacked again with redoubled force. Between October and April 1,435 men died from cholera, 5,301 from diarrhoea and dysentery, 2,355 from fever. The total deaths from disease – 10,914 – represented thirty-five per cent of the strength of an already weakened army. By January 1855, it was estimated that only about a third of the army was fit for duty. One regiment, the 63rd, reported a bayonet strength of seven.

Of those fit for duty, many were ill by any normal standards, but

either reluctant to leave their comrades or, even more under-
standably, reluctant to report to one of the overflowing hospitals.
Douglas Reid, a newly joined assistant surgeon attached to the 90th
Regiment, was taken on arrival to see that regiment's hospital.

'I expected to see a hut or building of some kind, and was much
astonished when he pointed out a row of bell-tents pitched, like all
the others, in the mud. I looked into some of them and found them
crowded with sick, ten or twelve men in each tent with their feet
towards the pole and their heads towards the curtain. They were
lying on the bare ground wrapped in their greatcoats. It struck me
that whatever was the matter with them they had a very poor chance
of recovery. They were being sent down daily in batches to Balaklava
for embarkation to Scutari or England. The diseases from which
they suffered were chiefly dysentery and fever. The regiment had
then been more than two months in camp, and this was the best
they could do for their sick and wounded.'

For the men bound to Scutari, the journey to Balaklava was a
torment. Fanny Duberly saw some arriving at the harbour. 'We have
no ambulance wagons,' she wrote, 'they are nearly all broken down,
or the mules are dead, or the drivers dead drunk; as well one as the
other, as far as usefullness goes. Our poor Cavalry horses, as we
know full well, are all unequal to the task of carrying down the
sick; and the French have provided transports for us for some time.
They were complaisant enough at first, but now (the men I mean)
begin to grumble and to do their work cruelly. One poor fellow,
wounded and frostbitten in the hands and feet, was taken roughly
from his mule and huddled down in the mud, despite his agonised
screams and cries. Another Frenchman drove his empty mule so
carelessly past one that was still laden as to cut the poor sufferer's
legs with the iron bar, and cause him cruel pain.

'Why can we not tend our own sick? Why are we so helpless and
so broken down?

'Oh England! England! blot out the lion and the unicorn: let the
supporters of your arms henceforth be, Imbecility and Death!'

Conditions on the transports were even worse. Timothy Gowing,
bayoneted in both thighs at Inkerman, had been carried down to
Balaklava by the French, for whom he had nothing but the highest
praise. He was loaded onto a steamer bound for Scutari.

'It was a horrible scene – poor fellows having every description of wound; and many died before we left the harbour. We were packed on board anyhow – to live or die – and away we went. The sea was rather boisterous, and I was not very comfortable with poor fellows dying fast all around me. There were not sufficient medical officers to look after fifty men, much less three or four hundred.

'Picture a ship rolling and tossing about at sea with such a freight! The sight was heart-rending; many of our poor fellows had not had the slightest things done for them since they were wounded on that bloody field. They had fought and helped to uphold the honour of their country and were now left to die in agony.'

The Barrack Hospital to which Gowing was bound had been described to Lord Raglan by the Chief Medical Officer, Dr John Hall, as being on a very creditable footing, with nothing missing. The truth was very different. There was no bedding, no furniture of any description, no operating tables and no screens. Men lying on bare floors awaiting operations were forced to watch the horrors that would shortly be visited upon them.

There was no soap, no towels, no scrubbing brushes. There was no hospital clothing, no kettles, knives, forks or spoons. Rations were cooked in thirteen great Turkish coppers which rarely even boiled the water, let alone cooked the meat. There were no rations suitable for the sick or convalescent, and very few drugs. The laundry had been contracted out to a Greek who washed shirts and blankets – if at all – in cold water. There were twenty-three chamber-pots for a hospital containing 2,500 men, most of whom were too ill to crawl to the filthy, overflowing latrine tubs placed at the end of each ward. There was *nothing* that would make this fit to be described as a hospital, other than a staff of overworked doctors and a complement of reluctant orderlies composed of those soldiers for whom their regiments could find no other use.

W.H. Russell's despatches of 9, 12 and 13 October described the sufferings of the sick and wounded, and mobilised public opinion. On 13 October, Sir Robert Peel, third baronet and brother of Captain William Peel RN, opened *The Times Fund*, which raised the astonishing sum of £30,000 within weeks.

Florence Nightingale, whose wish to become a nurse – a class of person even more despised than the private soldier – had so horrified her family, was, with all her other formidable qualities, extremely well connected. The Secretary-at-War, Sidney Herbert, was a close and life-long friend; his letter to her, asking her to proceed at once to Scutari with forty nurses, crossed hers offering to go. Armed with sole discretion in the spending of *The Times'* £30,000 and unlimited power of drawing on the government, Florence and her party arrived at Scutari on 5 November, while – as yet unbeknown to any at the Barrack Hospital – the Battle of Inkerman was raging. She and her nurses received an insincere and patronising welcome from the military authorities and were quietly sidelines. The forty ladies were allocated six small rooms, one of them occupied by a dead Russian general.

Florence stayed her hand, curbing her nurses' desire to get to work. Piecemeal measures, she knew, would serve only to make a bad situation tolerable. Only a complete breakdown in the system would give her the absolute power she needed.

This was not long in coming. With casualties from Inkerman and the sick from the siege lines pouring in, the authorities turned in desperation to Miss Nightingale. Within weeks, bypassing officialdom and drawing on all the money at her disposal, she became, in effect, Purveyor-in-Chief to the army. For every imaginable necessity from the smallest to the greatest, the doctors – who, Florence wrote, worked like lions – applied to her, the so-called 'Lady-in Chief'.

Florence Nightingale is remembered chiefly as The Lady of the Lamp for the nightly rounds she made at the end of every twenty-hour day, talking to the men and treating them as Christian human beings. She was actually an administrator of the highest order. She re-organised the kitchens, with new boilers which *she* purchased, and provided special invalid diets. She oversaw the scrubbing of every wall, floor and ceiling in the hospital; she hired Turkish laundresses and personally supervised their work; she had new wards prepared by Turkish labourers and arbitrated when they went on strike.

One regiment – the 39th – had come out in tropical kit; she provided them with warm clothing procured in the markets of Constantinople. This particular incident prompted her to write to Herbert that she was now clothing the British army.

She opened a soldiers' dry canteen, a reading room, four schools and a remittance scheme by which soldiers could – and did – send money home. The 'proper' authorities – led by Dr Hall – opposed her at every turn, piled on petty persecutions, fermented trouble among the nurses, and indulged in whispering campaigns. Their voices were stilled at last, by a letter which arrived – via Sidney Herbert – from a lady whose word was unanswerable.

'Let Mrs Herbert ... know that I wish Miss Nightingale and the ladies would tell these poor noble wounded and sick men that *no one* takes a warmer interest or feels *more* for their sufferings or admires their courage and heroism *more* than their Queen. Day and night she thinks of her beloved troops. So does the Prince. Beg Mrs Herbert to communicate these words to those ladies, as I know *our* sympathy is valued by those noble fellows.'

The letter was read out in every ward, and men who had stormed the Great Redoubt, charged the Russian guns at Balaklava, or stood in the bloody butcher's yard of the Sandbag Battery, heard the message with tears in their eyes.

'She thinks of us,' they said. 'Queen Victoria is a Queen who is very *fond* of her soldiers.'

For all Florence Nightingale's work, death rates at the hospital remained obstinately high: unknown to her, or to anyone else, the hospital had a fatal flaw. The Sanitary Commission, sent out by the Government later in the year, made its report: it had a defective sanitation system which made it a death-trap. Men arrived from Sebastopol with diseases associated with starvation and cold; they died of those they picked up at the Barrack Hospital.

Regiments' death rates depended on how many men they had sent to Scutari.

Dr John Hall retired with a KCB – or Knight of the Crimean Burial Grounds, as Florence wrote. Florence Nightingale returned a national heroine, but broken, bereaved. Not even the ringing cheers of the soldiers in the batteries above Sebastopol, who had strewn her way with fresh flowers, could remove the sense of failure that dogged her.

'Oh my poor men,' she wrote, 'I am a bad mother to come home and leave you in your Crimean graves – 73 per cent in 8 regiments in 6 months from disease alone – who thinks of that now.'

By the time she was carried to her family grave by six sergeants, in 1910, she had transformed the public image of both nurse and soldier, established nursing colleges, advanced the cause of public health and sanitation worldwide and overseen far-reaching changes in the theory and practice of military medicine. The debt owed to Florence Nightingale by generations of British soldiers is incalculable.

Back in the Crimea, February brought some improvements. The army was now hutted – the pre-fabricated wooden huts which had arrived in early January had been erected all over the Heights and around Balaklava. On 13 February, three steamers, the *Ermina*, *Sarnia* and *Pioneer*, arrived at Balaklava bringing 1,000 tons of gifts provided by the British public via the Crimean Army Fund: flannel shirts, woollen jerseys, stockings, gloves, earless woollen hats christened – and still known as – Balaklavas, sheepskin coats, preserved meats and vegetables, bacon, cheese, porter, ale, wine, tobacco, Christmas puddings; there were even Fortnum's hampers, containing delicacies many soldiers sampled for the first and only time in their lives. The Duke of Portland sent out jars of old Welbeck ale, which were distributed among the regiments. Another ducal landowner donated a hundred deer which a pastry-cook converted into potted venison; an Argyll distillery sent cases of whisky for the use of the Highland Brigade; London booksellers sent books and periodicals.

These gifts – the luxuries, the necessities and the wholly superfluous – packed by enthusiastic local groups in village halls across the country and transported free of charge by the railway companies, arrived in great profusion, and went a long way to alleviating the miseries of life in the camps, the batteries and the trenches. Perhaps more than that, they told the troops that if the administration had failed them, the public knew of their plight and cared about it. The first was nothing new for the British soldier; the second was little short of a revolution.

In February, work began on a railway from Balaklava to the plateau. Fanny Duberly saw the first of the workmen arrive.

'A cargo of "navvies" came out today in the *Lady Alice Lambton*. Their arrival makes a great sensation. Some of them immediately went ashore, and set out for a walk "to see if they could see e'er a —— Rooshian".'

In the meantime, the arduous work of man-packing continued to affect morale. One witness was someone who might never have lived to see it: Timothy Gowing had been lucky. The Scutari hospital was too full to accept him, so his ship was sent to Malta. Pampered by the kind-hearted Maltese, he made a swift recovery.

Other men might have sought to extend their Mediterranean winter break; not so Gowing. By February, he wrote, 'Regiments and drafts kept passing on for the front, and I was longing to have a slap at them once more, just by way of getting out of debt. So, towards the end of February 1855 – after I had made some splendid purchases in the way of good blankets, two dozen good flannel shirts, two dozen ditto drawers, two dozen warm gloves for my comrades, a good supply of flannels for myself, and a brace of revolvers – off I went once more to fight for Old England, home and glory.'

Gowing duly returned to do his duty. He described accompanying a fatigue party down to the harbour.

'I was one of the sergeants with a party of men that had been sent to Balaclava to bring up supplies in the way of biscuit and pork, or salt junk (salt beef). We had a young officer with us, well mounted, who had but little compassion for poor fellows who were doing their best, trudging through the mud up to their ankles, with a heavy load upon their backs. The party were not going fast enough to suit the whim of our young and inexperienced commander, who called out to the writer: "Take this man's name Sergeant, and make a prisoner of him when we get home."

'The unfortunate man was doing his best to keep up, and he gave our young officer such a contemptuous look as I shall not forget as long as I live. Throwing his load of biscuit down in the mud, he exclaimed: "Man indade! Soger indade! I'm only a poor broken-down commissariat mule!"

'The poor fellow was made a prisoner of at once, for insub-ordination. But when I explained the case to our Colonel he took quite a different view of the matter, forgave the man, and presented him with a good pair of warm socks and a pair of new boots; for the poor fellow had nothing but uppers and no soles for his old ones. And in order to teach our smart young officer how to respect men who were trying to do their duty sentenced him to three extra fatigues to Balaclava – and to walk it, the same as any other man.'

By the end of March the line had reached the Col and the soldiers' days as beasts of burden were drawing to a close – but even the railway was not without its dangers, as Surgeon Robinson of the Scots Fusilier Guards recorded.

'A sad railway casualty occurred last night; a strange incident to allude to out here. A party of the 71st Highlanders was returning by railway, from the trenches to their camp near Kade-koi, when, it is believed, owing to remissness in not putting on the break early enough, whilst going down the inclined plane, the chain broke, and the train went off the line; consequently the carriages were upset. Three men, it is said, have been killed, and seven wounded. The majority, it would appear, seeing the result about to happen, jumped off in time to save themselves, and thus the officers all escaped.'

Another welcome development was the arrival of Colonel McMurdo, armed with independent purchasing powers, to oversee the formation of the Land Transport Corps, manned by old soldiers and new, specially selected recruits. McMurdo was soon assembling and organising horses, drivers' escorts and vehicles. The Treasury began to squeal. The Secretary to the Treasury, Sir Charles Trevelyan, wrote on one of McMurdo's requisitions, 'Colonel McMurdo must limit his expenditure.'

McMurdo sent it back, having written below, 'When Sir Charles Trevelyan limits the war, I will limit my expenditure.'

This new activity, and the new resources being allotted to the army, were part of the Government's response to the public outrage at the soldiers' plight. Another part was the search for someone to blame. Lord Raglan, already under fire from Russell of *The Times* and his editor, Delane, for being remote and uncaring of his men's welfare, fitted the bill perfectly. Forgetting that they had foisted this campaign on Raglan late in the year and against his better judge-ment; forgetting the years of Government neglect and parsimony that had shorn the army of its administrative tail; ignoring – or ignorant of – the fact that he was now working a twenty-hour day in appalling conditions at an age when he should have been pot-tering about his estate, they now laid all the campaign's perceived failures at his door.

It did not save them – the Government fell at the end of January – but the new administration were no more sympathetic. Lord Panmure, in the new post of War Minister, informed Raglan brusquely that a Chief of Staff was to be sent out to 'assist' him, and to act as an Inspector-General.

When Lieutenant-General James Simpson arrived, he soon won over doubters with his pleasing and sympathetic manner. He wrote to his political masters, 'I consider Lord Raglan the most abused man I ever heard of!'

There was a change of ministry on the Russian side as well. On 16 February, a Russian force of 19,000, with cavalry and artillery, attacked Eupatoria, which was held by Omar Pasha and 23,000 Turks. After a day-long battle, the Russians were driven off. Despite the presence of some French troops and British Marines, it was an unequivocal Turkish victory – by no means the only one in this war.

A few days after receiving the news, Tsar Nicholas fell ill. On 2 March he died. *Punch* published a cruel cartoon of the Tsar dead on his camp-bed, with a skeleton in Russian general's uniform standing by the bedside, above the caption 'General Fevrier turned traitor'.

His son, Alexander II, soon left no one in any doubt that the war would continue. In a message to the defenders of Sebastopol he wrote, 'Passed away into life eternal, the supreme chief of the orthodox warriors blessed from on high their unequalled constancy and valour.'

As Timothy Gowing had observed at Malta, the army was being considerably reinforced. Fresh regiments had arrived throughout the winter, among them Hedley Vicars' 97th. Despite their sufferings in Piraeus, Vicars' regiment – nicknamed the Celestials after their sky-blue facings – made a distinct contrast with the regiments already there.

Henry Clifford saw them arrive. 'The 97th have just marched up from Balaclava . . . They have taken up ground to our right, between us and the Guards, about $\frac{1}{4}$ mile from my tent. They look so clean and smart, alongside of our chaps who have been day and night in the trenches, but I guess a month will take all their shine out of them.

'We hear large reinforcements are coming from Marseilles in English steamers, and four more regiments from England. Large Mortars are sent too, from Malta. The siege is now only nominal.

We fire a few shots during the day, but all seems at a standstill, waiting, I am sorry to say, for ammunition principally and men.'

Sadly, Clifford was right: within a month the Celestials had lost fifty men to sickness, and the newcomers were feeling the same frustrations as the rest of the army. Vicars wrote home, 'We are all anxiously waiting for Lord Raglan to storm Sebastopol; for though we must lose many in doing it, yet anything would be better than seeing our fine soldiers dying as they are daily. What should be done is to go at once with no more dilly-dallying.'

This was not his only worry. There were a number of Catholic Sisters among Miss Nightingale's nurses at Scutari, and this upset him deeply.

He wrote, 'I am sorry to hear of the Romish nurses being sent to Scutari to attend promiscuously upon Roman Catholics and Protestants. I know enough of Popery to dread its artifices. I pray to God to prevent them from turning away, to other mediators, any dying eyes from a dying saviour.'

Vicars was not alone in his concern, but he found the company of the soldiers always proved a tonic:

'In the trenches, the other day, one of our men amused us much. At the first shell which passed close to him, he dropped down on his back, screaming aloud for a doctor, for he was "kilt entirely". The doctor ran up to him, and asked where he had been hit, when he exclaimed "Och, och doctor! clane through the blanket!!"'

As well as new regiments, there were new drafts of men for regiments that had been in the Crimea since the start of the campaign. Often young and hurriedly trained – the lack of an experienced reserve was making itself felt – these men were to fight and die heroically in the months to come. Many felt that this was now a very different army to the one that had waded across the Alma. Billy Russell commented that when visiting a favourite old regiment or division he often found himself among strangers. A number of senior officers had gone home, the Duke of Cambridge among them. When his replacement, Lord Rokeby, saw the haggard faces of the Guards officers, and how few they were, he wept. De Lacy Evans had also gone home, pleading the adverse effects on his health of sleeping on the cold ground at the age of sixty-eight. In the House of Commons – he was Radical MP for Westminster – he was awarded the thanks of Parliament for his services. Other, younger, officers with less excuse, had also put in their papers and gone home.

Lord George Paget, who had only stayed on in the army because war broke out, had handed over command of his regiment in November and returned home to his beautiful wife Agnes. A hero of the Charge of the Light Brigade, he dined at Windsor Castle with the Queen and Prince Albert, and was eagerly questioned about the events of the war. Paget quickly discovered that the outburst of public enthusiasm expressed in the Relief Fund had its darker side. The press were highly critical of him for coming home early, and Paget soon found himself being cut in clubs.

'I will throw a veil,' Paget wrote, 'over the next seven weeks spent in my grateful country – for the credit of my countrymen, I would say were it not that my countrymen had gone mad, and were not answerable for their actions; though it would be unjust to class all alike, for I can with truth say that the sympathy that was shown me, by the many who still retained their reason, would have compensated me for the criticisms of others who followed the public press, but for the misery it entailed on my wife, who had committed her happiness and welfare to my hands, and who, in spite of the entreaties of myself and others, insisted on returning with me to the seat of war.'

By the end of February, Paget was back in the Crimea, commanding the Light Brigade, with Lady George at his side.

The public involvement in the war was one new development; there were others. March saw the arrival of Roger Fenton, the most famous – though by no means the only – photographer of the war. Fenton was only there for four months, but his work, and that of his colleagues, served to give the public a picture of the war less idealised than the sometimes overblown productions of the war artists and print-makers.

It is at this point that the nature of the war itself starts to change. There was nothing new in siege warfare, but the officers' and soldiers' letters from the opening months of the campaign described the kind of actions their grandfathers might have fought in. From winter onwards, they prefigure those of a later generation. Details of life in the trenches, complaints about conditions and rumours of peace alternate with requests for more socks, gloves, scarves or little luxury items from home.

Many men in the armies around or in Sebastopol must have

revisited home many times in their dreams, as Hedley Vicars described, 'It is curious what delightful dreams I have every time I fall asleep: now I am at Terling, surrounded by all your beloved faces; then again at Beckenham, with those I love so dearly; at another time I am going to read for old Sophy; again sitting by the blazing fire in the drawing-room, telling tales of the war to dear John; and awake to find my teeth chattering in my head, a sharp stone sticking into my side, the wind howling in gusts and squalls, and a concert of cannon and small shot, with variations from English, French, Turkish, and Russian performers, instead of a chant in the hall.'

There was a general feeling that this war had gone on long enough – the army had set off the previous year confident of being home 'in time for the pheasant shooting'. This produced the occasional outburst of war weariness but, more than anything else, the men were impatient to storm Sebastopol, at whatever cost.

Vicars wrote to his sister, 'As the honour of my Queen and my country is involved in this matter, not even to return to you, dearest, would I leave the Crimea, save through the harbour of Sebastopol.'

Severe weather had not brought any cessation in the war of the outposts, even if there was, from time to time, some fraternisation. Somerset Calthorpe recorded how, one cold night in front of Inkerman, some unarmed Russian soldiers approached the British picquets.

'They made signs that they wanted a light for their pipes, which one of our men gave them, and then they stayed a few minutes talking to our sentries, or rather trying to do so, the conversation being something after this wise:

1st Russian soldier. – "Englise bono!"

1st English soldier. – "Russkie bono!"

2nd Russian soldier. – "Francis bono!"

2nd English soldier. – "Bono!"

3rd Russian soldier. – "Oslem no bono!"

3rd English soldier. – "Ah, ah! Turk no bono!"

1st Russian soldier. – "Oslem!" making a face, and spitting on the ground to show his contempt.

1st English soldier. – "Turk!" pretending to run away, as if frightened, upon which all the party go into roars of laughter, and then after shaking hands, they return to their respective beats.'

A few weeks later, he told of a young British officer – a prisoner of the Russians – who received via Russian headquarters a letter from his fiancée, in which she expressed the hope that he would capture Prince Menschikoff and send her a button from his coat.

'It appears Prince Menchikoff was shown this letter, which amused him not a little; so he wrote to Mr C—— saying how much he regretted not being able to oblige his fair young correspondent as regarded considering himself a prisoner of Mr C——'s, but that he had much pleasure in sending him the enclosed button off his best coat, which he trusted Mr C—— would forward to the young lady with his compliments. Rather fun I think. Prince Menchikoff must be a good-natured fellow.'

Such pleasantries could not last. As the Allies resumed work repairing the batteries, advancing saps and parallels, the Russians took their own steps, and the chess-like game of measure and counter-measure began in earnest. Across the front of their defences on the east side of the Man-of-War Harbour, particularly in front of the Malakoff and the Great Redan – where both sides now realised the siege would be lost or won – the Russians constructed a series of rifle pits. Having learned the power of the Minié rifle, they now set out to employ what riflemen they possessed to best advantage.

Timothy Gowing described the result. 'Rifle pits are holes – large or small – constructed in various ways and manned by crack shots, who tormented us considerably by picking off our artillerymen, and the sailors manning our heavy guns; if anyone showed his head among the parapets of our trenches he was almost certain to have a hole made in it.'

Hedley Vicars described the results of sniping during a cold day in the trenches. 'We were obliged to walk about to keep ourselves warm, regardless of the bullets which kept flying about our ears like bees. A marine was mortally hit in the breast . . . and I saw the fellow carried past on a stretcher. He died in less than half an hour. As one of my men was walking up and down close to the rampart, a Minié ball hit him behind the ear. He fell on his side and died without a groan. I buried him at dusk outside the trench. Poor Robert Turton! *What* and *where* were thy last thoughts as death met three in that short walk? The Russian sentries did not molest us whilst we were digging the grave, although they must have heard us quite distinctly. We can hear them coughing and talking in their works.'

The Allies responded with trench raids, Timothy Gowing's account of one has a curiously modern feel to it.

'The taking of these pits were ... fearful work, and it was all done with the bayonet. This work is generally done by volunteers from the various regiments that happen to be in the trenches at the time. I volunteered to form one of these "nice little evening parties" — but I wished to go no more ...

'About 100 or 150 (sometimes 300 or 400) men would be formed up at the point nearest the pit to be assailed, all hands sometimes taking off their accoutrements. At a sign from the officers who are going to lead, the men creep over the top of the trench and steal up to the enemy on all fours. Not a word is spoken but, at a given signal, in they all go — and in less time than it takes me to write this, it is all over; the bayonet has done its work. The defenders are all utterly destroyed or taken prisoners, while the pits are at once turned and made to face the enemy, or are converted into a trench.'

As well as sniper fire, the Russians launched a series of night sorties from these pits, to slow progress, disrupt work and demoralise the besiegers. Captain Wilson of the Coldstream described a typical raid.

'If a sortie, covered by the howling wind and driving rain of a tempestuous night, or by the pounding of a powerful artillery, contrive to leave the place unperceived by the besiegers, and, taking advantage of the ups and downs of the intervening ground, creep unnoticed within a few paces of the weary men, thrown out in advance to protect "the opening" of the trenches, the situation is serious. The assailants, making a sudden rush, hurl the "covering parties" slap bang upon the diggers, drive the entire crew harum-scarum before them, and then proceed to tear up the gabions, and, time permitting, to fill in a portion of the ditch. This sort of thing being effected with more or less success, the sortie, almost untouched, falls back on the town, just as the invester, having rallied the fugitives (not an easy task in a fierce night storm) and obtained reinforcements, reappears on the stage: to find only bleeding mess-mates, broken gabions, and half-demolished parapets.'

With large numbers of new, inexperienced troops, the British were particularly vulnerable to this sort of attack.

The Russians did not confine themselves to raiding. Five hundred yards in front of the Malakoff — which was now a French responsibility – there was a conical hill, the Mamelon*. The Allies had intended to occupy it as a prelude to any general assault, and had already sited a battery each to enfilade it, but on 22 February, the Russians beat them to the punch. The French awakened that morning to find the Russians in occupation of the Mamelon, and fortifying it with all their usual energy. An assault by five French battalions the following night was beaten back by seven Russian battalions, supported by the guns of the garrison and ships in the harbour.

Two days later the Russians began another fortification, the White Works, over to the left of Mamelon. This was a major setback for the Allies: not only would the Mamelon have to be captured before any assault could proceed, but as long as it was in enemy hands, it enabled the Russians to harass and attack both British and French trenches. They wasted little time in taking advantage of it.

On 22 March John Hume of the 55th was in the trenches with a party of men from his regiment. At eight o'clock, he was relieved by some of the Light Division, as he recorded.

'Parties from three regiments relieved the 55th. One party of the 97th was commanded by Hedley Vicars. I had known him for some time and liked him very much . . . a brave soldier and a good religious man. I gave him all the information I could, telling him what an unpleasant post he had to guard.'

Vicars left his mark on all who met him, including Timothy Gowing, who was among the relieving party with a group of the 7th Fusiliers. Gowing was pleased to be with Vicars, whom he had met a few nights earlier.

'He and I had a long chat in the trench . . . He was very affable and kind and his men appeared to be very fond of him. He appeared to be one of those cool, determined men that are sure to win the respect of all classes and will lead men at anything . . . I told him about my comrade at the Alma.

' "Well, Sergeant," he said "the Lord's time is the right time; who is best off now, you or he?"

'He invited me to his tent that night for prayer, as he told me a few who loved the Lord met there as often as they could.'

That very evening, before coming out to the trenches Vicars said

* See Map 3.

he had: 'had two tent services, in the morning at eleven, and in the afternoon at three o'clock; Vandeleur came both times. I spent the evening with Cay. I read Isaiah xli., and he prayed. We walked together during the day, and exchanged our thoughts about JESUS.'

At ten o'clock that night, under the cover of a heavy fire, some 15,000 Russians issued out of Sebastopol by way of the Mamelon. They stormed some French trenches, then moved up the lines and crossed to attack the British trenches from the right and rear.

Gowing said, 'They came on pretending that they were French, and in the dark we could not see them. The enemy got right in the midst of us before we knew anything of their whereabouts, and then we set to work with the bayonet. Talk about hard knocks – they were served out that night as freely as ever they were! It was foot and fist, butt and bayonet, as hard as they could go at it; in fact they could have it every way they liked: the fighting was desperate.'

Both the officers of the 7th had been struck down when Vicars' voice was heard calling out: 'Now 97th, on your pins and charge!'

Vicars' Celestials had, at his order, lain down as the unknown body of men approached in the darkness. Now they rose up, fired a volley and charged, as commanded. Vicars was in the forefront; he cut down two Russians with his sword and was in the act of striking a third when he was shot through the right arm. As his men drove the enemy from the trench and back down the ravine, Hedley Vicars was laid out on a stretcher. He cheerfully assured his men that he was only slightly wounded, but after a few minutes he was heard to whisper, 'Cover my face; cover my face!'

Gowing said, 'Our men took a terrible revenge for his death. A number of our bayonets were bent like reaping-hooks the next morning, and all around where that noble Christian fell the enemy lay thick, one on top of the other.

'The 97th seemed to feel his loss keenly and over his grave strong men wept like a lot of children who had lost a fond father, and then vowed they would revenge him the first opportunity; that vow was kept not only by the 97th – the Captain was a general favourite throughout the Light Division.'

Like Gowing's Alma comrade, Vicars had had a premonition. Before he left England he had taken a close family friend to one side and asked him, '*When* I am shot, comfort my Mother.'

Vicars' apotheosis as a true Christian hero, and the impression it made at the time, foreshadows that – many years later – of another deeply religious young captain, currently toiling in the Batteries above Sebastopol: an officer of Engineers by the name of Charles George Gordon.

The French were now reinforced to eight strong divisions, compared to the six depleted ones of the British, and they were the major partners in the siege. Not only had they taken over the defence of the northern and eastern flanks of the Inkerman Heights, but it was agreed that they would now be responsible for the attack on the Malakoff, while the British, squeezed between two wings of the French, would retain their Left and Right Attacks, on either side of the Woronzov Ravine, and attack the Great Redan.

The arrival, in January, of General Péllisier, fresh from governing Oran, had brought the Allies a new aggressiveness. At a council of war on 25 March it was agreed that the Allies would begin a new bombardment on 2 April. The French had 378 guns and the British 123; the British guns were heavier, so the total weight of shot was almost equal. This time the British fire would be augmented by 13-inch Naval mortars – with their high trajectory, they could lob shells into the heart of the city. Once the cannonade had produced the required effect, an assault would follow.

The bombardment was delayed until 9 April, but it still took the Russians by surprise. It was half an hour before the Russians began to reply with their 446 guns, by which time, Calthorpe estimated, the Allies had thrown upwards of 2,000 shot and shell into the town.

'At the commencement of the day,' wrote Calthorpe, 'our artillerymen were allowed to fire at will, though towards the middle of the day, when the enemy's fire had greatly diminished, orders were given not to exceed the rate of 120 rounds per gun in the twenty-four hours. We have between 500 and 600 rounds per gun in all of the English batteries, and from 600–800 rounds per gun in the artillery parks, besides as much more at Balaklava ready to be brought up to the front should it be required.'

On the first day, the Russians responded slowly, partly through lack of powder. A whole face of the Great Redan – in front of the British – was silenced, and the French inflicted immense damage on the Flagstaff Bastion*. As the sun set, the guns fell silent, except for the mortars which, having no need to keep sight of their targets, continued to lob shells into the city throughout the night. The following day the French reduced the White Works to ruin, and on 11 April the Mamelon fell silent.

Officers and men of both armies lived in daily expectation of an assault. On 13 April, Henry Clifford wrote, 'I cannot say I see any great results from the firing, and I must return to the old idea of some seven months ago, the Bayonet is the only key into Sebastopol. I don't pretend to say this will be sure of gaining us an entrance, but big guns at the distance, ours are from the Redans, can only help us a little in the Assault.'

The ground across which the British Left and Right Attacks were creeping towards Sebastopol was stony, which made digging and entrenching difficult; by contrast the French, on thicker, softer soil, had been able to advance their batteries and parallels much closer to the enemy's defences. Not only did this affect the fire of the batteries, but it meant that British assault troops would have more open ground to cross.

Clifford and his chief, General Buller, were in the trenches every fourth day, with scaling ladders ready, in expectation of assault. It was a dangerous post: the Russian fire, though hesitant at first, had intensified over the days.

'We had a very narrow escape of being rubbed out by a shell which burst about five yards from the General and myself in Gordons on Friday night,' wrote Clifford. 'Fortunately I saw it coming, and we lay down and it burst without doing us any injury. I could not help laughing at the General's face, as I took him out of the heap of earth and gabions with which the bursting shell had covered him. "Entre nous" this sort of work is rather too much for the nerves of a man of his age.'

Clifford, on the other hand, seemed to relish it. 'If it is fine weather I like it, for I see more of what is going on in the Batteries. It is sad to see the poor Artillerymen and sailors at the guns knocked over. I saw eleven sailors killed or wounded by the explosion of one shell on Wednesday in Gordon's battery about 15 yards from me.'

* See Map 3.

The Naval Brigade batteries, under Captain Peel, were in the thick of the enemy's fire and suffered heavily. Among them was Midshipman Evelyn Wood, commanding the fire of two guns.

'I had a telescope laid in my left hand along the gun, and was steadying my right hand on the shoulder of Charles Green, First Class boy, of H.M.S. *Queen*, who was sitting on the right rear truck of the gun. While I was calling the results of the targets made, a man handed round rum for the gun's crew, and Green asked me to move my elbow, so that he might not shake me while drinking his grog. We both stood up, and he was holding the pannikin to his mouth, when a shot from the Redan, coming obliquely from our left, took off his head, the body falling on me. At this moment Michael Hardy, having just fired his gun, was "serving the vent". Hardy had turned up his sleeves and trousers, and his shirt being open low on the neck and chest, his face and body were covered with the contents of the boy's head.'

Hardy was acting as 'vent man' for the gun. His job was to keep his thumb on the touch-hole as the new charge was being rammed down. If he removed his thumb, the rush of air caused by the ramming might ignite any traces of burning powder left from the previous firing and cause a premature explosion – which would be fatal to Numbers 3 and 4 at the gun's mouth.

'Hardy never flinched. Without moving his right hand, he wiped with his left the boy's brains from his face. Those sitting at my feet were speechless, being startled, as indeed I was, for I had felt the wind from the Russian shot which had passed within an inch of my face. We were brought back to a sense of duty by Hardy's somewhat contemptuous, "You ——— fools, what the hell are you looking at? Is he dead? Take his carcase away. Ain't he dead? Take him to the doctor."

' "Jim, are you home?" he asked of No. 3, the Loader, who was in the act of giving the final tap, after having rammed home the charge, and seeing him nod, without bestowing another look on us, or possibly even thinking of me, he gave the order, "Run out. Ready." '

Wood had made a new friend, and from then on, he saw a lot of Hardy. 'We generally went to battery together, for although I had become an Aide-de-Camp I remained at battery duty, when Captain Peel did not require me. Hardy carried down my blanket and tea-bottle, receiving my allowance of rum for his services. He was in many ways a remarkable man, for when stationed at Eupatoria in the autumn of 1854, he amassed by questionable means a number of ponies, and started a livery stable, hiring them out to officers of the Fleet. I cannot say more of his courage than that he was as brave as Captain Peel, but in quite a different way, for I doubt whether Hardy ever felt danger.'

The bombardment continued for ten days, but the expected assault was continuously delayed. Lord Raglan was keen to attack as soon as possible, but Canrobert was under instructions from the Emperor not to go unless he was certain of success, and not to attempt it at all if he thought the loss of life would be great. Under such sanctions, it was impossible.

Fanny Duberly, by now something of an old campaigner, had already guessed as much. 'I cannot believe that this bombardment will be productive of the slightest effect on a position which we have allowed to become so strong,' she wrote. 'If we could see any point on which to build a hope – any gun dismounted – any embrasure knocked in, we could find something upon which to fasten and feed an interest; but it seems to me very like a bombardment in a picture – blue sky overhead, a town, and innumerable puffs of smoke all round it.'

'Man cannot tell, but Allah knows, how much the other side was hurt.' The cancellation of all plans for an assault was frustrating to the men of the Allied armies, but the bombardment was having an effect on the Russians. It was Evelyn Wood's opinion that for all the losses inflicted on the enemy in the three great battles, it was the bombardments that were breaking his will. The Russians, in daily expectation of an assault, were forced to mass battalions of infantry close behind the threatened bastions and the casualties among these, and among those manning the batteries, were horrific.

During the ten days of the April bombardment the great ballroom of the assembly rooms in Sebastopol was crowded with wounded, with more constantly arriving. The great square outside was packed with wounded, lying on stretchers – others were carried to the cellars of the sea forts or, if fit enough, ferried to the north side of the great harbour. The road to Simpheropol was said to be so encumbered by dead men, horses and cattle as to be impassable for wheeled vehicles. The Sebastopol Naval Cemetery bears moving testimony to the sacrifices of its defenders.

The extension of the telegraph to the Crimea on 25 April linking the generals at the front with both London and Paris, was a decidedly mixed blessing. Napoleon III's strictures to Canrobert, which effectively ruled out an Allied assault, had been motivated by his plan to come out to the Crimea and take personal command. It had taken all the eloquence of his generals, and some more gentle persuasion by Queen Victoria and Prince Albert, to dissuade him from this, but he continued to interfere.

Realising that the Sebastopol garrisons were being constantly reinforced and re-supplied via the port of Kertch on the sea of Azov, Raglan and Canrobert had prepared an expedition against it. French and British troops were embarked and en route when, on 3 May, Canrobert was informed by his Emperor that reinforcements were on their way and he must now prepare to engage the Russian field army in the Crimea. A fast steamer was sent to recall the French troops and the assault was cancelled.

For General Canrobert this was the last straw. Ten days later he resigned and took command of General Pélissier's corps, while Pélissier assumed command of the army.

Pélissier was forceful and uncouth; he excited strong opinions.

'Pélissier will lose 14,000 men for a great result at once,' said one colleague, 'while Canrobert would lose the same number by driblets without obtaining any advantage.'

Another claimed, 'If there was an insurrection, I should not hesitate to burn one of the quarters of Paris. Pélissier would not shrink from burning the whole.'

Pélissier lost no time in overcoming his first great obstacle: the Emperor's demand for a campaign against the Russian field army. The capture of Sebastopol was the key to victory, he announced, and the first step towards that would be the capture of the Mamelon and the White Works: 'Whatever they cost,' he said, 'I mean to have them.'

In the meantime, the expedition to Kertch was relaunched. A mixed force of British, French and Turkish troops landed without opposition on 26 May and destroyed the port's batteries. An Anglo-French naval squadron sank two hundred Russian transports, the Russians scuttled almost as many themselves, and the town was looted – not without violence and rape – by the soldiers and sailors of three nations.

Atrocities aside, it was good news at last for the Allies.

More good news came with the arrival; under General La Marmora, of 15,000 Sardinians. The King of Sardinia had decided that the Allies were likely to emerge as the winners, and he had high hopes of political gains from being among the victors. If nothing else, it meant that the British were no longer the smallest Allied contingent – and the new reinforcements certainly cut a dash.

Fanny Duberly saw them arrive. 'The Sardinians were disembarked in great numbers to-day; and, as we rode towards Kadikoi in the evening, we met two or three regiments marching up . . . The appearance of the Sardinian troops gives general satisfaction. The Rifle corps, which we met to-day, is most picturesque. They are dressed in a dark tunic and trowsers, with a broad-brimmed glazed hat, with a bugle stamped in gold on the front, and long massive plumes of black and green cock's hackle flowing over the left side of the hat, reaching to the shoulder.'

The arrival of these fresh, well-equipped troops boosted morale in the Allied camps. Two days later, Fanny watched a second contingent. 'As soon as they came in sight of the Cavalry camp the men began to cheer them; and as they passed, regiment after regiment took it up, and such a storm of shouts filled the air as must have frightened the pale young crescent moon . . . such cheers as only Englishmen know how to give.'

Their band concerts were highly popular – Fanny Duberly thought them sublime – but not every lady needed an invitation. Lord George Paget's beautiful new bride, who had accompanied him when he returned to the Crimea, was lodged at his insistence in Captain William Peel RN's quarters on board *Leander*. Agnes, Lady George, soon drew a host of admirers, including Omar Pasha, Lord Raglan, and the new arrival, General La Marmora. Paget noted in his diary for 13 May:

La Marmora paid Lady George a visit, his band having played for her night and morning since his arrival. He struck us much as being a thorough gentleman.

On the evening of 7 June, after a two-day bombardment, the French assaulted the Mamelon and the White Works. As the battalions marched down, the Algerian Zouaves (headed by their *vivandière*, the uniformed female sutler, attached to each regiment), the French Zouaves and the Green Chasseurs, General Bosquet spoke words of encouragement to each.

Fanny Duberly was beside him. 'The men had more the air and animation of a party invited to a marriage than of a party going to fight for life or death. To me how sad a sight it seemed! The divisions begin to move and file down to the narrow ravine, past the French battery, opposite the Mamelon. General Bosquet turns to me, his eyes full of tears, my own I cannot restrain, as he says, *"Madame, à Paris on a toujours l'Exposition, les bals, les fêtes; et – dans une heure et demi la moitié de ces braves hommes seront mortes!"* '

Paget and his wife watched the battle with Lord Raglan, the whole party lying at ease on the grass, as if at a picnic. Lord Raglan, hitherto starved of agreeable female company, had been out riding with Lady George the day before when, according to her husband, 'Lord Raglan had during this ride kept inquiring of her – where she saw the different clusters of men in their shirt-sleeves waiting for him, or running towards him – with the object always of trying to avoid them and their cheers; so characteristic of his *retiring* nature. His dislike of applause, or even of any ebullition of feeling of which he might be the object, is well known; a quality, so much to be admired in ordinary life, became in his case a weakness, having its drawbacks to one in his position. It was this which gave such a handle to malice, in imputing to him neglect of his soldiers during the winter months, during which period he visited his camps and hospitals more, I believe, than his brother Commander-in-Chief.'

Henry Clifford watched the French attack from an outpost in front of the Light Division's position. 'Our numbers drew upon us the fire of the Russians, and a round shot taking off the head of one of the onlookers soon left us more elbow room . . .

'Soon after 6, three rockets fired by the French was the signal for attack. The fire of shot and shell from all the Batteries Russian, as well as our own, had been very heavy for some hours previous, but the moment the French rushed out of the trenches, some 5,000 strong, and swarmed up the slopes of the Mamelon, the fire of shot, shell, grape and musketry on them was too awful to behold . . .

'It was as splendid as it was awful to see the brave Frenchmen rushing up under such a fire and my heart beat as I never felt it before and the tears ran down my face when in less than ten minutes after they left the trenches I saw the "tricolore" flag flourishing over the parapet of the Mamelon.'

Emboldened by their swift success, the French troops now swarmed over towards the Malakoff itself. 'I could hardly believe my eyes, for the brave fellows pressed on. Helas! not contented with having taken the Mamelon, the Round Tower was before them and they thought it within their grasp. On they went, rushing furiously on, till they came to the edge of the earthworks, and then it became too evident the trench was too great an obstacle to cross.

'The Russians under cover of their Batteries opened a deadly fire of grape, musketry, shot and shell. On it was a dreadful sight to see the brave fellows falling in heaps; they had dared too much.'

Worse was to come. As the French fell back to their new prize, the Russians followed, driving them out of the Mamelon and back to the trench lines from which they had started. Living up to his reputation, Pélissier counter-attacked, throwing in his reserves.

Clifford watched, 'On they dashed once more, the Russians in their turn fled, 20,000 French covered the "plateau" and swept up to the Russians, and the tricolore was seen once more on the hard-fought-for hill.'

Once again, however, the French stormed forward, as if they could sweep over the Malakoff and end the siege at a stroke. They had not been ordered to attack the Malakoff, nor were they provided with ladders for such an assault. Again they were slaughtered and fell back, but by now thousands more French soldiers had poured into the Mamelon, and this time it held. While the Mamelon was being taken and retaken, two of Bosquet's brigades had captured the White Works. The French had won both of their objectives, but at a cost of 5,440 killed, wounded and taken prisoners. The British had borne the brunt of the fighting up till now, but the French were now taking their share.

The French capture of the Mamelon was the signal for a British assault on the Quarries, a series of entrenchments in front of their ultimate objective, the Great Redan. About 700 men of the Light and 2nd Divisions attacked on both flanks and quickly drove the Russians out of their positions, although not without loss, as Timothy Gowing recorded.

'The old Light Division sustained another heavy loss in Colonel Egerton of the 77th, who had from the commencement of the campaign proved himself one of Britain's truest sons. He fell dead at the taking of the rifle pits that were ever afterwards named "Egerton's Pits"; he was one of the biggest men I ever saw in uniform. The old Pot-Hooks (the 77th) fought in a most dashing manner . . .

'The enemy tried hard that night to retake the pits, but it was no go. They were met with a fire that mowed them down by wholesale; then they got the bayonet. The 77th were backed up by a good strong party of the 33rd, and detachments of almost every regiment of the Light Division – the 97th could be heard distinctly shouting: "Remember Captain Vicars, boys!"

' "Stick it to them!"

' "Give it home, my lads!" '

The works, unenclosed behind, offered little cover from Russian guns on the Redan itself, and the Russians made repeated attacks through the night, but the Quarries remained in British hands. The following morning there was a truce, for both sides to remove their dead and wounded.

Edward Hyde of the 49th Regiment had an unusual encounter: 'Some of us waved our hands in a friendly way to the Russians who mingled with us in our work. I was not a little surprised to find among them an Irishman. I believe he had been a sailor, and had married a Russian woman but we had no time to gossip. He said there were two or three more in their ranks, but he declined to come back with us.'

All was now in place for a major assault – on the Malakoff by the French, and the Great Redan by the British – designed to end the siege. The date agreed upon was 18 June – the anniversary of Waterloo, it was hoped, would give the British and French something they could celebrate together. For the British, the focus of the siege was now narrowed down to the Great Redan, a giant V-shaped earthwork with the point of the V pointing at the British siege lines. On top of it there were Russian heavy guns, and firesteps from which the infantry could pour a murdering fire down its smooth sides. In front of it was a further obstacle, a deep ditch created by the digging of the earthwork, and in front of that, on the swept open ground known in military parlance as the glacis, was yet another obstacle: the abbatis, sometimes called a *chevaux de frises*. This was a thick tangle of trees, logs and brushwood, defined by the American writer Ambrose Bierce as *Rubbish placed outside a fort to prevent the rubbish outside getting at the rubbish inside*, it performed the function that barbed wire took on in later wars.

To storm this fortification, the British assault parties would have to rush forward over four hundred yards of open ground, under cannon-fire and musketry from the Redan, as well as flanking fire from the Garden and Flagstaff Batteries*. Skirmishers would fire at the enemy's ramparts to keep their heads down while the stormers tried to hack their way through the abbatis. That done, they would rush up the glacis – an area quite devoid of cover – to the ditch. The ladder parties would lower the ladders to allow the stormers to drop into the ditch and then, once across it, use them to climb up the other side and onto the steep slopes of the V. Some men would carry woolsacks to fill lesser ditches, and detachments of Royal Engineers would help clear any other obstacles and fortify the position once it was taken. All the time the stormers were in the ditch they would come under rifle and artillery fire at point-blank range from the enemy directly above them.

Once they had climbed the slopes of the V and were into the fortification, either through the embrasures or over the top of the parapet, the stormers would have to deal with further barricades inside, manned by more infantry, and would be subjected to counter-attack by enemy troops massed at the back of the position. The stormers' job was to hold on to what they had gained until the supports could arrive and push on through into the town.

Heavy casualties were expected in assaults of this nature and the stormers, who were often offered money or immediate promotion as an incentive, were known as the Forlorn Hope. The term derived from the Dutch, *Verloren hoop*, meaning lost troops (the French term was *enfants perdues*), but the English mistranslation was appropriate enough.

On 17 June, the Allied guns began a bombardment. By the end of the day it had disabled the Malakoff and the Redan, with huge losses. It was agreed that after a two-hour bombardment the following morning, which would undo any repairs the Russians had been able to do overnight, the French would take the Malakoff and, once they were in, the British would attack the Redan. Two British columns

* See Map 3.

would make the assault. The left column, drawn from the 4th Division, would be led by General Sir John Campbell, the right, drawn from the Light Division, would be led by Colonel Lacy Yea. With the Light Division would be a party from the Naval Brigade led by Captain Peel. Midshipman Evelyn Wood had been ill, but he was determined to accompany his chief; Peel reluctantly agreed that Wood could go with them as far as the Battery, but no further.

That evening the officers of the Naval Brigade discussed their chances of survival.

'On entering one of the Messes of which I was an honorary member, the conversation turned on the impending Assault, and one of the officers laughed at me, though in a friendly way, for having been forbidden to go beyond the battery,' Wood wrote. 'I said, "Barring accidents, I'll bet you I go as far as my Chief." Another officer observed, "I'll lay five sovereigns to one, young Wood is killed to-morrow." Dalyell replied, "Done; but bet's off if I'm killed."

Still weak from his illness, Wood decided to get an early night. 'At ten o'clock that night having instructed a Bluejacket standing sentry near my tent to rouse me when the ladder parties paraded, I fell asleep. The sentry, however, did not awake me, having been cautioned by Captain Peel that I was not to be aroused. The men "falling in" awoke me at midnight however, and my brother Aide-de-Camp coming to see if I was awake, we agreed that if, as was probable, our Chief was killed in the assault, one of us should stand by him, or bring in his body.

'I had been taking heavy and frequent doses of laudanum for three days, and when Daniels left me, feeling thoroughly worn out, I turned over and slept again, until Michael Hardy came into the tent and shook me. I told him to go away, as I was too ill to move, to which he replied, "Shure you'll never forgive yourself if you miss this morning's fun;" and against my will he proceeded to dress me. It did not take long, for my attire consisted of cap, jacket, trousers and low shoes. Hardy having propped me up against the tent-pole, brought my pony, on which he put me, being obliged however, to hold me in the saddle, for I was too weak to grip with my legs . . .

'When I reported myself to Captain Peel, he was seeing the men told off in parties, six men to each ladder, and a petty officer to every two ladders. I asked if he had thought to bring down a Union Jack, that we might have it up in the Redan before the Regimental

Colours, which, as I found later, were not taken out. He regretted that he had not thought of it, but agreed that it was then too late to obtain the flag.'

Before dawn, Pélissier decided to drop the opening bombardment and assault at once. It was a disaster. Three French columns climbed out of their trenches and charged forward into a hail of fire. Despite having a much shorter approach run – their trenches were only one hundred and sixty yards from the Malakoff – most of the men were mown down before they reached the abbatis. A few soldiers on the left managed to mount the fortifications and engage the enemy with the bayonet, but the supports could not reach them, and they were driven back.

Evelyn Wood was still with the Naval Brigade party despite having been sent by Peel on a succession of pointless errands designed to get him out of harm's way. He wrote, 'When the French went out from their trenches, 7 officers, 60 Petty officers, and Blue-jackets, of the Right Naval Brigade Ladder party, were all crouching close together, as much under cover as possible, behind a bank two feet high. I was lying next to Mr Parsons, a Mate, when suddenly he knocked against me violently, and as I thought in rough play. I was asking him to leave off skylarking, when I noticed he was insensible; he had been thrown over by a round-shot, which had killed another man and covered me with dust.'

As dawn came up it was clear that the French assault had failed at all points. Watching this from an advanced position near the Quarries, Lord Raglan, according to Calthorpe, who was with him as usual, 'Seeing and admiring the gallant efforts the French were making, felt that he would hardly be doing them justice, if he were not to second their endeavours by ordering our assault on the Redan, which would necessarily take off a portion of the enemy's fire from our allies, and thus make a diversion in their favour.'

The signal for the British to advance was given. Evelyn Wood was the first of his party to see it. 'Next to Captain Peel's detachment of 60 men was a party of soldiers of similar strength, and 50 men carrying wool bags. These were either volunteers or picked men of the Rifle Brigade, and in the words of their gallant leader, Captain (afterwards Sir William) Blackett, "among the best in the battalion". While we were waiting for the signal, a mortar-shell fell amidst the storming party, and blew a soldier and his accoutrements into the air. When taking my eyes off the body as it fell, I saw the signal flag as it was being run up, before it was "Broken", and shouting "Flag's Up", jumped on the little bank which had sheltered us, thus inducing a shower of grape and musketry, which knocked down several men.

The Russians now manned their parapets, and thence poured on us a succession of steadily aimed volleys.'

Leading the Light Division column was Colonel Lacy Yea, the martinet of the 7th who had bellowed, 'Come on, anyhow!' at the Alma, and later stood wringing his hands on the Heights, weeping for his poor dead Fusiliers. Just before the assault, Timothy Gowing, who was one of the stormers, said Lacy Yea had walked along the length of the trench addressing the men one after another: ' "Men, when we advance, move your legs. Remember not a shot – all must be done with the bayonet."

'When the order was given to advance, we all rushed over the trench, the Colonel shouting, "Fusiliers, follow me, and prove your-selves worthy of your title!" I was close to him. He ordered a number of active non-commissioned officers to keep up with him; and as we bounded over the plain he waved his sword and shouted "Fusiliers, follow me! Come on!" '

The stormers were met by a devastating cross-fire. Lord Raglan, who had witnessed the bloody stormings of Cuidad Rodrigo and Badajoz in the Peninsula, later wrote: 'I never had a conception before of such a shower of grape.'

A young captain of the 90th, Garnet Wolseley – the future Field Marshal – was heard to say, 'There is no hope for them.'

Henry Clifford echoed the sentiment: 'All hope left me the moments I saw the tremendous fire opened upon our poor fellows as they left the trench in front of the "Quarry".'

Somerset Calthorpe watched in horror as the British were cut down in swathes. 'The Russians were quite prepared for their appearance, for they instantly opened a most tremendous fire of grape and musketry. Colonel Johnstone was almost immediately severely wounded, and had his arm shattered. Seeing their leader fall, the men naturally got dispirited, and the torrent of grape-shot which swept through and through them sensibly diminished the thin line of British troops. The men began to waver when Colonel Yea, perceiving the state of affairs, saw there was nothing for it but to endeavour to form the men up in some sort of way, and lead them to the attack. This he did by voice and gesture, and then putting himself at their head, gallantly led the way towards the Redan. He was some yards in advance of his column, when a charge of grape-shot struck him in the body and head, and he fell to the ground, pointing out with his sword the direction the troops were to take. Thus gallantly fell, at the head of his men, one of the bravest and best officers in the British army.'

Timothy Gowing was near Yea when he died. 'Our Colonel fell dead, our Adjutant the same, and almost every officer we had with us fell dead or wounded; but still we pressed on until we were stopped by the *chevaux de frise*, and in front of that our poor fellows lay in piles. We were there met with a perfect hell of fire, at about fifty yards from us, of grape, shot, shell, canister and musketry, and could not return a shot.'

With the Naval Brigade, Evelyn Wood was not far behind. 'Various kinds of projectiles cut up the ground all around us, but not continuously in their fullest force, for, while there was no cessation of the shower of missiles, which pattered on the ground like tropical rain when the monsoon breaks, at times there were death-dealing gusts of increased density, which swept down the hill, felling our men as a reaping-machine levels standing crops. Captain Peel, standing on the parapet waving his sword in the dim light, cheered on our men, shouting, "Come on, sailors; don't let the soldiers beat you." At this appeal the whole of the ladder party, some of whom had taken cover at the first outburst of the Russian fire, ran forward at a steady double, simultaneously with the skirmishers and wool bag carriers. The skirmishers had started 50 yards in front of us, and went straight up to the abatis, where I was speaking to one of the leaders when he was mortally wounded. Although Daniels and I had previously determined to remain with Captain Peel, from the moment we started I lost sight of both my friends.'

Like many another that day, Wood found physical reserves he didn't know he possessed. 'When I was riding down to the battery, I felt so weak as to be incapable of fighting hand to hand even a boy of my own size, for I had been living on tinned milk and rice for over a week, and I instinctively realised the value of Michael Hardy, who was holding on to my pony, as a fighting man. Thinking I would secure at all events the support of one strong arm, I said,

"Hardy, when we go out I shall stick to the Captain, and you must stick to me." Hardy replied, somewhat evasively, "Yes, I will stick to him if he goes well to the front;" and this indomitable Irishman carried out his resolve, and permitted no one to surpass him in the assault. Now invigorated by excitement, I ran forward in front of the ladder parties. Before we had gone 100 yards, several sailors were struck down, and I was hit by a bullet while cheering on the Bluejackets and waving my sword, which was knocked five yards from me. My arm was paralysed by the jar, and I thought it was off, as I instinctively dropped on one knee. On looking down, I saw that it was only a flesh wound of the hand, and jumped up hastily, fearing that anyone passing might think I was skulking. Picking up my sword, I found it was twisted like a corkscrew, so threw it down, and with it the scabbard which had got between my legs. I had no pistol, and thus was without any weapon, but that did not occur to my mind as I ran on to overtake the leading ladder. Before I had rejoined it, my comrades had suffered considerably; the Senior Lieutenant had been slightly wounded, and Dalyell had lost his left arm, shattered by grape shot.'

Worse than this, Wood's revered chief was hit. 'Captain Peel was hit, when halfway up the glacis, by a bullet which passed through his left arm. He became faint and was accompanied back by Mr Daniels, who was the only unwounded officer out of the seven who went out with the right ladder party. He escaped injury, but his pistol-case was shot through in two places, and his clothes were cut by several bullets. Thus, within about 250 yards, or about half the distance to be passed over, I was the only Naval officer remaining effective. It was possible that I unconsciously brought up my left shoulder to avoid the fire from the Redan; but anyhow, having no weight to carry, I again outstripped the leading ladder men, and then retraced my steps for 100 yards, although unwillingly, for I was intensely anxious to reach the Redan, although with no clear idea what to do when I got there.'

By now the naval party, which had started out with ten ladders, was reduced to four. The soldiers' ladder party to Wood's right had been shot down in the first volley. Seconds later, all the army officers accompanying them were on the ground, dead or wounded. By the time Wood and his remaining sailors had reached the abatis, on the forward edge of the ditch, he said, 'I had with me only two ladders;

these were carried by three and four men respectively, and I was in front of the leading ladder. Its carriers were reduced to three, and then the right hand rear man falling, I took his place. The second ladder now fell to the ground, the men being killed or wounded by a blast of case-shot, and when we were 25 yards from the abatis my ladder carriers were reduced to two. The man in front was only a few years older than myself, an Ordinary Seaman, but he had shown no other feeling than the desire to be first up. I had not carried it far when the man alongside of me was killed, and then the Ordinary Seaman in front, feeling no doubt he was bearing an undue share of the weight, not knowing I was under the ladder, turning his head as far as he could, addressed me as his messmate, "Come along, Bill; let's get our beggar up first." Before he recognised me, while his face was still turned backwards, he was killed, and with him tumbled the ladder.'

Held up at the abatis, redcoats and bluejackets alike were slaughtered. Timothy Gowing recalled, 'Our men could not advance and would not retire, but were trying to pull down the barrier or *chevaux de frise*; we might just as well have tried to pull down the moon ...

'The enemy mounted the parapets of the Redan and delivered volley after volley into us. They hoisted a large black flag and defied us to come on ...

'The cry of "Murder" could be heard on that field, for the cowardly enemy fired for hours upon our countrymen as they lay writhing in agony and blood. As some of our officers said, "This will never do – we'll pay them for this yet!" We would have forgiven them all had they not shot down poor, defenceless, wounded men.'

Having lost his ladder party, Wood confessed, 'In my heart I experienced a sense of relief, from the feeling that my responsibility was over, as even my most gallant Chief, William Peel, would not expect me to carry a ladder 18 feet in length by myself. It was now lying within 30 yards of the abatis, under the shelter of which a few scattered soldiers were crouching: some were firing, a great many shouting, while on the parapet 15 feet above us stood Russians four and in places six deep, firing at, and calling on us sarcastically to walk in. I looked round and at once saw that there was no chance of our accepting the invitation. The abatis where I was standing, between 60 and 70 yards from the salient, was a strong fence 4 feet thick, and 5 feet high in places, made up of stout trees, and beams from 6 to 8 inches in diameter, closed with brushwood. There were places where a man could have squeezed through the holes made by our shells, but only one at a time, and even then, assuming that he crossed unscathed the open space intervening between the abatis and the ditch, there was a still more formidable obstacle. From the bottom of the ditch the top of the parapet on which the Russians were standing was 26 feet high.

'The storming party had dwindled down to 100, and I perceived at once that unless heavy reinforcements came up there was no chance of carrying the work.'

Officers and NCOs did their best to induce the men to go forward. Wood himself witnessed two very different attempts.

'An officer detaching a bough from the abatis waved it over his head, and cheerily called on the men to follow him, but while shouting he was pierced by several bullets and fell lifeless. I was greatly impressed by the courage of a young Sergeant, who was trying to collect men to accompany him through or over the abatis. After calling in vain on those immediately to follow him, he lost his temper, and shouted, "I'll tell my right-hand man to follow me, and if he fails I'll shoot him." He brought his rifle down to the "Ready", and said, "Private —— will you follow me?" I was almost touching them, and seeing by the Sergeant's eyes that he was in earnest, stood for a few seconds studying the determined look on the man's face. The Private looked deliberately on the hundreds of Russians above us, and then ran his eye right and left of where we were standing, as if estimating the number of his comrades, who certainly did not exceed 100, and with as much determination as the Sergeant said, "No, I won't." The non-commissioned officer threw his rifle to his shoulder with the intention of carrying out his threat, but in doing so, struck by grape-shot, he fell dead.

'I now dropped on one knee to talk to an officer sitting under the abatis as to our chances of getting in, when he was hit just above the waist-belt by a bullet. He tossed about in great pain, calling on the Almighty. I was somewhat perturbed, but had seen too many men killed to be seriously affected, until he apostrophised his mother; this allusion distressed me so much that I rose, and walked slowly in the direction of the Malakoff, looking to see if there were any weaker spots in the abatis. I had only gone a few yards, when glancing upwards I saw a section of Russians "following" me with their muskets. Instinctively throwing up my left arm to shield my face, I was walking on, when a gun was fired with case-shot close to me. The missiles came crashing through the abatis, and one weighting $5\frac{1}{2}$ oz struck my arm just below the funny-bone. This sent me screaming to the ground, and I rolled some yards down the slope of the hill, where I lay insensible.'

The left column did at least gain a foothold, according to Timothy Gowing, thanks to the men of the 18th (The Royal Irish). 'Major-General Eyre addressed them in Irish and said that he hoped their deeds that morning would make many a cabin in Old Ireland ring again. The men of that Regiment were wrought up to a state of madness ... and it was not lost upon the Norfolk Regiment. Not a shot did those two noble regiments fire, but with a cheer they pitched into the enemy. No power was wasted, but the Russians were fairly pitched out of their works. Their General's appeal had touched them to the quick, and these gallant regiments seemed to vie with each other in the rapidity of their movements and in their deeds of valour.

'A few prisoners were taken. One huge Grenadier, profusely bleeding, might have been seen dragging by the collar of his coat a monster of a Russian. Pat had fought and subdued his antagonist, and then remembered mercy, exclaiming, "Go it lads! There are plenty more of them yonder. Hurrah for ould Ireland!"'

At length, said Gowing, 'The "retire" was sounded all over the field but the men stood sullen and would not heed it. Our men, and those of other regiments, were fast dropping. At last the remnant of the attacking column retired to the trenches amidst a storm of grape which nearly swept away whole companies at a time.'

Wood did not hear the signal. 'I don't know how long I was unconscious, but it cannot have been many minutes; for the whole affair did not last more than half an hour. I was aroused by an Irish corporal, who shook my arm saying, "Matey, if you are going in, you had better go at once or you'll get bagoneted." I presume it was the pain in my arm which brought me back to consciousness, but I answered the man with an outburst of bad language. He drew himself up erect, and bringing his hand across his body to the rifle said, "I beg you pardon, sir, I did not know you were an officer. Can I help you?"

' "Yes, help me up, but by the other hand." He then told me the "Retire" had been sounded some minutes earlier, and that all our people were going back. In spite of the number of men firing at us at less than 100 yards distance he helped me up carefully, taking care not to hurt my arm, and then bending down his head, ran as hard as he could towards our trenches. I followed him towards the 8-gun battery, but very slowly; for although I had not previously felt my weakness since the moment we crossed the trenches to assault, I had now become faint, and could walk only slowly, although grape and case shot fell thickly around me.'

The retreat was as bloody as the advance, Gowing said. 'The columns of the attack had not been driven back by weight of numbers. Nay, they were mowed down with grape, canister, musketry, and broadside after broadside from the shipping. And the enemy seemed to take a delight in shooting down poor helpless, wounded men who were trying to limp, or drag their mangled bodies, away from the devouring cross-fires.'

Even in the last moments, as Evelyn Wood discovered, there was danger. 'As I approached the trenches in front of our 3rd parallel, from which we had started, the last of the Covering party which had remained out to fire on the Russians, were returning inside the trenches. I made for a place where the slight bank was worn down, in order to avoid the increased exertion of mounting up four feet, when a young soldier passed me on my left side, and doubtless not noticing I was wounded knocked me heavily on the arm, saying, "Move on please." As he crossed the parapet, I caught the butt of the rifle to pull myself up, and he turned his face, saying, "What are you doing?" A round-shot passing over my right shoulder struck him between the shoulders, and I stepped over the remains of his body so exhausted as to be indifferent to his death and to my preservation, due to his rudeness in jostling me out of my turn at the gap.

'On the safe side of this little parapet, there sat a sailor who made me feel ashamed of my own powers of endurance. He had been severely wounded in the right hand, and had lost two of his fingers, and thinking how helpless I had become, I stood still to admire the man's coolness and self-possession. With his left hand he had pulled out of his trousers the tail of his shirt, and holding it in his teeth, had torn off nearly three strips when I approached. With these he was bandaging up his hand in a manner which would have done credit to a class who had gone through "First Aid for the Wounded", and he answered my question as to his wound quite cheerily.

'When I reached the foot of the parapet of the 8-gun battery I was unable to walk up it, and fell to the ground at the first attempt. When I did surmount it, I hesitated to step down to the banquette, fearing to jar my arm, and paused so long that a sergeant, probably not wanting to see more fire drawn on to the spot called out, "Jump, jump, you little devil, or you will get killed." I consigned him to a hot place, and sank down where I was, when two officers seeing my state came out and carried me inside the work.

'I was taken to a doctor (an Irishman) whom I had known for some time, and was greeted warmly with the exclamation, "Sit down, dear boy, an' I'll have your arm off before you know where you are." I steadily but with some difficulty evaded his kind intention, and was eventually put into a stretcher and carried to camp by four Bluejackets.'

Here Wood faced another battle: to save his arm. 'Whilst I was waiting in the operating-tent for my turn for the table, I was interested by the extraordinary fortitude of a Bluejacket, who discussed the morning's failure without a break in his voice while the doctors were removing two of his fingers at the third joint. When my turn came, I had a heated argument with the surgeons, who wished to amputate the arm above the elbow. The Navy had then an officer dangerously ill from a wound received a few days earlier, in which case amputation had been delayed too long, and all but the senior Doctor wanted to take off my arm. To him I appealed to be allowed the chance, and to persuade him I underwent considerable pain. The eight who were removing the limb declared that it was impossible that any use could be obtained from the arm, the elbow joint of which had been shattered. To prove that it was not, I, doubling my fist, raised the arm as high as I could, until the case-shot met the fore and upper arm, on which the Senior Medical Officer decided that he would at all events try to save the limb.

'As soon as I had recovered consciousness after the anaesthetic Captain Peel came to see me, and telling me that he had got halfway, asked how far the remainder had advanced. Having told him, I enquired anxiously for my friend Michael Hardy, of whom I could learn nothing. At the time of the Truce next day, his body was found in an embrasure of the Redan, the only man as far as I know who crossed the abatis and ditch that day.'

For their actions on the glacis of the Redan, Captain Peel and his ADC, Edward Daniell, were both to be among the first recipients of a new award which had been discussed in *The Times* editorials, mooted in the House of Commons and enthusiastically taken up by the Queen herself. Designed as a classless equivalent of the French *Legion d'Honneur*, it was to be cast from the bronze of a captured Russian gun. It was named the Victoria Cross.

The medal was finally instituted in 1856, and other early recipients were Captain Rowlands of the Welch Regiment, who had rescued his Colonel and started the battle of Inkerman, and Henry Clifford, for his conduct in that same battle. Edward Daniell – Evelyn Wood's friend and fellow ADC – had the sad distinction of being the only officer ever to forfeit the VC, for misconduct on the China station. By the war's end, one hundred and eleven VCs had been awarded to soldiers and sailors. Like Captain Peel and Edward Daniell, Evelyn Wood was invalided home, but he didn't stay home for long. Keen to get back to the Crimea, Wood applied to join the army, and was granted a commission without purchase in the 13th Light Dragoons, the start of a military career that was to win him a Victoria Cross, and the rank of Field Marshal.

The assault on the Redan had been a costly fiasco: 1,505 British soldiers and sailors fell, and 3,500 French. The Russians had lost 5,500 men, but had held on to both the Malakoff and the Redan. The French assault having failed, Raglan's decision to commit the British troops to a hopeless attempt was a catastrophic error. He must have known this. As he visited the wounded, he came upon a young officer lying on a stretcher. As he enquired after the man's injuries the officer, according to Captain Wolseley, 'in the rudest terms and most savage manner denounced him as responsible for every drop of blood shed that day'. To a man of Raglan's sensibilities, such a scene must have been mortifying.

CHAPTER EIGHT

The dead and wounded from the failed assault lay out all the next day under a blistering sun. It was not until 4 o'clock in the afternoon that the signal for a truce was given. Timothy Gowing thought it further evidence of Russian savagery. 'The black flag (or flag of defiance) was flying upon all their batteries while some hundreds – yea thousands – of our poor fellows were lying with every description of wound, exposed to a burning sun – and the heat of the Crimea in summer is equal to that of India,' he wrote.

Henry Clifford saw: 'One poor fellow ... waving his hand at 9 o'clock in the morning and asking for help, but without a Flag of Truce it was impossible to go out to him. By 4 o'clock so bad had been the wounds and so great that heat that the faces of the poor Dead could hardly, and many could not, be recognised. Their faces were quite black and many of them had swollen up and burst.

'I was obliged to go about among the corpses to get the men to carry them away, and I was sick and vomited many times, and the greater number of men who carried the stretchers did the same ... Our men are so strange. You have no idea how very hard it is to get a man of another Regiment to touch one belonging to some other Corps. The 33rd will only look after the 33rd men, Rifles after Rifles and so on. I had great trouble obliging some 7th men to carry away a wounded man of the 17th.'

Gowing and his comrades of the 7th felt the Russians added insult to injury. 'The enemy placed a strong chain of sentries all along the front of their works – evidently picked men – and they had actually had a wash, and some of them a clean shave.

'All our men that had fallen in front of the *chevaux de frise* they brought and laid for us to take away. This was humiliating to the feelings of a Briton. They were, moreover, very insulting, and it would not have taken much, if our officers had not been firm, for our men (some of them at least) to have dashed their brutal heads off with one straight from the shoulder; for they had no arms, except the sentries placed in front of our trenches. Our men were very quiet and sullen, but one could read revenge written on their countenances.'

Even amidst the carnage, Clifford was able to feel some sympathy for the Commander-in-Chief. 'I have no doubt there will be a very great out cry against poor Lord Raglan in England when our would-be Assault of the 18th is heard of and our sad loss. Poor man! he has a hard part to play to satisfy our Government and the French too. It is hard to judge him and I am very careful how I speak of him to anyone.'

The humiliating defeat of 18 June – on Waterloo Day, of all days – and the loss of 1,500 of his men was not without its effect on Lord Raglan, although he made great efforts to cheer his staff.

'Lord Raglan is perhaps the most cheerful of anyone,' wrote Somerset Calthorpe, 'considering how much he has had lately to worry and annoy him; but at the same time, I fear that it has affected his health; he looks far from well, and has grown very much aged latterly.'

Lord George Paget and Lady George dined with Raglan on 23 June, and Paget noted, 'He has been ailing, and did not look well, and though at dinner his spirits seemed to be good, one could see that he was out of sorts after the 18th of June. Some of the fellows told me after dinner, that a day or two before, when they had been looking gloomy, he kindly upbraided them, saying – "We must not have grave faces; one would think an army had never received a check before. All armies are subject to them &c." '

Another blow was about to land. A severe storm blew up that night and Lord Raglan insisted on Lady George going home in his carriage. That same storm brought on a worsening of the condition of General Estcourt, already ill with cholera. A long-standing colleague and close personal friend of Raglan's, Estcourt had been nursed by his wife and sister. On the morning of 24 June he died.

Calthorpe noted the effect on his uncle. 'The night before his death, Lord Raglan, although himself far from well, from an attack of dysentery, went to take leave of the poor general, who was an old and dear friend of his. His death had been a great shock to him. He had intended to have been present at his funeral, and got up for that purpose, but he found the trial too much for him, and for the first time his wonted composure left him, and he was quite overcome with grief.'

On the following evening he was not well enough to come to dinner. He remained in his bed the following day, watched over at all times by one of his staff. On the morning of 28 June, Paget and Lady George rode up to Headquarters to enquire about his health.

'We had ridden most days to enquire about Lord Raglan and each day with a better report, and so we were ill-prepared for the news of this afternoon, when about five o'clock Steele and Burghersh came out to see us on our arrival at headquarters, and told us he was all but given over. We went in and remained with him till all was over, his death taking place about 7 p.m., calm and peaceable, but he did not recognise either of us. It reminded us both so much of a death-bed we had witnessed only a year before! The features of Lord Raglan and of my father were sufficiently of the same character to render them strangely alike under such circumstances; with the paleness of death upon them, and their attitude was similar; with the head inclining to one side, and the same calm repose in each case. The motto of each the same – "Duty".'

'It seems as if some pulse in this vast body had ceased to beat, the army is so quiet,' wrote Fanny Duberly on hearing the news. 'Men speak in low voices words of regret.'

'All flags at half-mast and not a smile to be seen,' noted Lord George Paget in his journal for 29 June.

That same day, according to Calthorpe, 'The Commanders-in-Chief of each army, and the Admirals of the Allied Fleets, came up to Headquarters ... to take a farewell look at their late colleague. All seemed deeply impressed by the event. It was a touching sight to see these old warriors who had so often looked death in the face unmoved, shedding tears of regret over the body of our late beloved Commander. General Pélissier stood by the bedside for upwards of an hour, crying like a child.'

Sir George Brown, Lord Raglan's natural successor, was himself ill and about to be invalided home, so command fell to General James Simpson. He was a diffident newcomer, too shy to attend at

Lord Raglan's death-bed until Paget coaxed him in. It soon became clear that the Allied generals had little regard for his opinions.

Almost as if to confirm the reduced status of the British in the alliance, the next blow dealt to the enemy scarcely involved them. On 16 August, in a final attempt to break the siege, Prince Gortchakoff – now commanding all the Russian forces in the Crimea as Menschikoff had been dismissed by the Tsar after the defeat at Eupatoria – launched four divisions and two artillery brigades across the Tchernaya River. His aim was to recapture the Fediukine Heights as a base against the Sapoune and Balaklava. In a five-hour battle, during which the Russians proved they had learned *nothing* from Inkerman, throwing massed columns against Allied rifles, the French and Sardinians drove them back with a loss of 8,000 men, including one of their column commanders, General Read.

The Tchernaya offensive had been the Russians' last hope. Their resources – even of manpower – were not limitless, and now they were stretched to breaking point. Shortly before the death of Tsar Nicholas it had been estimated that the war up to that point had cost them 240,000 men. Death and disease, as well as the relentless Allied bombardment, had taken their toll within Sebastopol; between March and August, they had lost a further 81,000 men. Nor could they rely on reinforcement any longer as long marches across desolate country meant that out of every three Russian soldiers despatched to the Crimea, two fell by the wayside.

Inside Sebastopol conditions were truly appalling. The defences were under bombardment, day and night now, by Allied mortars, and now they were crumbling. Repair work, even at night, was ever more difficult, and increasingly costly in dead and wounded. Much of the city was in ruins and hospitals were full and overflowing into the streets and squares. Moving the wounded was well-nigh impossible by day, and they lay where they fell, under the same pitiless sun that had tortured the Allied wounded at the Redan.

A renewed Allied bombardment by 775 Allied guns began on 17 August – and confirmed Prince Gortchakoff in his earlier decision to abandon the southern portion of the city altogether. To this end, he began the construction of a pontoon bridge across the harbour, sixteen feet wide, and strong enough to bear the weight of heavy vehicles.

On 24 August, Fanny Duberly, staying on board the warship *St*

Jean d'Acre, anchored off Sebastopol, was able to survey the city through a telescope.

'The bridge across the harbour, in front of the men-of-war moored at the entrance, which they commenced a week or two ago, is now complete. The traffic over it is perpetual both of men and horses. For two days as the stream set principally from the south to the north, we fancied that the Russians were removing their goods, previous to evacuating the south side; and this appeared more probable, as they were busily employed in erecting fresh earthworks on the north side; but lately opinion has changed on the subject.'

Opinion had changed in Sebastopol too. Gortchakoff suddenly decided – after a visit on 20 August – that to defend the south side to the last extremity was the only honourable course. He reinforced the garrison, which was by now losing between 800 and 900 men a day, with 25,000 men from the field army, and set to work once more restoring the defences.

By now the French trenches had been pushed so far forward that the closest were as close as twenty-five yards to the Malakoff. An Allied Council of War named 8 September as the date for an assault by the French on the Malakoff, the Little Redan, and the Flagstaff and Central Bastions*. In the centre the British would assault the Great Redan.

The Malakoff had long been seen as the key to Sebastopol. Pélissier had learned that the relief of the Malakoff garrison took place at noon, and that to avoid crowding the fortification with troops – and presenting a tempting target for Allied gunners – the old garrison was marched out before the new one moved in. An assault timed for midday would find the Malakoff weakly defended; the problem would not be getting *into* the Malakoff, but *holding it* against the massive Russian counter-attacks that would surely follow. To apply pressure all along Sebastopol's defences, to pin the defenders and prevent them concentrating against the Malakoff, once taken, was the real purpose of all the other assaults, including the British assault on the Redan.

For the assault on the Malakoff, Pélissier had chosen General M.E.P.M. MacMahon's division. The British assault force was to be found – once more – from the Light and 2nd Divisions, a total of

---

* See Map 3.

1,900 men, commanded by Lieutenant-General William Codrington and Major-General J. Markham respectively. The British trenches were still two hundred yards to the Redan, so the assault troops would have that much open ground to cross under a cross-fire from the Garden, Barrack and Gervais Batteries*. Among the British, fears of a repeat of the 18 June débâcle were widespread, and there were anxieties about the quality of some of the new troops.

'I hope we shall not be so foolish as to attempt another assault on the Redan,' Henry Clifford wrote home, 'but I suspect we shall make a sham attack at all events. We have commenced two new trenches – one a zigzag running towards the angle of the Redan, the other a straight sap running down a ravine between the Malakoff and Redan, and only meant to end in a rifle pit. Last night the Russians attacked the latter trench; they were not in force, and I am sorry to say that our men behaved exceedingly badly, and although superior in numbers they fairly bolted, trampling over the assistant engineer who tried to rally them. The Russians advanced and destroyed two nights' work.'

Clifford felt that trench work – gabion-dodging, as it was called – was not the best training for raw recruits.

'It will be worth several thousand men to our little Army if we can get rid of the Trenches, not from the loss of some sixty men (our casualties in twenty-four hours) but the Trenches are the worst possible school for young soldiers. Many a young fellow who would fight like a lion in the open and die at the point of a bayonet, loses all nerve and confidence in a trench in the dark, with no knowledge of the number of the attacking force, or in what direction they are attacking; hardly distinguishing friend from foe, and exposed at any moment to be killed or wounded by shell, grape, round-shot, falling in the trench without being able to avoid them, and in the cool blood without the excitement of fighting. Great excuse is to be made for young soldiers wavering and not always displaying the characteristic bravery of the English soldiers, and if you see these sorties and their consequences roughly handled in the papers, you must not judge too harshly of the Regiments mentioned, or think that our friends the brave French are not subject to the same sad mistakes as ourselves, for they only speak of success, but they

* See Map 3.

have their full share of reverses and runs away in the advance Trenches.'

The new young officers also gave cause for concern. Serving in the trenches as an assistant engineer was Captain Colin Campbell of the 46th Regiment (no relation to the commander of what was now the Highland Division; this army appears to have had a never-ending supply of Colin Campbells). Campbell noted that trench warfare had a high attrition rate among young officers.

'The officers lately out from England knock up very fast, particularly the young ones, "cheepers" as we call them. Out of a batch of seven engineer officers who arrived here in June, not one remains, three being killed and four gone home sick.'

On the morning of 8 September, the 350th day of the siege, one young Engineer officer, Lieutenant George Ranken, was awakened early. 'Between five and six o'clock, a.m., the Adjutant came in and confirmed my conjecture, that I was to lead the ladder party,' he wrote. 'Soon after Anderson came into my tent, and informed me he was told off for the working party, to follow when the storming party were well in possession, and form a storming party across the Redan. I rose and dressed; I put on my red shell jacket to look as much like the men as possible, and carried in my pocket besides a tourniquet, portion of a night-shirt torn into strips for bandages . . .

'I had an interview with Nicholson (now Major Micholson, RE), to whom I gave my brother's address, with a request that he would communicate with him in the event of my death. He promised to act for me in every thing, as he felt I should have wished him to act, and tried to re-assure me as to my chance of escape, though (as he told me afterwards when I came back) he had not the slightest expectation of ever seeing me again safe and sound. These matters settled, I rode down to the trenches . . .'

By the time Ranken arrived, the men from the two assaulting divisions – stormers and supports – were already crowded into the trenches. The commanders of the assaulting brigades, Brigadier-General Charles Windham of the 2nd Division and Lieutenant-Colonel Thomas Unett, 19th Regiment of the Light Division, tossed a coin to decide which brigade should lead the way. Unett won, and vowed he would be the first man into the Redan.

Timothy Gowing was with the supports. 'We fell in at 9 a.m. A dram of rum was issued to each man as he stood in the ranks; all

THE THIN RED LINE

hands had previously been served out with two days' rations. There were in our ranks a great number of very young men, who had not much idea of the terrible work that lay before them; but there were others who knew only too well, having had near twelve months' hard wrestling with the foe – and no mean foe either . . .

'As the hour of 12 drew near, all hands were on the alert; we knew well it was death for many of us. Several who had gone through the whole campaign shook hands saying, "This is hot! Good-bye old boy!"

' "Write to the old folks at home if I do not return," was the request made by many.

'Nothing is more trying than to have to stand under a dropping fire of shell and not be able to return a shot. The enemy had the range of our trenches nicely and could drop their shells into them just as they liked. We lost a number of men, before we advanced to the attack, by this vertical fire.'

Also among the supports was another old friend, John Hume of the 55th. 'My Company, No. 6, was formed in the rear of the Light Company commanded by my brother, Captain R. Hume. We were told off to lead the regiment when the supports got the order to advance. The salient angle of the Great Redan was the point we were ordered to make for. All thought that as far as the arrangements for the British attack went, they were in many ways similar to those of the 18th June, as on the 8th of September we were no nearer the Redan then on the former occasion, and the same 250 yards had to be passed over without a particle of cover before the salient angle could be reached. But "ours not to reason why", so we waited impatiently for the order to advance . . .'

While waiting for the French to attack, George Ranken had plenty to occupy his mind. 'The Batteries were firing heavily on the Redan and the Russian works; the enemy replying with grape and round-shot. I found the ladder party, composed of men from the 3rd Buffs, and 90th and 97th Regiments, lining the sap in front of the Redan (called the sixth parallel), the trench which Cooke and myself commenced on my first night's duty in the trenches.

'The party consisted of 320 men, who were told off to forty scaling ladders, each twenty-four foot long. My instructions were, to advance with my sappers, armed with crowbars and axes for cutting through the abatis, and with the ladder party immediately after the skirmishers had been thrown out. The party was under command of Major Welsford, 97th Regiment, with whom I conferred for several minutes and to whom I explained the point where the ladders were to be placed, in order to screen them as much as possible from the fire of the enemy. I then told my party of sappers what they were to do, and assembled the non-commissioned officers to point out the measures to be taken under their directions, in the event of my being killed or wounded.

'These arrangements being made, I awaited the signal to advance; silently calling upon God to aid and assist me in doing my duty, and if it were His will, to preserve my life.'

At noon, MacMahon's leading brigade rushed out from their trenches, sweeping forward across the open ground and using planks to cross the ditch in front of the Malakoff. Intense study of the Malakoff by French engineers had revealed that the fortification, which was round, to conform with the round tower on which it was based, had a fatal weakness: at one point on its circumference it could not be covered by its flanking batteries. It was on this point that the French stormers converged.

Pélissier's plan had worked brilliantly. Within minutes, MacMahon's Zouaves were in the Malakoff. There the struggle began in earnest as the Russian garrison and their supports defended the numerous rows of traverses inside the fortress. The Russians now launched a succession of bloody counter-attacks, and as casualties on both sides piled up inside the works MacMahon announced his determination to hold fast, with the immortal words, 'J'y suis, j'y reste.'

Crucially for the British, the Tricolore now floated above the Malakoff.

In a forward trench, standing beside General Codrington, Henry Clifford had watched the French assault go in. 'About ten minutes had elapsed since the French first left their advance trench, when I told General Codrington in our advance trench that the flags were up. Our parties for covering the advance, the assaulting party, and the working and ladder parties had all received their orders, but the moment they heard the Flag was up, and before the General could prevent them, half had jumped up on the parapet and Sir William seeing it was no use checking them gave the word to advance.'

In the forefront was Lieutenant Ranken. 'Suddenly there was a shout that the French were attacking the Malakhoff. I looked over the parapet, and saw them rushing up the salient. They were apparently unresisted. The French flag in a minute was seen waving on the ramparts. All this happened so instantaneously, that it took us all by surprise.

'We had anticipated a hard struggle, and we were ordered not to advance till a decided success had been achieved; but, as it were, in a second the dreaded Malakhoff had fallen into the hands of the French. Our men could no longer be restrained; before there was time to get the ladders to the front, and before the sappers could advance to cut away the abatis, they rushed in a straggling line over the parapets, and dashed onwards to the salient.

'I hurried up my sappers as fast as I could, shouting to them till I was nearly hoarse, and ran forward with them and the ladder party, with a drawn sword in my hand (my scabbard and belt I left behind). In the hurry and confusion many ladders were left behind. There was, however, little excuse for this, as the men had had their places distinctly assigned to them, and should not have left the trench without their ladders. It was of course impossible to perceive that anything of the kind had occurred, and still more impossible to have rectified it had it been known. The only word was – "Forward"; the only course to pursue – to advance as rapidly as possible. Nearly 200 yards of rough broken ground and an abatis to be crossed under the enemy's fire. The men advanced with the greatest spirit. I could see bodies dead and wounded lying along and strewing the ground on each side of me, as I pressed forward, shouting continually to the men to advance, and not pause for an instant.'

As on 18 June, the British were hit by a storm of roundshot, grape, canister and musketry. Colonel Unett was killed almost immediately, leaving General Windham in sole command, but the stormers pressed on to the ditch.

Henry Clifford watched them go. 'The distance between the advance trench and the Redan is about two hundred yards. The Russians, prepared by the advance on the Malakoff, received our troops with a volley of musketry and grape from three guns on the proper left of the Redan, shot and shell, in spite of which, tho' with considerable loss, the 90th and 97th and covering party of the Rifle Brigade, 2nd Battalion, reached the Ditch.'

At the ditch, all was confusion. Unlike the Malakoff, the smooth slopes of the V-shaped Redan were swept by fire from the flanking Russian batteries. At the abatis, Ranken said he: 'found five men nearly exhausted carrying a ladder and trying to get it over the opposing branches; the remaining three men composing the party of eight had probably been killed or wounded in the advance. I lent them my aid and urged them on. The edge of the ditch was soon reached, and I was relieved to find the ditch not nearly so formidable as it had been represented, and as I had good reason, from the solidity and extent of the Russian defences, to suppose it was likely to prove . . .

'I kept my ladders rather to the right of the salient angle, having been warned that the flanking fire would probably be severe up the proper left face. Half-a-dozen or so were lowered and reversed in a minute, and the men poured up them with eager haste. I set to work with every sapper I could get hold of, or to whom amid the din I could make myself audible, to tear down the rubble-stone work with which the salient of the escarp was revetted, and form a ramp practicable for ascent without ladders.

'I had to work, however, with my own hands; it was difficult to get anyone to do anything; the men as they straggled up to the assault in support of the advance, seemed stunned and paralyzed – there was none of that dash and enthusiasm which might have been looked for from British soldiers in an assault; in fact it required all the efforts and example of their officers to get the men on, and these were rendered almost ineffective from the manner in which the various regiments soon got confused and jumbled together.

'The men, after firing from behind the traverses, near the salient, for half-an-hour at the enemy – also firing behind his parados and traverses – began to waver. I rushed up the salient with the view of cheering them on, and the officers exerted themselves to sustain them; the men gave a cheer and went at it afresh.'

Despite the enemy fire from both flanks and from above, a party of the 97th – Hedley Vicars' Celestials – clambered to the top of the parapet and gained a lodgement inside. They paid a heavy price.

Henry Clifford wrote, 'Colonel Handcock, commanding the 97th, was shot through the head and expired in the arms of his young wife in Camp this morning. Major Welsford of the same Regiment had his head blown off, trying to get in at an embrasure, and a great number of Officers and men of the three Regiments were killed and wounded.'

Even so, the British had a foothold in the Redan. It was time to order up the supports. With the 55th, John Hume had been taking some last-minute precautions when he and his men were called forward.

'While waiting, some of us read our prayer books. After reading I put mine in the breast of my coatee; I may have thought that it might stop a bullet. Just before we got the order to advance a shell from the enemy fell amongst us, burying itself in the trench close to my brother. Private O'Brien, of the Light Company, seeing the shell pitch, pulled my brother down to try and save him; the shell exploded under my brother and blew him some paces down the trench, wounding him severely, but not dangerously. I had not time to speak to him before I got the order to take out two companies out to support the stormers who had reached the Redan and were hotly engaged. The remaining companies of the 55th were to follow as soon as they could be brought up. There was only room enough in the trench to form up two companies at a time.

'I sprang over the parapet followed by the Light Company and No. 6, and we made our way across the space between our trenches and the Redan as quickly as we could under a very heavy fire of round shot, shell, and grape. Several men were knocked over. A grape-shot struck me on the breast, glanced off my prayer book, cutting through my sword-belt, and denting the Light Company whistle which was on my belt, but beyond the shock doing me no harm. Fortunately I was waving my sword at the time or I must have been struck in the right arm. Part of my water-bottle was shot away soon after; it was hanging by my side.'

Timothy Gowing was crossing the same ground with his comrades of the 7th. 'We, the supports, moved forward to back up our comrades, but anyone with half an eye could see that we had not the same cool, resolute men as at Alma and Inkerman, though some of the older hands were determined to make the best of a bad job. I am happy to record that the old Inkerman men took it very coolly; some of them lit their pipes – I did the same.

'A brave young officer of ours, a Mr Colt, told me he would give all he was worth to be able to take it as comfortably as some of our people did – it was his first time under fire. He was as pale as death and shaking from head to foot, yet he bravely faced the foe. The poor boy (for he was not much more) requested me not to leave him; he fell dead by my side, just outside the Redan.'

Another young officer, who had been in the Crimea exactly one month, was twenty-year-old Lieutenant Boscawen Trevor Griffith of the 23rd (Royal Welch) Fusiliers.

'We heard a tremendous row in our front (no doubt the 97th Storming) and soon after a staff officer came rushing to us and called us to the front. We rushed madly along the trenches, grape-shot flying about our ears. Several officers we met coming back wounded said they had been in the Redan and that the supports were only wanted to complete the victory.

'On we rushed impeded more and more by the wounded officers and men carried back from the front. We gained the 5th parallel, our most advanced trench, and "On the 23rd! this way!" cried the staff officers. We scrambled out of the trench into open ground.

'That was a fearful moment. I rushed across the space about 200 yards I think, shot striking the ground all the way and men falling down on all sides. When I got to the edge of the ditch of the Redan I found our men all mixed up in confusion but keeping up a steady fire on the enemy. Radcliffe was just before me – he called on the 23rd to follow him but as they wavered at the head of the ditch he asked me if I would follow him – on we both rushed over the next of the glacis into the ditch – here were lots of men of different regts. all huddled together – scaling ladders placed against the parapet crowded with our fellows – Radcliffe and I got hold of the ladder and went up it to the top of the parapet where we were stopped by the press – wounded and dead men kept tumbling down on us – it was indeed an exciting and fearful scene.'

'Griffith's commanding officer was Colonel Dan Lysons, who guided the guns across the river at the Alma. In a letter to his mother, he described the advance towards the Redan.

'I led my men forward in line; they advanced beautifully, all the young officers in front ... we found the fire of grape from the Garden and Barrack Batteries and the batteries on the opposite side of the ravine on our left tremendous. There were also three guns firing into our teeth, and as soon as we had passed the salient angle of the Redan, where Windham was, the Russians manned the parapet and fired down upon our right shoulders.

'Close to the ditch, near the re-entering angle, I got knocked over by a ball in my thigh ... when I looked round for my men very few were untouched. I got into a hole with other wounded men and managed later to get back to the salient angle.'

It fell to the younger officers to lead the men over the parapet, where the few stormers were still hanging on against a fierce Russian counter-attack. There, young Griffith met an old school friend. 'Here I saw Deane of the 30th Regt who you have heard me mention (when I was at Barton's at Reading) rush over into the ditch with his cap raised on the end of his sword cheering on a party of the 30th. He recognised me (I had not seen him since I was at Barton's) on the parapet, we shook hands, he rushed on and I believe was killed a few minutes after. Was that not a strange meeting!'

By now, Timothy Gowing had reached the ditch. 'How ever anyone lived to pass that 200 yards seemed a miracle. Our poor fellows fell one on top of the other; but nothing but death could stop us. The musket balls whistled past us more like hail than anything else I can describe, and the grape-shot cut our poor fellows to pieces; for we had a front and two cross-fires to meet. It seemed to me that we were rushing into the very jaws of death, but I for one reached the Redan without a scratch.

'While standing on the brink of the ditch, I considered for a moment how best to get into it, for it appeared to be about twenty feet deep, with no end of our poor fellows at the bottom, dead and dying, with their bayonets sticking up. But the mystery solved itself – our men came rushing on with a cheer, and in we went, neck or nothing, scrambled up the other side the best way we could, and into the Redoubt we went with a shout truly English.'

The ditch and the slopes leading up to the parapet were crowded now by a jumble of men who could push on no further because of the fierce fire-fight raging above them between the few British troops who had gained a lodgement in the Redan and its defenders. The interior of the work was as strongly defended – with lines of traverses – as the Malakoff, and with the Russians feeding in their supports from behind, the few stormers who had fought their way in soon found themselves hemmed in the bottom end of the V, outnumbered, outflanked and subjected to a withering crossfire.

By the time John Hume and his men of the 55th arrived, the

situation was desperate. 'On arriving at the Redan I found the salient angle crowded with men of various regiments, the stormers who had been driven back. Some had penetrated into the Redan, but the fire from the flanks of the work was too much for them, broken up as they were by having to cross the 250 yards under a very heavy fire. Some had stopped short under cover instead of rushing the work, and they impeded those who came after them.

'I found it quite impossible to get my men through the crowd on the salient in any kind of formation, so the only thing to be done was to get through as best we could; but it was fatal to our chance of doing much to be stopped in our advance, and whatever formation we had was quite destroyed; it was too late, under the heavy fire we were exposed to, to try another part of the work. I, with some of my men, went down one of the scaling ladders and up another until we got near the crest of the parapet. Two of my men, real plucky fellows, got through the crowd on the crest and helped me up. They were both Irishmen, Privates Jeremiah Whelan and James Dunn. When I got up I had a good view of the interior of the Redan, and saw a number of our men lying dead where they had been killed by the fire from the flanks of the works and some guns in the rear. There were no Russians to be seen in my immediate front, but I could see numbers behind the traverses on either flank, and they kept up a hot fire upon us.

'Whelan said to me, "Ah, sir, let us charge them!"

'I turned to the men of various regiments behind me who were crowding the salient angle, and said, "If these men will go with us we will; three of us are not enough to do any good." They did not respond. My men kept firing into the Russians quite coolly, and it was a marvel how they escaped being killed. I noticed a fine tall Russian officer about twenty-five yards from us on our right front. He was quite in the open. He had loaded muskets handed up to him, which he fired at us as quickly as he could.

'Whelan said, "Sir, there's a fine shot for your revolver." I wanted to keep my shot for closer quarters, so told Whelan he had better shoot him; and I believe he did, as the brave Russian disappeared apparently shot. It was a pity, but as he was killing our men it was a relief to get rid of him. I hope he was only wounded.'

Timothy Gowing had also clambered into the Redan. He too saw the fighting at first hand. 'The fighting inside the works was desperate – butt and bayonet, foot and fist. The enemy's guns were at once spiked. Some of the older hands did their best to get together sufficient men for one charge at the enemy, for we had often proved that they were no lovers of cold steel; but our poor fellows melted away almost as fast as they scaled those bloody parapets, from a cross-fire the enemy brought to bear on us from the rear of that work. The moss of that field grew red with British blood; after our stormers had entered the Redan the enemy came at us in swarms, but were kept back by the bayonet.'

On the slopes beneath, unable to advance and subjected to fire from both flanks while they waited, the men's morale was beginning to crumble – Lieutenant Campbell, watching from the advanced trenches, could see what was happening.

'The mass of our men, instead of going boldly into the Redan, remained clinging to the outside of the parapet and shooting over at the Russians, who ensconced themselves in shell-holes and behind a small entrenchment.

'I cannot account for the behaviour of the men in not following their officers, and I do not know what version of the story may reach England: but the plain truth is, that from the time they reached the parapet they showed the most arrant cowardice. On mounting the parapet of the Redan, you see before you a large open space, and the sight of this appeared to paralyze the men.

'No one can deny the fact that, in spite of all the exertions of the officers, the men clung to the outside of the salient angle in hundreds, declining to go in, although they were swept down by the flanking fire in scores. The officers, as usual, behaved as well as possible; I saw many of them – mere boys just from school, who had not been a month in the Crimea – standing on the parapet, and endeavouring to get their men on in the most gallant manner.'

In the Redan, casualties were mounting. One of them was John Hume.

'A Russian threw either a hand-grenade or a stone, which hit me on the back of my head, knocking me down under a scaling ladder. A man of the 41st Regiment, shot through the head, fell over me, and I had some difficulty in getting out of a very unpleasant place. I was a bit bothered by the blow on my head. Private Dunn came to me with a bullet-hole right through his shoulder. He said to me when he was hit, "Ah sir, I'm done at last!" I don't think he meant to make a joke on his name. He did not die but lost his arm out of the socket. Private Whelan escaped unhurt.'

General Windham, who had been in the forefront of the fighting inside the Redan, had sent repeated requests to General Codrington to commit the Highland Brigade, now waiting in the third parallel. Having sent several messengers to no effect – presumably killed in the fire that still raged across no man's land – he now ran the gauntlet himself to request reinforcements for his handful of stormers and the supports hugging the sides of the Redan.

John Hume was in no doubt that the Highlanders would have tipped the scale. 'If the Highland Brigade, whose ranks were filled with splendid old soldiers, had been sent at the Redan when it was seen that the salient angle was held, but that there was no chance of the works being carried, they would, I feel certain, have swept all before them, and those of the attacking party that were left would have joined the Highlanders, and the Russians would have been driven out.'

He was less sure about General Windham's decision to leave at that moment. 'Whether he did right or wrong to leave his command I cannot say. No one ever doubted his courage. It may have been an error of judgement, but no doubt he meant it for the best, knowing that if he could bring up sufficient fresh troops the work might be held. One regiment would not have been enough. If, as I said before, the general commanding had sent the Highland Brigade forward when he saw that the attack had partially failed, the Redan would have been ours. When the French took the Redan I could see the Russians streaming from that work towards the Redan.'

Right or wrong, it was in Windham's absence, that disaster struck. Down in the ditch Lieutenant Ranken was among the supports crowded on the slopes of the Redan, unable to go forward, unwilling to go back.

'They refused . . . to retreat, and seemed to look round for aid; I trembled when I saw no one coming, and looked continually, anxiously, round for the reserves I considered as a matter of course, would be advanced immediately it was perceived that the leading columns had failed to carry the position and were commencing the waver.

'It was in vain, however, to look; our Generals had left the reserves about an hour's march in the rear, so that even if our soldiers had charged forwards, as they should have done, they would probably have found themselves compromised, surrounded by the enemy, and immolated, before any assistance could have been brought to them.

'I had just given directions to the fraction of the working party of 100 men told off to me, which reached the ditch, what they were to do, and was returning towards the salient, when the sad repulse took place. What brought matters completely to a crisis I have never exactly ascertained: I heard directly after I regained our trenches that three officers of the 41st, after vainly trying to induce the men to advance, rushed forward together, and were all three shot down like one man by the cross-fire of the Russians behind their parados. This was the turning point, according to this account, of the men's indecision – they wavered and fled. I was near the counterscarp when I saw the whole living mass on the salient begin wavering to and fro; in a moment I found myself knocked down and lying on my face, with a number of men scrambling over me – their bayonets running through my clothes.'

Just below the parapet, Lieutenant Griffith had been trying to urge his men on. 'Do as we could we could not get the men to come up the parapet in sufficient numbers. The officers at the top kept calling out that those inside could not hold their ground unless ammunition was passed up to them, as theirs was expended. We passed it up as quick as we could but suddenly a panic seized our men and I grieve to say but the truth must be spoken, they deserted their comrades inside and retreated in confusion towards our trenches.

'In vain we bellowed out to them and tried everything to rally them – it was no use – the ladders were suddenly pushed down upon us and after remaining as long as they were able the officers were forced to follow their men.'

There was nothing the officers or NCOs could do to prevent a general stampede to the rear. Many officers were scathing in describing the men's conduct, but they had done all that could be asked of them. Crowded onto the sheer sides of the Redan, with most of their officers dead or wounded, and raked from both flanks by heavy artillery firing grape and canister, it was small wonder that they finally broke and ran back to the only cover there was: the trenches from which they had first started.

In the stampede, Ranken had been trampled underfoot. 'I expected to have been stunned and bayonetted, and to have been left insensible in the ditch, or shot by the enemy before I could drag myself out of it. However, at last I saw an opening, and holding on by my hands and knees, managed to force my way to it through the moving mass, and regain my legs. I ran then as fast as I could towards our advanced trenches, the grape whistling past me like hail, and the Russians standing on the top of their parapets, and firing volleys into the crowd of fugitives.'

Timothy Gowing didn't even remember leaving the earthwork. 'I myself was carried thither, having received five wounds in different parts of the body, my left hand shattered, and two nasty wounds in the head. I was totally unconscious when taken out of the Redan, and for some hours afterwards. An Irishman named Welsh was instrumental in saving my life. He had noticed me fall, and when he found that he had to retire from the Redan, he carried me up to the ditch and let me slip in, and then, with assistance, got me out of it and carried me across that terrible 200 yards, being shot through both legs in doing so. Before he reached our leading trench, some other good Samaritan picked me up and ran away with me.'

Meanwhile, in the reserve trenches, the Highland Brigade remained uncommitted. With the 42nd Highlanders, the Black Watch, was Lieutenant R.H. Stewart. All day they had waited, relying on scraps of information from men returning from the Redan. He wrote to his mother, 'We knew things must be going well, for we saw large quantities of prisoners coming up, some looking as happy as anything could be and no wonder. A rifleman had taken a prisoner and so he didn't see why he should carry nothing and we were much amused by seeing the prisoner carrying the Rifleman's rifle, bayonet and pouch whilst the victor walked behind with a revolver and his hand on the trigger. All this time the number of wounded being carried by was something awful! . . .

'Every officer who went by was questioned as to how affairs were going on, at first it was; "Oh alright, we've been inside the Redan half an hour."

'One of the 88th, an Irishman, was questioned as to what we were doing in front. "Och, bedad, we'se been in the Redan the last hour, nor don't mean to lave it" at which we all laughed and cheered the poor fellow, but as you already know, we did not keep our word about "not laving it".

'We were in a most nervous anxiety all day, for we could see nothing from the smoke and the accounts were gradually worse and worse. We were beaten out of the Redan: we were re-formed again and were again beaten back and then we learned the truth that the British soldier had turned tail and refused to mount the parapet.'

By now the survivors of the stormers and supports were slumping thankfully back into the British trenches. In a ghastly rerun of 18 June, the retreat had been as bloody as the advance.

Lieutenant Griffith wrote, 'Feeling disgraced, tho' I had done my best, unwillingly turned to follow the men. I saw our trench at some distance but I never expected to reach it. The fire was fearful and I kept tumbling over the dead and wounded men who literally shrewed the ground. At last to my great joy I gained our Parallels and tumbled somehow into the trench Lawrence tumbling upon me. I should have said that on the way a bullet hit my water bottle which was slung at my side, spilt all the water and glanced off. A stone thrown up by a grape-shot hit me in the leg but didn't hurt me much. Soon after we found Capt Drewe and a few men and by degrees mustered most of the unhurt. It was very melancholy we found so many missing.'

When Ranken jumped down into a British trench, 'All was shame, rage and fear – the men were crowded together and disorganised. It was hopeless to attempt to renew the attack with the same troops. My sappers all went to the Quarries, but I remained for more than half-an-hour in the most advanced trench with the shattered remains of the assaulting column. An officer of the 97th came up to me and shook me by the hand, saying that he was glad to see me safe and sound, and that of his regiment he was the only officer left . . .'

When Ranken did go to the Quarries, he said, 'I passed Sir William Codrington, who was charged with the direction of the attack, sitting in one of the trenches with his aides-de-camp about him. I repeated to him a few words I had heard fall from an officer of the 33rd, to the effect, that if it were possible to collect the men of the various regiments together, under their own officers, he would be willing to renew the assault. Sir William said the fire of the grape was too heavy to admit of the attack being repeated that day.'

Codrington had seen enough. As the men had come running in from the Redan, some of his staff, one of them Henry Clifford, had tried unsuccessfully to rally them.

'When the men ran in from the parapet of the Redan, Glyn, who was on General Shirley's staff, came up and we drew our swords and beat the men and implored them to stand and not to run, that all would be lost; but many fled. The trench where they ran in was so crowded that it was impossible to move without walking over the wounded who lay under our feet, without any possibility of removing them. By degrees we got the Regiment into a little order. I forgot to tell you that from the commencement they were all broken in advancing on the Redan, by the heavy fire of grape and musketry.

'Sir William decided it was no use attempting a second assault, our men would not go at it.'

Not even General Windham's urgings could persuade Codrington to renew the assault. Codrington moved the Highland Brigade forward, but by 6 p.m., when they were finally in place, it was deemed too late to assault and they were warned off for an attack at dawn.

Lieutenant Campbell, the assistant engineer, met Windham on his return from the trenches. 'I was so glad to see him come back safe from the trench that I rushed up to shake hands with him, and ask him for some account of the proceedings. He put his hand on my shoulder and said: "My dear Campbell, look here, this is the greatest disgrace that has ever fallen on the British soldier. I could have forgiven them if they had been beaten out, but they would not go in. These may be the last words I shall ever say to you, but I declare they are true. The men would not follow the officers; all the dash seems to have gone out of them."'

The attack had been another costly failure: 2,610 men had fallen, 550 of them dead, including 29 officers. Perhaps what made it worse was that as evening fell, the Tricolore still floated over the Malakoff. MacMahon had been as good as his word: the interior had become a charnel house, as both French and Russians had poured reserves into the battle. Unlike the rear of the Redan, which was open and allowed easy entry for Russian reserves, the gorge at the back of the Malakoff had been blocked to protect it from rear attack by any enemy who entered the city elsewhere. This meant that once they had seized the Malakoff, the advantage lay with the French.

Five Russian counter-attacks were beaten off, at appalling cost —
MacMahon's division had climbed out of their trenches with 4,520
men and 199 officers; of these 29 officers and 292 men were killed
and 89 officers and 1,729 men wounded. Other French assaults,
against the Central and Flagstaff Bastions and the Little Redan, had,
after initial successes, failed: they had been beaten off with heavy
loss.

Nevertheless, by nightfall, the key to Sebastopol was in French
hands.

Among the British, the recriminations were already starting.
Timothy Gowing blamed it on the extreme youth of the soldiers.
'We had a great number of very young men with us who had come
out with drafts to fill up the gaps. Many of them had not seen
seventeen summers; plenty of them had not had two months'
service. We wanted 20,000 tried veterans; but through some mis-
management, they were kept back.

'Had we even ten thousand men with us, the Russians would
have gone into the harbour at the point of the bayonet, or else been
made to lay down their arms. But no; men were sent up in driblets,
to be slaughtered in detail.'

Some blamed the press for starting a scare-story that the Redan
was mined and that once British troops were swarming over it they
would all be blown sky-high. Most criticised the selection of the
Light and 2nd Divisions: they had been in the forefront of all the
fighting since the campaign began, had suffered the most casualties,
and consequently had the highest number of new recruits.

John Hume was certainly of this opinion. 'There is no doubt that
the men of the 2nd and Light Divisions, who had borne the burden
and heat of the trench work from the commencement to the end of
the siege, ought to have been the reserve instead of being the
attacking force. There were numbers of young soldiers in the two
divisions who had been taught to keep under cover as much as
possible when in trenches, who on reaching the Redan sought for
cover instead of rushing the work.

'The 1st Division, fine old soldiers who had not done as much
trench work, would most likely have taken the Redan and held it,
but the great distance between our works and the Russian work
was one of the principal causes of our failure. It was impossible to

keep any steady formation under the very heavy fire we were exposed to while crossing the 250 yards, and there not being sufficient space in our trenches to allow more than two companies to be formed up at a time, obliged us to move out in driblets instead of in a strong column such as is usual in an attack on a strong position.'

Hume had been wounded in the left arm while staggering, dazed, through the ditch, but he had made it back to the British trenches. Now, like Evelyn Wood before him, he faced a battle to save his arm.

'I went to my tent, where some of the surgeons of the 2nd Division held a consultation as to whether my arm was to be amputated. They all agreed that it ought to be cut off with the exception of Cowan, our assistant-surgeon, a clever young Scotchman, who said, "I know Captain Hume's constitution and habits, and think I can save his arm; at all events leave it on till tomorrow." The others agreed, and I owe the saving of my arm to the old regimental system of having surgeons belonging to regiments who know the habits and constitutions of officers and men from constant observation.'

Hume had reason to be thankful. His regiment had suffered heavily. 'Lieut. Johnson, 55th, was severely wounded in the ankle. A Russian threw his musket and bayonet at him. Captain Richards was also wounded ... Brigadier-General Warren and his aide-de-camp, Lieutenant Morgan 55th, were both wounded, the latter very severely. His arm was broken in two places by a blow from a rifle which was knocked out of a man's hand by a round shot. The 55th had 1 officer killed and 7 wounded, 2 corporals and 24 men killed, 8 sergeants, 14 corporals and 92 privates wounded, making a total of 8 officers and 140 non-commissioned officers and privates killed and wounded.'

Even more poignant than mere lists of numbers was Hume's observation. 'Out of the 2nd Division cricket eleven who played in a match against the 4th Division on the 1st of September seven were killed and wounded. The four bowlers were killed.'

Colonel Dan Lysons of the 23rd, who had been wounded at the base of the Redan as he brought his regiment up in support, had hobbled back unaided to his camp, only to find that his life had been despaired of.

'When I approached our camp, my faithful groom, Styles, was the first to see me. He ran out and seized me in his arms, and hugged me like a child, crying out, "They told me you were killed." I looked into the hospital, and I was put in bed in my tent.'

The mood in the British camps was one of despondency. Of all the hard lessons of the war, the hardest – taught first on 18 June, and repeated again on this day – was that British troops *could*, and sometimes *did*, run away.

Henry Clifford described his emotions that night in a letter to his family. 'My head is throbbing, my ears are ringing with the booming of the cannon, the whistling of the grape and the musket-ball, the wild shouting of the soldiers, the groans and yells of the wounded and the dying, my eyes almost blinded with dust, have before them the brave officers leading on their men, waving their swords over their heads on the parapet of the Redan, *alone*, falling wounded, and perhaps less dreadful, dead into the ditch or amongst the enemy into the Redan. I see yet the mangled piece of flesh that your foot must tread on alive, yes, alive, and that you must stand by and pass by, and be implored, and cursed and upbraided by, without means to help. And what almost breaks my heart, and nearly drove me mad, I see our English soldiers that I was so proud of, run away.'

He finally closed his eyes to sleep with one last melancholy thought: 'About nine o'clock I lay down on my bed with my clothes on, I never remember feeling so low-spirited. Sebastopol will never give in till we have fought for every inch of ground, thought I.'

He did not sleep well. 'Throughout the night heavy, dead sounds awoke me, but I thought it must be the state I was in and the constant booming of the cannon the previous day. At last a tremendous explosion thoroughly awoke me. I jumped on my horse, and in a few minutes, Sebastopol all in flames was before my eyes. English soldiers were in the Redan, English soldiers and French were in the town. I looked at the Bridge; it was crowded with the retreating foe. I looked for the Russian Men-of-War; they had been sunk. Was it a dream?'

If it was, he was not the only one dreaming it. Lieutenant George Ranken described how he: 'was awakened from a broken slumber at about four . . . by a tremendous explosion, and soon after heard Nicholson (who had just come back from a night's trench duty) assert, that the Russians had evacuated the town, and were firing their magazines by galvanic batteries.'

Ranken dressed, and with Nicholson and a few others, rode towards Sebastopol. 'We had not gone far before we saw an immense cloud rise in the air accompanied by a deep sullen sound, the explosion of another large magazine. The whole of Sebastopol was in flames; but half of the burning city was hidden by an impenetrable cloud caused by the explosion. The huge line-of-battle ships which formerly lay like grim floating towers, blocking up the harbour, had been sunk. Nothing of them but the tops of the masts remained visible. A few steamers, looking melancholy and isolated in the midst of the general wreck, alone remained of the fleet which had spread terror over the Black Sea.'

From the moment the French had seized the Malakoff, Sebastopol's fate had been sealed. Before darkness had set in, Prince Gortchakoff had given the order to evacuate the south side of the city. In a brilliantly executed operation, the Russian garrison, who had held the city for almost a year, withdrew from their works, collected by the harbour and began crossing by the bridge of boats on the north side. The city's thirty-five magazines were ignited, starting at eleven o'clock and continuing through the night. At the same time, fires were started all over the city.

Lieutenant Stewart was out with a fatigue party of the 42nd Highlanders, making gabions for an assault that he increasingly suspected was not going to take place.

'That night I saw a sight which beggars description, the Russians performed the old trick of Moscow, whatever they could not take away they destroyed, burnt or blew up. And most unpleasant and dangerous were the blow-ups to the working parties, as the pieces of stone, and trunks of trees were falling about our ears very unpleasantly, and we had one or two men hurt, though none seriously I am happy to say.'

As a grand finale, at daybreak the bridge of boats itself was blown up, leaving the Allied and Russian armies divided by the waters of the main harbour.

Riding up towards the Redan, Henry Clifford could hardly believe what had happened. 'I rode on, I came to our trenches. I rode over the open – there, where for months no man has dared to go, even on foot. Those trenches, so crowded with our troops for months, were empty, not a sound. I passed the Batteries, all was still as death, not a breath of air, and the smoke from the burning City hung like a shroud over the ground, every yard almost of which has been moistened by the blood of men. Never was I so alone, never was silence so awful. I felt that the sound of a cannon would have been a relief.

'I wandered on and found myself at the advance trench. Voices of the rough soldiers caught my ear, a few yards more, and the theatre of our strife, of our pride, of our shame, was there. No, it was no dream. The Russians had abandoned the south side of Sebastopol! A few yards further and I stood inside the Redan! and I looked at Sebastopol on fire!!! and I heard a fearful roar, and I saw a dark solid mass of smoke rise in the air from the Town, some large magazine had blown up. Yes I stood in the Redan, and the Redan was ours.'

Lieutenant Stewart was already inside. 'At about 5 a.m. I went into the Redan with Dr McKinnon of ours to help the wounded, and I staid there about an hour giving away water and putting the men on stretchers, etc. The 93rd behaved infamously; I saw the men rifling the pockets of our dead Officers and didn't I pitch into them? The brutes would not lend a hand in carrying the stretchers, so intent were they on plunder. I myself did not take a single thing then, as I could not find time.

'I left the Redan at last, being rather afraid of being blown-up, as whilst I was in several blow-ups occurred close by, and we felt rather nervous the whole time, having heard of such things as galvanic wire.'

Surveying the British dead, Stewart thought, 'It was a great absurdity letting the assaulting party consist of regiments that had been dreadfully cut up during the war. I can assure you that the men I saw lying out and inside the Redan were perfect children. Some I should think not more than 17 or 18. How then can you expect children like that to perform feats of valour unequalled in ancient time?'

Ranken and his friends had come supplied with brandy and water, which they gave to the wounded, British and Russian indiscriminately. 'We emptied four or five bottles, which I hope did some good. I saw Sir Colin Campbell, who seemed to approve of what I was doing, and told me I was playing the good Samaritan.'

Lieutenant Stewart had a more bruising encounter with Sir Colin. 'When I got outside, the first person I met was Sir C. Campbell. "Are you here on duty, Sir?" was his first question.

' "I came with Dr McKinnon to help with the wounded, Sir."

' "That was not my question, are you sent here by your commanding officer?"

' "No, Sir."

' "Very well, you had better get back as soon as possible, as you have no right to be here."

'This was rather hard, as I would have got leave in a minute, being requested by the Surgeon to come with him. However, I got off much cheaper than some officers in the Rifles, who got a most tremendous wigging.'

'The salient of the Redan presented a terrible appearance,' Ranken wrote in his journal that night. 'Outside the ditch and a little to the left of the salient angle, in a small hole, lay the bodies of fifty or sixty English soldiers, thickly piled together. Near the crest of the counterscarp was an officer with his hand stretched out as if in the act of waving his sword. His features were not distorted, but noble, composed, and manly, though a portion of his head had been shot away by a grape-shot.

'The ditch near the salient was full of bodies, gabions, and debris, lying in horrible chaos together. Inside the Redan few bodies were to be seen, but a handful of our men having penetrated into the interior. At a point, however, more than twenty yards from the salient, I saw the body of a young English officer, and close to him, three or four soldiers lying side by side, or across the bodies of several Russians. The attitudes of the various figures bespoke the energy of their death struggle.'

Standing on top of the Redan looking down on the fallen city, Henry Clifford felt anything but triumphant. 'If a few days before I had been told "on the morning of the 9th September at five o'clock Sebastopol will be in the hands of the Allies and you will stand in the Redan held by the English," I should have said, "Oh that will be a proud and happy moment, that will repay us for all we have gone through, even the loss of so many lives, so much suffering and hardship will not have been thrown away in vain!" But no, I stood in the Redan more humble, more dejected and with a heavier heart than I have yet felt since I left home.

'I looked towards the Malakoff and there was the French flag, the Tricolour planted on its Parapet. Yes, the French had taken the Malakoff, but the English had not taken the Redan. No flag floated on the Parapet on which I stood and if it had, I could have seized it, and dashed it into the ditch we could not pass, or hid it in the bosom of the young officer, dead at my feet inside the Redan.'

Clifford's judgement was too harsh. The capture of the Malakoff was the key to the city's fall, but it might not have happened had the fire directed at the Redan been switched to the Malakoff, or if the Russian reserves committed to defending the Redan had moved and been deployed against the French. Even if the French had taken the lion's share of the fighting in the last months, the capture of Sebastopol was truly an Allied effort.

Not everyone was as low-spirited as Henry Clifford, but the main reaction was one of weary relief. Lieutenant Campbell wrote home, 'I suppose all in England are in a great state of excitement about the fall of Sebastopol. To us out here it is the greatest relief you can imagine. Our sensations are more like those of a person enjoying a quiet Sunday in the country after a week of dissipation than anything else I can think of. The incessant boom of the guns, the constant passing of wounded men, and the daily question as to which of your friends or acquaintances had been killed the night before, had become almost intolerable. Can you fancy a greater strain on the mind than passing three nights in the week within a hundred yards of the enemy, never knowing at what moment you are to be attacked, and always ready to exchange the spade for the firelock?'

Visitors to the city found it in ruins. Campbell was appalled at the conditions he found. 'I will not attempt to describe to you the scenes that I witnessed after we entered the town. I do not believe that history tells of anything more dreadful than the state of the Russian hospitals. The slaughter about the batteries, particularly opposite to the French, was terrific, and nothing is more painful in scenes of that sort then the utter helplessness of the looker-on. What can one man with a flask of sherry do among 10,000 wounded men, mostly speaking in an unknown tongue? I passed men lying terribly wounded, and twenty-four hours afterwards passed them again, and found them in the same spot still alive, nothing having been done to them. No blame is to be attributed to anyone for this, as it is impossible to relieve all where there are such numbers.

'Generally speaking, the wounded Russians bore their wounds with the greatest patience, and were gentle and grateful for anything that was done for them; there were a few who looked as if they would like to shoot even those who assisted them, but they were the exceptions.'

Others were less sympathetic. Fanny Duberly, who had observed the burning city from the heights, wrote in her journal: 'It was a magnificent sight, and one which afforded me, in common I fancy with many more, more satisfaction than pain. I could not think at such a moment of the destruction and desolation of war. I could only remember the long-coveted prize was ours at last, and I felt no more compunction for town or for Russian than the hound whose lips are red with blood does for the fox which he has chased through a hard run. It was a lawful prize, purchased God knows! dearly enough, and I felt glad we had got it.'

Once in possession of the city, the Allies embarked on the systematic and wholesale destruction of its dockyards and fortifications. For their part, the Russians strengthened their fortifications at the Star Fort and kept up a sporadic artillery fire against the Allies from across the harbour, which soon rendered parts of southern Sebastopol untenable.

At home, the general rejoicing over the fall of Sebastopol was cut short by impatience at General Simpson's inability to capitalise on the Allied success. The Russians were still on the northern side of Sebastopol, and maintained a force of some 14 divisions beyond the Tchernaya; the public wanted to know why the Allied armies were not acting against them. The expedition had achieved its strategic objectives – the destruction of Sebastopol and the Black Sea fleet – but that appeared to have escaped the politicians. In the opinion of Captain Garnet Wolseley, the whole siege had been 'a game at brag' from the start. Now that the Russians had folded, they might have considered this and thought themselves lucky.

The fact that Pélissier was also under pressure, from the Emperor, was little consolation to Simpson, who resigned his command in November and handed over to Sir William Codrington.

Codrington was no more eager than Simpson to embark on any new ventures this late in the season, especially with an exhausted army. In truth, the Russians and the Allies had fought each other to a standstill. The main harbour was, in Codrington's words, 'a mutual wet ditch under fire from both sides', and apart from an occasional desultory exchange of roundshot, hostilities had ceased.

On the Upland, the armies settled down for another winter.

Supplied by rail and an improved road, housed in huts and abundantly supplied with warm clothes and rations, the British fared much better than they had the previous winter. Surgeon Robinson of the Scots Guards believed that the men in his brigade were better off than they would have been at home.

'The contrast, in every point of view, between the condition of the troops at the termination of the year 1855, contrasted with that of the preceeding, cannot fail to be forcibly brought to the minds of all who witnessed the sad sufferings of the first period ... Taking my own Corps and the other two regiments of Guards as examples, I conceive the ratio of sickness at this time to be less (from disease generally) than would probably have been the case had the men been quartered in London, or any other town at home. ... From one class of disease, notoriously the most fatal in troops on home service – particularly in the Household Brigade – experience has shewn, I think indisputably, that very few cases have originated in the Crimea. I allude to consumption.'

This winter it was the French who suffered most. Their administrative system, the admiration of British officers the previous year, now buckled under the strain imposed by the massive reinforcement of their army. Typhus and cholera broke out and 53,000 men were admitted to the French hospitals. Some 10,000 men died, mostly from typhus.

It was perhaps as well that by January Austria was taking the initiative in bringing about a peace. The previous month, Count Esterhazy had been to St Petersburg to deliver a paper stating the demands of the Allies. They wanted confirmation of the autonomy of Wallachia and Moldavia; free navigation of the Danube for all nations; the neutralisation of the Black Sea, with the abolition of all military installations on its shores; and a guarantee of the rights of Christian subjects in Turkey. The Holy Places in Jerusalem – which had provided the *casus belli* for the war – were not even mentioned. Prussia urged the Tsar to accept these demands, and Austria added that if they were not accepted, she would declare war on Russia herself. Two days before the deadline, Tsar Alexander II accepted the terms. On 28 February 1856, news of the armistice came to Sebastopol by telegraph from the Paris Peace Conference. The armistice was to last until 31 March.

On that same day George Ranken, who had commanded the

engineer party at the Redan and was now promoted to Major, was engaged in blowing up the Naval Barracks in the Karbalnaya suburb. Several of the mines missfired, so Ranken went back in to relight the fuses. As he did so, one of the powder hoses to which the fuses were attached ignited and the resulting explosion brought the building crashing down. It was not until the next morning that Ranken's body was found: the last British casualty of the Crimean War.

The following day representatives of both sides met at the Traktir Bridge to discuss the terms of the armistice. Reviews of each other's troops were arranged by both sides, and at the end of the discussions, Sir William Codrington invited the Russian officers to a race meeting.

The war was over.

'But what good came of it at last?' asked the small boy at the end of Robert Southey's poem 'The Battle of Blenheim'. The old man answered,

'Why that I cannot tell,' said he,
'But t'was a famous victory.'

Under the terms of the Peace, Sebastopol was returned to the Russians, who immediately set about rebuilding it. Within fourteen years the Tsar had repudiated the Treaty of Paris and was once again threatening Turkey. In 1877 a war broke out which saw Russian troops marching through Bulgaria, almost to the gates of Adrianople. This time the Russians were stopped by diplomatic means. By the end of the century Lord Salisbury was wondering out loud whether Britain had backed the wrong horse in the Crimea. By 1916 the British and the French were again at Gallipoli, this time being fought to a standstill by Johnny Turk, who was engaged in the east against Britain's ally, the Tsar of Russia.

To have sided with the Russians in 1854 would have been wholly unacceptable to the British public. The Crimean War was a just war, and, ultimately, a successful one. The Allied armies effected a landing on the coast of the most powerful nation in Europe, took her largest naval base and destroyed her fleet. The price, in blood and treasure, was high. The British had spent more than £50,000,000. Of the 22,500 soldiers, who died, only 4,000 were killed in action or died of wounds. The remainder, 18,500 men, died of cholera, typhus and other diseases.

The chief benefit of the British nation was the reform of the British army. This war, fought at the mid-point of the nineteenth century, had many elements that would have been familiar to those who fought under Wellington. There were as many new elements introduced that would have been equally familiar to the soldiers of the Great War. Rifled firearms and artillery, conical bullets and shells, the electric telegraph, iron-clad, steam-driven warships, railways, war photography, war-reportage: all of these developments, new at the start of the war, were accepted as normal by its end. Tactics changed dramatically; both cavalry and infantry learned to adopt more open formations, and relied far more on firepower, which itself was far more predictable. The Minié rifle had been replaced in the latter stages of the campaign by the Enfield, which were so effective that they were soon being sent out to India, to be issued to the sepoys.

More significant even than the technological changes were the administrative reforms that resulted from the Crimean War. The old tangle of prerogatives and responsibilities was swept away. The fourteen or so authorities responsible for the army were replaced by one civilian – the Minister for War – and one soldier, the Commander-in-Chief. In the following years there was considerable progress in the staff system, and in the training of officers – although the Duke of Cambridge occasionally applied the brakes. In due course the purchase of commissions was abolished, and improvements were made to the lot of the private soldier, including the abolition of flogging.

Improvised solutions to military inadequacies during the course of the war became permanent institutions. The British army had gone into battle with no transport and totally inadequate medical services; it emerged with a Land Transport Corps – later to become the Military Train, and eventually the Army Service Corps – and a Medical Staff Corps. Florence Nightingale began reforms in military medicine, which she continued during her long life and were taken up by others. It was not until the Great War that enemy munitions killed more British soldiers than disease, but the Victorian army would never let its soldiers down that badly again.

Above all, the Crimean War was the training ground for a generation of young officers. Some of those who served in the Crimea as young men became the generals of the future: Hamley, Gordon, Adye, Wolseley. Midshipman Evelyn Wood became a Field Marshal, and Sergeant Luke O'Connor, who had refused to relinquish the 23rd's Colour in the Great Redoubt, died a Major-General and a KCB. These were the men who went on to extend, defend and police the Empire, and in general, they did it well. The wars they fought were against natives rather than regular European armies, but they posed huge strategic, administrative and logistical problems. In later years, in bushveldt, jungle or desert, under palms or under pines, when they looked back on their Crimean days and reflected on what they had learned, they might have answered, as had Wellington when asked what he'd learned in Flanders under the Grand Old Duke of York.

'I learned how not to do it, and that is always something.'

APPENDIX

Of the individuals we have followed through the Crimean campaign, the following is known of their subsequent careers:

Lord George Paget became a Major-General in 1861, by which time his wife Agnes had died, leaving two children. That same year he married Louise Heneage. He commanded the cavalry at Aldershot 1860–2, and the Sirhat Division of the Bengal Army from 1862–5, when he returned to England and was appointed Inspector-General of cavalry. He was nominated a Lieutenant-General and KCB in 1871, and General in 1877. He died at his Mayfair residence in 1880.

Henry Clifford VC married, in 1857, Josephine Anstice. They had six daughters and three sons (the middle son, Henry, was killed in action in 1916, a Brigadier and a holder of the DSO). After serving in China, Clifford held a series of Staff appointments in England before, in 1870, now a CB and a Brevet Colonel, being appointed ADC to the Commander-in-Chief, the Duke of Cambridge. He and the Duke had been on the best of terms since the Crimea, and Clifford knew how to defuse the Duke's notorious rages. When on one occasion the Duke called him a 'damned fool' in front of a mixed bag of junior and senior officers, Clifford disarmed the Duke with his reply, 'Sir, I am not prepared to stand here and be called a damned fool before all these other damned fools.' He was Assistant Adjutant-General at Headquarters from 1873-5, and in 1877 was gazetted Major-General. In 1879 he was chosen to command the Lines of Communication for Lord Chelmsford's campaign against the Zulus. After the death of the Prince Imperial Clifford, with his Catholic faith and fluent French, was the obvious choice to accompany the Empress Eugenie to the site of her son's last moments. In 1882 Clifford was appointed to command Eastern District, with

Headquarters in Colchester, but was already ill with cancer. He died at the family home, Ugbroke in Devon, the following year.

Fanny Duberly's wish that her life not 'rust away' was granted, at least in part. Her journal, published in 1856, proved a popular success and she enjoyed a measure of celebrity, although permission to dedicate the book to the Queen was refused. When the 8th Hussars were inspected by the Queen and Prince Albert she was pointedly ignored by the couple; only the Princess Royal, Vicky, cried out 'Oh, there's Mrs Duberly' before being hurried away. Fanny never received the Crimean medal she had hoped for.

A year later the 8th Hussars were again on campaign, this time in India, during the Sepoy Mutiny. True to form Fanny braved official opposition and accompanied her husband. When the Regiment charged at Gwalior in 1858, she could not restrain herself and charged with them, leaving Henry watching from the sidelines. Among the enemy cavalry was another woman, the scimitar-wielding Rani of Jhansi, who was cut from her saddle by a trooper of the 8th. After India the Duberlys returned to England and a life which Fanny found intolerably dull. She died, aged 73, in 1903.

Sergeant Timothy Gowing served a total of twenty-two years with the Royal Fusiliers, eighteen of them in India, returning to England in 1874. He married three times and had nineteen children, only one of whom survived him (seven died of cholera in one day, in India in 1864). An immensely strong man – even in old age he could lift two loaded coal scuttles above his head hooked onto his little fingers – he spent his last years wandering the industrial areas of Lancashire selling copies of his memoirs in factories and offices. He died, aged 74, in 1908.

John Hume got command of the 55th in India in 1874, taking over from his brother Robert, who had commanded it for the previous sixteen years. John retired a Major-General; his brother, Robert, a Lieutenant-General and KCB. Their brother Gustavus served during the Indian Mutiny with another brother, Walter, and became Lieutenant of the Queen's Bodyguard, the Gentlemen at Arms.

Somerset Calthorpe's comments, recorded in these pages, about

Lord Cardigan's conduct at Balaklava, involved him in a long-running dispute with the 'Noble Yachtsman'. A cousin of the Duke of Beaufort, Calthorpe was one of the few people with political and social clout to stand up to Cardigan, who first of all attempted to have him court-martialled and then brought an action against him for libel. The case was finally heard in 1863, with Cardigan objecting to, among other things, Calthorpe's comments on the Sore-Back Reconnaissance, Captain Morris' protests to Cardigan after the Heavy Brigade action, and Cardigan's alleged absence at a critical juncture during the Light Brigade charge. The Lord Chief Justice ruled that as an 'expression of his own feelings' Cardigan had been libelled, but that due to a number of factors including the death of a number of witnesses; the absence of others in India; the time elapsed; and the fact that 1,000 copies of Calthorpe's book had previously been destroyed by a private agreement with a friend of Cardigan's (an agreement of which Cardigan denied all knowledge) the ruling could not be made absolute. The case was dismissed without costs. Calthorpe married in 1862. He died, by now the 7th Baron Calthorpe, in 1912, aged 81.

Having transferred from the 13th Light Dragoons to the 17th Lancers in 1857, **Evelyn Wood** served in India during the Mutiny, where in 1857 his gallantry during the Central India Campaign won him a Victoria Cross. Returning to England he served on the staff until in 1871 he purchased a commission into HM 90th Light Infantry. Here he attracted the attention of fellow Crimea veteran Garnet Wolseley. Having served with distinction in Wolseley's Ashanti campaign, he became a member of that General's favoured 'ring' of senior officers. After commanding the 90th in the Ninth Frontier War in South Africa, he was appointed commander of No. 4 Column, for Lord Chelmsford's invasion of Zululand. At the battle of Kambula, Wood inflicted heavy casualties on the Zulus, in part at least redeeming the disaster to the Centre Column at Isandhlwana. During the first Boer War, Wood took command of British forces following the death of General Colley at Majuba, after which he commanded the 4th Division in an independent role during Wolseley's Egyptian campaign. Having successfully reorganised the Egyptian army, Wood went on to command the lines of communication during Wolseley's attempt to relieve General Gordon (another Crimea veteran), later serving as Wolseley's Chief of Staff. Returning home with failing health, Wood held a number of important posts at Colchester and Aldershot and in 1893, by now a Lieutenant-General and GCB, he became Quartermaster-General at the War Office. His last command, as a full General, was 2nd Army Corps. Wood died, aged 81, in 1919 having risen from Midshipman to Field Marshal.

Wood's boyhood hero **Captain William Peel** also served in the Indian Mutiny commanding a battery of heavy guns, this time 500 miles inland, from his frigate *Shannon*. Peel served with distinction, under Sir Colin Campbell of Balaklava fame, at the second relief of Lucknow. As in the Crimea, Peel's cool courage and laconic manner won him many admirers and it was later held that, had posthumous VC' s been awarded at this time, Peel's conduct during this campaign would have won him a bar to his Crimean VC. He died of smallpox at Cawnpore in April 1858.

SELECT BIBLIOGRAPHY

Books

Adkin, Mark, *The Charge* (1996)

Adye, John, *A Review of the Crimean War* (1860)

Airlie, Countess of, *With the Guards we shall go: A Guardsman's letters in the Crimea (1854-5)* (1933)

Angelsey, The Marquis of, *A History of British Cavalry Vol 3* (1973)

Anon, *Memorials of Captain Hedley Vicars* (1856)

Bell, Sir George, *Rough Notes of an Old Soldier* (1867)

Bonham-Carter, Victor, *Surgeon in the Crimea: The experiences of George Lawson* (1968)

Campbell, Colin Frederick, *Letters from Camp to his Relatives during the siege of Sebastopol* (1894)

Calthorpe Lieut. The Hon S J G, *Letters from Headquarters; or the Realities of the War in the Crimea by an Officer of the Staff* (1857)

Chapman, Roger, *Echoes From the Crimea: Eyewitness accounts by members of Her Majesty's 19th Foot* (Green Howards Museum 2004)

Clifford, Henry, *Letters and Sketches from the Crimea* (ed. C Fitzherbert) (1956)

David, Saul, *The Homicidal Earl: The Life of Lord Cardigan* (1997)

Duberly, Mrs Henry, *Journal* (kept during the Russian War) (1855)

Fletcher, Ian and Ischenko, Natalia, *The Crimean War: A Clash of Empires* (2004)

French-Blake, Lt-Col R L V, *The Crimean War* (1971)

Fortesque, The Hon. J W, *History of the British Army Vol. XIII* (1930)

Franks, Sgt Major Henry, *Leaves from a Soldier's Notebook* (1904)

Gowing, T, *A Soldier's Experience: a Voice from the Ranks* (1895)

Hamley, Sir Edward, *The war in the Crimea* (1891)

Hibbert, Christopher, *The Destruction of Lord Raglan* (1961)

Higginson, General Sir George, *Seventy-One Years of a Guardsman's Life* (1916)

Hodasevitch, Robert Adolf, *A Voice from within the Walls of Sebastopol* (1856)

Hume, Major-General J R, *Reminiscences of the Crimean Campaign with the 55th Regiment* (1894)

Jocelyn, Col. J R J, *The History of the Royal Artillery, Crimean Period* (1911)

Kinglake, A W, *The Invasion of the Crimea* 9 Vols. (1877-88)

Lysons, Daniel, *The Crimean War from First to Last* (1895)

Mawson, Michael Hargreave (ed.), *Eyewitness in the Crimea; the Crimean War Letters of Colonel George Frederick Dallas* (2001)

Moyse-Bartlett, Lt-Col. H, *Louis Edward Nolan and his Influence on British Cavalry* (1971)

Mercer, Patrick, *Give Them a Volley and Charge! The Battle of Inkerman, 1854* (1998)

Mitchell, Sgt A, *Recollections of one of the Light Brigade* (1885)

Morley T, *The Man of the Hour* (1892)

Munro, W, *Records of Service and Campaigning* (1887)

Paget, General Lord George, *The Light Cavalry Brigade in the Crimea* (1881)

Pemberton, W, *Baring Battles of the Crimean War* (1962)

Ranken, W, Bayne *Six Months at Sebastopol* (1857)

Regimental Officer, A (Col. CT Wilson), *Our Veterans of 1854* (1859)

Ross-of-Bladensburg, Lieutenant-Colonel John, *A History of the Coldstream Guards (1815-1885)* (1896)

Russell, W H, *The War in the Crimea* (1855)

Seaton, Albert, *The Crimean War: A Russian Chronicle* (1977)

Small, E, *Told From the Ranks* (1897)

Steevens, Lieutenant-Colonel Nathaniel, *The Crimean Campaign with the Connaught Rangers* (1878)

Sterling, Anthony, *The Story of the Highland Brigade in the Crimea* (1895)

Stirling, Richard, *Seth Bond, A Warwickshire Hero at the Charge of the Light Brigade* (1994)

Strachan, Hew, *From Waterloo to Balaklava: Tactics, Tehnology and the British Army, 1830-54* (1984)

Thomas, Donald, *Charge! Hurrah! Hurrah! A Life of Lord Cardigan of Balaklava* (1974)

Ward, S G P, (ed.) *The Hawley Letters* (1970)

Warner, Philip and Richard Temple Godman, *Fields of War; A young cavalryman's Crimea campaign* (John Murray, 1977)

Wolseley, Field Marshal Viscount, *The Story of a Soldier's Life* Vol I (1903)

Wood, Sir Evelyn, *The Crimea in 1854 and 1894* (1895)
> *Midshipman to Field Marshal* Vol I (1906)

Woodham-Smith Cecil, *Florence Nightingale* (1951)
> *The Reason Why* (1953)

Letters and Periodicals

Diary of Major G V Mundy – The Duke of Wellington's Regiments Museum

Illustrated London News

Leamington Spa *Courier* – Warwickshire Records Office

Letters of Boscawen Trevor Griffith – Royal Welch Fusiliers Museum

National Army Museum: Letters of: Lieut Hugh Annesley; Lieut-Col G L Carmichael; Maj-Gen F P Haines; Ensign Robert Lindsay; Lt A MacDonald; Cornet the Hon. Grey Neville; Captain the Hon Henry Neville; Lt E A Seager.

INDEX

Abbott, Private 152
Adams, Brigadier 211–2
Adye, Lieutenant-Colonel 3–4, 323
Agamemnon, HMS 117
Ainslie, Colonel 238–9
Airey, General Sir Richard 39, 43, 77
Aladyn 10, 12–13
Albert, Prince 4
Alexander II, Tsar 262, 320
Alma, battle of the
    night before 46–7
    deployment 49–54
    the Great Redoubt 50–51, 70–74, 75, 82, 91,
      188
    the Lesser Redoubt 50–51
    allied advance 54–64
    assault on Bourliouk 59–62
    river crossing 63–4, 81
    assault 64–74, 188
    Russian counter-attack 74, 76, 78–80,
      82
    advance of the support line 75–8, 82
    Lord Raglan's role 80–83
    advance of the Guards 84–91
    advance of the Highland Brigade 91–3
    Russian collapse 93–4
    aftermath 95–9, 101–9
    pursuit abandoned 95
Almatamack 49, 54
Annesley, Lieutenant Hugh 86, 102, 106
Anstruther, Ensign 73
artillery
    British 3, 125–6, 128, 132
    ammunition 49–50
    Russian 49–50, 72
    siege 121–2
Ashton, Sergeant 191–2
Austria 2, 15–16, 17, 320

Balaklava
    seizure of 117–8

defences 137–8
as supply base 251–2
    railway 259, 260–61
Balaklava, battle of
    charge of the Light Brigade: *see* Light
      Brigade, charge of the
    the Causeway Heights 137–8, 143, 156–7,
      159
    opening moves 137–41
    the Redoubts 138, 141–3, 183
    Russian cavalry charge 144–7
    charge of the Heavy Brigade 147–54
    Russians begin to withdraw 155
Balchik Bay 31
Baltic, the 28
Bancroft, Private 225
Barnston, Lieutenant 210
Bell, Captain 73–4
Bethlehem 2
Black Sea 40–41
Bloomfield, Private 55–6, 58–9, 59–60, 60–61,
    63, 68–9, 196, 196–7
Bond, Sergeant Seth 161, 179–80
Boothby, Ensign 46, 73
Bourliouk 49, 59–62, 188
Bosquet, Pierre 124, 233–4, 276
Braybrooke, Captain 106
Britannia, HMS 23
Brite, General 160
British army
    strength 3–4, 8, 124, 246
    artillery 3, 125–6, 128, 132
    organisation 3
    administrative responsibilities 4
    commanders 4, 5, 7–8, 41–2
    lack of baggage train 5
    officers 5, 13, 26, 62
    other ranks 5
    mobilisation 6–7
    initial deployment 8
    voyage east 8–9

at Varna 8, 10–19, 21, 26
women 11–12, 30–31, 31–2, 145
facial hair 13–14
floggings 14–15
departs Varna for the Crimea 28–34
landings in the Crimea 35–40
supplies 39–40, 250–53, 259–61
advance on Sebastopol 39–47, 109–17
tactics 52
ambulance corps 102
siege artillery 121–2
bands 244–5
diet 254
reinforcements 262–4
lessons of the war 322
British formations
1st Division 3, 10, 25, 36, 42, 52, 76–8, 82,
   113, 140, 154
1st Royal Fusiliers 6
1st Royal Dragoons 151
2nd Division 3, 10, 25–6, 36, 41–2, 51, 52,
   55, 57–61, 62–3, 64, 113, 188–9, 193, 202–
   3, 277, 295–6
3rd Division 3, 10, 42, 52, 55, 76, 113
4th Division 3, 10, 39, 42, 114, 140, 154, 216,
   280
4th Dragoon Guards 151
4th Light Dragoons 28, 38–9, 114, 158, 163,
   165, 167–72, 172, 174
5th Dragoon Guards 24–5, 148–52
7th Royal Fusiliers 41, 59, 61–2, 67, 70, 268
8th Hussars 11–12, 24, 158, 163, 164, 165,
   172, 176–7, 326
11th Hussars 158, 158–9, 160–61, 165, 167–
   72, 174
13th Light Dragoons 44, 115–6, 158, 161,
   166, 174
17th Lancers 158, 161–2, 166
18th (Royal Irish) Regiment 287
19th Green Howards 22–3, 41, 69–70, 70, 75,
   88–9
20th Regiment 216
21st (Royal North British) Fusiliers 236, 238,
   239
23rd Royal Welch Fusiliers 41, 70, 73, 303–4
30th Cambridge Regiment 41, 210
33rd Duke of Wellington's Regiment 41, 70,
   278
39th Regiment 257
41st Welch Regiment 41, 188, 211
42nd Black Watch 42, 91–2
46th Regiment 223
47th Lancashire Regiment 41, 188, 208

49th Hertfordshire Regiment 41, 188, 189–
   90, 204, 211–2
55th Westmoreland Regiment 4, 37, 41, 44,
   59, 62, 68–9, 188, 210, 236, 237, 237–8,
   268, 302, 304–5
57th Foot 112
63rd (West Suffolk) Regiment 236, 238, 254
68th Light Infantry 183, 223
71st Highlanders 261
77th East Middlesex Regiment 41, 75, 206–
   7, 208–9, 239, 277–8
79th Cameron Highlanders 42, 93
88th Connaught Rangers 41, 75–6, 205–6
93rd Sutherland Highlanders 42, 92–3, 138,
   144, 144–7, 152
95th (Derbyshire) Regiment 4, 41, 46, 55–6,
   57–8, 58–9, 59–60, 60–61, 61, 63, 67–8,
   70, 73, 188, 190, 202, 203, 216
97th Regiment 26, 27–8, 262–3, 268, 269,
   278, 301–2
Army of the East 3, 16
Brigade of Guards 10, 16, 25, 36, 42, 55, 56,
   76–8, 84–91, 154, 200–01, 207–8, 212–23,
   224–5
Cavalry Division 3, 10, 138, 139
Coldstream Guards 31–2, 42, 85, 87–8, 94,
   213
Grenadier Guards 42, 57, 85, 87, 88, 89–91,
   93–4, 212–3, 224–5
Heavy Brigade 3, 39, 144, 147–54, 174
Highland Brigade 10, 42, 55, 56, 91–3, 253–
   4, 307, 309, 311
Inniskilling Dragoons 147–52
Land transport Corps 261, 322
Light Brigade 3, 17, 18–19, 45, 144, 153–4,
   155–86
Light Division 3, 8, 10, 14, 21, 22, 25, 41, 51,
   52, 55, 56–7, 58, 63, 64–5, 66–74, 76, 78–
   80, 82, 84–6, 113, 117–8, 201–2, 205–7,
   277–8, 280, 282, 295–6
Medical Department 4
Medical Staff Corps 322
Naval Brigade 125–6, 130–31, 132–3, 230–
   31, 272–3, 280–81, 281, 281–2, 283–5
Rifle Brigade 35, 41, 58, 59, 61, 117–8, 216,
   281
Royal Artillery 4, 83–4, 145
Royal Engineers 4, 279
Royal Marines 138, 140, 145
Scots Fusilier Guards 42, 84–6, 212–3
Scots Greys 112, 114, 147–52
Brown, Sir George 8, 13, 20, 41, 56, 65, 67, 73,
   79, 90–91, 96–7, 233, 293

Buckton, Trooper 170–71, 178
Bulganak river, action at 43–5
Buller, General 96–7, 206, 208–9
Burgoyne, General Sir John 111
Burnaby, Captain 224–5

Cadogan, Colonel 16
Calamita Bay 34
Calthorpe, Lieutenant Somerset
  at Varna 10, 30
  reconnaissance of Sebastopol 33
  on the assembled fleet 34
  landings in the Crimea 35, 36
  advance on Sebastopol 41, 42–3, 109, 110,
    111–2, 115, 116, 117
  at the Bulganak river 45
  at the Alma 51, 55, 80–81, 81, 82, 83, 95, 96,
    104
  on medical treatment 102
  first sight of Sebastopol 113
  on seizure of Balaklava 118
  at Sebastopol 120–21, 124–5, 127–8, 129–30,
    131, 132–3, 133–4
  on the death of St Arnaud 123
  at Balaklava 138, 141–2, 143, 151, 155
  and the charge of the Light Brigade 160,
    172
  on Cardigan 172, 327
  at Inkerman 203–4, 236–7, 245
  on Raglan 237, 292, 292–3
  council of war, 7 November 245–6
  storm, 14 November 249–50
  fraternisation 265–6
  on the April bombardment 271
  on the Malakoff 281
  at the Redan 282–3
  on Raglan's death 293
  post-war 326–7
Cambridge, Duke of
  command 42
  at the Alma 76, 77, 78, 86
  at Balaklava 140
  at Inkerman 212, 212–3, 215–6, 226, 230, 231
  returns home 263
Campbell, Lieutenant 306, 311, 318–9
Campbell, Sir Colin
  at the Alma 53, 58, 87, 91–3, 96
  at Balaklava 138, 139, 140, 144, 145, 145–6,
    152
  at Sebastopol 316–7
Campbell, Lieutenant-Colonel Colin 228
Campbell, Captain Colin 297
Campbell, General Sir John 280

Canrobert, General Francois 32–3, 113, 118–9,
    131, 134, 239, 241, 245–6, 274
Cape Tarkan 34
Caradoc, HMS 32, 34
Cardew, Ensign 72
Cardigan, James Brudenell, 7th Earl of
  background 17–18
  and Lucan 17–18, 39
  Sore-Back Reconnaissance 18–19
  and Fanny Duberly 31
  at the Bulganak river 44, 45
  advance on Sebastopol 114
  at Balaklava 153–4
  and the charge of the Light Brigade 157–8,
    158, 162, 166, 167, 172–3
  damns Captain Nolan 184
  criticism of conduct 184, 327
  post-war dispute with Calthorpe 327
Careenage Ravine 187, 188, 207–8
Carmichael, Lieutenant 57–8, 61, 196, 197,
    198–9, 202, 203, 217–8, 225, 230, 234
casualties
  to disease 21, 22, 23, 24, 27, 28, 123–4, 254,
    258, 263, 320
  first 45
  the Alma 67, 79, 80, 97–9, 101, 102–7
  Sebastopol 132, 134
  Balaklava 152–3
  charge of the Light Brigade 185
  Inkerman 219–21, 241
  the Mamelon 277
  the Redan 290
  Russian total 294
  Tchernaya offensive 294
  second assault on the Redan 311
  second assault on the Malakoff 312
  British total 322
Cathcart, Sir George
  background 42
  dormant commission 42
  advance on Sebastopol 114
  at Sebastopol 120–21, 128
  at Balaklava 140
  at Inkerman 215–6, 223–4, 227–9, 233
  death of 228–9
cavalry charge, experience of 148–51
Champion, Major 79, 190–91, 216–7, 225, 226
Chester, Colonel 79
cholera 21–8, 32, 37, 105, 109–10, 122–3, 254,
    320
Clifford, Henry
  background 16
  reservations 21

on cholera 22, 23
at Varna 30
illness 34
at the Alma 75–6
at Sebastopol 122, 126, 129, 246, 291, 296–7
and the charge of the Light Brigade 160, 182
at Inkerman 206–7, 208–9, 240, 243–4
on Cathcart 229
on Menschikoff 245
storm, 14 November 247–8
on supplies 251, 252
on reinforcements 262–3
on the April bombardment 271
on the capture of the Mamelon 276–7
at the Redan 282
VC 290
on Raglan 292
second assault on the Redan 299, 300, 301–2, 311, 314
the fall of Sebastopol 315–6, 317–8
post-war 325–6
Clifford, Hugh 123, 125
Codrington, Sir William 65, 73, 74, 88, 296, 307, 310–11, 319
Colour Parties 70–71
Connolly, Lieutenant John 189
Connor, Trooper 163, 170
Cox, Gunner 82, 82–3
Crimea, invasion of 35–40
Crimean Army Fund 259
Crimean War
    origins 1–3
    cost 321–2
    winter, 1855 319–20
    assessment 321–3
Crosse, Captain 205–6
Culloden, the 9

Dallas, Lieutenant Frederick 224, 228
Daly, Private Pat 206
Daniell, Edward 290
Dannenburg, General 194, 194–5, 211, 239, 240
Danube river 3
Daubeney, Lieutenant-Colonel 187, 237, 238, 244
Dawson, Vesey 201
de Lacy Evans, Sir 41–2, 62–3, 77, 188, 190, 200, 246, 263
Delane, John T. 107
Deschenes, Vice-Admiral 28
Devna 10
Diamond, HMS 130

Dickson, Colonel Collingwood 234
disease 21–8, 32, 37, 109–10, 122–4, 247, 254–5, 258, 263, 320
Dobrudja 17
Douglas, Colonel 174
Drummond, Captain Hugh 84–5, 93
Duberly, Frances Isabella (Fanny)
    background 11–12
    at Varna 12, 15–16, 18
    on the Light Division 14
    on the Sore-Back Reconnaissance 18–19
    on disease 21
    departs Varna for the Crimea 31
    aboard the Himalaya 32
    landings in the Crimea 38
    on the Alma 108–9
    at Sebastopol 126, 128–9, 135, 294–5, 319
    at Balaklava 141, 143, 144
    and the charge of the Light Brigade 182
    at Inkerman 243
    storm, 14 November 248–9
    on Balaklava as supply base 251–2
    evacuation of sick 255
    on 'navvies' 259
    on the April bombardment 273
    on the Sardinian army 275
    on Raglan's death 293
    post-war 326
Dunn, Private James 305, 306–7

Edward of Saxe-Weimar, Prince 207–8
Egerton, Colonel Thomas 208, 277–8
Elder, James 179
Elliott, Captain Granville 153, 201, 214–5
England, Sir Richard 42
entertainment 244–5
Ermina, the 259
Estcourt, General 292
Esterhazy, Count 320
Eupatoria, battle of 262
Evans, Private William 73

Federoff, Colonel 187, 191
Fenton, Roger 264
Fevrier, General 247
Filder, Commissary-General 250
Fitzgibbon, Lord 180
Fore Ridge 188
France, war aims 1
Franks, Sergeant Major Henry 24, 149, 150–51, 151–2, 152
Franz-Josef, Emperor 2

French army
  strength 8, 10–11, 124, 246
  punishments 15
  departs Varna for the Crimea 30
  landings in the Crimea 35
  advance on Sebastopol 39, 40, 41, 109
  at the Alma 51, 54–5, 81, 88
  at Sebastopol 122, 124, 130, 131, 133, 134,
    189, 267–8, 270, 271–2, 295
  at Balaklava 138, 154
  and the charge of the Light Brigade 181–2
  at Inkerman 231–4, 236, 237–8, 239, 241, 246
  supplies 251
  Péllissier takes command 274
  capture of the Mamelon 275–7
  assault on the Malakoff 278, 279, 281, 290
  and the Tchernaya offensive 294
  second assault on the Malakoff 295, 299–
    300, 311–2
  winter, 1855 320
French formations
  Zouaves 11, 275–6
  Chasseurs d'Afrique 181–2
  Corps of Observation 189
  7th Léger 236
French navy 131–2

Gallipoli 8
Gambier, Colonel 204, 234
Gascoigne, Private John 206
Giffard, Captain, RN 15
Goodlake, Captain 191–2
Gordon, Charles George 270, 323, 327
Gortschakoff, Prince 89–90, 91, 294–5, 315
Gowing, Sergeant Timothy
  departure from Manchester 6
  voyage east 9
  on the French 11
  landings in the Crimea 35, 36–7
  and religion 46–7
  at the Alma 59, 63, 66, 67, 67–8, 79–80, 97,
    98, 107
  at Sebastopol 126, 277–8, 291, 291–2
  at Inkerman 201, 221–2, 233, 240–41
  evacuation 255–6
  return to duty 260
  trench raid 267
  battle at the Mamelon 268, 269
  at the Redan 282, 283, 285, 287, 288
  second assault on the Redan 297–8, 302–3,
    304, 305–6, 309, 312
  post-war 326
Grant, Trooper Robert 163, 169–70, 171

Grant, Major Thornton 204
Great Britain, war aims 1
Great Redan, Sebastopol 120, 130, 133, 134,
    271, 316–7
  assault on 278–90
  second assault 295–311
  aftermath of second assault 312–4
Green, Charles 272
Griffith, Lieutenant Boscawen Trevor 303, 304,
    308, 310
Grigg, Private Joseph 163, 168, 168–9, 171, 176

Haines, Major 238–9
Hall, Dr John 103, 107, 256, 257–8, 258
Haly, Colonel 199
Handcock, John 243
Hardy, Michael 272–3, 283–4, 289–90
Herbert, Colonel 190
Herbert, Private Harry 150, 168, 169
Herbert, Sidney 256–7, 258
Heyland, Captain 46, 73
Higginson, Captain George 57, 89, 90–91, 93–
    4, 99, 212, 230–31, 231–2
Highflyer, HMS 33
Himalaya, the 31, 32
Hood, Colonel 90
horses 9, 164, 185
hospital ships 105–7
Howells, Private 22, 56
Hume, Captain John
  on quality of men 4
  voyage east 9
  at Varna 14
  on the cholera outbreak 25–6
  aboard the Timandra 33–4
  first night in the Crimea 37
  advance on Sebastopol 44
  at the Alma 53–4, 59, 62, 96
  at Sebastopol 127
  and Little Inkerman 187, 193
  at Inkerman 195–6, 210, 237, 244–5
  storm, 14 November 248
  battle at the Mamelon 268
  second assault on the Redan 298, 302, 304–
    5, 306–7, 312–3
  post-war 326
Hume, Robert 96
Hyde, Private Edward 199, 211–2, 278

Inkerman, battle of
  terrain 187–8, 195
  Little Inkerman sortie 187–93
  Russian plan 193–5

opening moves 195–9
Russian assault 200–10
Sandbag Battery 210, 241
battle for the Sandbag Battery 211–20, 220–22, 224–5, 230–32, 233–4
casualties 219–21, 241
British charge 222–30
French forces arrive 231–4
final attacks 234–9
Russian retreat 239–40
aftermath 240–41, 243–6
Inkerman, Mount 187–8, 189

Jacob (Clifford's African servant) 97
Janvier, General 247
Jarvis, Lieutenant 167
Jason, the 37

Kadikoi 138, 140, 144–7
Kangaroo, the 105
Katcha river 110
Kertch, expedition to 274–5
Kirwin, Private 63, 71, 73–4, 79, 89, 97–8
Kirwin, Margaret 22–3
Korniloff, Admiral 111, 119, 134
Kourgane Hill 49, 50, 94, 95
Kvetzinski, General 91

le Marchant, Colonel 24
Lidwill, Lieutenant George 63–4, 69–70, 78–9, 88–9, 96–7, 116, 202
Light Brigade, charge of the
    orders 155–7
    advance 158–62
    dispositions 158, 159
    the charge 162–6
    at the Russian guns 165–71
    beyond the guns 167, 171–2, 173–5
    Cardigan's withdrawal 172–3
    withdrawal 175–84
    blame 184–5
    aftermath 184–6
    casualties 185
Lindsay, Ensign Robert 85–6
Liprandi, Lieutenant General 137, 185–6
Little Inkerman sortie 187–93
London, HMS 23, 106
looting 104, 112
Lucan, Lord
    and Cardigan 17–18, 39
    background 18
    Paget on relationship with 39
    at the Bulganak river 44, 45

at the Alma 95
advance on Sebastopol 114
at Balaklava 138, 139, 148
and the charge of the Light Brigade 156–7, 159, 174, 181, 184
Lyons, Sir Edward 118
Lysons, Colonel Daniel 60, 82, 86–7, 124, 303–4, 313–4

Macdonald, Captain 244
MacDonald, Lieutenant 67–8
Macdonald, Major 226–7
Mackenzie's Farm 117
MacMahon, Major 139–40
McMurdo, Colonel 261
Malakoff, the, Sebastopol 120, 129, 277, 317–8
    assault on 278, 279, 281, 290
    second assault 295, 299–300, 311–2
Malta 260
Mamelon, the, Sebastopol 267–9, 275–7
Markham, Major-General J. 296
Mauleverer, Colonel 210
medical treatment 101–3, 105–7, 255–9, 289
Megara, the 34
Menschikoff, Prince 2, 45, 49–50, 111, 115, 137, 155, 193, 240, 245, 266, 294
Miller, Lieutenant, R. A. 206
Mitchell, Trooper Albert
    departure 7
    voyage east 9
    on floggings 14–15
    at Varna 14, 29–30
    landings in the Crimea 37–8
    at the Bulganak river 44, 45
    advance on Sebastopol 46, 115–6, 116
    at the Alma 52–3, 95–6, 104
    on the ambulance corps 102
    on casualties 103
    at Balaklava 142, 149
    and the charge of the Light Brigade 161, 172–3, 181, 182–4
Monastir 22
Montenegro 2
Morgan, Captain 60, 61–2, 70–71, 108
Morley, Corporal Thomas 161–2, 166–7, 174–5, 182
Morris, Captain 153–4, 159, 162, 174
Mundy, Major 63
Munro, Surgeon George 42, 53, 94, 101–2, 109–10, 145, 145–7, 253–4
Murphy, Sergeant Pat 227, 244

Napier, Sir Charles 28

Napoleon III 2, 274
Neville, the Hon Grey 150–51, 152
Neville, Henry 219
Newcastle, Duke of 13–14, 20, 21, 42
Nicholas I, Tsar 1, 1–2, 21, 193, 262
Nicholson, Private William 7, 38
Nightingale, Florence 256–9, 322
Nolan, Captain Louis 55, 156, 156–7, 159, 184
Norcott, Major 58, 59, 61, 65, 67, 72–3, 79

O'Connor, Sergeant Luke 73, 323
Odessa 15
Oltenitza, battle of 3
Omar Pasha 2, 8, 16
Osman Pasha 3
Osten-Sacken, General 15

Paget, Agnes, Lady 275, 276
Paget, Lord George Augustus Frederick
    background 28–9
    arrival in Varna 29
    fire at Varna 30
    landings in the Crimea 38–9
    on relationship with Lucan 39
    on Raglan 40, 276, 292
    on St Arnaud 40
    advance on Sebastopol 43, 114
    at the Alma 103–4, 108
    at Sebastopol 120, 128
    at Balaklava 138–9, 139–40, 143, 148, 149,
        151
    and the charge of the Light Brigade 157–8,
        159, 162–3, 164, 165, 167–72, 175–6, 177,
        178, 181–2
    criticism of Cardigan 184
    return home 264
    returns to Crimea 264
    on Raglan's death 293
    post-war 325
Pakenham, Lord 219–20
Palmer, Sergeant John 221
Panmure, Lord 261
Parkes, Private Sam 169, 171, 186
Paskevitch, General 8, 17
Paulet, Lord William 139–40
peace talks 320–21
peace terms 321
Peel, Sir Robert 256
Peel, Captain William, RN 130–31, 134, 230–
    31, 272, 280–81, 283, 284, 289, 290, 328
Péllissier, General 270, 274, 281, 293, 295, 319
Pennefather, General Sir John 69, 107, 200, 202,
    216, 235–6, 239, 240

Percy, Henry 90
Peters, James 105–6
Pioneer, the 259
Piraeus 27–8
Portland, Duke 259
Price, Private Samuel 206
Prince, the 249, 250
prisoners of war 116, 243–4

Quarry Ridge 188
Queen, HMS 23, 130

Raglan, Fitzroy Somerset, Lord
    background 7–8
    on the enemy 10
    staff 10
    at Varna 10
    on officers uniforms 13
    instructions 19, 20
    and the decision to attack Sebastopol 20, 21
    'meeting' with St Arnaud 32
    landings in the Crimea 36
    Paget on 40, 276, 292
    at the Bulganak river 44
    at the Alma 51, 55, 77, 80–83, 93, 95, 96,
        108
    visits wounded 102
    options of attack at Sebastopol 111, 112–3
    advance on Sebastopol 115
    meeting with Canrobert 118–9
    at Sebastopol 129, 133, 133–4, 292
    at Balaklava 141, 144, 151, 152, 155
    orders to the Light Brigade 155–7
    and the charge of the Light Brigade 184
    at Inkerman 203–4, 237
    council of war, 7 November 245–6
    criticism of 261–2
    and Lady Paget 276
    assault on the Redan 281, 282, 290
    death of 292–3
Ranken, Major George 297, 298–9, 299–300,
    301, 307–8, 309, 310, 314–5, 316, 317,
    320–21
Reid, Douglas 255
resurrection men 208
Rhyzov, General 143, 144
Robinson, Surgeon 102–3, 153, 220, 261,
    320
Rokeby, Lord 263
Ros, Lord 39
Rowlands, Captain Hugh 197–8, 199, 290
Royal Navy
    bombardment of Odessa 15

cholera casualties 23–4
Baltic actions 28
at Sebastopol 125, 132
Russell, Henry 5–6
Russell, William Howard 107, 144, 185, 250, 256, 263
Russia, war aims 1
Russian army
advance to the Danube 3
strength 8
lifts siege of Silistria 17
Cossacks 35–6, 142
at the Bulganak river 44
artillery 49–50, 72
at the Alma 49–50, 51–2, 59, 66, 67, 68–70, 71, 72–4, 83, 84, 87–8, 89–90, 91, 92–3, 97–8
tactics 52, 247
counter-attack at the Alma 74, 76, 78–80, 82
collapse at the Alma 93–4
move into interior 115–7
at Sebastopol 119, 124, 127–8, 129, 131, 133, 134–5, 266, 271, 277, 296
at Balaklava 137, 141–4, 144–7, 147–52, 155
and the charge of the Light Brigade 159, 162, 166–7, 169–70, 175–8, 179–80
and Little Inkerman 187, 189–93
at Inkerman 193–5, 198, 200–10, 211–2, 211–9, 224, 226–9, 231, 234, 234–40, 241
officers 209
achievement at Inkerman 246–7
at Eupatoria 262
raids 267
battle at the Mamelon 269
defence of the Redan 278, 285, 290
total casualties 294
Tchernaya offensive 294
evacuation of Sebastopol 315
Russian navy
Black Sea Fleet 3, 19
at Little Inkerman 191–2
Ryan, Private James 73–4

Sanders, Colonel 22
Sardinian army 182, 275, 294
Sarnia, the 259
Scarlett, General Sir James Yorke 147, 148, 148–9, 152, 152–3, 184
Scutari 8, 39, 106–7, 124, 255–8, 263
sea-power, importance of 40–41
Seager, Lieutenant Edward 164–5, 176–7, 186
Sebastopol
decision to attack 19–21

strategic importance 19
reconnaissance of 33
harbour 110–1, 119
defences 111, 119–20, 266
first sight of 113
engagement on advance to 115–7
Sebastopol, siege of
dispositions 118–9
defences 119–20
Allied preparations 120–29
the Barrack Battery 120
Bastion du Mat 120
the Great Redan 120, 130, 133, 134, 271, 316–7
the Malakoff 120, 129, 277, 317–8
cholera outbreak 122–3
bombardment 129–35
British defensive picquets 189
council of war, 7 November 245–6
storm, 14 November 247–50
conditions 250–8, 259–62, 262–6, 291–5
fraternisation 265–6, 278
snipers 266
battle at the Mamelon 267–9
raids 267
April bombardment 270–73
capture of the Mamelon 275–7
assault on the Quarries 277–8
assault on the Malakoff 278, 279, 281, 290
assault on the Redan 278–90
second assault on the Redan 295–311
second assault on the Malakoff 295, 299–300, 311–2
aftermath of second assault on the Redan 312–4
fall of 314–9
Shegog, Trooper 148
Shell Hill 188
Sheridan, Trooper 180–81
Shewell, Colonel 158
Silistria 8, 16–17, 120
Simpson, Lieutenant-General James 262, 293–4, 319
Sinope 3
Snow, John 26
Soimonoff, General 195, 198, 204, 209
Sore-Back Reconnaissance 18–19
Soulbey, Corporal 73
St Arnaud, Marshal 11, 32, 40, 51, 54, 95, 113, 123
Star of the South, the 126, 248–9
Steevens, Captain 205–6
Stewart, Lieutenant R. H. 309–10, 315, 316–7

Strangeways, General Thomas Fox 236–7
strategic situation 1–3, 8, 319–20
Suvarov, Alexander 52

tactics 52, 121–2, 247, 322
Talbot, Sergeant 161
Tchernaya offensive, the 294
Telegraph Height 49, 51, 55
Tennyson, Alfred 186
Tiger, HMS 15
Timandra, the 33–4
Times Fund, The 256
Times, the 20–21, 107
Todtleben, Colonel 111, 119–20, 134, 135
Torrens, Captain 223–4
Torrens, General 223–4
Tower, Captain 201, 215, 218–9
Trevelyan, Sir Charles 261
Troubridge, Major Sir Thomas 221–2
Turkey 1, 2–3
Turkish army 30, 51, 109, 138, 141–3, 145, 189,
    252, 262

Unett, Major Thomas 64, 66–7, 297, 300
Usherwood, Sergeant Charlie 71–2, 78

Varna 8, 10–19, 21, 26, 28, 29–30
Vicars, Captain Hedley 26–8, 263, 265, 266,
    268–70
Victoria, Queen 21, 258, 274
Victoria Cross, the 290
Ville de France, HMS 32
Vulcan, HMS 105, 106

Walker, Colonel 212–3
weapons
    Minié rifles 9–10, 68, 200, 246
    revolvers 170, 171, 218
    swords and sabres 150, 152–3, 218
Whelan, Private Jeremiah 305, 307
Williams, Sergeant-Major Francis 196
Wilson, Captain Townsend
    on Zouaves 11

at Aladyn 12–13
on facial hair 13–14
rumours 16
on the siege of Silistria 17
on the Sore-Back Reconnaissance 19
on the cholera outbreak 25
on women 30–31
landings in the Crimea 35–6
advance on Sebastopol 42, 43, 47, 112,
    113–4
at the Alma 56, 57, 77, 87–8, 94, 95, 96, 103,
    104–5
on seizure of Balaklava 117–8, 118
at Sebastopol 123–4, 125, 127, 130, 132, 133,
    134–5
on initiative 154
and Little Inkerman 192
at Inkerman 200–201, 207, 213, 214–5, 215,
    218, 219, 222–3, 229–30, 231
on Russian night sorties 267
Windham, Brigadier-General Charles 297, 300,
    307, 311
Wolseley, Captain Garnet 319, 323, 327–8
Wombwell, Cornet George 162, 166
Wood, Midshipman Evelyn
    on cholera 23–4
    at Sebastopol 125–6, 129, 130–31, 134,
        272–3
    at Inkerman 243
    storm of 14 November 247, 248, 250
    on supplies 253
    at the Redan 280–81, 281, 281–2, 283–5,
        285–7, 287–8, 288–9
    post-war 323, 327–8
Woodham, Trooper Edward 160, 169, 170, 178–
    9, 185
Wootton, Trooper, 160
Woronzov Ravine 122
Wrightman, Trooper 161, 174–5
Wroots, Trooper Thomas 160–61, 178

Yea, Lieutenant-Colonel Lacy 6, 65–6, 97, 280,
    282, 282–3